Western Europe: The Trials of Partnership

Western Europe: The Trials of Partnership

Critical Choices
for Americans

Volume VIII

Edited by
David S. Landes

Lexington Books
D.C. Heath and Company
Lexington, Massachusetts
Toronto

Library of Congress Cataloging in Publication Data

Main entry under title:
Western Europe.

(Critical choices for Americans; v. 8)
Includes index.
1. United States—Foreign relations—Europe, Western—Addresses, es-
says, lectures. 2. Europe, Western—Foreign relations—United States—
Addresses, essays, lectures. I. Landes, David S. II. Series.
JX1428.E8W47   327.73'04   75-44726
ISBN 0-669-00423-5   Sept 6 77

Copyright © 1977 by The Third Century Corporation

Published simultaneously in Canada.

Printed in the United States of America.

International Standard Book Number: 0-669-00423-5

Library of Congress Catalog Card Number: 75-44726

Foreword

The Commission on Critical Choices for Americans, a nationally representative, bipartisan group of forty-two prominent Americans, was brought together on a voluntary basis by Nelson A. Rockefeller. After assuming the Vice Presidency of the United States, Mr. Rockefeller, the chairman of the Commission, became an ex officio member. The Commission's assignment was to develop information and insights which would bring about a better understanding of the problems confronting America. The Commission sought to identify the critical choices that must be made if these problems are to be met.

The Commission on Critical Choices grew out of a New York State study of the Role of a Modern State in a Changing World. This was initiated by Mr. Rockefeller, who was then Governor of New York, to review the major changes taking place in federal-state relationships. It became evident, however, that the problems confronting New York State went beyond state boundaries and had national and international implications.

In bringing the Commission on Critical Choices together, Mr. Rockefeller said:

As we approach the 200th Anniversary of the founding of our Nation, it has become clear that institutions and values which have accounted for our astounding progress during the past two centuries are straining to cope with the massive problems of the current era. The increase in the tempo of change and the vastness and complexity of the wholly new situations which are evolving with accelerated change, create a widespread sense that our political and social system has serious inadequacies.

We can no longer continue to operate on the basis of reacting to crises, counting on crash programs and the expenditure of huge sums of money to solve our problems. We have got to understand and project present trends, to take command of the forces that are emerging, to extend our freedom and wellbeing as citizens and the future of other nations and peoples in the world.

Because of the complexity and interdependence of issues facing America and the world today, the Commission has organized its work into six panels, which emphasize the interrelationships of critical choices rather than treating each one in isolation.

The six panels are:

Panel I: Energy and its Relationship to Ecology, Economics and World Stability;

Panel II: Food, Health, World Population and Quality of Life;

Panel III: Raw Materials, Industrial Development, Capital Formation, Employment and World Trade;

Panel IV: International Trade and Monetary Systems, Inflation and the Relationships Among Differing Economic Systems;

Panel V: Change, National Security and Peace;

Panel VI: Quality of Life of Individuals and Communities in the U.S.A.

The Commission assigned, in these areas, more than 100 authorities to prepare expert studies in their fields of special competence. The Commission's work has been financed by The Third Century Corporation, a New York not-for-profit organization. The corporation has received contributions from individuals and foundations to advance the Commission's activities.

The Commission is determined to make available to the public these background studies and the reports of those panels which have completed their deliberations. The background studies are the work of the authors and do not necessarily represent the views of the Commission or its members.

This volume is one of the series of volumes the Commission will publish in the belief that it will contribute to the basic thought and foresight America will need in the future.

WILLIAM J. RONAN
Acting Chairman
Commission on Critical Choices
for Americans

Members of the Commission

LEO CHERNE
   Executive Director, Research Institute
   of America, Inc.

JOHN S. FOSTER, JR.
   Vice President for Energy Research
   and Development, TRW, Inc.

LUTHER H. FOSTER
   President, Tuskegee Institute

NANCY HANKS
   Chairman, National Endowment for the Arts

BELTON KLEBERG JOHNSON
   Texas Rancher and Businessman

CLARENCE B. JONES
   Former Editor and Publisher,
   The New York Amsterdam News

JOSEPH LANE KIRKLAND
   Secretary–Treasurer, AFL-CIO

JOHN H. KNOWLES, M.D.
   President, Rockefeller Foundation

DAVID S. LANDES
   Leroy B. Williams Professor of History
   and Political Science, Harvard University

MARY WELLS LAWRENCE
   Chairman and Chief Executive Officer,
   Wells, Rich, Greene, Inc.

SOL M. LINOWITZ
   Senior Partner of Coudert Brothers

EDWARD J. LOGUE
   Former President and Chief Executive Officer,
   New York State Urban Development Corporation

CLARE BOOTHE LUCE
Author; former Ambassador
and Member of Congress

PAUL WINSTON McCRACKEN
Professor of Business Administration,
University of Michigan

DANIEL PATRICK MOYNIHAN
Professor of Government,
Harvard University

BESS MYERSON
Former Commissioner of Consumer Affairs,
City of New York

WILLIAM S. PALEY
Chairman of the Board
Columbia Broadcasting System

RUSSELL W. PETERSON
Chairman, Council on Environmental
Quality

WILSON RILES
Superintendent of Public Instruction,
State of California

LAURANCE S. ROCKEFELLER
Environmentalist and Businessman

OSCAR M. RUEBHAUSEN
Partner, Debevoise, Plimpton, Lyons
and Gates, New York

GEORGE P. SHULTZ
President
Bechtel Corporation

JOSEPH C. SWIDLER
Partner, Leva, Hawes, Symington, Martin
& Oppenheimer
Former Chairman, Federal Power Commission

EDWARD TELLER
Senior Research Fellow, Hoover Institution
on War, Revolution and Peace,
Stanford University

ARTHUR K. WATSON*
Former Ambassador to France

MARINA VON NEUMANN WHITMAN
Distinguished Public Service Professor
of Economics, University of Pittsburgh

CARROLL L. WILSON
Professor, Alfred P. Sloan
School of Management,
Massachusetts Institute of Technology

GEORGE D. WOODS
Former President, World Bank

Members of the Commission served on the panels. In addition, others assisted
the panels.

BERNARD BERELSON
Senior Fellow
President Emeritus
The Population Council

C. FRED BERGSTEN
Senior Fellow
The Brookings Institution

ORVILLE G. BRIM, JR.
President
Foundation for Child Development

LESTER BROWN
President
Worldwatch Institute

LLOYD A. FREE
President
Institute for International Social Research
*Deceased

Preface

It is customary, when referring to the ties between the United States and Western Europe, to speak of a "special relationship." And, indeed, our ties to the nations of this area of the world are like no others. We have allies around the world, but our Western European allies are the ones we think of as stable and enduring. We are bound to Western Europe by kinship, history, common causes, and common values. Our sense is that the diminution of Western Europe would be our diminution; their loss, our loss. No other part of the world has evoked the same emotional response. Yet, today this special relationship is strained; it has become at best a "troubled partnership."

Western Europe: The Trials of Partnership is one of seven geographic studies prepared for the Commission on Critical Choices for Americans, under the direction of Nancy Maginnes Kissinger. Companion volumes cover the Soviet Empire, China and Japan, Southern Asia, the Middle East, Africa, and Latin America. Interdependence has long been a fact of the twentieth century—our neighbors to the north and south and across the oceans to the east and west are clearly a part of America's future. The critical choices we face as a nation—the food, energy, raw materials, and national security which we once solved with our resources at home—can now be solved only in the context of our relations with other nations.

David S. Landes' study of Western Europe and the contributors to it point to new directions in our ties with a centuries-old friend and ally. Their essays bring a new awareness to all of us of a new relationship taking shape with a Western Europe that has come of age financially and politically.

—W.J.R.

Acknowledgments

This study has benefited from the critical comments of Charles Kindleberger, professor of economics and management, Massachusetts Institute of Technology; John Newhouse, counselor, Arms Control and Disarmament Agency; Fritz Stern, Seth Low Professor of History, Columbia University; and Richard Ullman, professor, Department of Politics, Princeton University and of the Council on Foreign Relations—all of whom participated in a discussion of early drafts of these papers in New York in March of 1975.

We were also fortunate in the early participation of Ralf Dahrendorf of the Commission of the European Communities and Theo Sommer, editor-in-chief of *Die Zeit*, whose heavy commitments prevented them from staying with us to the end, but who participated in a planning and discussion conference in Paris in the summer of 1974.

We should also like to thank Patricia Scanlon and the many staff members of the universities and organizations of the contributing authors who helped in the preparation of the manuscript. Also those of the Commission staff who have assisted the project from conception to delivery, Anne Boylan and Charity Randall in particular. Finally we owe a debt of gratitude to Guido Goldman, who has counseled us all the way.

D.S.L.

Contents

List of Tables

I   Introduction

David S. Landes

Technology has so shrunk space and time that, as the cliché has it, the world has become a global village. As a result, a great power such as the United States has interests and relations everywhere; and insofar as these constitute a seamless web, we have no security frontier. Every place matters. But it is easier to say that than to act upon it. Even the greatest power does not have unlimited resources and must allocate them according to rational criteria of strategic advantage and tactical opportunity. In a system of national security ordered by such criteria, Western Europe has been and continues to be at the top of our list. No place in the world has been more the object of American commitment and solicitude. Only the Europeans and the Canadians have been defined as though they were flesh of our flesh, and their independence guaranteed by American men and arms—all our arms.

It is not hard to account for this priority. In the first place, there are compelling geographical considerations. The great geopolitician Halford Mac-kinder already pointed out at the beginning of this century that the United States would of necessity have to concern itself not only with its coasts and the oceans that wash them but the lands on the other side. One can conceive of reviving an earlier isolationist policy in the twentieth-century guise of Fortress America; but it is hard to believe that if hostile nations stood across the sea from us, we would be comfortable or even safe in the long run. It is this strategic dependency, which has grown with advances in transportation and communication, that has helped persuade American governments on two occasions to lead us into European wars. In both instances, our concern was to prevent the domination of Europe by a single power: in effect, we took over from Britain the role it had played going back to the seventeenth century—that of offshore

1

guarantor of European freedom—because we understood, as Britain always had, that we were defending our own freedom as well.[1]

A second consideration is the importance of Europe as a factor in the balance of power. There are more populous areas, and there are many places more richly endowed with the raw materials that make for economic wealth and military force. But no other region, except for the United States itself, contains so large a pool of highly educated and skilled persons and such a large stock of the most up-to-date plant and equipment. Western Europe is one of the great workshops of the world. It is also one of the few regions of the world that is capable of feeding itself and more. Even if nothing positive drew us together, we would not want to see this factory and granary incorporated into or subordinated to a hostile camp.

Third, we are bound to Western Europe by more than the negative fear of losing it as friend and ally. For one thing, we are members together of the endangered species of elective democracies. There have never been many of these; indeed, there are those who would argue, sometimes in mitigation of the tyranny that prevails over most of the globe, that democracy may be some kind of Western political aberration—a delicate wine that travels badly. (I can remember my friend and colleague Pat Moynihan defending his concern for India, at a time when India was rather unfriendly to the United States, by arguing that democracies have to stick together. India, he noted, represented about half the world's democratic population. We are now down to the other half.)

Fourth, we are also members of the rare species of market economies. The usual term is "capitalist economies," but Western economies have long since diverged so much from the ideal type that gave rise to the word "capitalism," that the designation is more polemical than descriptive. We have a common interest in relative freedom of trade in goods and services, and even freedom of movement of the factors of production; also in the technological creativity generated and sustained by a market system. As a result, our economies have become increasingly interdependent, to the point where each of us has an enormous pecuniary stake in the security and prosperity of the other. The stakes are not equal: in economic things, Western Europe still needs us more than we need it and thus is affected more by what we do than we are by what it does. But these are matters of degree rather than kind. We both need each other.

Finally, we are bound by ties of sympathy and experience. The vast majority of Americans are of European origin; we speak a European language; our culture is impregnated with European folk memories, moral values, and artistic achievements. England in particular has been almost a second country for many Americans—not only those of English descent, but those whom the King James Bible and Shakespeare and Mother Goose have made Englishmen by adoption. It is no accident that we have fought two wars on the side of the once hated colonial mother country: independence, as many former colonies can testify today, is not the end of a relationship.

These four factors—geographic, political, economic, sentimental—have been of unequal and varying weight. The sentimental tie has been strongest in time of conflict and in the glow of camaraderie thereafter. It has much weakened of late, for reasons I shall turn to later. The economic bonds have grown stronger with time, though increasing competition for raw materials and markets has given them an ambivalent quality. Political affinities have had their ups and downs: when Europeans and Americans look at the abuses of other systems, as when Soviet troops suppress the Hungarian revolt or bring the Czechs to heel, they get a keen sense of the preciousness of their common heritage of civil and political freedom; but when they look at one another, which they do most of the time, they have no end of invidious and critical comparisons to make. Freedom is an asset best understood and most appreciated in its absence. Besides, the argument runs, there is no point in wasting ammunition on totalitarian societies, which are of their nature more or less unresponsive to opinion. Far better to save it for vulnerable targets, that is, those close enough to us to care. The effect is more ambivalence.

I

The bonds that link the United States with Western Europe were at their strongest during and immediately after World War II, though even then we had some problems. We were engaged in a common endeavor to defeat nazism/fascism, and when the war was won and a prostrate Europe was threatened by domination from the east, we recognized the need to furnish aid and continue the alliance in peacetime. This was in itself a marked departure from American tradition and, along with the earlier participation of the United States in the creation of the United Nations, constituted a belated but timely recognition of the political realities of the twentieth century. In those days of revival and "economic miracles," of crises overcome (the Berlin airlift) and restrictions eased, the alliance was very much a marriage of love as well as of convenience.

The alliance found its institutional expression in the North Atlantic Treaty Organization (NATO), which united the United States and Canada on this side and most of the nations of Western Europe (including Iceland and Portugal) in a mutual defense pact. It reflected a recognition that the victorious nations of Western Europe had been so exhausted by the war that even together they could not match the power of the Soviet Union; that the entire continent was therefore liable to victimization and subjection by a triumphant autocracy assisted by a "fifth column" of Communist party members and sympathizers in the still incompletely organized postwar polities; in short, that the danger of one-country dominion that had brought the United States into war in the first place had not been ended; only the threat had changed.

The alliance, as formalized in NATO, eventually rested on three elements: joint, integrated armed forces; nuclear arms and a commitment to use them;

United States leadership, reflecting the disparity between our power and that of our allies and, specifically, our commitment of and control over atomic weapons. This domination by one country of a coalition of some of the world's oldest and proudest nations was intrinsically unstable. Aside from those on the left who opposed the alliance as an act of provocation and hostility to the Soviet Union, there were those on the right who saw it as an unacceptable hegemony incompatible with the dignity and independence of its members. It was, to be sure, a most benevolent hegemony, not to be confused with the totalitarian darkness that had descended on Eastern Europe in a series of coups that took on the character of standardized scenarios. But it was a hegemony nonetheless, and already in 1951 de Gaulle, from his retreat at Colombey-les-Deux-Eglises, was denouncing NATO as an insult to national sovereignty.

Still, in those early postwar years, most countries were too busy rebuilding and modernizing with American help to make an issue of United States superiority. For the hard-pressed, impecunious British, the Alliance was a welcome continuation of a happy wartime partnership, an additional source of help with military responsibilities, and an employment outlet for supernumerary personnel. For Germany NATO was an insurance policy against aggression by next-door neighbors. Only France of the larger European powers had cause to grumble. It received a very small share of NATO commands; and unlike Britain, it had no part in atomic technology and weaponry. All of this was no doubt an extension of the relative unimportance of defeated, occupied France in the wartime alliance; also an expression of the special relationship within a special relationship of the United States and Great Britain—what the French group together as the Anglo-Saxons; also perhaps an unexpressed reservation concerning French political stability and reliability. France's latent grievance was exacerbated by a long history of Anglo-French rivalry, damped in two world wars, but never extinguished. The French could not help but infer from NATO a sense not only of American domination but of American favoritism at their expense.

These incipient or potential discontents were much mitigated by the advantages of American friendship. After an initial disastrous attempt to plunge postwar Europe into a world of free trade, open exchanges, and arms-length credits, the United States recognized the need for positive measures of assistance and protective restraints of trade. The new aid policy was signaled by General Marshall's famous speech of June 5, 1947 and carried out through the so-called European Recovery Program, entrusted by Congress in April 1948 to the Economic Co-operation Administration. The tolerant trade policy found expression in American encouragement to such cartel-like institutions as the European Coal and Steel Community (ECSC); in our acceptance of monetary controls that discriminated against the dollar; and in our willingness for the time being to live with European subsidy of exports to the United States (dumping) and quotas on dollar imports.

Marshall Plan aid was initially offered to all of Europe, but the Soviet Union and its satellites rejected it from the start as an instrument of American imperialism and an arrant interference in the domestic affairs of sovereign nations. Even in Western Europe there was occasional resentment of the conditions of American aid: I recall a friend high in the French Ministry of Finance who chided us for our intrusive concern for French productivity: "Does a gentleman tell his mistress what kind of soap to buy with the money he gives her?" Many Europeans, moreover, were unwilling to credit the United States with an act of generosity. We were giving the money and goods, they said, to sustain the American economy, which would otherwise have sunk into depression. Such cynicism told more about the cynics than about the United States.

The primary concern of the American leadership was to build a European barrier to further Soviet expansion, and we felt that an impoverished, disunited Europe would be easy prey to domestic subversion and foreign intimidation. The Marshall Plan was intended to be the occasion for collaboration among the recipient European nations, who were invited to concert on the manner of its distribution and use. They responded with alacrity, convening a series of conferences that gave rise in April 1948 to the Organization for European Economic Co-operation (OEEC), to administer the aid program, and two years later, the European Payments Union (EPU), to serve as a multilateral clearing agency for international money flows. The success of this invitation to collaboration reflected not only the rational advantage of these arrangements but a certain ideological preparation. Already during the war a number of European thinkers and statesmen had come to the conclusion that Europe could not afford more of these internecine conflicts; that some kind of supranational federalism was desirable to soften if not eliminate the bitterness of past aggressions and tenaciously competitive nationalisms; and that the Franco-German rivalry in particular had to be laid to rest once and for all if Europe was to survive. Even those who were less critical of the nation/fatherland as a focus of action and loyalty felt that the waste of Europe's substance in two bloody wars and the concomitant rise of a Soviet-American world diarchy made some coalescence of European forces a precondition of international influence. If European countries wanted more of a voice, they had better create more of a Europe.

This was also the conviction of the United States, which did its best from the early postwar years to encourage all moves to European unification, even at the expense of American economic interests. The ECSC, for example, was more than a device to rationalize and develop the coal and steel industries of Western Europe. It was consciously a vehicle for mitigating Franco-German discord in a most sensitive domain and "a first step in the federation of Europe."[2] The preamble to the treaty establishing the Community (signed April 18, 1951) spoke explicitly of "economic community" in the broader sense and saw it in turn as "the foundation of a broad and independent community among peoples long divided by bloody conflicts." This broader economic community was realized by the Treaty of Rome (signed March 25, 1957), which provided for the establishment of a European Economic Community (EEC) that would put into operation over the next twelve years a common market in goods plus sundry other features of an integrated economy.

A more obvious example of American support for European unification, because in this instance we actually initiated the move, was the effort to establish a European Defense Community. The aim was to make it possible for Germany to rearm, not as a nation, but as part of a larger framework. For this purpose the French *government* was persuaded to propose the creation of a separate European force that would operate within NATO, hence under the orders of the Supreme Allied Commander Europe (SACEUR), that is, an American (at the time, Eisenhower). The proposal encountered fierce resistance, especially from the French, who still had the gravest reservations about German rearmament; besides many of France's troops were engaged at that point in Indochina, and the French felt that the Germans were bound to dominate a largely German force. In 1954, after months, even years, of tedious negotiations and horse-trading, EDC failed of passage in the French Chamber. The United States, mistaking the wish for the deed, was stunned and angry. Anyone who knew France could have warned us—if we had been ready to listen.

It must be said (though few said it) that United States support for European unification, however enthusiastic and self-sacrificing, at least on one level, was always tacitly conditional. We were all for a united Europe because we took it for granted that a united Europe would be for us. This is not because we believed, like the Soviet Union, that we knew what was good for Europe and had the right and duty to impose our will and interests even against manifest opposition. There are hegemonies and hegemonies, and the use of the same word to describe a relationship of superior strength on the one hand and superior force *cum* violence on the other is inaccurate and sometimes deliberately misleading.

What we did believe was that the common interest of the United States and Western Europe would lead us to want the same thing; and that insofar as there might be differences of perspective or advantage, these could be easily resolved by friendly, honest give-and-take. So we brought pressure to bear on those recalcitrants who balked at the surrender of pieces of sovereignty to supranational bodies; and we deplored the repeated failures to extend the manifest successes of economic integration to the political and military spheres. In the beginning, the major opponent of unification was Britain, which clung to its imperial and Commonwealth ties, its mini-isolationism (FOG OVER CHANNEL, CONTINENT ISOLATED), its special relationship to the United States. From the late fifties on, however, it was France that took the lead in defending sovereignty and independence against supranational authority, not only on the European, but even more on the Atlantic plane, for reasons that we shall explore later on.

For more than a decade, American-European relations were predominantly harmonious. This is not to say there were no serious quarrels. One thinks, for example, as Raymond Aron does, of the crises attending decolonization: the American refusal to give the French military help in Indochina, our lack of support for the French effort to hold Algeria, Dulles' peremptory veto of the Anglo-French Suez expedition. These instances of nonassistance, even opposition, could not help but leave a legacy of disappointment and distrust. To this day there are Frenchmen who are convinced that American policy in North Africa in the 1950s was shaped primarily by our desire to secure oil concessions from the indigenous population that would have otherwise gone to their colonial or ex-colonial masters; and who is to say they are entirely wrong?

Yet there were in Europe enough dissenting voices on colonial issues to soften the impact of American opposition and sustain our underlying friendship. In general, it was possible in those years (up to the mid-1960s) to bypass points of friction and concentrate on areas of potential accomplishment. These were primarily economic: every year saw European product and incomes grow, trade increase, welfare improve. It was not only Germany that enjoyed a miracle; Italy had one, France also, Benelux as well. Europe had more than a generation of lag—depression, war, occupation—to make up, and it threw itself into growth and productivity with a zeal and an intelligence that put its American teacher in the shade. How much of this growth was due to the Common Market is hard to say. What is less debatable is that economic integration was enormously facilitated by this expansion (it is always easier to reduce protection when everyone, or almost everyone, is getting richer); that the United States profited by this prosperity, among other things, by the implantation in Europe of American multinational firms; and that the Western alliance grew stronger as the West European region changed from convalescent to a major force in the world economy.

II

More precisely, the Alliance grew stronger as a congeries of resources (population, industrial capacity, wealth), but weaker as a team. A number of factors conjoined to this result:

1. *From economic tutelage to parity*. European economic parity (or near parity) was bound to alter the relationship with the United States. On our side, we no longer felt so much stronger that we could concede to Europe the privileges of a double standard in commercial policy. For years the Europeans had been allowed to discriminate against American exports, to subsidize their own exports or engage in dumping, to grant special favors to Third World countries, essentially former colonies, in return for preferential treatment of European products. All of this was part of reconstruction, and besides, Europe was not yet enough of a rival to trouble our own producers. By the late sixties,

however, the Europeans had caught up in technology and business practice. The burst of postwar revival and expansion was just about over; a generation of pent-up demand had been satisfied; and competition with the United States for third markets intensified. European economies seemed less and less a suitable object of American solicitude and benevolence.

There were also grievances on the European side, not so much in the economic domain proper as in the area of political economy. They focused on the dollar. Under the gold-exchange standard established at Bretton Woods, the U.S. dollar became the reserve currency for most of the world outside the Socialist sphere and was preferred even there for exchanges with market economies. During the first fifteen years or so after the war, the shortage of dollars both for purchases in the United States and for use in international payments was such that the United States was in effect free to export as much paper money as it wanted, that is, to spend abroad without regard to the balance of payments. Even after the dollar gap disappeared (from about 1958 on), the United States was able to continue spending without penalty, first, because of the readiness of other countries, principally our allies, to accumulate dollar holdings, and second, thanks to the institution of programs (the "gold pool," foreign exchange swaps, special drawing rights [SDRs]) designed to minimize the impact of a growing overhang of dollars. In effect the dollar was now overvalued, just as it had been undervalued in the years immediately after the war—hence the proliferation then of black and "parallel" currency markets whose rates were openly quoted in the daily newspapers of Europe. This was in the event an ideal sequence for European industry: it could buy the raw materials and equipment it needed so desperately in the years of reconstruction at an artificially favorable price; and when it had recovered enough to go over to large-scale exports, it had the converse advantage of an artificially low exchange price for its products. In the commercial sense, then, the privileged dollar was a subsidy to European economic expansion.

It was a subsidy in another way, and this gave rise to trouble. American businessmen, as we have noted, took advantage of the overvalued dollar to invest heavily in foreign enterprise. Some of this was no more than a transfer of ownership, and in such cases the dollars exported constituted an addition to the European money supply and a source of inflation. Some of it, though, paid for new plant and equipment, and in such instances the dollar made possible an increase in Europe's productive capacity and employment opportunities. Most investments combined something of both. Whatever the circumstances, though, all these investments constituted an invasion of European economic "turf," with all the disadvantages entailed by alien ownership: management less responsive to local interests and influence, comparatively mobile capital, income less vulnerable to taxation.

Moreover, it was not only private enterprise that was spending dollars abroad. The American government was an even bigger spender, especially after our involvement in the Vietnam War. We simply poured the dollars out, billions of them, without much regard to effectiveness or legitimacy of expenditure; that is the way of war. This freedom to print all the money we needed to pay for a foreign policy that many Europeans disapproved of reinforced opposition to the privileged dollar, the more so as the growing accumulation of dollars fueled inflation abroad. The French in particular were quick to perceive that the special status of the dollar was at once the source of our prodigality and the chink in our armor. They began to attack the dollar from every angle—by bullionist critiques from de Gaulle on down (the French have always had a love affair with the gold standard), by conversion of most of their dollars into gold, and by a summons to other countries to follow their example. In a matter of years, the United States gold reserves in Fort Knox fell to where they were grossly insufficient to pay claims outstanding. The day of reckoning was not far off.[a]

2. *Competition in third countries.* Where economic interests diverge, can foreign policy be far behind? The growth of European productive capacity and the progressive satisfaction of domestic demand stimulated European interest in outside and overseas markets, hence in extra-European relations. The Socialist countries of Eastern Europe, which could once be easily ignored as marginal trading partners, in part because the United States wanted it that way, took on a new attraction. The Middle East, long more or less abandoned to American enterprise (the British had the short end of the stick, and the French even less), now looked ripe for prospecting, the more so in view of United States support for Israel. European ministers, with the French in the van, took on the functions of traveling salesmen—what might be *déclassé* at home was glamorous abroad in the service of the nation; and foreign policy was adjusted to maximize exports. Inevitably the United States found that outside the area covered by the Alliance its allies were more and more its competitors, even its adversaries.

3. *The raison d'être of the Alliance weakens.* This trend toward rivalry was fostered by the apparent subsidence of the Soviet threat to Western Europe. Whereas in the late forties, at the time of the Berlin airlift, American military personnel in Europe carried extra jerricans of gasoline in their cars so that their dependents could flee to safety on a moment's notice, such a precaution would have seemed ludicrous only a few years later. A number of developments conduced to this growing confidence, among them: the death of Stalin, the Russo-Chinese split and the multipolarization of the world balance of power, the moderately successful conclusion of postwar settlements regarding Austria and Germany, Europe's increasing sense of its own strength and bargaining power, the coming-of-age of a generation that had to learn about the origins of the cold

---

[a]The French government also resisted the dollar invasion by refusing when possible permission for American purchase of French enterprises or even construction of new plants. But there de Gaulle ran into the penalties of a multinational Europe, that is, he was hoist by his own petard. Other countries were happy to receive job-creating American investment, especially when it could be directed to less prosperous regions. In the end even Gaullism had to yield to the facts and subordinate foreign policy to domestic advantage.

war from the history books. The last, to be sure, is not precisely true: from time to time, as in Hungary in 1956 and in Czechoslovakia in 1968, the Russian bear showed his claws. But these episodes were quickly explained away by those who wanted to avert their eyes—and no one had any stomach for fighting with the Soviet Union—as an understandable, if not quite legitimate, enforcement of discipline within the accepted Soviet sphere of influence. They would not do that to us.

This self-tranquilization in turn fostered, and was fostered by, the process that has come to be known as détente. This is an ambiguous word even in French; in English it has been so often redefined by statesmen and political scientists that it may well have to be relegated to the junkheap of slogans.[4] Perhaps the broadest definition is the safest: détente is a relaxation of tensions, a process that is supposed (intended?) to bring the Soviet Union and the West from the perils of cold war and segregated coexistence to a happier state of peaceful commerce.

As a policy, that is, as a guide to action, détente is most closely associated in the public mind with Henry Kissinger and the Nixon administration, going back to 1969. In fact, however, it was the French who took the first initiatives in this direction in the mid-sixties: General de Gaulle, exploiting to the limit the shelter offered by the United States military commitment, wooed the Soviet Union with a vision of one Europe from the Atlantic to the Urals, free of Yankees, and with Germany safely sandwiched between East and West. This hint at a resurrection of the Franco-Russian entente of the 1890s never came to much, essentially because the Soviets weighed France in the international balance of power and found it wanting; besides, de Gaulle was shocked to learn in 1968 that his vision of a relaxed Soviet withdrawal from Eastern Europe was just fantasy.[b] Even so, the very fact that he could indulge such fantasies is testimony to the diminution of earlier anxieties.

Moreover, Prague was not enough to reverse the trend: Michel Debré, de Gaulle's vociferous caddie, called it a "traffic accident" on the road to a new Europe, and the bilateral contacts initiated in 1967 between some of the smaller West European countries and some of the satellite nations to explore the possibilities of military détente were scarcely interrupted. The subsequent American entry on the scene (the United States and the Soviet Union began preparations for SALT in 1969) gave some Europeans cause for concern, lest we make deals behind or on their backs; but it also confirmed the general impression that a Soviet military threat to Europe was the obsolete bugbear of an earlier generation.

4. *France opts out.* Analytically this factor may not seem to be on the same

---

[b]The honeymoon had already ended in 1967, when de Gaulle visited Warsaw and permitted himself to invite Poland to follow the French example and establish its independence vis-à-vis its Soviet Protector. (It was in that same year that he provoked a scandal by visiting Canada and crying out, "*Vive le Québec libre!*") The Russians were not amused.

level as the three general considerations outlined above. After all, France is just one country among many; and it is not hard to show that other West European nations have had their differences, sometimes important, with the United States.

Yet as the essays in this volume make clear, France has been a country apart in the evolution of European-American relations. All of the chapters on general, transnational topics must give a special place to France, even where, as in the Stanley Hoffmann essay, an effort is made to minimize these differences by highlighting the support other countries have given France, openly or silently, and by presenting French positions as European. The record of the last fifteen years or more shows France opposing the United States at almost every turn, on large issues and small, in European forums, international organizations, and the media of communication—sometimes at the price of self-isolation.

Why? France, after all, is America's oldest ally: our friendship, though not smooth, can be traced back to the French assistance to the colonists during the Revolutionary War. In this century, we have twice sent men to Europe to defend France or free it. And our commitment to the defense of Western Europe applies as much to France as to any other country. Is this the way to treat a friend?

On one level the answer is simple. That master turncoat Talleyrand enunciated the principle over a century and a half ago: nations know no gratitude; they know only interest. It is a principle that has continued to govern French foreign policy in our time. Here, according to Stanley Hoffmann, was de Gaulle's first precept of operation:

International politics is a battle. Interests often converge, and possibilities for common action result from them, but nothing assures that this convergence will last. Indeed, it may have to be provoked, so to speak. As a result, friendships or enmities are never permanent, and one must always be on one's guard. The international milieu is a kind of jungle, moderated only by the beasts' self-restraint and by the combinations of power that force or encourage self-restraint, and the statesman must act accordingly. There is no point in expecting even partners to show "mutual trust" . . .[5]

Yet even if we put gratitude or friendship aside, surely the interests of France and the United States ought to coincide or converge more than they seem to. Presumably we both have the same concern to keep the Soviet Union out of Western Europe, the same desire to promote European economic development, the same care for elective democracy and civil liberty. In the long run, we ought to agree on just about every important goal and value.

We agree on all except one: the relative position of France and the United States; or to put it differently, the position of France in Europe and the larger world. Here history is all-important. France is an old country that has known moments of grandeur and hegemony. Under Louis XIV it was the first power in Europe, and only a general coalition of just about everybody else was able to curb its expansion. Its *Grande Révolution* of 1789 opened a new era in history:

the abolition of authoritarian monarchy and seignorial servitudes; the conversion of the subject into a citizen; the invention of the nation-in-arms; the injection of ideology into politics; the apotheosis of the *patrie* and the dissemination of the potent seed of nationalism. Europe and the world were never the same again. The Revolution made France the *grande nation*, and under Napoleon it momentarily established a dominion over Europe not seen since the days of Charlemagne. Again it took a great coalition to bring France down, and this high tide was followed by a long retreat. In an industrializing world, France changed more slowly than her European rivals; in a period of demographic explosion, France was the first country to find a population equilibrium. By the twentieth century, France had fallen well behind Britain and Germany; and although it was to be on the winning side in the great wars to determine a new balance of power in Europe, it paid dearly for victory. World War I bled it white; and World War II was such an unhappy experience—collapse in 1940, collaboration under Vichy, of necessity a small contribution to allied victory—that it left a bitter and humiliating aftertaste.

For someone like Charles de Gaulle, who had long warned his countrymen against the German danger and urged them to change their military doctrine and tactics before it was too late, these wartime disasters were a calvary. He was already a proud and tough Frenchman when, from London, he summoned his countrymen to resist in 1940; but his character was forged in the fire of resentment—resentment that France should have to be a mendicant for allied assistance and that it should have to insist upon respect. These wartime years gave de Gaulle a mission and a sense of his role in history. He would restore his country to the greatness that was its character and the honor that was its due.

The first postwar years gave him little scope for action; he was too busy mending wounds. And when his countrymen preferred to his leadership the games and intrigues that were to make the Fourth Republic, unjustly, a byword in futility, he chose to go off to Colombey and meditate on his destiny. There is something in the role of leader-prophet that seems to demand or thrive on this sequence of withdrawal-and-return. De Gaulle spent his time thinking on and writing history . . . and waiting for fate and his countrymen to summon him to power.

When the Algerian War and the threat of a right-wing putsch brought him back to Paris in 1958, he had long made up his mind on a number of issues, among them that of the relations that should obtain between France and Europe on the one hand, France and the United States on the other. His primary aim was to destroy the hegemony of the superpowers and make room for France to play a role worthy of its greatness; to do that he was determined to involve France in "vast enterprises" that would strain its resources and engage its passions. His first task was to free his hands by liquidating the Algerian War—which he did with a determination that alienated some of his most devoted partisans but earned the gratitude of most of his countrymen and of history; and by forcing the Americans to say no to him—which he did by offering to join with the United States and Great Britain in a trinational directorate of world strategy for the West.

It is clear that he expected a negative or elusive reply to this proposal from Eisenhower and Macmillan, but one should remember that this had also been his line in the days of the RPF [Rassemblement du Peuple Français], and that if it had by miracle been accepted, it would have allowed him to pursue his design—by blocking American inclinations toward a direct dialogue with Moscow, and by acting, in this triumvirate, as the only genuine voice of Europe.[6]

By 1962 de Gaulle was firmly installed in power as the first strong executive that France had known, except for Pétain, since Napoleon III. He had just successfully survived the threat of a putsch by dissident generals in Algiers (1961) and put an end to fighting in Algeria. He now turned to Europe and the United States. He tried to undermine "Anglo-Saxon" domination of NATO by wooing Germany (Franco-German treaty of January 1963); then offered the Soviet Union his vision of Europe *de l'Atlantique à l'Oural*, in which France and Russia would join hands in domesticating Germany. He had French representatives resist efforts of the European Commission to wield supranational authority, proposing instead the so-called Fouchet Plan of intergovernmental consultation; and when Britain, after years of voluntary separation, proposed to join the Common Market, he vetoed what he saw as a threat to French predominance. After all, it was still easy for France to dominate Germany, for moral as well as political and military reasons, but Britain's entry might open the door to an Anglo-German alliance within the Commission (shades of the 1920's!). Besides, France saw Britain as a catspaw for the United States. There was even the intrusion of the English language to be guarded against; French had become the common language of the Common Market; could it hold that place in competition with English? Here again we can appreciate the significance of this concern only in the larger historical context: the French see the prestige and diffusion of their language as a measure of their own status, and they hark back nostalgically to the days when French was the accepted official language for international relations.[c]

France's determination to limit the supranational functions of the Common Market was a shock. It was not that de Gaulle wanted to renege on the Treaty of Rome; on the contrary, his government anticipated great advantages from a commercial union that would open Western Europe to French agriculture and finance the costly price-support policy that was the condition of rural tranquility and peasant political support. The point was that the Europeanist founders of the Common Market saw it as a step on the road to political unity and

---

[c]Hence substantial expenditures for French language teaching overseas; a requirement that French diplomats and scholars use only French at international meetings; even a battle to make sure that Concorde be spelled with an E.

envisaged an operation similar to that of the supranational Coal and Steel Community. When de Gaulle chose to put France on a nationalist course, then, he was running head on into long-ripened plans, specifically, expectations of Community control over its own funds and preparations for popular election of a European parliament. De Gaulle wanted to stop the clock; Europeanists felt he was trying to turn it back. So did the United States, which in those days was whole-heartedly committed to the idea of European unification.

On the NATO front, de Gaulle moved to free France from subordination to United States command. He determined that France should have its own nuclear arms. He complained bitterly of "Anglo-Saxon" preeminence within the command structure. And he sent up some *ballons d'essai* concerning a European defense entity that would exclude the United States and would necessarily be dominated by France. This was perhaps the greatest advantage of French nuclear capability: since the Soviet Union would presumably never allow Germany to become a nuclear power, a *force de frappe* would permanently establish a relationship of inequality between France and Germany.

These overtures found no response, primarily because the Germans saw no advantage in exchanging an American protector for a French one—the less so as the tone and content of the two commitments were so different. Thus although the United States was in Europe because it felt that Europe's security was its security, that is, for selfish reasons, it had construed this interest generously, particularly as regards a former enemy such as Germany. It had chosen to define its goals in idealistic terms, as a contest between freedom and tyranny that, however simplistic or self-deceiving, contained an element of sentimental loyalty and constituted a political commitment.

By way of contrast, Charles de Gaulle did not believe in sentiment or friendship in international relations, except as window dressing. He saw the key to peace, not in agreement, but in balance; and the balance is never stable. To quote Hoffmann again:

De Gaulle told Adenauer that as long as there was a threat of German *revanche*, he had to throw his weight on the Soviet side, but, as the threat now came from the East, he wanted to side with Bonn. Later, he said that if Bonn was won over to the Soviet side, he would have to cling to the United States. When Bonn clung to the United States, he moved again toward the Russians.[7]

All of this was no doubt very astute and cunning. It represented an effort to maximize France's weight in the international arena: Have Nation, Will Travel. But it worked better in the short run than in the long. The Soviets were initially most pleased to welcome this *trouble-fête* into their midst and to announce the imminent break-up of the Western coalition; but they were not ready to bet their security on a Franco-Russian entente. If France's long-standing allies could not count on its loyalty, why should the Soviet Union? The Germans made a similar calculation. They were delighted to receive these overtures of collaboration and to be accepted by their traditional enemy as an ally in good standing. But they were perfectly aware of France's deep-rooted reservations, its insistence on precedence and military superiority, and the conditional character of its friendship.

All of these moves were directed in the last analysis against the leadership of the United States. The French made much of their determination to be free of foreign domination and painted the hegemonies of the two superpowers in the same colors. According to Stanley Hoffman, whose defense of the French position is as good as ever the Quai d'Orsay devised, there was nothing "personal" or even critical in all this. The United States and the Soviet Union were behaving, indeed had to behave, as dominant, hence domineering, powers; and it was up to the smaller powers to defend themselves as best they could. Efforts to distinguish between the two adversaries "were both dangerous and futile."

The French were thus prepared to shift their support and smiles from one to the other, as circumstances required. In the 1960s, it was the United States that was de Gaulle's principal *bête noire*. He tried to force a break-up of NATO, and when that did not work, pulled the French forces out and expelled it from France. He mobilized all France's financial resources to mount an attack on the dollar and invited other countries to do the same. He did his best to block the long-cherished objective of European unity, but trotted out at opportune moments the vision of a different kind of Europe—a true Europe—by which he meant one free of the American presence or influence. These salutes to a *Europe européenne* have encouraged some to call de Gaulle a great, or real, Europeanist, but they never fooled the Europeanists, who recognized that de Gaulle's Europe also meant a Europe under French hegemony, that it was a summons to his Europe or no Europe.

De Gaulle did not confine himself to diplomatic maneuver. A master of words, he took every opportunity to chide the Americans for what he saw as their mistakes, to read them lessons in foreign policy, to undermine their authority and prestige. He traveled to Latin America in 1964 and offered (in Spanish) to help France's Latin cousins throw off the *yanqui* yoke; to Cambodia in 1965 and denounced the United States role in Vietnam; to Canada in 1967 and, deliberately snubbing the central government in Ottawa, invited what he called les Français du Canada (not Canadiens français) to look forward to a free Quebec.

De Gaulle's patronizing manner, the aloof certainty of his little sermons, his readiness to bring down the house to teach the builders a lesson—what the French call *la politique du pire*—all of these proved self-defeating on balance. The other members of the Common Market came to resent France's bullying and sulking; the Germans especially proved a disappointment; and the Americans, surprised, then shocked, then disenchanted, came for the first time in memory to look upon the French as adversaries. De Gaulle's officials did not disabuse them: when a top general was asked whom France was defending itself against with its *force de frappe*, he replied, *"Tous azimuts"*—all directions.

Yet for de Gaulle at least, success in specific conflicts was less important than the larger objectives: to throw France's weight around and make other nations take account of it; to exploit his nuisance value to the limit; to undermine American preeminence and break up as much as possible the power blocs that divided Europe. Here he did leave his mark. In the space of a decade he made France the most important medium-sized power in the world. The sixties did see a serious decline in American power and prestige, along with the dollar, and while most of this was our own fault, France hastened the process. And NATO has never been the same since the French withdrawal. How could it be? Any serious defense of Western Europe requires the control and use of French territory, to say nothing of the assistance of French forces. Finally, even though most of our European allies disapproved of de Gaulle's tactics and continued to prefer the protection of the United States to a Gaullist Europe, they did not want to have to choose between Paris and Washington. They needed the first for the Common Market; the second for security.

In the meantime, the French policy of opposition to the United States on every available issue had its effect even within the Alliance. No civil servants are so highly selected and well trained as the French; no country prepares its briefs so carefully, lobbies so assiduously, logrolls so skillfully. The French found sympathizers where they were to be found and gave them every encouragement; and since no alliance is without conflicts of interest and personality and no leadership without friction or challenge, the French were able to nourish a spirit of anti-Americanism that was there for the using.

The resignation of de Gaulle in 1969 did not mark an end to this quarrel. For one thing, Gaullism outlived de Gaulle. The general left behind a party of loyal, sometimes worshipful adherents who were if anything more papist than the Pope. For another, the policy of independence and grandeur that de Gaulle had pursued was more than a party program. It gave expression to deeply felt needs of the French people (as the General well understood), and even those who deplored the growing split with the United States or the sabotage of European unification could not but take satisfaction from their country's new-found eminence. Nationalism, Freud pointed out, is related to narcissism, one of the most profound and powerful aspects of the ego. De Gaulle was psychotherapist to a nation.

5. *Anti-Americanism.* Hardly had the euphoria of victory faded before the hardships of reconstruction, than graffiti began appearing on the walls of France and other European countries: "Yankee Go Home." This sentiment was in no way representative of the population at large, but was rather an attempt by Communist and Communist sympathizers to mobilize opinion against the American presence in Europe—then, and for a long time thereafter, a major Soviet objective. (The Soviets may have now changed their minds about this: our

forces provide a useful justification for the maintenance of Soviet occupation troops in the Warsaw Pact countries.) How much echo this agitation had is hard to say: it takes only a handful of people to paint slogans on every surface and give the widest currency to what may be the most eccentric opinion. The subject needs investigating; and if political scientists and historians have done so little with it, this may be due to the difficulty of the inquiry—how does one weigh the changing components of variegated opinion?—and not its importance.

Within the limits of our knowledge, it seems reasonable to assert that anti-American sentiment has grown in Europe over the past generation. Not steadily perhaps; but the overall trend seems indisputable. In the early years the Communists and left-wing opponents of so-called Yankee imperialism, atomic terror, and capitalist exploitation led the chorus, with substantial help from American expatriates. These were the years of peace marches, Picasso's dove, the Rosenberg trial, the McCarthyite purges. As time passed, these themes yielded ground to an even older right-wing anti-Americanism, which drew its strength from the resentment that many Europeans felt at their misfortunes and their displacement in the world arena by what they perceived as a younger, less experienced, less cultured or civilized people. This resentment long antedated World War II, as any study of, say, French writing on the United States makes clear. But it was enormously magnified by the experience of war and occupation—de Gaulle, as we have seen, is an excellent example—and further reinforced, in a process well known to psychology, by the aid-and-dependency relationship that prevailed for some years thereafter.

The anti-Americanism of distaste and disdain often found expression in trivia—trivia, that is, to Americans, but not to aggrieved Europeans. Thus the battle to keep Coca-Cola out of France in the fifties: the principal opponents were the manufacturers and distributors of the traditional apéritifs and soft drinks, which is perfectly understandable; but they were able to mount a tremendous campaign to defend French independence against *"coca-colonisation,"* and there was even one reputable scholar (Etiemble) who solemnly warned his compatriots that Coca-Cola would necessarily lead to quick lunches and love-making in automobiles; and then what would happen to French civilization?

The fact was that Western Europe *was* to a great extent Americanized in these years. As economies prospered and incomes rose, everyone wanted those hard goods that had become characteristic of "the American way of life": automobiles first, but also refrigerators, television sets, washing machines, record players, telephones. With these came new habits: supermarket shopping, packaged and prepared foods, motor outings, youth culture, the diversions and satisfactions of the consumer society. The cinema played its usual role, but so, too, did television, and also the rapidly increasing flow of American tourists, often decried but even more often copied—and often decried and copied by the same people. It became fashionable to dress and eat and play American while criticizing the shallowness and materialism of American culture; indeed the criticism was a means of self-exoneration.

While this widespread cultural and spiritual anti-Americanism no doubt served the useful purpose of bolstering European egos in painful circumstances, it created a reservoir of animus that could be tapped for political purposes. France, with its complexes about the "Anglo-Saxons," was the most receptive to this appeal, which the Gaullists were able to convert into hard votes. But it also became a factor in the domestic politics of other countries, where, as in France, it became fashionable to equate independence with standing up to the Americans, which was only a short step away from opposing them. The Vietnam War gave considerable stimulus to this sentiment by providing an issue on which both left and right could agree: even old imperialists now found it convenient to condemn us.[d] Racial conflict contributed to this negative image. It was the old half-full, half-empty dilemma: some Europeans stressed the achievements of the civil rights movement and noted that Americans were not alone in matters of racial prejudice; other preferred to dwell on our shortcomings, which were and are many.

In short, the sixties turned the United States for many Europeans into a villain. This was no small matter. A villain, after all, is not simply someone who is a victim of misfortune, or who makes a mistake, or gets caught in the machinery of miscalculation. A villain is someone who does wrong because he is bad and wants to do wrong. The diffusion of this negative stereotype—the association of the adjective "ugly" with what had always been the good name of American—inevitably handicapped us in our relations with our allies. Like "bad breath," it was not the kind of thing that they would discuss with us: "Even your best friends won't tell you." But it could hardly be ignored, if only as a force in European domestic politics.

Here the passage of time aggravated the problem. The younger Europeans came to remember little or nothing of the common struggle against Nazi Germany or the American contribution to European reconstruction or the airlift that saved Berlin. As a result, they were little inclined to accept as given the postulates of the Western alliance, and their own anxieties for peace in an atomic age made them singularly susceptible to the equation of the two superpowers. They were a rich generation, in the sense of income and material temptations, so much so that they have transformed the taste and demand patterns of the entire population; yet their sensitivity to privilege loaded them with guilt that was easily displaced onto that bastion of materialism, the United States. In this regard the young were a particularly marked example of the Americanization-anti-Americanism syndrome.

---

[d] The scope and nature of the destruction in Vietnam also gave Europeans pause: might a nation that destroyed villages to save them do the same thing in Europe? The qualms about American intentions as embodied in the notion of flexible response could only be revived and aggravated.

Within the younger generation, university students constituted a group apart: wealthier than their contemporaries; destined by education and connections to positions of authority; exposed to every current of ideas and opinion; segregated by residence and activities, hence easily mobilizable. Their numbers had grown rapidly in postwar Europe—one more instance of catching up with American patterns. In France, the 122,000 of 1939 became 514,000 in 1967; in Germany, the 137,000 of 1954 grew to 316,000 in 1968.[8] Facilities had not kept pace, and the inconveniences and discontents of mass instruction rendered a naturally sensitive group that much more susceptible to political agitation. In all of Western Europe, the students tended to be more highly organized and politicized than in the United States, and in most universities, especially those located in the great urban centers, the dominant affiliation was with the Left. This did not necessarily redound to the advantage of the Soviet Union, since Communism had limited appeal to a generation that rejected the discipline and subordination entailed by Party membership. But it did imply an anti-imperialist, anti-Vietnam War, antiracist (often anti-white), anticapitalist, anti-Establishment, hence anti-American stance. It also threw the political support of the young to those parties that were hostile or indifferent to European unity—a big change from the idealistic commitment to Europe in the immediate postwar years—and the Western alliance. The effect was to shift the political center of gravity leftward, more and more on balance every year.

It would be a distortion, however, to see this change of values and loyalties as confined to the European side of the Atlantic. In the United States also, the younger generation found it hard to relate to the fears and commitments of their elders. Here too the youth came to constitute a powerful constituency apart, closer in some ways to Youth International than to their own parents. Thanks to the new media of communication and the unprecedented cheapness and ease of travel, ideas and aspirations spread from university to university, hostel to hostel, festival to festival. Within five years the student riots at Berkeley found imitators around the world. The slogan of the rioters at Chicago in 1968 was, "The whole world is watching." That was the point of the exercise.

In the United States the student fight against the war in Southeast Asia was, for obvious reasons, even more influential than in Europe. A good part of a generation was disabused, became disenchanted and decommitted. The verities of the postwar years rang hollow; the distinction between two drastically different systems took on the appearance of a fraud, the more so as it was often advanced as an argument against social and political criticism at home. Revisionist historians did their best to shift the blame on the United States for the postwar estrangement of the Soviet Union and found a large audience among their students. Their thesis is bad history; but that is not the point; it had and continues to have an alienating effect on those who want to believe the worst of the United States. All of this tended to undermine the American commitment to our allies in Europe and to promote a new isolationism.

III

As a result of these changes, the decade of the seventies opened on an alliance in serious trouble. The marriage of love and convenience had turned sour; and as is the wont, each partner found fault with every action of the other. Even gestures that were intended to appease somehow went wrong.

Where to begin? It is impossible to say. In domestic quarrels, every action has its antecedent. For purposes of convenience, let us take our start from the American decision of March 1968 to end support for the private market in gold. Gold was put on a two-tier basis: an official price (still $35 an ounce) at which the United States would continue to sell gold for dollars to central banks; and a free price for private buyers and sellers. This ended private speculation using gold against the dollar, but it did not end official speculation of the kind that France had engaged in since 1962 or private speculation against the dollar in foreign-exchange markets. Now the continuing American deficit on balance of payments came home to roost. By August 1971 the pressure on the dollar had become irresistible, in the sense that the cost of supporting it was too much for any and all interested parties. Without much warning the United States suspended convertibility, in effect inviting other currencies to revalue upwards against the dollar. By so doing, it unilaterally abrogated the gold-exchange standard it had conceived and instituted at Bretton Woods over a quarter-century earlier. It also imposed a temporary 10 per cent surcharge on most imports, to be lifted when our trade balance had improved sufficiently.

These measures were only the opening salvos of what President Nixon called a New Economic Policy. By fall of 1971 American representatives pressed Japan to impose quotas on those exports that were making heavy inroads in the American market; and urged the Common Market to lower barriers to American farm products imposed by the high support-price structure of the Common Agricultural Policy. We also raised objections to the reverse preferences built into the European Community's special arrangements with ex-colonies in the Third World. And then, in December 1971, we devalued the dollar, and again in February 1973, after which we decided simply to let it float with supply and demand.

None of this was new. Devaluation was a familiar resort of such countries as France and Great Britain; so were import surcharges and quotas. But for the United States to have recourse to these unilateral breaches of commercial continuity constituted a revolution. For a generation the Western alliance had rested on the tacit assumption that the United States was strong and Europe weak; that the United States would sacrifice its interests if necessary to further the prosperity of Europe; and hence that Europeans would be permitted to do things that we would not do. Now we were telling Europe that the pact was null and void. We would have to defend our own commercial interests, as they theirs.

Benjamin Cohen describes this reversal as a "bargain come unstuck." That represents a misreading, I think, of the American commitment. "Repeatedly," he writes, "the United States emphasized its willingness to sacrifice short-term economic benefits for the longer-term advantages of partnership with a united Europe. Its attitude was that what was good for Europe was also good for the United States."[9] That is true so far as it goes, which is only part of the way. American readiness to make sacrifices for the sake of European prosperity and unity was never intended to be permanent; certainly no Americans, from the leadership on down, would have accepted such an undertaking if it had been put in those terms at the beginning. Our commitment was to Europe's revival, and by 1971 no one could argue that Europe had not been thoroughly revived. What did change at that point was the readiness of the United States to impose on itself a higher standard of abnegation than was expected of our allies. We were saying that we too would have to consider our interest in these matters. And since long-enjoyed privilege has a way of becoming vested right, this may well have appeared to many as a breach of contract.

In the event, the Europeans (and the French in particular) were not happy. They did not so much attack the new principles of American policy as the manner of execution: unilateral, abrupt, inconsiderate. They could hardly complain about the devaluation of the dollar, which they had done much to bring about; but they were upset to find that the desacralization of the dollar did not end its role as an international reserve currency (what else was there?), and that the floating of exchange rates tended to undervalue the dollar and handicap the strong-currency countries (Germany, Switzerland, and to a lesser degree, France) in commercial competition. The French were particularly inconvenienced by the new situation, for the franc tried to tie itself to the mark, which was not easy to keep up with, so that French exporters found their goods overpriced and France was compelled for a while to drop out of the European monetary snake. The remedy, the French argued, was a return to fixed parities. They found American indifference to the exchange rate of the dollar hard to understand: in Europe exchange rates are as much a matter of national prestige as of economic interest.

In the meantime, the United States was trying to set its own house in order by getting out of Southeast Asia, a process that required complicated diplomatic preparation, a vast reexamination of national priorities, and the liquidation of important international commitments. Given the enormous material and psychic American commitment to the conflict, one can understand the misdirection, the reversals, the deception and self-deception that characterized a process that will some day look obvious and unavoidable. It was a time, among other things, for building bridges to erstwhile adversaries—of rapprochement with China and reinforced détente with the Soviet Union. It was also a time of reconsideration of the American military commitment in Europe.

For the Europeans these efforts at disengagement were welcome in principle (they had long condemned or deplored our role in Vietnam) but worrisome in practice. The French in particular, always sensitive on this point, saw here one more example of superpower dominion, of negotiations conducted over their heads, of deals that would surely affect them concluded without their say-so. And all could not but be troubled by hints of United States retrenchment or withdrawal (even the French needed our umbrella to play odd man out)—to say nothing of the genuine anxiety they felt regarding the obvious decline in American power and prestige.

It is in this context of unhappiness and concern that Nixon and Kissinger tried to reassure our allies by declaring 1973 "the year of Europe." The intention was no doubt good: to efface or minimize sources of disagreement, to reaffirm the American commitment to European security, to accept the pursuit by European governments of bilateral ties with the Soviet Union and Eastern Europe, to propose such issues as energy for common consideration and action. They also summoned our European allies to join with us in defining a (new) "basis of co-operative economic relations"—tacit confirmation that for the United States, European economic parity implied equality of give-and-take. "We need," Nixon said, "a new affirmation to our common goals, to give political direction to our economic negotiations and promote co-operative solutions."[10]

Tact is in the ear of the listener. The intentions may have been good, but the overture was received with a mixture of indifference, resentment, and hostility. Again the French proved most umbrageous. At that time the French foreign minister was Michel Jobert, an ardent nationalist in the Gaullist (Gallic?) tradition. Jobert had little faith in the friendship of other nations.[11] When a friend reproached him for ingratitude—he had worn an American uniform and used American equipment during the war—he quipped that when you put on blue jeans to mow the lawn, you're not making a gift of your person to America.

Jobert and Pompidou reacted badly to the Year of Europe. The reference to the "regional security interests" of the Europeans in juxtaposition to America's "vital interests outside of Europe" was singled out as particularly offensive. Kissinger and Nixon may have thought that they were giving evidence of good will: justifying European bilateral arrangements with the Soviet Union (which America had once wanted to discourage) as well as U.S.-Soviet negotiations on strategic and global issues. Jobert saw this as "an exposé without prudence of American geopolitics: Europe confined to a purely regional vocation and the world revolving around the American power like the Celestial Empire of old, with its seven moons turning around it." As for the invitation to draft a new "Atlantic Charter," "the very brutality of the proposal" filled Pompidou with "a cold determination not to associate himself with a gesture that was maladroit in form and made light of France's interests."

So much for good intentions. According to Jobert,[12] Kissinger was later to defend himself by saying that he had spoken of these things with Pompidou ahead of time and found him receptive. Jobert does not think that argument is even worth refuting. That is the way of sour marriages (partnerships). Neither partner seems to understand the other; neither will give the other the benefit of the doubt; and each side enjoys marking points whose subjective importance far exceeds their real meaning.

This was the mood when the Yom Kippur War broke out and the Arab oil embargo changed all the rules of the game. It is roughly at this point that the contributors to this book take up their story.

Notes

1. Cf. the excellent analysis of Hans Morgenthau, "The United States and Europe in a Decade of Détente," in Wolfram Hanrieder (ed.), *The United States and Western Europe* (Cambridge, Mass.: Winthrop, 1974), pp. 1-7.

2. The words are those of Robert Schuman on May 9, 1950, cited in Roger Morgan, *West European Politics since 1945: The Shaping of the European Community* (London: B.T. Batsford, 1972), p. 87.

3. Ibid., p. 133.

4. See, for example, the biting analysis of Theodore Draper, "Appeasement and Détente," *Commentary* 61, 2 (Feb. 1976): 27-38.

5. Stanley Hoffmann, *Decline or Renewal: France since the 1930s* (New York: Viking, 1974), p. 312.

6. Ibid., p. 295. Among other things, acceptance of the proposal would have entailed full French membership in the nuclear club, an act of proliferation that would have seemed provocative to the Russians and politically reprehensible to the Americans. In those days, we still cherished the hope that there would be no extension of nuclear capabilities to other powers.

7. Ibid., p. 314.

8. John Ardagh, *The New French Revolution: A Social and Economic Survey of France 1945-1967* (London: Secker & Warburg, 1968), p. 323; Alfred Grosser, *Germany in Our Time: A Political History of the Postwar Years* (New York: Praeger, 1971), p. 252.

9. Benjamin Cohen, "The Revolution in Atlantic Economic Relations: A Bargain Comes Unstuck," in Hanrieder (ed.), *The United States and Western Europe*, p. 106.

10. From "U.S. Foreign Policy for the 1970's: Shaping a Durable Peace," a report to the Congress by Richard M. Nixon, May 3, 1973, as given in Hanrieder (ed.), *The United States and Western Europe*, p. 311. Kissinger's version of the Year of Europe was announced in a speech in New York on April 23.

11. He writes in his *Mémoires d'avenir* (Paris: Bernard Grasset, 1974), p. 11: "Nothing seems more suspect and pitiful to me than the enthusiasm my countrymen have shown in turn for Great Britain—let's say nothing about Germany—the United States, the U.S.S.R., Cuba, China, India. And I don't have to go back in time! My older brother, who went to Saint-Cyr, was a member of

the class of 1939, called "Franco-British Friendship." I attended the graduation ceremonies. A few months later we had Dunkerque, then Mers-el-Kebir. Louvois, Vauban, Surcouf, Montcalm, Dumouriez, Hoche—any of these would have made a better name for that class and at that point in history."

12. Ibid., pp. 231-32.

Europe and the United States: The Relations Between Europeans and Americans

Raymond Aron

The subject of European-American relations seems to me, more than ever, a false good subject or, if one prefers, a fruitless subject. Having tried for twenty-five years now, too often, to explain French policy to the Americans and American to the French, I experience in advance, at the moment of writing this text, a sense of boredom as well as a fear of boring. Those responsible for this book would have done better to entrust the task to a commentator from another generation. But rather than settle for a failure, let us try once again.

The present conjuncture—that of summer 1975—makes my task difficult for four principal reasons.

1. In a sense, or in certain respects, the conjuncture in Europe is the same as it has been for thirty years. The Old Continent is divided into two zones: one ruled by Communist parties, where, if necessary, the Soviet army is prepared to impose discipline; the other composed of liberal democratic states allied to the United States. The western part of the Old Continent does not have the capacity to maintain a military equilibrium, not for lack of resources, but of will and especially of unity. It has been thus since 1945. The result is that the Europeans—I shall use that name for those who are west of the line of demarcation—are "protected" by the United States. Anyone can easily imagine the variations of humiliation, resentment, bitterness of protégés—variations that any commentator can easily enlarge on at will.

This situation lends itself the less to original analysis or to critical choices in that, for the moment, Europeans do not seriously fear either an invasion by the Russian army or the breakdown of the Atlantic alliance. Even the fear of an American withdrawal, which was relatively genuine at the time of Richard Nixon's resignation, seems to have more or less died down in the wake of the collapse of South Vietnam.

25

2. The present conjuncture, which is much like that of the last quarter of a century so long as one looks only at the political-military situation of the Old Continent, nevertheless differs from it considerably in other respects. The disintegration of the British Empire, which the independence of India, proclaimed in 1948, announced and made inevitable, still lay in the future when the North Atlantic Treaty was signed in 1949 and the idea of the Coal and Steel Community was launched in 1950. France, whether in 1945 or 1950, was still exercising its authority on both shores of the western Mediterranean. In the course of the last quarter-century, the countries of Western Europe have lost or liquidated their empires while at the same time they have risen from their ruins and have effected an economic expansion of unprecedented rapidity.

Since the end of the war in Algeria, the major countries of Western Europe have ceased to be "colonialist" (Portugal did not heal itself of this sin until 1974-75), and as a result, it is the United States that has been placed in the front line and exposed to the charges of anti-imperialist propaganda, while the Europeans have been trying to take their distance from a protector that compromises them. And then, even more than this reversal of roles, which the second Vietnamese war has encouraged, it is the change in the economic climate that makes any speculation on the future uncertain.

The Atlantic Alliance constituted historically a strange alliance because it limited the engagements of the partners to a specific geographic zone, while creating an integrated military structure. During the years of decolonization, the paradox of a geographically limited alliance gave rise to tensions between the United States and Great Britain (1956) and between the United States and France (until the end of the Algerian War). The same paradox threatens to engender other tensions in the next phase: insofar as the United States expects support from its European allies in regions outside the Alliance (for example, the Middle East) or in regard to economic and monetary questions, not covered by the Alliance, the quarrel that the French were picking with the Americans twenty-five years ago (one cannot be at the same time allies here and adversaries there) threatens to revive, with reversal of roles, the Americans demanding this time more solidarity than the French are disposed to accord.

3. I have just substituted for the dialogue between the Europeans and the Americans the dialogue between the French and Americans. There is no valid reason to treat the relationships between the citizens of different European countries and the citizens of the United States as if the former belonged to a single political entity, economically and culturally comparable or of the same type as that constituted by the United States. Even in the cultural sphere it is not at all true that all Western Europeans have more in common than certain of them have with the Americans. The Scandinavians, for example, seem to me in every respect closer to the Americans (or to the Anglo-Americans) than to the Greeks and Portuguese. As for Great Britain, even though it has now entered the European Community, it has retained in some regards a special relationship with the United States.

In order to do a better job of analyzing the relations between Western Europe and the United States, one has to consider successively the dialogues between Bonn and Washington, London and Washington, Paris and Washington, all of which differ from one another. More precisely, it is desirable to separate two problems: (a) the attitude of the American government toward the European Community, or more generally, the effort to create a European unity; and (b) the attitude of the American government toward the different European governments in respect to the various problems posed. There is no global dialogue taking place between Europe as an entity and the United States.

4. Once one sees things this way, it becomes difficult to know what crucial choices might confront the American government after the elections of 1976, or why a question of crucial choices should arise at all if a new president should enter the White House.

In his report, Stanley Hoffmann tries to define these choices in relation to the formulas, of Gaullist origin, of European Europe and Atlantic Europe. He is perfectly aware that these formulas are the creations of rhetoric or polemic. Algerian Algeria enjoyed a short life as something intermediate between French Algeria and an independent Algeria. Western Europe belongs in fact to the Atlantic Community, whether it is a question of defense or money; Europe is in fact, as of now, Atlantic. The crucial choices that Mr. Hoffmann presents to the leaders of the United States concern their attitude toward the European Community—ranging from effective hostility, even if not declared, to determined support. Now the fact is that in view of the American political system, that is, the practices normal in a democracy, the choice that will be made will almost surely be simply more of the same, with a slight tipping in one or another direction according to the persons in charge and the issues.

In short, if it is a question of the original function of the American presence in Europe, of the military balance between the two blocs, we are not going to leave familiar paths. On the other hand, if one envisages the new world economic order, the monetary system, the energy crisis, the common struggle against stagflation, then we are entering into technical controversies and little-known terrain. Finally the attitude regarding the European Community is not going to change fundamentally from what it was; rather it will vary ever so slightly according to circumstances or problems.

In spite of these introductory remarks, which may well discourage the reader, I should like to seek the answer to a simple question: since Western Europe was never in so much danger as now, why do the Europeans persist in acting as though they did not know this? Why do the writings on the relations between Europe and the United States ignore more often than not the heart of the matter?

The Routinization of the Atlantic Alliance

I mean by routinization of the Atlantic Alliance the fact that it no longer arouses enthusiasm or hostility. When it was created, Hubert Beauve-Mery (editor-in-chief of *Le Monde*) denounced it as the prelude to the rearmament of Germany. In this, he was a good prophet; which does not mean that in the absence of the Alliance, this rearmament would not have happened. The Alliance persists, even though two of the member states, Turkey and Greece, are on the point of leaving it (or at least of leaving NATO). Routinized, the Alliance survives without a strong consensus among the partners, without a common goal. When Mr. Kissinger, on the eve of the Paris agreements, launched the idea of a "Year of Europe," he failed miserably; or rather he obtained a result contrary to what he had envisaged: whereas he wanted to restore to the West the sense of a common concern, he only succeeded in highlighting the absence of such a common interest, or rather the deep disagreements on what such an objective could or might be. Was the Year of Europe condemned in advance, or was it rather condemned by clumsiness of execution?

The Original Function of the Alliance

The Atlantic Alliance was born of a European desire for support at the time of the Korean War. The Alliance fulfilled in the beginning, and continues to fulfill today, a function that the European governments considered and continue to consider necessary: that of symbolizing and consecrating the interest that the United States has in maintaining an independent Western Europe and in giving to that Europe a sense of security resting on a true military balance. I shall not enter here into a detailed analysis of the measures available for reinforcing this balance or preserving it at less cost. I shall ask only why this function is sufficient today for a Community held together by habit rather than will.

The reason normally invoked to account for this is the disappearance of a sense of peril. This is true enough, but in a paradoxical sense: the objective circumstances are such as to justify anxiety today much more than in 1948 or 1949, when the United States held a monopoly of atomic arms and the Soviet Union had not yet recovered from the destruction of the war. The Soviet Union of Stalin inspired fear, even though it was weak, whereas that of Brezhnev neither hypnotizes nor terrifies, even though it continues to pile up armaments.

Could the United States awake the Alliance from its routinization? The American critics of the personal diplomacy of Henry Kissinger assert as much, and one can easily imagine a debate between those who emphasize dialogue at the summit between the two superpowers and those who consider more important the maintenance of coordination between Americans and Europeans (with Japan included). Would a change of style and priority on the part of American diplomacy allow us to look forward to a revitalization of the Alliance? Without attempting for the moment to pass judgment on the advantages of such changes, I should like to indicate why I do not see such a change, even in the most favorable circumstances, producing more than limited consequences.

Diplomacy at the Summit and Joint Dominion

The Atlantic Alliance is necessarily routinized to the degree that it is limited to its initial function—that of guaranteeing the military security of Western Europe by means of a solemn engagement on the part of the United States. The direct negotiations that have taken place and are taking place between Washington and Moscow only accentuate an evolution that is more or less inevitable.

American diplomacy, at least since Kennedy, perhaps even earlier, has sought a dialogue with Moscow in order to reduce the risks of a catastrophic collision. Today numerous Frenchmen denounce the Russian-American "condominium." Non-French Europeans also do so, but only French officials have given explicit expression to this charge. The present president of the French Republic, unlike his predecessor Georges Pompidou, has rejected the charge. As he puts it, Russians and Americans are trying to work out between them problems that concern them alone and that they are the only ones in a position to resolve (for example, the limitation of strategic arms). Which of these two interpretations is closer to reality?

I shall begin by observing that in such matters it is not easy to distinguish between appearance and reality. It is enough for Nixon and Brezhnev or Kissinger and Gromyko to meet regularly and sign from time to time an agreement, or join in resolving a crisis, for Europeans to get the feeling that they have been reduced to the role of spectators and to give expression to their bitterness by denouncing this joint dominion.

In the precise sense of the term, condominium means a common exercise of power or domination. Such a condominium does not exist and cannot exist so long as there is rivalry of power and ideological competition between the two superpowers. More loosely construed, condominium implies simply that the two partners, even if they are not agreed on ruling together, exclude others, in particular their respective allies, from their deliberations and decisions. It is this weak version of condominium that best describes the direction of Russian-American relations over the past few years. Within the context of that version, moreover, there are two aspects to be distinguished.

The first of these concerns the negotiation of a limitation of strategic arms. This negotiation concerns the allies of the United States, but it is only the latter that makes the decision. What is more, the technical complexity of these negotiations is such that few officials in European foreign services are capable of following them in detail. The Europeans are informed of these matters, at most consulted, but in the end, decisions on the proportions of strategic forces are taken by the Soviets and the Americans, in common so to speak. And so far as I can see, I do not think it can be done any other way.

Does this mean a weakening of the American deterrent, of the guarantee given by the American commitment? Logically, no. The alteration of the proportions of nuclear forces, the substitution of equality for American superiority, theoretically weakens the value of the American guarantee. The fact that the Americans officially sanction the new situation of parity is less important than the situation itself. What is more, the last agreement, prepared at Vladivostok, did not bear on the forward bases of the United States (in other words, on the tactical nuclear arms in Europe) any more than it did on the French and English forces. The American negotiators thus seem to me justified in pleading that the limitation of strategic arms was negotiated without diminishing the obligations, both written and informal, of the United States toward its allies.

The second aspect of "condominium" concerns the temporary settlement of the Middle East crisis following the Yom Kippur War. These events touched directly and seriously the most vital interests of the nations of Western Europe. Now these had hardly been consulted in advance on the policy followed by the United States. When invited by the Americans to place their bases at the disposal of the American air force so as to make possible the reequipment of the Israeli army, they refused. They were compelled to stand by, almost passively, and watch the mobilization of American forces in the confrontation with the Soviet Union and to witness in the same way the cease-fire imposed by the two superpowers. They vented their frustration, to the great indignation of Henry Kissinger, by signing declarations favorable to the Arab position.

In the Middle East, it would be absurd to speak of joint dominion, since the American-Russian rivalry is permanently installed there. There the Russians and Americans tested their new arms by the intermediary of Egyptians, Syrians, and Israelis. On the other hand, it is easy to see there an example of "condominium" in the weak sense: neither Russians nor Americans left any share there for their respective allies in the settlement they imposed. If by "condominium" one means simply the exclusion of the others, the crisis of autumn 1973 certainly justifies this use of the word.

Europeans react sharply, there is no doubt, to this second aspect of "condominium." But in fact this is a necessary result of their military weakness and their historic abdication. The Middle East has been since 1948 the theater of a war, in the classic sense of the word, interrupted from time to time by truces. It is a single, continuing war, and the return to regular combat is possible at any moment. Now the Europeans devote just about all of their military resources to their security vis-à-vis the Soviet Union. The nuclear forces of Britain and France are of no use whatsoever in military conflicts outside the zone covered by the Atlantic Alliance. Under the circumstances, the Europeans are perfectly logical in refusing as much as possible any solidarity with American diplomacy. The Americans, in advance or in return, do not seek the aid of European diplomacy (whether in the form of the joint efforts of the Community or the diplomatic efforts of the several European states), except insofar as it hopes for support for its own conceptions. In effect, it is less a question of knowing what goal one is aiming for, but rather by what route and at what speed.

Europeans and Americans, if one is to believe their official declarations, both claim to support the existence of the state of Israel (within secure and recognized boundaries)—whatever that may mean. At the same time they seek to impose a return to the frontiers of 1967, with minor modifications, and the restoration of the rights of the Palestinian people, whatever that may mean. Under the circumstances, they might have some advantage in working together, but the French have little desire to join with the Americans in this matter. At the same time, the Israelis would perhaps resist European-American pressure even more stubbornly than they have an exclusively American pressure. It is possible that at a certain time, in the course of the long process leading from the precarious cease-fire of today to a general peace, the collective participation of the European states or the participation of certain European states might be useful. I do not think that it makes any sense here to speculate about possible scenarios.

The Europeans thus have to live with these two versions of "condominium." One is legitimate; the other, inevitable as a result of circumstances.

In addition one can probably find examples of a third version: Russian-American agreements on problems that concern the Europeans as much as the Americans, where the Americans have at the very least made promises to the Russians with the aim of facilitating a global accord with them. At Vladivostok, for example, President Ford surely gave Leonid Brezhnev to understand that he could have his meeting of heads of state at the end of the Conference on Security and Co-operation in Europe. This is something Brezhnev wanted very badly. There were probably other cases of this sort of "diplomacy" at the Russian-American summit, and they aggravate the sense of powerlessness felt by the Europeans. In the event of a change of personnel in the United States, bringing in a team whose manner of thinking and style were like those of the first teams of the postwar period, these two versions, legitimate or inevitable, of "condominium" would probably become less prominent, and the third (that of settling problems common to all of the West over the heads of the Europeans) would disappear. The effect eventually would be to produce a modification, in appearance at least, of American diplomatic priorities. The unity of the West would once again be in first place, and the dialogue with Moscow would fall back to second.

Beyond that, it is necessary to push the analysis further and inquire into the consequences of détente in general, the implications of the German *Ostpolitik*, and the so-called privileged relationship of France with Moscow.

Détente

Kissinger's diplomacy at the summit is the result in part of the constraints imposed on the United States by the Vietnam War. In order to extricate the

United States from South Vietnam without capitulating, the Nixon-Kissinger team had recourse to traditional diplomatic procedures, resuming relations with Peking and thus, indirectly, stimulating Moscow to deal with Washington and to give counsels of moderation to Hanoi. Kennedy and Johnson had themselves both sought a dialogue with Moscow on nuclear armaments (the first agreement on the subject dates from July 1963, when Kennedy was still in the White House). Nixon and Kissinger succeeded in going much farther, partly because they had made contact with China, partly in all probability because the Soviets had made up a good deal of their weapons lag and found themselves for the first time in a position to deal on the basis of parity and symmetry.

The French and Germans had preceded the Americans in Moscow. But the Russian-American détente produced for the system as a whole consequences that were altogether different from those formulated by de Gaulle: détente, entente, cooperation, or "Europe from the Atlantic to the Urals." Gaullist policy tended to seduce or irritate the rest of Europe, which was either tempted to follow suit or convinced that only the Atlantic discipline of the other Europeans made it possible for France to play this brilliant but solitary game. The *Ostpolitik* of the Germans already marked a breaking point: the West Europeans had in effect lost since 1956 the hope (if they ever had it) of once again putting in question the partition of Europe effected by the armies in 1944-45. Even so Western Europe refused to recognize the territorial arrangements produced by the Second World War and protested, in the name of the principle of legitimacy, against regimes whose first leaders, Walter Ulbricht, for example, had come in the pack wagons of the Red Army. The transition from de facto acceptance to de jure recognition—which is what *Ostpolitik* was all about—was of some historical moment. So long as the West Europeans said *No* with a capital *N*, they remained in conflict with the Soviet Union. The day they ratified the status quo, the conflict vanished, at least so far as they were concerned.

The Russian-American summit negotiations did not deal in principle with the political conflict between the two Europes. But the Russian-American dialogue, the declarations of Moscow (1972) and Washington (1973), once again reinforced the sentiment that the world was entering on a new phase and that the cold war belonged to the past. Nothing in principle now prevented countries of different social regimes from contracting and maintaining the best relations, or, if one prefers, normal relations. New slogans became the order of the day: the end of the postwar era, diplomacy without ideology.

To be sure, the Europeans did not lose sight of the growing military power of the Soviet Union and, out of habit, they became anxious each year at the proposals of a few American senators that the United States withdraw part of its forces in Europe. That would leave the heart of the alliance—the integrated command of NATO; nothing more. No matter how much the Soviets insisted that détente (peaceful coexistence) concerned only interstate political relations and had nothing to do with ideological competition, the Europeans, or at least most of them, saw in this only formulas and worn-out slogans. Even when the bear showed his teeth, they preferred to believe he was smiling.

In such a climate, what common objective could have possibly animated within Europe in 1973 the partners of the Atlantic Alliance? As for the rest of the world, the Europeans either could not or did not want to maintain solidarity with the Americans.

Regional Powers and World Power

No phrase of Henry Kissinger aroused more indignation in Europe than his remark about the regional interests of the Europeans as against the global tasks of a world power like the United States. Let us put aside the intentions of Mr. Kissinger or the meaning that he subsequently gave to these words. The question for us is how much truth is there in this antithesis?

In one sense, the American secretary of state was obviously right. No European country possesses substantial military forces east of Suez. In that respect Great Britain is no different from France or Italy. Even in the Mediterranean, the European nations taken together could hardly match the Soviet fleet. Unless the Soviet fleet were prepared to leave the Mediterranean at the same time as the American Sixth Fleet, the latter's withdrawal would not serve to return the "eternal sea" to the countries along its shores but rather to the Third Rome.

On the other hand, Kissinger's formula does not hold water in economic or cultural matters. The European Community constitutes the most important commercial unit in the world. It buys and sells on all continents; it is more important than the United States in Africa. The Chinese understand better than the Americans the place that Western Europe could occupy in the global system if and when it realized its potential.

These last remarks concerning military importance and economic power throw light on the achievement, at first glance paradoxical, of the quarter-century since the conclusion of the Atlantic Alliance: the Europeans, encouraged by the Americans, have abdicated politically and devoted themselves exclusively to the prosaic task of material prosperity. This abdication has been a complete success, but it is a success that, however brilliant, seems once again to be in question.

The American reader will ask me what I mean when I say that the leaders of the United States have encouraged this European abdication. My answer is, they have done so in two ways. First by the strong support they gave to anticolonialist movements; and secondly by the doctrine of nonproliferation of nuclear arms. I do not say that they are wrong in either of these, but the doctrine of nonproliferation (which only yesterday Professor Kissinger approved of with considerable reservation) contained the germ of the SALT agreements and the perpetual dependence of Europe on American protection. As neither the Congress nor American public opinion is conscious of American responsibilities in this respect, the leaders of the United States demand concessions from their European allies in order to appease the revolt of some senators against the burden of the common defense. Even more, they have retarded the development of a European armaments industry, intentionally or not, by insisting on compensation for troop outlays in Europe by European arms purchases in the United States. France developed a nuclear strike force in the face of the most determined opposition of the American government. This government supports American arms exports with as much vigor as the French government does French arms exports. The recent battle over the sale of a new fighting aircraft to four European states, Norway, Denmark, Holland, and Belgium, ended, as everyone knows, in an American victory.

I am neither criticizing nor approving; I am simply stating facts. When it is a question of defense, Europe, whether as a community or not, *is* Atlantic, whatever individual national preferences may be. The Americans wanted it this way, and even with hindsight it is hard to see how it could have been otherwise. But to recognize this is to understand that a change in attitude on the part of the United States in this regard is not a plausible prospect. America's policy, which prefers Atlanticism to European unity, would change only in response to changes in Europe.

These changes could come only from France, because it alone could one day adopt a European objective acceptable to its partners that the United States would perhaps agree or resign itself to.

Before considering these possibilities, it is useful to look a moment at the other side of the coin: in matters of defense and high policy, there is nothing fundamentally new. The style and sometimes the crudeness of Kissinger have brought out fully the dependency and impotence of Western Europe—a dependency that is aggravated by the increase in Soviet forces and the damage wrought by recession and higher petroleum prices on the European economy.

Political Alliance and Economic Competition

Marxists and "para-Marxists," in the tradition of Hobson and Lenin, explain the wars of the twentieth century by economic conflicts among capitalist states. Since 1917, and especially since 1945, the creation of what they call a world Socialist market outside the world capitalist market, as well as a political alliance among the principal members of the world capitalist market, have apparently given rise to arrangements contrary to this interpretation. I recall a Soviet article, written on the morrow of the Second World War, that contained the following lines (I quote them as I remember them): the major contradiction within the capitalist world is that between the United States and Great Britain, but it is developing in the form of an intimate cooperation.

The fact that the Marxists, working within their system of thought, continue to explain the breakdown of alliances among capitalist countries by economic rivalries—a dogma contradicted by history—should not prevent us from inquiring into the relations between these partner-rivals and into the political consequences of commercial competition. This inquiry is the more legitimate in that in certain domains, in particular that of armaments and nuclear industry, exporters, if not congruent with states, benefit considerably from the support of their governments.

A recent remark by Valéry Giscard d'Estaing illustrates the perhaps trivial idea that I am putting forward here. The French president was explaining why relations were easier with the Soviet Union than with the United States. The relations with the Soviet Union, he said, concern only states; this favors equality of partners and diminishes the number of occasions for meeting and disagreeing. By way of contrast, Franco-American relations concern the two societies at the same time as the two states; they are an expression for one thing of the respective weight of the two societies. This remark of the French president, in all its apparent naïveté, is worth citing, the more so as it tends to moderate Franco-American quarrels. It reminds us nevertheless of this indisputable fact: the reader of a French journal, even one favorable on balance to the Atlantic Alliance, will find many more criticisms of the United States and many more commentaries on Franco-American differences than criticisms of the Soviet Union or references to Franco-Soviet quarrels.

The recent episode of the "contract of the century," of the choice by four small European countries of a new fighter plane, constitutes an extreme caricatural case of the scope that export competition can sometimes attain when businessmen are supported by their governments. In such circumstances, the United States appears to French opinion not only as a competitor—in a market economy, competition is by definition unavoidable—but as an adversary that profits from its weight and, using extracommercial arguments, tries to monopolize the market and maintain France as well as the rest of Western Europe in a state of permanent dependency. (It goes without saying that both sides argued that their plane was incontestably better.) French exporters also felt that the Americans enjoyed an unfair advantage by reason of the undervaluation of the dollar.

Nuclear energy offers another propitious terrain for export quarrels that turn into political quarrels. The most recent example, in July 1975, is the German-Brazilian agreement. The leaders of the United States, concerned to prevent the enlargement of the nuclear club, reproach the Germans and, in other cases, the French for concluding less rigorous agreements than they have imposed on their own clients. Here it is the Europeans who are accused by the Americans of taking risks with the security of all in order to win markets.

Let us put aside for the moment these pathological excrescences of commercial competition. Let me go back instead to the two trivial propositions that at the macroeconomic level each of the economies of the world capitalist market has an interest in the prosperity of the others even if, on the microeconomic level (or rather, the microcommercial level), the success of one is the failure of the other. What gives rise to problems, is the intermediate level, that of the rules of the game or the utilization (or manipulation) of the rules of the game by different governments or groups of governments. During the last few years, American negotiators have bitterly reproached the European community for injuring American exports, in particular by the Common Agriculture Policy and by the special arrangements with Mediterranean countries. The French in turn bitterly blamed the United States in the sixties for exploiting the international function of the dollar to export capital—that is, to exempt itself from the constraints imposed on all other states by a deficit of the balance-of-payments. Today they reproach the United States for the reverse, but with equal bitterness (greater tomorrow perhaps): they blame it for devaluing the dollar—a devaluation which is camouflaged and justified by the alleged floating of the exchanges but whose consequences are in no way different from the "competitive devaluations" of the '30s. (When this report appears, the situation will perhaps be reversed and the dollar overvalued.)

I should like first, before analyzing some of these problems in greater detail, to sort out the structural causes of these quarrels. Three of these seem to me to be worth consideration:

1. Within the capitalist world economy, the United States has held since 1945 a place apart. Its superiority over other nations has been such that it has contributed, more than all the others together, to the preparation of the statutes of the International Monetary Fund and the General Agreement on Tariffs and Trade (GATT). These rules are today out of date. Those of the IMF are obsolete because the fixed exchange rates have disappeared and the free-floating rates do not seem to function satisfactorily, at least not in the opinion of most economists and political leaders; nor do they offer by themselves a valid substitute for the Bretton Woods agreements. The rules of GATT are also now placed in question by the tariff policy of Brussels and especially by what are called nontariff barriers to trade. Since 1973, however, the negotiations that were already being called the Nixon Round have lost in advance some of their interest: so long as the most important currency, the dollar, undergoes such wide and unforeseeable fluctuations, how can anyone discuss tariff duties or even nontariff barriers? Relations with the Third World are more important now than free trade among industrial countries.

2. Even in an international market governed by rules, as it was from 1948 to 1971, the dissymmetry between action and reaction, between the impact on France of decisions taken in Washington and the impact on the American economy of decisions taken in Paris, threatened to give rise in Paris to resentment whenever decisions taken in Washington seemed contrary to French interests (or, to be more cautious, to the interests of France as the French leaders understood them). American economists do not deny the responsibility

of American leadership for the economic and monetary welfare of the West as a whole. But in their immense majority, they give evidence of the same naïveté as a certain president of General Motors, who declared: "What's good for General Motors is good for the United States; and what's good for the United States is good for General Motors." In the same way American economists judged in 1945 that fixed rates of exchange were good both for the United States and for the world; whereas today they have decided that floating exchange rates are good both for the United States and for the world. I have no doubt that certain French economists, Jacques Rueff for example, are convinced in similar fashion that their preferred solution is good for France and for the United States and for the world. The difference is the American economists are justifying a system that Washington leaders are able to impose on their partners, while heaping scorn on those who think otherwise. Not without reason: the solution that the American leaders reject becomes, by virtue of their dominance, in effect impossible.

3. The world capitalist economy has known over the last quarter-century an exceptionally rapid growth of commercial exchange and capital movements. In effect, the economic sovereignty of European states has been infringed upon in many ways, in matters of credit, money, and industry. The margin of autonomy of each government is limited by the policy of its partners, by capital movements, by the strategy of so-called multinational firms. Insofar as the conjuncture of the world market is greatly influenced by decisions taken in Washington, Europeans resent, not without some justification, their dependence on the world market. This dependence remained irritating even when, in the past (between 1950 and 1971), it entailed numerous advantages and favored a more rapid economic progress in Europe than across the Atlantic. Today it is a handicap in a competitive industrial market.

Now, the European community is in agreement eventually to negotiate as a single commercial unit with the United States; though in my opinion, even if it spoke with one voice, it would not be certain of matching the weight of the United States. In any event, the Community is least successful in this when it is a question of two issues, both decisive at this time: money and energy. Once again, I should like to look at the causes or reasons for these difficulties.

Let us consider first the international monetary system. At the first level of analysis, everyone will agree that at the time of Bretton Woods, American negotiators were right to fear that the United States might be compelled to finance the deficits of its partners, or that these might be inclined to repeat, at the expense of all, the competitive devaluations of the 1930s. The Americans therefore imposed rules of conduct on countries suffering from payments deficits and established the obligation of fixed exchange rates. The American government, of its own accord, added to these the convertibility of the dollar into gold. There was obviously no Machiavellian intention behind this: the American leaders, acting on the basis of their appreciation of the situation at the time and the fears inspired by past experience, established a system that they felt was in conformity with their national interests (a limitation of American engagement, the obligation of deficit states to take appropriate measures, etc.) and the interests of Western nations as a whole. They were not wrong in this, and until the early 1960s, the system functioned in a satisfactory way. The European economies advanced rapidly, and the peculiar role of the dollar as the pivot of the system, a currency of exchange and a reserve currency as well as one of account, gave rise to no discussion.

Beginning with the presidency of Kennedy in 1961, a new period began, which ended in 1971 with the termination of the convertibility of the dollar into gold and the devaluation of the dollar vis-à-vis other currencies. When Kennedy entered the White House, he asked a task force to report to him on the American deficit on balance of payments. Every year the United States was incurring short-term debts in the amount of $2-3 billion, ordinarily in respect of central banks which added these dollars to their reserves; while at the same time it increased its long-term claims abroad. This increase consisted largely of direct investment: either American firms founded branches abroad, or they bought up foreign enterprises.

At that time, the best American economists, in particular Professor Samuelson, concluded that the dollar was simply overvalued and that the rates of exchange adopted in 1948, which perhaps corresponded to the exceptional postwar conjuncture, were no longer appropriate to the normal ratios of purchasing power between countries. And yet, for reasons that seem to me even now incomprehensible, the American experts kept this diagnosis to themselves. For ten years, from 1961 to 1971, successive American administrations took multiple measures to combat the deficit, all of which proved ineffective. Beginning in 1965 and the inflation produced by the Vietnam War, the deficits grew or, if one prefers, dollar balances abroad built up, up to the moment when, in August 1971, President Nixon and his secretary of the treasury, Connally, cut the Gordian knot and broke the ties between gold and the dollar.

During these ten years, economists and presidential advisers poured out interpretations and analyses justifying the American deficit. Rather than accept a change in the price of gold or a devaluation of the dollar with respect to gold and other currencies, they took up the ideas of Keynes concerning this "barbarian relic" and used the demonetization of gold as a menace against those who criticized American manipulation of the Bretton Woods agreements.

Did the maintenance of an overvalued dollar correspond to the special interests of the United States from 1961 to 1971? Personally I do not think so at all, and I feel that the United States and the world would have been better off with a change in the rate of exchange between the dollar and European currencies and a revaluation of gold (even if this had been accompanied by a progressive modification of the monetary function of gold). To be sure the Europeans would have resisted the devaluation of the dollar, as their behavior in

August 1971 shows. But if the American economists had made use of their ardor and talent to plead the case (which they themselves thought was just) of devaluation, instead of justifying the situation as it was—a situation that was in the long run impossible to maintain—the presidential advisers would probably have been able to move American politics in this direction. In brief, I venture to blame the majority of American economists for having placed their knowledge at the service of the state in such a way that one can no longer grasp the ultimate motivation of their behavior—intellectual self-interest or pride, interest in the national economy, or the wish to dictate the rules of the system?

A reading of the liberal press—say, the *New York Times* or the *Washington Post*—invariably nourishes my surprise. These are newspapers that have played a large role in forcing out a president, which chop the CIA into little pieces, which are prepared to take the risk of weakening the United States abroad and compromising foreign men of state. Yet when it comes to monetary matters, they follow the directives of the government with docility. So long as the American government is sustaining, against all fact and opposition, the system of Bretton Woods, these newspapers are prepared to argue that the dollar is as good as gold. As soon as the same government indicates its readiness to abandon the system, these journals call for the demonetization of gold. They are not above using, in all naïveté, the argument that the revaluation of gold would favor those who have preferred gold to the dollar, as though docile submission to the contradictory successive conceptions of the American government constituted a special virtue. To be sure, this government is not the only one which wants to recompense its friends, but these same newspapers are pitiless in speaking of the South Vietnamese. Only those who have given expression to doubts about the dollar seem to have committed an inexpiable crime or sin.

I do not claim here to be taking a position, whether in a few words or a few pages, on the problem of the international monetary system. I am simply saying that the determination of the United States to impose on other states the demonetization of gold represents in my eyes an abuse of power. Undoubtedly the Americans would allow the other states to make use of their reserves of gold to borrow dollars. The fact remains that the United States has never ceased, in the monetary sphere, to confuse its ideas with truth and the good of all.

At the present time the Americans are going too far in the direction of devaluation, just as earlier they went too far in the direction of overvaluation. Overvaluation gave a commercial advantage to the Europeans, particularly the Germans, and to the Japanese, and led these in return to accumulate dollars. The present undervaluation, which is facilitated by the large dollar balances held abroad, favors American exports. In these circumstances there is no reason why the market should establish valid exchange rates by itself: the large mass of liquid, mobile capital is big enough to push the dollar up or down as the case may be.

The above analysis does not reflect either French government opinion or that of economists. It is strictly mine, cannot even be called French, and can the less be called European. In monetary matters the European community does not exist or, insofar as it does exist, it is Atlantic. Let me make clear what I mean.

There cannot be a European Europe in monetary matters for the following reasons:

a. No British government will ever adopt a monetary policy opposed to that of the United States. Besides, the London market continues to receive foreign capital, placed there at short term and subject to transformation into long-term investments outside. As a result, even if there were to be created a European monetary zone, it could not take in all the members of the Community.

b. So long as the monetary system takes the form of floating exchange rates, certain European states can do no more than constitute a zone of relative stability or coordinated float. Such a zone, in its turn, implies compatibility among them in regard to credit policy, monetary policy, and budget. One might also say, by way of simplification, that a coordinated float presupposes comparable rates of inflation from one country to another. All that remains from the first such attempt at a coordinated float is a Deutsche Mark zone (the German Federal Republic, Benelux, Denmark) which France has just rejoined (July 1975) after being compelled to pull out in January 1974. Even if this zone can be maintained, it makes possible only a restricted autonomy for this rump of Europe. It continues to depend on the price of the dollar, which it experiences more than it determines.

Regional integration was a failure in the monetary sphere between 1970 and 1974 for two principal reasons. It was justified less in itself than as a means. Europeans wanted monetary unity in order to reinforce economic unity, and beyond that, political unity. Monetary unity depended in turn on a political will which was lacking among certain Europeans, for the reasons given above. In the monetary sphere the Atlantic community is more immediately real than the European.

It was not inconceivable, however, and is not yet inconceivable, that a monetary Europe could be carved out within the Atlantic community. But for this the European states would have had to be able to coordinate their respective policies. Unequal rates of inflation and unequal severity of economic and social crises doomed any such effort.

Now let us consider the problem posed since 1973, that of energy, and in particular, that of the price of petroleum. The symbol of the nonexistence of Europe is the International Energy Agency, which France does not belong to but that a non-European country like Japan does. By "European nonexistence," I mean two things. The members of the European Community have not been able to define a European energy policy, and all of them, except for France, have joined the IEA. This inability to come up with a European policy is not the result of accident or of the absence of political will, but rather of the artificial character of Europe-taken-as-a-whole in respect of certain problems.

In matters of defense, Western Europeans share the fate imposed on them by geography: the Soviet army stations its troops permanently in Eastern Europe, especially in the German Democratic Republic. In the event of military aggression from the East, the battle would be fought on European soil, and American territory would not be affected unless the conflict escalated to the extremes of nuclear war and an exchange of intercontinental missiles. The proximity of the Soviet Union therefore tends to create a European solidarity, or at least a propensity to solidarity, and an awareness of this solidarity, with regard to the Soviet threat and American protection. German reservations, as well as French, concerning the doctrine of flexible response reflect this common geographical interest, or what I may call this geographic community.

Now let us return to commercial exchanges. The common external tariff of the Community and the intensity of intra-Community exchanges have created and reinforced a common European interest (at least to a degree), even though certain Europeans, whether by doctrine or special interest, are in some respects closer to American attitudes than to those of other Europeans. In the course of the last twenty-five years, the intensification of exchanges among developed countries has been accompanied by regional integration, in Western Europe on the one hand, in North America on the other. When the United States some years ago limited foreign access to the American capital market, they exempted Canadian borrowers from these restrictions, thereby discriminating in their favor in the same way that Europeans have discriminated commercially in favor of states associated with the Common Market.

The question that was posed beginning in 1973, that is, rapid inflation and a sharp increase in the price of petroleum, can be formulated in these terms: do we have here problems that the European Community can and ought to take a common stand on vis-à-vis the United States, if not in opposition to it? I am more inclined to say no than yes. In energy matters, the situations of Holland, with its large reserves of natural gas, and of Great Britain, which is counting on North Sea petroleum, are different from those of Italy or France, possessing no energy resources to speak of, now or in prospect. On the other hand, one might argue that the real distinction is that between the United States, which has enormous resources of coal and, beyond that, petroleum-bearing shale and asphalt sands, and the European states taken as a whole, which are almost entirely dependent on oil from the Middle East. Even so, the Europeans were unable, before or after the crisis of fall 1973, to define a common interest and a policy reflecting it. As importers of energy and members of the industrialized world, Europeans, Japanese, and Americans found themselves in the same camp. A European community in this area was neither excluded nor imposed by circumstances, but it could not come into existence except with the cooperation of all Europeans. The American secretary of state, exasperated by the behavior of all the Europeans during and after the Yom Kippur War, took as his objective an Atlantic or rather tricontinental coalition. As a result the French minister of foreign affairs lost a battle that he perhaps never wanted to win.

The case of energy seems to me symbolic of the economic problems that Europeans as well as Americans face today, to say nothing of the Japanese. The world economy has left behind the phase of rapid and continuous growth that we enjoyed during the last quarter of a century. Failing radical measures, the next phase, which will last at least until the breakdown of the cartel of oil-exporting countries, will be characterized by a lower rate of growth and the permanent threat of inflation. The British pattern of stop-and-go will come to characterize the whole of the world economy, outside of the Socialist sphere.

No one knows at the moment what this so-called new world economic order will be like—what the terms of exchange, how much aid to development, where free trade will give way to constraints. This review of themes daily evoked in the press has no other purpose than to introduce a banal idea, trivial if you will: how much do Europeans think alike in these domains? How much do they constitute a unit in the face of imminent difficulties and a post-Keynesian economy?

It is frequently asserted that economic and monetary problems, and not only tariff negotiations, are now part of what was once called high politics. There is no doubt of this, but one may put it differently: whether it is a question of organizing exchanges with the Third World or reestablishing an international monetary system, whatever the technical language the negotiators may employ, the positions of the negotiating parties are shaped by a mixture of national ambitions, interest, and theoretical preferences. The reorganization of the world economy is more difficult today than it was in 1945-48. At that time, for better or for worse, one major power dominated, and that power knew more or less what it wanted. Today the Americans, who dominate the field of political economy both at home and abroad, do not seem to know what they want or do not all want the same thing. In addition, the influence of the United States, its ability to convince without compelling, has diminished along with its prestige, its military superiority over its enemies, and its economic superiority over its allies. As is normal, its generosity has diminished along with its superiority.

The Probable and the Desirable

In the first part of this study, entitled "The Routinization of the Atlantic Alliance," I tried to show that the original function of the Alliance—the maintenance of a military balance in Europe—remains necessary, but that it does not suffice to give to the allies the sense of a common objective. In the second part of this study, devoted to the economy, I tried to throw light on two facts, one old and the other new. Within the world capitalist economy, the United States, thanks to its weight, imposes on its partners more constraints than it is subjected to by them. So long as these constraints were experienced in the context of an expanding economy, protests, bad humor, and polemic remained within the limits of good behavior, and it did not seem to require much effort to surmount conflicts of interest or doctrine. Since 1971, or more precisely 1973, it has been another story. It is the prosperity of the Atlantic Community, or even of the world economy, which is today in question. An agreement between Europeans and Americans on problems pending is obviously badly needed, but in itself it is not enough, since the participation of the Japanese and the Third World would also be required. Furthermore it is legitimate to ask if or where the European partners in the Atlantic Alliance can and should act together, if and where Europe can and should constitute a unit, speaking with a single voice in dialogue with the United States.

The United States and European Unity

According to the report of Stanley Hoffmann, the decisive choice for American policy in the next few years concerns the attitude regarding the European Community. I have said from the beginning that of the three attitudes that he judges possible, two can be eliminated with almost perfect assurance. Nothing could be more obvious. American diplomats will seek neither to build nor to destroy what remains of the European Community. They will not try to destroy it, because it may once again become useful, perhaps even necessary if Congress continues to paralyze the foreign policy of the country. They will not try to build it, because they do not have more than mediocre resources to that end and because only a modification of French diplomacy would dissipate the suspicions that they entertain with regard to such an enterprise insofar as it is inspired by the Quai d'Orsay.

It might perhaps be a good idea, before examining possible choices for the United States, to summarize briefly the present state of the European Community. This Community, first the Europe of the Six, now the Europe of the Nine, represents a prosaic and partial accomplishment of the ideas of Robert Schuman and Jean Monnet. It is admittedly an accomplishment: Franco-German reconciliation, opening of frontiers to men and merchandise, common work projects, a sense of common destiny—all of that, which was nothing but a dream in 1950, is a daily experience for the Europeans of 1975. Yet a prosaic accomplishment: the role of culture and ideology in European integration has been reduced to a minimum; whereas that of the economy, of industrial exchanges and fights over agricultural prices, seems exaggerated to the point of taking over the whole front of the stage. Finally, a partial accomplishment: even in economic matters, the opening of frontiers and the intensification of exchanges have produced neither a harmonization of laws nor even a coordination of management. Neither the Six nor the Nine have been able to get beyond the stage of the Common Market, the customs unit; as for politics, if one defines it by diplomacy and defense, the Europeans are still only on the threshold.

Would the Europeans have gotten on with these things more rapidly if the breakdown of the Bretton Woods agreements and the rise in oil prices had not nipped in the bud the efforts of Pompidou, Heath, and Brandt to relaunch the idea of a wider community? It is always difficult to answer such questions with certainty: what would have happened if . . .? I would confine myself to saying that in 1970 the goal of a monetary and economic union of Europe seemed to me unrealizable, condemned in advance because the governments of Europe did not appreciate the conditions of such a union and probably would not have accepted these if they had been able to appreciate them.

In the present state of things, where can Europe get a new boost? If one thinks of defense, only France is in a position to wrench the Atlantic Alliance out of its rut. France, alone among the Continental states, has left the integrated command of NATO and possesses nuclear arms. It therefore conserves in principle the choice, if not of returning to the integrated command (most unlikely given the distribution of political forces within the country), at least of adopting a doctrine of European inspiration.

Nuclear arms, like all arms, are by definition tools of policy. They are means to an end, in this case strictly defensive. It is inconceivable that France should use a nuclear threat with the aim of modifying the status quo. But there remains the choice: either the objective is simply to prevent an attack against French territory; or it is to prevent an attack against the Atlantic allies of France. Only the second of these responds to the spirit of the Atlantic Alliance, but the first shows up often in the writings of military leaders, influenced by the books of General Gallois. If, as some believe, the territory of a state possessing nuclear arms is *ipso facto* a sanctuary from attack, regardless of the inequality of the destruction wrought on one side and the other, France, with its nuclear arsenal, is free to choose between two defense doctrines: either armed neutrality, that is, recourse to arms only in the event of a direct aggression against France itself; or participation in the defense of Western Europe. The *Pluto* missiles (tactical nuclear arms) have now acquired a symbolic value. If France were to place them in Germany, that would imply a decision to participate in the defense of Western Europe. Placed in France, they imply the choice of armed neutrality, with their use reserved to the defense of the home territory. They are now placed in France, but French ministers hint that they might, in case of crisis, be moved forward. In this way they hope to avoid the necessity of defining the French choice.

In the circumstances, the objection that many American readers will raise, namely, that so small a nuclear force as the French makes very little difference anyway in a Western Europe defended by seven thousand American warheads, is of little import. Leave aside the political-technical disagreements, whether for example French tactical nuclear arms would be able to reinforce deterrence of Soviet aggression by lowering the nuclear threshold or threatening a potential aggressor with a lower threshold. What interests me here is today's political reality: the German government attributes a symbolic significance to the French doctrine regarding use of the *Pluto* missile. It interprets this as a clue to French intentions concerning European defense. In the present circumstances, the most indulgent interpretation possible is that the French are still unwilling to make a choice.

The above analysis, for all its brevity, serves to dissipate the illusions created by propaganda slogans. In the area of defense, what is meant by the term "European Europe," as opposed to Atlantic Europe? Surely the French government does not want Germany to acquire its own nuclear arms. Nor does it want to merge the British and French nuclear forces. By choosing to walk out of an integrated European command, France was counting on profiting from the advantages of particpation in the Atlantic Alliance while enjoying the freedom conferred by its own defense doctrine.

There is no point here in criticizing, much less praising. What is important is to understand: French diplomacy in this area is neither European nor Atlantic but strictly French. At the same time, France's leaders do not want to set an example to other European nations, for if these followed suit, France would soon lose the advantages of the American guarantee, which both General de Gaulle and Georges Pompidou saw as the foundation of France's independent diplomacy. Our geopolitical situation, in which the potential enemy, for the first time in French history, is not across a border but beyond the territory of an allied state defended by a German-American army, gives us now the opportunity to those in the second rank—that of reserving, in case of crisis, freedom of choice to help or stand by.

It may be objected that in the event of conflict in central Europe, this freedom would quickly vanish, and that the Soviet Union would compel France to declare itself in one way or another. It might also be objected that once the Soviet armies arrived at the French frontier, the game would be over and that France would inevitably be incorporated into the Soviet imperium—to which certain French would answer: at least this Sovietization would not be so costly as war and would be gently and gradually imposed.

These objections (one can easily imagine others and multiply the scenarios) do not invalidate the simple propositions that I should like to oppose to journalistic slogans. In regard to defense, the world being what it is, the notion of a European Europe, in opposition to an Atlantic Europe, makes no sense. French doctrine is for the moment French and not European. American diplomacy has never favored a European Europe, since the United States wanted to maintain a monopoly of nuclear arms in Europe. France, which has developed a nuclear force in the face of an American veto, is not placing these arms at the disposal of a European defense system or an autonomous Europe. French leaders prefer to maintain the ambiguity: they do not rule out the possibility that French arms may one day add to the margin of autonomy of European states within the Atlantic Alliance. But the doctrine put forward in the press and the military academies is much closer to what I have called armed neutrality than to European defense.

What are the chances that this situation will change in years to come? I would say, very poor. The one thing that might change this prognosis is a decision by the American Executive or the Congress, together or separately, to weaken the American guarantee to such an extent that fear compels the Europeans, including the French, to make new and radical decisions.

Barring that, it is hard to see the French government's making a choice in this matter. Here the balance of domestic opinion and politics has to be taken into account. Valéry Giscard d'Estaing took part in the last war only toward the end of the fighting; he volunteered in 1944 and fought in the battle of Germany. He belongs to a generation imbued with a European spirit. He never had the sense of Germany as the hereditary enemy, but neither did he know in any deep way the menace of Stalinist Communism. At this moment, he is trying above all to save the hard core of the European Community: the Five rather than the Six, since the political future of Italy is too uncertain to count on. But he has avoided getting involved in defense matters, because he does not see them as an urgent problem and never interested himself in the subject before his election as president. He will thus avoid challenging the UDR (the majority party of the governing majority), because this political custodian of the Gaullist tradition would react violently to a new defense doctrine that appeared to abandon the policy of independence in all directions. On the other hand, so long as it was not necessary to deny this Gaullist legacy, the French president would probably not be opposed to military measures of genuine cooperation between the Germans and French within the Atlantic Alliance.

As for American decisions, a Frenchman such as I has few comments to make. Personally I feel that the American government should choose between two attitudes: either recognize explicitly that the military balance in Europe ought to be maintained, in the American interest as well as that of Europe, and that even a partial withdrawal of American troops would have unfortunate consequences, at least psychologically, out of proportion to its financial advantages; or declare openly that the Europeans, taken as a group, now have the resources needed to arm the number of divisions required for European security, with the support of American nuclear arms, and then withdraw some of the American forces in Germany. Such a choice is just as rational as the French one presented above (armed neutrality or joint defense). In both cases, it is unlikely that a choice will be made. Just as the French government prefers to maintain ambiguity, so the president and Congress, by their hesitations and disagreements, will probably allow their resolution in this matter to remain in doubt. Following on the disaster in Vietnam, Senator Mansfield did not present this year his famous resolution on withdrawal of troops from Europe. This is no proof, however, that it will not be moved again next year.

The gap between the probable and the desirable is not in this case a dramatic one. It is simply the kind of thing that is characteristic of a democratic system, even in regimes where the executive possesses, as in the United States and France, a certain margin of maneuver with regard to public opinion.

Passing Now from Defense to Diplomacy

This very phrase conveys the paradox of the effort of the Nine to establish a common foreign policy ("Let us speak with a single voice") in the absence of a common defense policy. Let us concede for purposes of argument the possibility of a functional integration or unification, that is, one achieved sector by sector.

Is it probable, is it even desirable, for the Nine to speak with a single voice? As for what is desirable, an American will reply: everything depends on what that voice says. If the desires of the Nine go against the national interests of the United States or Western interests as the Americans conceive them, Washington will no longer see European unity as desirable. To be sure, Henry Kissinger said in his book *The Troubled Partnership*, which he wrote at a time when he was still a professor, that if and when Europeans united, they would surely not see their common interest as coinciding with that of the United States. He added that even so, the United States should favor European unification because these inevitable disagreements were less important in the last analysis than the advantage offered by allies conscious of themselves and their wishes as against passive, submissive partners. Those for better or worse were the thoughts of a professor. A secretary of state thinks and acts in the immediate: when he is trying to bring together Israelis and Arabs, he is not ready to forgive Europeans for complicating his task, and he is inclined to forget that a united Europe, even recalcitrant, is a better ally than divided Europeans, docile but full of resentment.

Let us consider now the various areas in which Europeans might speak with a single voice, or engage in common action, apart from the United States. So far as the Soviet Union is concerned, Europeans and Americans have the same attitude. They both support détente and are eager to develop commercial relations. European unity on this matter is evidenced by the delegation to the Commission of Brussels of authority to negotiate customs agreements with COMECON, the Soviet Union, or the several states of Eastern Europe—a delegation envisaged by the Treaty of Rome and applicable to all negotiations of this type, but not yet achieved.

As for Germany or Berlin, wherever the four allied powers continue to have responsibility, the Americans, British, and French cooperate closely with the German Federal Republic and among themselves. No one contemplates extending to the Nine (which is not interested in any case) the responsibility of the two European states among the four occupying powers.

I see then, so far as diplomacy in the traditional and limited sense of the term is concerned, only one region in the world where the Nine might perhaps want to maintain a presence, or even a common policy of action, without joining themselves to the United States; and that is the Middle East and the Mediterranean. In this area, the European desire for unity, of varying strength from one country to another, seems to me more than just a fiction or pious hope.

One should distinguish between diplomacy proper (in the narrow and traditional sense) and economic or commercial diplomacy. The Nine claim to have the same objective as the United States in the Arab-Israeli conflict. There is thus no clash of principle between what the Nine claim to want and what the Americans are doing their best to bring about. And yet, when Israel is under attack in international organizations, the Europeans tend to abstain whereas the United States votes against the anti-Israeli resolutions. The European stand in these matters does not seem to be the kind of thing that Europeans can be proud of. In general, although Americans and Europeans have a common objective, the Americans are playing the role of mediators, whereas the Europeans confine themselves to declarations or symbolic gestures.

Does the dialogue between Europe and the Arab countries deserve all the passion it has aroused? Some, in France, have seen in it the potential for an autonomous European diplomacy. Others, in the United States particularly, have seen in it a weakening of American leadership and, by the same token, of the capacity of the United States to play its role. The fact is that so long as two fleets dominate the Mediterranean, the American and the Soviet, agreements among the neighboring states will continue to be primarily symbolic, except insofar as they concern economic matters. This symbolic value is not necessarily in itself insignificant, since it may open interesting possibilities in the future. All that I want to say here is that diplomats on both sides of the Atlantic must use their talent to dedramatize the opposition between the European-Arab dialogue and the American-Arab dialogue and to make the two approaches complementary rather than contradictory. And even when certain Europeans want, on the contrary, to dramatize the conflict between the two dialogues in order to emphasize European autonomy, observers should not allow themselves to be deceived by such concessions to the necessities, real or supposed, of national politics.

On the other hand, the Mediterranean economic agreements and such accords as that of Lomé with the African and Caribbean countries seem to me eminently desirable. And it seems equally desirable to me that the United States should admit this, in spite of the most-favored-nation principle. The extension of the Common Market to the south and Africa does not compromise any major interest of the United States and opens the way perhaps to a regional integration that is possibly a specifically European mission.

Turning Now to Economic Diplomacy

Let us consider the primary task of the years to come: the elaboration of the rules of a new world economic order, a new international monetary system. The thesis that I would submit on this subject is the following: when it is a question of the Kennedy Round or the Nixon Round, of customs negotiations, it is legitimate to speak of a European-American dialogue and of a potential conflict of interests, with each of the two entities defending its own and seeking to obtain suitable trade-offs for its concessions. But this does not hold true for energy or money. There is no European energy policy and no reason that there should be. There is no European monetary doctrine and no reason there should be.

So far as money is concerned, the Europeans (excepting the British) used to reproach the United States for its deficit on balance-of-payments, or if one prefers, for the large dollar balances that they were compelled to accumulate. Today they are complaining about the undervaluation of the dollar (with good reason six months ago, no more so in December 1975), but they are not agreed on calling for fixed exchange-rates or the consolidation of dollar balances. And although one may perhaps speak of a French gold doctrine, there is certainly no European doctrine.

Americans and Europeans have the same interest so far as petroleum prices are concerned. They are both of them consumers and importers and want to pay as little as possible (which, narrowly conceived, might be interpreted as selfishness). Certain European journals have accused American leaders of being less opposed to high fuel prices than they pretend, since high prices encourage the search for substitute sources of energy by rendering these alternatives more profitable. Among all the participants in the action, those least opposed to the rise in prices would seem to be the major oil companies, although in all fairness it is hard to see how these can resist the cartel. What is clear is that Western Europe is more vulnerable in the medium run than the United States to the manipulation of prices by exporters of raw materials. In this sense, it has learned that its prosperity is not enough to confer autonomy. It has also discovered that the action of OPEC has reinforced the bonds between the different world economic regions. The European countries have been compelled to borrow dollars on the money market, and the United States has become a lender of last resort.

The formula of a new world economic order, launched by the less developed countries, covers a complex of problems regarding which there exists *a priori* neither an immediately defined European interest nor an inevitable opposition or divergence of interests between Europe and the United States. Europeans and Americans would both like to protect themselves against cartels of producers of raw materials and to ensure the regular supply of such materials to their industries, while maintaining the regime of free trade in manufactured products. The major differences between them concern agricultural products, especially the external tariff of the Common Market, which hurts American exports but which the Europeans, the French especially, see as a minimum condition of autonomy.

The oil producers would like to maintain as long as possible the high prices that they have succeeded in imposing and to index these prices in such a way as to beat inflation. This goal obviously conflicts with that of the advanced industrial nations, most of which are importers rather than exporters of oil. Even a general indexing of the prices of all raw materials, almost inconceivable, would be of no use, since the developed countries are as much exporters of primary products as the poor countries. The best placed in this respect is still the United States, which is the granary of the entire world and producer of the greatest surpluses of basic food products.

How to solve these problems? Proposed solutions are a dime a dozen. But these conflicts, where the stake is economic, are tenacious by reason of their ambivalence: they are a function neither of military force nor of market conditions exclusively. The model of non-zero-sum games with multiple coalitions offers an approximate image of the kind of conflict that characterizes today's world economy. In the last analysis, the maintenance of the prosperity of the industrialized countries does not exclude increased aid to development for the poorer nations. The latter, unfortunately, cherish the illusion that a change in the terms of trade would constitute an effective instrument of redistribution of wealth and that this redistribution could be effected by a manipulation of prices. In this they are wrong: what the oil producers have been able to do, the rest of the Third World cannot do.

The old issues of disagreement between Europeans and Americans—multinational firms, Mediterranean accords, common external tariff, nontariff trade barriers—have little weight in the last analysis by comparison with the common concerns: inflation, the cost of energy, the monetary system. Yet common concerns do not necessarily produce common doctrines.

International interdependence in economic matters has reached the point where the autonomy of each state, even of the European Community as a whole, is narrowly limited. Now, the fact is that in the world market, the United States exercises, willy-nilly, a dominant influence. It is the United States that has fixed the monetary system over the last fifteen years: overvaluation, then a more or less dirty float of the dollar. The Europeans can complain all they want; they can do little about this whether united or not.

Personally, I think that the American government will pursue in years to come its policy of floating exchange rates and demonetization of gold. It will perhaps try to give special drawing rights (SDRs) the status of a transnational money. Although in the long run, especially once the international community has become a political reality, such a system may be viable; although money can in principle be detached from any material base in its international functions as it already has in domestic exchanges; I persist in holding to certain ideas which were those of the American economists of thirty years ago. I do not believe that floating rates favor a return to a noninflationary economy. I do not believe that SDRs constitute in the short run a real money. I do not believe that the dollar can once again play the role that it did between 1948 and 1960. The probable, then, in this matter seems to me to be different from the desirable. The probable is a continuation for another half-dozen years at least of the search for a post-Keynesian economy, with a changing order of priority between growth and stability. The desirable would be a clear and clean breach with the inflationary economy of recent years.

In itself, an ambiguous phase of slow inflation and expansion would not in itself constitute a catastrophe. After all, it is neither surprising nor shocking that no one has a sure-fire solution. Meanwhile national economies have become so involved with one another that the world market needs a transnational money. This cannot be the dollar or gold alone; and all other solutions are necessarily experimental. The United States picks the experiments. And Americans have never been so interested in international economics as the British were at the time the pound played the same role as the dollar today.

The Dangers

It would seem that I have not yet found an answer to the question posed above: why this contrast between almost ritual exchanges of reproaches between Europe and the United States and the feeling of a new peril? The preceding pages contain the elements of an answer.

The economic climate seems to be shifting. The European Community will survive, one way or another, but make little progress. It is possible that after the retirement of Henry Kissinger, the new secretary of state may be more concerned to spare European sensitivities and to seek agreement from the Europeans on certain subjects. But one can rule out large changes. In defense, there is little likelihood of a French initiative that will change the present conjuncture. In economic matters—energy or money—the problems are neither European nor even Atlantic; they are worldwide. The Westerners will continue the so-called détente policy, even after Kissinger leaves, because they are politically incapable of opting for conflict. When the Soviets decide to speak the language of détente, the Westerners have to reply in kind. Besides, in today's economic conjuncture, every Western country is eager to secure contracts with Eastern Europe, even if on balance the credits granted the Soviet Union permit it to pick up the latest Western techniques and to shift its own resources to armaments.

All of that would not be dangerous in itself if it were not for the specific crises of Italy and Great Britain on the one hand and, on the other, the passage of Portugal and, in short order, Spain from right-wing authoritarian regimes to liberal or left-wing authoritarian ones. As soon as one keeps these crises in mind, it becomes obvious why speculation concerning European-American relations or such things as the benevolence or hostility that the secretary of state may show to the cause of European unity, is trivial or at best marginal to the real historical forces. In a way, we have gone back to the situation of 1946-48: the fate of liberal civilization in Europe was less a function then of relations between the United States and the Soviet Union than of developments within the several

European nations. At that time the victory of the West was ensured by Stalin's mad violence on the one hand and the Marshall Plan and American aid on the other. The battle today, twenty-five years later, is even more difficult, and it must necessarily vary from one country to another.

The elections of April 1975 showed that the majority of the Portuguese people want a government like those of Western Europe. A part of the Armed Forces Movement and the Communist party of Portugal, which built a solid clandestine organization under the old regime, are today apparently resolved to create a Left despotism. At the time of writing, July 1975, the Socialist party and Centrist parties have left the government. The Communist party has taken over most of the media. Catholics and Socialists are still able to demonstrate in the streets and give press conferences to foreign journalists. General Spinola has had to flee to Brazil, the the Constituent Assembly, shorn of all powers, is still meeting. By the time this essay is published, the revolutionary process will likely have worked itself out: either left-wing militants in the Communist party will have lost, probably after a clash of forces; or they will have consolidated their positions and established an authoritarian government and a command economy. The distribution of power between the military and the Communists in such an eventuality is impossible to predict. As of December 1975 it seemed that the leftists had lost after a very moderate clash.

The United States, which intervened in Chile, where it should have remained neutral, has lost almost any possibility of influencing events in Portugal. The European countries have only a moderate capacity to intervene. Nevertheless the Socialist parties of Germany, Great Britain, France, and Sweden can give support to Mario Soares. The European Community as a whole can and should make clear to the present leaders of Portugal that they have a decisive choice to make: either they respect the rules of free government, in which case they will receive the support of the Community; or they follow the Bolshevik path and thereby isolate themselves once again from Europe—unless the rest of Europe should end by following the same path.

No one doubts that the death of Franco will open a political crisis in Spain, and Juan Linz's report shows that it is impossible to say where the country will go. Europeans and Americans are no more in a position to intervene in Spain than in Portugal, or to impose what Eastern Europe has called the doctrine of limited sovereignty. The Russian army, with its Warsaw Pact allies, can impose ideological discipline by force. There is no army that can do this in Western Europe. This is not to say that Europeans must simply look by and observe the Spanish crisis as spectators, as they have done up to now in Portugal. But to do more, they would have to get together on means, economic and political. In particular, it would be desirable, though improbable, for François Mitterand and Valéry Giscard d'Estaing to get together and agree quietly on advice to their respective allies.

In Spain the Communist party and its leader in particular are said to be closer to Communism Italian style than Portuguese (or French). All Spaniards who favor the liberalization of the regime agree on legalizing the Communist party. Where they differ is on the question of Communist participation in government. The answer to that depends on another question: do we want to maintain continuity between the Franco regime and the one that follows? Or should there be a distinct constitutional break? Personally, I am convinced that continuity offers a better hope of a liberal succession than the so-called revolutionary process. But what matters here is not so much desires as events—such events as the data of Franco's death.

In Italy the same question arises, but in other terms, for here there has been a pluralist democratic government since the end of the Second World War. This government now seems to be at the end of the road, and all the observers are asking whether we ought to seek or fear a historic compromise, that is, the cooption of the Communist party. Would the Communist party, if it shared in power, respect the rules of the democratic game? If it did so, it would be the first example of a party of Bolshevik origin converting to social democracy. The event would constitute a historic watershed. If on the other hand, thanks to this historic compromise, the Communist party were able to push Italy into the totalitarian camp, the event would be equally significant and would constitute a major modification of the political map.

Stanley Hoffmann condemns in his report any intervention in the domestic affairs of other states. Diplomacy in his view, if I understand him correctly, should confine itself to interstate relations. Such a stand strikes me as either naive or hypocritical. The Bolsheviks do not hesitate on their side to make use of men and parties devoted to their cause. The Americans and the CIA have in certain cases modeled their action on that of the Soviet Union and the KGB; many of their operations have been either repugnant or useless. There was no justification, for example, for helping bring down Allende. On the other hand, the Europeans have the best of reasons not to be indifferent to what goes on in Spain or Italy, and certain types of intervention would be neither repugnant nor useless.

Here two questions arise: (1) Should American and European leaders bring pressure on the Christian Democrats in Italy to dissuade them from trying this historic compromise? And (2) If the Christian Democrats decide to go ahead with the compromise, what should be the attitude of Americans and Europeans? Personally, and this is only my opinion, I would do nothing to influence the Christian Democrats in this matter. Moreover, if and when the experiment is tried, Italy's allies should not behave as the United States did with regard to Allende, that is, immediately undertake a clandestine action with a view to bringing about a crisis. They should not move to thwart the experiment unless and until they are convinced by facts that the Italian Communist party does not intend to observe the rules of the game.

The case of Great Britain is radically different from that of Italy, even if both are suffering from hyperinflation. I do not intent to review here the Andrew Shonfield analysis. My own sense is that the current economic crisis derives in large part from the political crisis. The two-party system, which was once seen as a masterpiece, is today producing governments that rest on electoral minorities. What is more, it disperses men who think alike in the two parties and places men who differ in the same party. Thus the referendum on the Common Market produced a majority comprising elements from both sides and more effective than either.

What distinguishes Great Britain from Latin Europe is the absence of a Communist party and of a revolutionary potential. I will not try here to sketch out the various scenarios possible. The other Europeans, the Germans first of all, should under certain circumstances assist the British government. It would be useless to try and stipulate in advance whether this aid should be conditional or unconditional, linked or not to the temporary suspension of the rules of the European Community so far as Britain is concerned.

France is not for the moment among the sick nations. But it could fall ill quickly if, in 1978, the Left won the legislative elections. What is more, France also faces the urgent question of these years: how can liberal democracies resist economic depression?

The answer would be more confident if everyone, in Washington as well as in Paris, were not doing his best to lull the public. The Soviets are not building up their military forces in order to invade Western Europe, but they expect the growing disparity to bring diplomatic advantages. At Helsinki, in July 1975, Western Europe solemnly recognized the status quo. The effect is to make Soviet gains nonnegotiable while the West remains negotiable.

Everyone knows the next step: the recognition by West Europeans of superior Soviet power and hence a right of scrutiny of what happens in Western Europe. Thanks to the economic crisis and the willful obtuseness of the West, the Soviets seem to be well on the way toward reaching this next objective. This gloomy projection, it goes without saying, is not an affirmation of the desirable, not even a prognosis of the probable, only an expression of the possible.

III

Uneven Allies: An Overview

Stanley Hoffmann

This essay tries to examine the broad choices open to American foreign policy toward Western Europe in the near future—roughly the next ten years; this is about as far as any political scientist's horizon can be stretched. In order to do so, I shall first make some analytic remarks about the past, showing the elements of continuity in the U.S.-West European relations; and I shall assess the significance of the present moment, whose importance and novelty are well worth stressing. Only then will I discuss America's future choices. The story of U.S.-West European relations is so complex that a fair treatment would require a comprehensive essay dealing both with American and with West European achievements, fiascos, policies, and aspirations. This essay may appear unfair to the reader because it covers primarily the American side and addresses itself critically to American choices, past and coming. Let me reassure him, or cool his indignation: I have been at least as severe for the West Europeans in several essays, including one that I see as a kind of companion piece to this one—the other side of the coin.[1]

Past

My purpose in this first section is not to provide a sketchy history (although a book devoted to it is sorely needed). It is to point out the threads that run through the whole story, and the innovations introduced in the early 70s by the diplomacy of President Nixon and Henry Kissinger.

    A. There are three common threads that run through the story, from the late 1940s to the early 70s.

1. The first, and most obvious, is the broad range of common interests acknowledged, publicly or privately, in words or in actions, by Western statesmen on both sides of the ocean. These have, of course, provided the basis for the association since the beginning of the cold war. To the United States, Western Europe has been a major concern in all three ways.

a. The physical security of Western Europe has been a priority in U.S. strategic policy. The United States has seen world affairs as a huge contest for power and influence between Washington and Moscow and Western Europe as a decisive stake in the balance of power. The deterrence of a Soviet attack that could either have led to the conquest of Western Europe by the USSR, or—if limited but successful—exposed the inability of the United States to protect a vital interest abroad, has been an objective less important only than the deterrence of an attack on the United States. Washington therefore gave its nuclear guarantee to Western Europe, while deploying American forces and tactical nuclear weapons there to serve as links to America's strategic nuclear forces and as security for the guarantee. These moves have also had another aim: to deter our allies from the temptation of the kind of neutralism that (given the inevitable disproportion between Soviet and indigenous West European forces) might have amounted to "Finlandization," i.e., a neutrality "tilting" in Russia's direction.

b. The economic well-being of Western Europe has been a major objective of U.S. policy since the Marshall Plan. This was partly a reaction to the "economic consequences of Versailles," to the spectacle of Europe in the 30s; partly a result of the conviction that an economically weak Europe would be a breeding ground for communism, especially in light of the existence of strong Communist parties in Italy and France; partly a policy aimed at facilitating the reintegration of West Germany into a self-confidence and productive "neighborhood"; partly a foresighted calculation about the opportunities a prosperous Western Europe would provide for American trade and investment.

c. The close association of Western Europe with U.S. foreign policy in general was also deemed essential. In other words, the desired partnership was not limited to an American guarantee of Western Europe's safety and an American preoccupation with Western Europe's prosperity. Washington wanted, on the one hand, to be able to count on the support of its European allies, if not for military operations in the rest of the world (we realized Western Europe's fears of involvement and the risk of further depleting their meager forces), at least for America's major diplomatic moves, especially toward the USSR: the existence of a regular, two-way alliance strengthened America's hand in dealings with Moscow. On the other hand, Washington also hoped to be able to count on the cooperation of these allies (and of Japan) in the functioning of the international monetary system and in the various international institutions—the UN itself, or GATT, or the ILO, etc.—that provide the framework of global economic activities.

This third concern—for diplomatic support—is more than a logical extension of the first two; it transcends them, and deserves special mention because of its significance for our allies. Whereas the first two (physical security and economic well-being) were clearly in their interests (whatever difficulties might arise over a specific strategic doctrine or the terms of economic aid, for instance), the third one put a kind of unwritten obligation on them and could at times be a cause of diffuse distaste.

Nevertheless, Western European leaders have spoken and acted as if they too had no doubts about a broad range of common concerns. Without any way of influencing U.S. strategic policy directly, they have shown their interest in a strong American nuclear force (indeed de Gaulle's repeated questioning of the plausibility of America's guarantee was derived from his analysis of the effects of America's *loss* of its overwhelming superiority over the Soviet Union). They have, without exception, shown no desire to "appease" the USSR, and, when pursuing their own policy of détente, it was always from the base of a military situation of strength. Despite divergences among themselves on matters of degree, they have been favorable to a reasonably open trading system for industrial goods and have refrained from crippling regulations on capital movements and foreign investments, in conformity with American preferences and with the rules of international conventions and institutions predominantly based on American concepts. De Gaulle, the only West European statesman who seemed, after 1962, to launch a global challenge against the United States, did not remove France from the North Atlantic alliance, though he did pull it out of NATO; and his attack on the "dollar exchange standard," while stressing its drawbacks for France and Europe, was based on his conviction that this system would ultimately prove untenable for the United States as well—which it did.

2. A second thread might be called circumscribed support to West European unification.

a. On the one hand, American policy from the late 40s to the early 60s strongly encouraged the West Europeans to go "beyond the nation-state." There was, here, a remarkable blend of "ideals and self-interest," to use the title of Robert Osgood's fine study.[2] Self-interest suggested not a divide-and-rule policy, but American support for a European entity capable of overcoming the traditional enmities between Western Europe's nations (particularly between Germany and her neighbors) and of "speaking with one voice." The more united the partner, the more effective and reliable he would be. The disproportion between the United States and the several middle-size or small nation-states in Western Europe was seen as a source of trouble in the association, rather than a condition for American predominance. This was the case, not because altruism and self-abnegation had grabbed the minds and hearts of American policymakers, but because what they wanted from their associates—military cohesion, economic prosperity *and* liberalism, overall support—seemed to be more achievable through unity than through fragmentation. It was also an enlightened form of self-interest that dictated Washington's acceptance of the "non-liberal" or "inward-looking" features of the European enterprise, especially the Common Agricultural Policy and the overseas association agreements. For these concessions to regionalism and regional protectionism, limiting American access to several markets, were seen as the price to be paid for obtaining a more cohesive and united partner. Moreover—a point rarely stressed here—the establishment of a vast open market for industrial goods and capital in Western Europe allowed a prodigious expansion of U.S. investments there—so much so that Servan-Schreiber described American industries in Europe as the second largest industrial force in the world, second only to America's own.[3]

But there was also a strong streak of idealism, a conviction that what had proved so good for America's political development and economic growth—federal institutions and a vast, open market—would be beneficial for the Europeans as well. The support so markedly shown by American statesmen for so long for the "Monnet method" of European unification was based on a fascinating blend of calculation (the more "supranational" the institutions, the weaker the influence of those European nation-states that were still concerned with making *their* distinctive mark on world affairs) and ideological preference (the latter being at times expressed so vigorously as to delay or complicate further West European unification). That Americans should be the "best Europeans" was often a hindrance and an irritant.

b. On the other hand (and this may explain why there was, after all, no contradiction between the ideology and the calculation), there always was a hidden (and at times not so hidden) condition to American enthusiasm for European integration: it had to be, so to speak, fitted into the overall design of U.S. diplomacy and strategy. The United States did not support *just any* kind of West European entity. Insofar as it expressed a preference for a certain kind of institutional formula, it was because Washington hoped that the "right" institutions would produce the "right" outcome. What American policy demanded, in effect, was that the West European "partner" observe one restraint and two imperatives. The restraint was in the military realm: especially after the procedural rejection of the European Defense Community (EDC) by the French National Assembly, defense was considered in Washington to be a *NATO* domain. This meant a jealous concern for keeping in American hands the power to decide on the right strategy, for preserving the structure of military integration that put West European conventional forces under an American commander-in-chief, and above all for keeping the monopoly of decisions regarding escalation. Hence Washington's opposition, strongly expressed by the Kennedy Administration, to "independent" nuclear forces. Hence the tortuous episode of the Multilateral Nuclear Force (MLF), invented to keep France's neighbors from being tempted to imitate her independent course and to join her in military "separatism." Hence also the strong pressure put on our allies to equip their forces with American weapons. There could be a "European voice," a "Eurogroup" within NATO, and there could be a nuclear committee for consultations, but there was not going to be a *separate* West European defense entity, however much we were in favor of a West European economic and even political community.

As for the imperatives: one was specific; one was broad. Specifically, we wanted an "outward-looking Europe" in economic matters, i.e., a Europe that would lower its external tariff, organize its agriculture in a way that did not shut out American goods, and refrain from turning association agreements with developing nations into *chasses gardées*. Broadly, we wanted what the French called an "Atlantic Europe," i.e., a Europe giving priority to the American connection, and we disliked the Gaullist concept of an *Europe européenne* concerned above all with defining a separate identity. For such a quest could not help magnifying differences with the United States and would result in Europe's taking global policy stands of and on its own. Here we come back to the third American concern I had mentioned above: we desired European support in global policy, but it was to be *our* global policy. Indeed, we took—in the UN or at Suez—our own approach to colonial matters and did not hesitate to dissociate ourselves from the policies of some of our European allies. We never considered that our alliance should keep us from engaging in "summitry" with the Soviet Union, particularly over arms control. In other words, the imperative of an Atlantic Europe turned out to be a second restraint on Western Europe, having to do with the higher reaches of foreign policy. And if we opposed the "Fouchet plan" approach to European institutions, while supporting Britain's application for admission to the Common Market (even though Britain was most unlikely to accept any federal scheme for Europe, indeed anything much beyond the Fouchet plan), it was because we thought that an international scheme would give too much influence to French views and vetoes, unless Britain became a member and helped isolate and neutralize France.

3. This brings us to the third thread: uneasiness and division among the West Europeans. I have analyzed elsewhere the reasons that come out of the separate histories, political and social systems, and national perceptions of the leaders and elites in Europe's nation-states.[4] Here, I want to stress only the reasons that are related to American policy and to European-American relations, my point being that ever since the beginning, the United States has been as much a factor of division as of integration.

a. Uneasiness was bred by what could be called a genteel, often unconscious paternalism in American attitudes. We are here in the treacherous realm of psychology more than in that of politics, but that does not make it any less important. To be sure, as Dean Acheson once blurted out in reply to a question, alliance politics isn't pathology or therapy. Yet the United States, having emerged from the Second World War as the most powerful nation on earth, was confronted with allies who had all experienced, or were in the process of experiencing, a calamitous decline in prestige, power, and influence, along with huge internal problems of material reconstruction, moral rehabilitation, or "identity." What America displayed was an extraordinary release of energy and a joyous, meddling, and universal exercise of leadership. To European statesmen, inevitably preoccupied by domestic priorities and, in many cases, colonial turmoil, America's "can-doism" became something of an alibi for dependence, an excuse for leaving global problems to the Protector—and this could always be rationalized as the safest way of keeping him involved in Europe's fate. Thus, insensibly, inevitable dependence (on America's military might, on American economic aid, and later on American capital, technology, and internal welfare) became a rationale for what could be called external subordination (by contrast with the satellites of the Soviet Union, subjected to internal as well as external *Gleichschaltung* [homogenization]).

Moreover, America's hearty encouragement for federal formulas had a way of overshooting the mark: such schemes as the draft for a European Political Community (1953), prepared with the help of distinguished American scholars and officials, or the European Defense Community, being premature, not only failed but backfired, for every setback dampened the enthusiasms and lowered the sights of the "Europeans" themselves. Indeed, their own tendency to concentrate on the institutional issues (supranationality, majority vote, the role of the European parliament, etc.) both reflected and reenforced a tendency to leave shrouded in ambiguity the external purpose of the "European enterprise." Should it be a Third Force, a "second pillar in the West" (probably Monnet's notion), a separate entity *à la* de Gaulle, or an "Atlantic Europe" as described above? Should it turn its back on power altogether and merely provide the world with a model of "depoliticized" community relations, to be imitated by other regional groups in search of peace and welfare? For a while, the Chinese and the Russians, rather than attack each other, talked about Albania. The various schools of thought about Europe could avoid facing both the depth of their disagreements on goals and the constraints on their opportunities by focusing on the juicy legal issues.

b. Uneasiness developed also because American policy toward Western Europe was based not merely on the accurate assumption of common interests, but on the broadest possible reading of the range of community, and on the subtle postulate that in realms where there could be some doubt or debate about Europe's interest, the United States knew best and had the best interests of Europe in mind. This was manifest on the colonial issue. To be sure, Washington correctly identified the long-term trend (and indeed made a terrible mistake when cold war considerations led it to endorse a colonial power, as in Indochina after January 1950). But being right and making it clear nevertheless breeds resentments when one is the dominant power.

At least the colonial issue was liquidated. But the same problem arose in connection with all three of the areas of common interest described above. In the realm of strategy, there was the subtle difference due to geography, between a Protector who, rationally, could afford to choose between a strategy of deterrence and a strategy of defense for Western Europe, and protégés for whom defense, i.e., war, whether conventional or nuclear, meant death. The Protector could envisage a "graduated" strategy of intermediate solutions between a "classical" conventional fight and the suicidal resort to strategic nuclear weapons, with the conviction that the very existence of such intermediate solutions would in fact reenforce deterrence, since an "all or nothing" strategy would appear quite hollow to the enemy. But the protégés would fear that any strategy which seemed to reassure the foe that he did not risk immediate incineration if he moved, would be only too plausible and encourage him to take risks. So that even on the subject of deterrence (the only one the Europeans wanted to hear), there was an uneasy tension between America's search for a strategy of "rational" deterrence and the Europeans' preference for the "rationality of irrationality"; between America's fascination with "flexible response" and limited nuclear counterforce, and the Europeans' obstinate embrace of strategies creating the maximum of uncertainty, the better to maintain the enemy's fear of escalation. Their distaste for devising "rational use" strategies against a failure of deterrence has persisted. Hence also the paradox of more than 7,000 tactical nuclear weapons placed by the United States into Western Europe, but no NATO agreement on their proper role. The West Europeans have never entirely lost their fear that the United States, with its monopoly of nuclear decision, might be just a bit too prudent and too slow for Europe's good. Hence the reluctance of the European members of NATO to endorse the MLF, which would in no way have ended that monopoly.

In the realm of economic and monetary affairs, uneasiness was concentrated in two areas. There was some resentment at American efforts to get the European Economic Community (EEC) to lower its external tariff at once—one of the few cements of a community initially rather poor in common policies—and at American protests against the Common Agricultural Policy (CAP). More seriously, in the 60s, there were rising misgivings against the cavalier way in which the United States, rather than take potentially painful domestic measures to reduce its balance-of-payments deficits, counted on its allies' willingness to absorb huge quantities of dollars without demanding their conversion into gold and used its commercial surplus to invest heavily in Europe.

Finally, the American desire to have general diplomatic support never went over well. There was a fear of being dragged into American anti-Communist adventures overseas; and the Europeans either tended to believe that Washington exaggerated the worldwide aggressiveness and cohesion of communism, or else thought that they were too weak and too exposed to share the front lines with Washington everywhere. Fearful of total destruction, they never saw any contradiction between their demand for a total American commitment to the deterrence of Moscow's threat to Western Europe, and their determination not to be dragged into a confrontation between Washington and Moscow or Peking in Asia, Africa, or the Middle East—between their desire for total solidarity where they were (i.e., in Europe and in their own colonies) and their preference for dissociation elsewhere. The Europeans rather felt that the Americans were the ones who contradicted themsleves, insofar as they seemed to expect global support while keeping their own hands free, for instance, in arms negotiations with the USSR. Moreover, once they had gotten over their fear of American rashness in the days of the "rollback" rhetoric, many West Europeans believed that the United States could much more easily live with the Continental status quo—i.e., the division of Europe—than they. Whether they dreamed of a grand reunion of the two halves, or believed that the best that could be obtained was a lowering of barriers and a multiplication of contacts between these halves, they felt that this was a specifically West European interest—indeed, perhaps a specifically European interest—which collided both with obvious Soviet resistance or hostility and with U.S. complacency.

c. Uneasiness, however, led to division, not to rebellion. For reasons that lie outside the scope of this essay, the West Europeans split between "orthodox Atlanticists," ambivalent Atlanticists, and Gaullists. It was not, or only in appearance, a split between France and all the others, even though Washington sometimes read it that way. There were various politicians and interests in France who disapproved of de Gaulle's tactics and objectives. But there also were, among France's neighbors, many political figures who sympathized, if not with de Gaulle's style, and certainly not with his nationalist emphasis, but with his critique of America and his ambitions for Europe. Thus—especially in West Germany—there were leaders who could be called *pro forma* Atlanticists yet hidden Gaullists. Given West Germany's particular geographical position along the Iron Curtain, precedence had to be given to the security relation with the United States; but they were not unhappy to hear the French statesman draw global perspectives different from Washington's and raise sharp questions about American practices, for this was a way of having Washington's complacency shaken without having to pay any price.

Yet the practical result of this division (and of the purely intra-European factors of discord) was that the Community remained a rump. Politically, there was neither supranational federation (de Gaulle dealt it one last killing blow in 1965) nor Fouchet-plan intergovernmental leadership: the combined opposition of Holland, within, and of the United Kingdom and the United States outside, had killed *that* in 1962. After EDC, there was no attempt at a common defense, since the United States did not favor it, and France's secession from NATO in 1966 made such prospects even more remote. There was no coordination of foreign policy. There was merely a free market for goods, capital, and labor, a complicated agricultural policy, a foreign economic policy essentially limited to trade negotiations with associates and with the United States. From 1963 to the fall of de Gaulle from power in 1969, the EEC was deadlocked. This deadlock in effect kept the Community alive, a truncated testimony to the high hopes of the

50s, but it also preserved American predominance and prevented the birth of any "European nationalism" that might have challenged Washington. Western Europe's impotence was demonstrated at the time of the Soviet invasion of Czechoslovakia; the West Europeans deplored the casualness of America's reaction—the United States had its eyes on Vietnam and on Chicago—yet they themselves said little, did nothing at all, and were rather relieved to see the crisis stay local.[5]

B. To what extent have these general trends been transformed by the new leaders and events of the period 1969-73? Again, having dealt with this period in more detail elsewhere,[6] I will limit myself to what is most essential for an understanding of the present and of the future.

1. With the benefit of some hindsight, one can now see that, from the viewpoint of West European unification, this period constituted a remarkable—and lost—opportunity.

a. At its most superficial level (but is it?), this period saw the coming to power in Paris, Bonn, and London of three men—Pompidou, Brandt, Heath—whose feelings and calculations toward Washington were not identical, but for whom the creation of an effective West European identity was a common priority. Brandt was less "Atlantic" by far than Erhard or Schroeder had been, partly for *Ostpolitik* reasons; Heath wanted to prove that England in the EEC would not be Washington's Trojan horse; Pompidou, for all his Gaullism, accepted as a fact the death of de Gaulle's dream of a "Europe from the Atlantic to the Urals," as a reality the dangers and limitations of a French solo performance, and as a necessity the resulting priority for what Gaullism had sometimes derisively called "la petite Europe."

b. Moreover, some of the intra-European factors of discord had been fading away. The gap between pseudovictors (France and Britain) and losers of World War II (Germany and Italy) had vanished. Colonial distractions were over. Bonn was less unsure of itself; Paris (after May '68 and the financial crisis of November '68) and London (facing economic sluggishness, social strains, and payments problems) were less sure of themselves. The three countries' *Ostpolitiken* were finally on the same wave length; all three were seeking a détente, yet with the hope that recognizing the status quo would help soften it up.

c. Finally, there was a new French strategy. It aimed at a revival of the EEC after the years of deadlock. It lifted the veto on Britain as a precondition to that revival; and it set aside the issues of ultimates de Gaulle had raised, for they had provoked American opposition and intra-EEC paralysis. Thus, on the one hand, precedence would be given to what might be called a "safe," internal issue, monetary unification, as a way of linking the West European economies more tightly. On the other hand, the West Europeans would refrain from deliberately challenging American preferences or policies: a common European foreign policy, a separate defense were not on the agenda. (Indeed Pompidou proclaimed the necessity of American forces in Europe.) Since the new American president and his chief adviser had, on their first trip abroad, come to Paris to bury the hatchet, and in particular to indicate both continuing support for the idea of a European entity and indifference to its institutional make-up, this prudent French policy of reenforcement without collision seemed to have a good chance of success. But its success depended on one prerequisite: a calm external environment, so that the entry of Britain *and* the "deepening" of EEC could take place and be digested without outside interference. In other words, the new strategy rested on the hope that with the removal of two major irritants—de Gaulle's grand challenge and the Johnson policy in Vietnam—there would be no reasons for new friction between a prudent, if "inward-looking" Europe, and Nixon's United States. But things did not turn out that way.

2. American policy toward Western Europe underwent several important changes. To be sure, the conviction that there were crucial common interests persisted. So did the specifications about the limits and the content of West European unity: given the West Europeans' own avoidance of the issue of defense autonomy, the Nixon-Kissinger team did little to encourage any alternative to or reform of NATO in defense matters (even if overt hostility to the French nuclear force disappeared). Nor did the United States move away from the preference for an economically "outward-looking" Europe. But there were two major innovations.

a. The first was the new priority to transforming relations with the two major Communist powers. To be sure, the West Europeans had preceded the United States on the road to Moscow (Kissinger had initially been critical of Brandt's approach). They had regretted America's refusal to deal with "Red China." Washington had been more skeptical than its allies about the Soviet-sponsored Conference on Security and Co-operation. But this was not really the point. The new political strategy of the United States seemed to imply a subtle demotion of Western Europe's importance. Western Europe had to remain an ally because its safety and prosperity provided the United States with essential trump cards in dealing with the USSR, but even this suggested that an end-in-itself had become a tool. Only yesterday, the global policies of the United States, which the Europeans were either told to support or were kept away from, had seemed less central than the U.S.-West European relationship; and whenever the latter appeared to lose its relative dominance—as during the Vietnam years—many Europeans and Americans screamed bloody murder. Now these global policies were taking clear precedence. Indeed, the rise within the U.S. Congress of a strong pressure for the reduction of American conventional forces in Western Europe, while resisted by the administration, seemed both to underline this fall from grace and to be its perhaps unintended yet plausible consequence. In other words, in the grand attempt to turn relations of enmity into merely adversary, indeed partially cooperative, relations, it seemed that Western Europe mattered less. But was this not something that would actually serve the designs of Pompidou?

b. It might have, except for a second innovation. The first left Western Europe aside; the second quite literally attacked it. I refer to a double change. It was a switch in style: the return to a "national interest" approach, after years in which the dominant mode of U.S. policy had been the "interest of the free world" style. If the new compass was to be the *national* interest (in part because, on such a basis, a new approach to Moscow and Peking was much easier), then the old American sense of urgency about West European unification, the preference for dealing with one composite partner instead of nine national ones was gone, and in fact notice was being served that the new criterion would be applied to past policies, for instance, in the realm of economics. Indeed, there also came to be a switch in substance after August 1971: the import surcharge, the suspension of convertibility, the devaluation aimed at recreating a trade surplus, the proposals for world monetary reform aimed at eliminating payments surpluses abroad, the offensive against the CAP, the protest against trade diversion resulting from Britain's entry, the drive against reverse preferences and the "Mediterranean policy" of the EEC, the pressure toward a new round of trade negotiations pointing to a zero tariff on industrial goods (and also, in NATO, the demand for "fairer" burden-sharing and new offset agreements)—all of these amounted to a revocation of past "concessions" consented in exchange for the hoped-for political advantages of a united Europe. The latter was obviously felt to be either unlikely or less necessary; while America, in its own time of economic and monetary difficulties, would not refrain from putting pressure on, and trying to dissolve, the glue of the EEC.[a]

c. The two separate innovations came together in Kissinger's "Year of Europe" speech of April 1974. On the one hand, the old notion of an Atlantic Europe was reasserted: i.e., Europe's unity was not an end in itself; it had to be subordinated to a higher goal, which transcended Europe and included not only the United States but Japan. On the other hand, this diminution of Western Europe was taking on an entirely new dimension for two reasons. First, Kissinger was demanding in effect that the Europeans join the United States in a whole (if vague) series of worldwide undertakings. Second, he was obliquely asking for concessions in trade matters, because of the interrelatedness of security and economic issues ("linkage"), while raising once again the security issue in terms that could not help but revive European fears, since he stressed the impact of "nuclear parity" on deterrence and the need to define the "requirements of flexibility" anew. Later, in the lengthy discussions on a joint Atlantic declaration, he raised the issue of consultation in a way that suggested that despite his repeated assurance that Washington still favored European unity, the United States wanted not only to make sure that its *outcome*, in policy terms, be right (i.e., "we will expect to be met in a spirit of reciprocity") but also to take a more active part in the *process* so as to have more of a say in the outcome. Thus

---

[a]This was the time when members of the administration were complaining that it was often easier to deal with Moscow or Peking than with the allies.

subordinated to a far more ambitious and global American policy, told to make adequate economic and monetary concessions, and asked to consult more intimately with the United States, the European entity, whose unity Washington said it was still supporting, was not left with a great deal of autonomy. In exchange, it was told merely that "the United States will never knowingly sacrifice the interests of others . . . consciously injure the interests of our friends": obviously, defining these interests for them was not felt to be injurious.

d. This far more heavily conditional and confining approach to Western Europe corresponded to two changes in U.S. policy-making: one, so to speak, at the top, the other in depth. At the top, I refer to the mode of operation of Kissinger. Convinced that creativity and bureaucracy are enemies, that leadership is personal, that flexibility and maneuver and secrecy are the highest attributes of a creative diplomacy, that control is the precondition to success (all very Gaullist attitudes), Kissinger proved far better at dealing with responsible statesmen in command of their own policies than with collective structures, whether coalition governments or international organizations. Hence his preference for man-to-man rather than institutionalized diplomacy, for dealing with French, German, or British leaders rather than with the heavy Brussels machinery. In the latter, he could not fail to see either a rigid complication, or a smokescreen that European statesmen could hide behind in order to resist American pressures or delay response to American demands. (Tolerance, if not enthusiasm, for the rather clumsy and inefficient bureaucracy of Brussels, requires considerable faith in Europe's capacity to overcome national habits and institutions, and nothing allows one to believe that Kissinger ever had such faith. So—as usual—his behavior turned into a self-fulfilling prophecy.) Further, in order to unfreeze situations that had been marked by sclerosis or inertia, he would lean on a "pivot": Chou En-lai, to unblock the relations with both Communist powers; Brezhnev, to get SALT and détente going; both these men, to act on Hanoi; Sadat, to launch the post-Yom Kippur piecemeal settlement policy; Faisal (without result) to have some leverage on OPEC. But in the Pompidou-Brandt-Heath period he found no comparable pivot on the European scene.

At the deeper level, his policy unfolded at a time when the attitude of the relevant American publics was changing both toward Western Europe and toward the outside world in general. Congress was growing more restive about U.S. military engagement abroad, and more critical of Western Europe's trade policies and alleged failure to "neutralize" (i.e., pay for) the balance-of-payments losses incurred by the United States because of its forces in Europe. The foreign policy establishment that had guided diplomacy and strategy in the cold war days and nurtured the belief in Western Europe's importance and unity was now partly depleted by age, partly demoralized and splintered by Vietnam, partly disconnected from the new administration. Nixon, always suspicious of the "Eastern establishment," and Kissinger, its product and protégé but reluctant to take advice and intent on protecting his initiatives and calculations, were keeping it in the dark. The priorities and attention of the public-at-large were turning inward (as any teacher of international relations or reader of newspapers has observed). And yet the public was satisfied with the maintenance—at lower cost in blood and crises—of U.S. predominance. And it was pleased both by the prospect of a détente with enemies and by the new toughness toward increasingly competitive allies (suspected of wanting to take advantage of their access to the American market after having fattened on American investments, which, some said, meant fewer jobs in the United States). The public thus left Nixon and Kissinger free to pursue their global acrobatics. Complacency instead of the old consensus, voyeurism (or mere appreciation of the fine spectacle provided by the two men) rather than the participation that had verged on hysteria in the days of Joe McCarthy—this was the new public mood, and it was not very friendly to Europe.

3. The effect of the new policy and mood on Western Europe was complex. At the cost of "roughing up" chronology, I would stress the following aspects.

a. Superficially, the new American approach seemed, unwittingly, to goad Western Europe to greater unity. While de Gaulle had been the aggressor, so to speak, the partners of France refused to follow him. Now that Nixon and Kissinger were firing the shots, there was a tendency to close ranks. The new American policy toward the USSR was applauded as long as it merely tended to slow down the strategic arms race (the acceptance of approximate equality with Moscow did not provoke in Western Europe the same anxieties as in Senator Jackson's mind). But there was a fear of direct U.S.-Soviet talks and deals that could create an imbalance dangerous for Western Europe's security (and, even more, self-confidence), even while preserving the global balance; hence considerable anxiety regarding Mutual and Balanced Force Reductions (MBFR), even among those Europeans who endorsed the idea. There was a fear that—at the Conference on Security and Cooperation in Europe (CSCE) or at the summits— the Big Two might be putting the development of their own mutual relationship ahead of West European concerns. The statement on the prevention of nuclear war at the 1973 summit seemed to indicate that the superpower dialogue had been given public precedence over NATO obligations, and Kissinger's perfectly justified denials about the letter did not quite dispel doubts about the spirit. All of this made it possible for the West Europeans to begin—at last—foreign policy coordination with the preparation of a common stand for the CSCE; and it led Pompidou to allow Jobert, in 1973, to raise for the first time since the early 60s the issue of a separate European defense.

As for the "direct attack" on the EEC, it ended up (also on the surface) reenforcing the Community. The common float of six of the nine currencies in 1972 was an attempt to create an "island of stability" in a chaotic world, pending an agreement on a new global system. The CAP was preserved, and

American demands for other concessions warded off. Kissinger's request for "a new Atlantic Charter" allowed Jobert to rally his colleagues behind the idea of a separate document stressing Western Europe's own identity. Thus America's new, more stringent attempt to define the limits and nature of European unity, which previously had contributed to arresting it, now seemed to help it move along—in a direction that was not what Washington had wanted.

b. At a deeper level, however, centrifugal forces were at work, precisely because a *solid* reenforcement would have required a quiet world. On the one hand, the reaction of many West Europeans to the first aspect of Kissinger's diplomacy had been symptomatic of the craving for dependence I have mentioned. They complained of being neglected; they kept pulling Kissinger's sleeves (which explains in part why he thought that his "Year of Europe" speech was meeting their demand for attention). To be sure, when he did pay attention again, they did not like what he requested, but at least it seemed to suggest, however contentiously, that the old relationship still mattered. It was bad to be so publicly demoted to a lower place in what Jobert called America's cosmogony,[7] but it was good to be shown that one fitted in it. Thus, even in the summer of 1973, behind the facade of European solidarity that so irritated Kissinger (obliged to receive a Danish EEC spokesman with no powers of negotiation), there were subtle differences between French activism—which rejoiced at Kissinger's *gaffes*—and the attitudes of several other countries, which deplored them and had no desire for a break.

On the other hand, the attempt to strengthen European unity found its most serious limit in the uneven impact of outside winds on a heterogeneous group. The "monetarist" approach to economic unification was a short cut that required intense internal cooperation (a pooling of reserves, a reevaluation of gold, comparable credit policies) as well as a stable environment. But periodic reshufflings of currency rates among the major powers, huge speculative movements of private capital, and different domestic priorities at a time of rising inflation exposed the monetary "serpent" to recurrent distortions between its component parts, and neither the lira nor the pound was even able to join it. External storms meant that energy had to be spent on simply keeping whatever had been accomplished from being blown away. Different internal economic priorities doomed attempts at finding new areas for common policies: there was not sufficient will; attention was mobilized by domestic tasks. Hence the futility of the Paris summit of 1972. And Britain, far from bringing a new dynamism into the EEC, turned out to be a headache even under Mr. Heath. Britain's economic weakness and the persistence of political opposition to the EEC in Britain obliged him too to beg out of some of the common enterprises (thus, the float) while demanding specific aid in other respects (regional policy).

This explains the kind of West European *Götterdämmerung* of October '73 - Spring '74. At first, the fear of the consequences on Western Europe of the Arab oil embargo and restrictions, the unwillingness to be drawn, if not into the conflict, at least into a de facto alliance with the United States by America's use of European bases for its airlift to Israel, indignation at being left out of the resolution of the crisis by the superpowers produced apparent unity—a unity of lamentation, in the form of a common statement on the Arab-Israeli dispute. But soon all appearances exploded: internal solidarity was not strong enough to produce a statement of support to Holland; the Copenhagen summit ended in deadlock on regional and energy policies; each member looked after its own bilateral deals; the common float disintegrated when France, faced with a run on the franc and the impact of the quadrupled price of imported oil, jumped out in January '74; and Secretary of State Kissinger, in proposing a consumers' front under American leadership, provoked an open break between Jobert and his partners. This time, France was isolated, not merely—as so often in the past—within EEC, but far more seriously, by the fact that her eight associates chose to join a new agency outside EEC. In a grand symbolic finale, the three leaders of the phase that was coming to such a crashing end—Heath, Brandt, and Pompidou—all disappeared, while Kissinger remained.

Present

What is the significance of the present moment—the situation which has prevailed since the Organization of Petroleum Exporting Countries (OPEC) decisions on the price of oil and the general derangement of the "American world economic system" of the postwar period? This is the system characterized by the supremacy of the dollar, low industrial tariffs among the developed non-Communist powers (free trade playing the same ideological role of bulwark and ram for the most advanced power, as in the British system of the nineteenth century), a high rate of economic growth, the spectacular rise of largely American multinational corporations, and cheap access to the energy and raw materials of the Third World. We are at a turning point.

A. The objective conditions have been deeply transformed.

1. For all the industrial powers this is a period of intense crisis.

a. Cheap access to oil abroad is over, and there is a risk of "more OPECs" covering other raw materials. Moreover, economic nationalism in the developing countries is liable to lead them to nationalize basic resources and industries producing them, to restrict the multinationals to a commercial role, and to try to limit their profits. Even if no cartels comparable to OPEC emerge, the developing nations are unlikely to give up their current offensive against the postwar world economic order, their demands for a redistribution of the world's wealth, and their determination to exploit whatever assets they possess, whether these consist in products needed by the industrial powers, or in masses of votes in international bodies, or in sympathy for their cause among fractions of the ruling elites or intelligentsia of the advanced nations.

b. Unevenly (see below) but quite generally, the increase in the cost of oil has created balance-of-payments problems for most of the industrial countries, and there is a danger that each one will try to seek remedies in bilateral deals with oil-producing countries, in export subsidies aimed at making the execution of these deals possible, or in import restrictions and exchange controls, in sum, in the destruction of the "open" economy. Moreover, the accumulation of huge reserves by the OPEC countries, far in excess of what several of them can use productively for their development, or even for shiny weapons, creates new risks of financial strain on the banking system of the industrial nations, especially if much of the revenue acquired by OPEC is used for short-term, easily maneuverable deposits.

c. In addition, and quite apart from the oil drama, the "open" world economy is suffering from a combination of inflation and recession. The inflation has, undoubtedly, many causes, and experts disagree about the fundamental ones. Some point to the decreasing productivity of capital, others to the pull of demand and the push of pressure groups, others to the inflationary effect of American monetary practices both at home and—until the switch to floating rates in March 1973—abroad. The result has been a depreciation of the currencies of those countries most affected by inflation (and this has undoubtedly been one incentive for OPEC's action).

Measures taken, in the United States and elsewhere, to fight inflation by restricting credit and curbing the resources of enterprises have provoked a decline in investments, a fall in industrial activity, and a rise in unemployment. Where the government has decided to combat recession with budget deficits (through tax cuts), there is a new danger of inflation, unless the capital market can be tapped without competing with private enterprises eager for funds. This means that, in order to absorb the inflationary impact of such deficits while paying for imported oil, such governments may need the help of OPEC. That is, the creditors may be asked to keep the debtors afloat! Meanwhile both the inflation and the recession are fed by the oil crisis. Imported oil costs much more, and the hike in prices constitutes a tax on the industrial powers. Some of the measures they will have to take in order to cope with it—a reduction in imports, domestic conservation programs—may contribute to the recession; others—a shift from production for the domestic market to exports, the development of substitutes for imported oil—may contribute to inflation, as well as to economic dislocation and domestic shortages. Further inflation in turn might provoke further OPEC price rises. A spreading recession in the industrial world would make paying for OPEC oil more difficult; while a quick recovery would increase the level and the load of oil imports.

d. There is, at present, nothing more than a stopgap, de facto international monetary system. The "dollar exchange standard" collapsed in part because Japan and Western Europe could no longer absorb gigantic amounts of dollars, in part because fixed rates could be maintained only by painful and politically unacceptable domestic monetary and credit constraints so as to eliminate imbalances. Short-term capital flows made possible by the "open" economy were putting intense, speculative pressure on the weaker currencies, and domestic priorities (inevitably the first concern of governments) made the external goal of exchange stability seem arbitrary or perverse. But the successor system of "dirty floats," whether or not it is inflationary (as is argued by those who point to all the structural factors that prevent a decline of prices in interdependent industrial economies), is no more than a *pis aller*. If "a major drawback of a system of freely fluctuating rates is that it substitutes market reconciliation of inconsistent payment objectives for the reconciliation of objectives through international cooperation and agreement,"[8] managed floating rates add to this drawback the risks of constant maneuver. The establishment of an international monetary system capable of imposing effective constraints on international liquidity and of inciting governments to create the internal conditions for the stability of their currencies has been postponed because of present uncertainties—which this postponement feeds.

2. But there is a second objective change—*among* the industrial powers.

a. On the one hand, the United States has emerged as a relative winner: OPEC did for Henry Kissinger what he had not been able to achieve by himself. OPEC's coup may have been a disaster, or at least a major headache, for the industrial world as a whole, but it had windfall aspects for the United States. Far less dependent on imported oil than Europe or Japan, the United States faced a less stringent payments problem. It is in the United States, the most advanced industrial power, with a stable political system and a currency that, for all its recent weakness, remains the world's most demanded reserve, that OPEC funds are most likely to be invested. It is from the United States that OPEC countries can best buy the technology, industries, and brains they need for their development and the weapons they covet for their ambitions. It is the United States which, as a major oil producer and a leader in technology, has the greatest opportunities to develop substitutes for imported oil and for oil generally—and to sell them to its allies. It is the United States which is most able to be the "lender of last resort" in secondary recycling, i.e., to raise the money needed by countries with balance-of-payments crises and insufficient OPEC investments, loans, or orders. In other words, whereas a drastic reduction in the price of oil would be a blessing for its allies and save them from having to slave for OPEC, Washington could live well with a merely moderate reduction—just enough to keep the development of oil production and new sources of energy at home profitable. Of course, the United States has suffered some very hard knocks: the recession, the crisis of political authority at home, the debacle of Indochina abroad. But on the subject of the so-called "ungovernability" of Western democracies, it is hard to say whether Western Europe is better or worse off than the United States; the recession has not been limited to the United States, and the lamentable end in Indochina was but the inevitable outcome of a long course of error.

b. On the other hand, the crisis has demoted a Europe that had become used to seeing itself, along with Japan, as a major "civilian power," more important to world trade and more productive than the United States. It has also aggravated Europe's internal heterogeneity. As we have seen, France in 1974 had to leave the joint float so as not to become a dependent of the strong Deutsche Mark, and if it decided to rejoin it by mid-1975, it was largely in order to prevent the revaluation of the franc against the falling dollar from continuing and thus undermining a French export drive that, for all its successes, was still far more fragile than Germany's. Bonn, with a low rate of inflation, a somewhat smaller dependence on imported oil than its neighbors, a very strong currency, exports that had triumphed over four revaluations, and huge payments surpluses, is in a much more enviable position than its partners (even though this strength has its own drawbacks, while recession has hit Germany too). Britain, for deep structural reasons, and Italy, for primarily political ones—but is it easier to change a stalemated political system than a sluggish economy?—are in very serious trouble: their currencies are under constant pressure and their reserves are running out. France is in temporary trouble—temporary insofar as the restoration of its payments equilibrium without continuing recession depends partly on the smoothness of domestic events, partly on the prosperity of its biggest client, West Germany, whose own prosperity depends on the United States. This vulnerability of the West European economies to America's is another factor that, in the present phase, casts a pall over Western Europe; but unlike the oil problem, this one can hardly be said to give a relative advantage to the United States.

3. The consequence of these events and problems is a sudden change in the context of U.S.-European relations. Yesterday's issues either related to the "Soviet problem" (i.e., the complex of problems concerning the physical and political security of Western Europe), or else they were "bilateral" U.S.-European issues concerning trade, agriculture, offset agreements, the negotiation of mutually acceptable exchange rates, etc. Today, in addition to the Soviet-related issues, whose very persistence underlines Western Europe's dependence on America's might, the new problems on the agenda are global. The bilateral issues are either gone or look trivial. They have been blown away by the storms and made irrelevant by the removal of the taproot of discontent: America's sense of relative decline, compared to her allies, in the period 1969-73. Instead, we are faced with issues such as a new monetary system, the price of oil and the payments difficulties resulting from it, the link between raw materials or energy prices and the prices of industrial goods, food and famine, the disposition of the oceans, new technologies to replace or complement oil, the plight of the oil-poor countries of the Third World, the hideous question of nuclear proliferation, the stuffing of conventional weapons into powder kegs, and of course the perils of a spreading recession and the Arab-Israeli dispute. The ugly word "globalization" reflects both the shift and the headaches.

B. The subjective conditions have of course also been transformed.

1. This is a period of reexamination on both sides of the Atlantic. But here again there are deep differences.

a. The United States, ever since 1941, has been used to "living globally." Coping with world-wide issues is not exactly new: indeed, both George Ball and Henry Kissinger have remarked that the United States is the only non-Communist power with global responsibilities. Kissinger's activism has aimed at replacing one set of global issues (those of the cold war confrontation) with another; his "state of the world messages" bear testimony to this. He has succeeded beyond expectation. But the "shock of recognition" for the United States consists in discovering (rather angrily and partially) that the kinds of global issues that crowd today's agenda are not those which the neoclassical or neo-Bismarckian design and diplomacy of the Nixon-Kissinger era had hoped to bring to the fore. They centered on the relations between the superpowers; insofar as they paid attention to economic issues, it was either in order to use them as baits (with respect to the Soviets) or in order to redress imbalances with the allies—i.e., as a kind of political warfare, at our initiative. Instead of this we now find ourselves faced with a host of issues involving above all the Third and Fourth worlds, and these issues, largely economic, are raised by others in such a way that they actually endanger our long-range "situation of strength" vis-à-vis the Communist powers—either because our challengers, while active in the open international capitalist economy, attack the rules of the game as drafted by the industrial powers, or else because our critics actually reject the capitalist model both for their economies and for the world economy. It is therefore not always clear whether Kissinger is the sorcerer, or the sorcerer's apprentice. Moreover he has discovered that, in the realm of Soviet-related issues, NATO's military strength cannot prevent a possible weakening of Western Europe through domestic developments, especially in Mediterranean countries; while détente, at Helsinki or in arms talks, did nothing to curtail the long shadow of Soviet might on Europe's façade; indeed that it perhaps made these domestic changes behind it easier.

b. Reexamination is even more painful on the other side of the ocean. However damaging to some Europeans' pride the "fall from grace" in America's eyes and moves may have been in 1969-73, it corresponded to a period of high hopes for Europe's development and world influence. Now there is a genuine fall; gone is the faith in constant growth, which had accompanied the whole European enterprise. Instead, there is awareness of economic insecurity, added to the never-departed sense of military insecurity. Strategically, Western Europe knows that it can less than ever match the Soviet Union. Economically, it has been made rudely aware of its dependence both on the United States (inflation, recession, etc.) and on the OPEC countries (and the other raw materials producers). The latter dependence was always there, but it had remained hidden, unlike the Red Army—one more proof of the importance of perceptions and of the "necessity" of crises. Meanwhile domestic shifts in southern Europe have added a sense of political insecurity.

This overall European fall does not affect the perceptions of all countries in the same way. Bonn, used to dependence in the fields that have been central to its diplomatic strategy and foreign policy, aware of economic fragility because of historical memories in part, and yet least affected by the change in Europe's fortunes, can afford to see in its relative eminence not only a reward for sound management but an opportunity for external assertion. The shift from Brandt to Schmidt both expresses and symbolizes this new perception. Britain, under Labour party management, can see in the change a new reason for skepticism regarding the higher ambitions of the European enterprise and in the North Sea oil a saving card, to be kept strictly national. But France, which had been the most ambitious for Europe—while the most niggardly on common institutions, lest too big a dose of supranationality divert Western Europe from those far-reaching distinctive goals—is the most seriously hit, both because (by contrast with Britain and Italy) it has been hurt while operating at a (relative) peak—at least in terms of growth and foreign trade—and because the new global issues have provoked one more European identity crisis. The fact that Jobert, a convinced and committed "European," turned intensely nationalist in his last weeks in office, while Giscard, another "good European," seems to turn *mondialiste* ("the world has moved from a civilization of groups to a global civilization") indicates both disarray and distress.

2. From the changes in perceptions, let us proceed to changes in policies, which set the stage for our consideration of future options.

a. American policy toward Europe has changed in tone, pace, and substance, but only partly in significance. The "Year of Europe" speech had called for a joint declaration of intent to transcend petty issues and turn toward new common problems. It was friendly, indeed pleasing, in tone; it suggested no pressing deadline; and while calling for collaboration on energy, it remained vague. By the time the declaration was signed in June 1974, it had been overtaken by events. Kissinger, irritated by the troubles he had encountered in the process of getting it, by Western Europe's attitude toward the Yom Kippur War, by the reluctance he felt among his allies toward his rather militant (although not military) approach to OPEC, switched from a tone of patient sympathy to one of increasing and public contempt. He pressed the allies very hard for a rapid alignment of the consumer countries: the International Energy Agency (IEA) was set up fast and given vast amounts of work, and the same happened a little later with the recycling facility he proposed. As for substance, instead of a mere commitment to face new problems and to solve existing ones, the new policy entails the eclipse of the old ones and action—not mere talk—on the oil crisis in its various political and economic dimensions.

And yet, if the "attack" on the EEC has therefore apparently stopped, it may well be only because the two main implications of the Nixon-Kissinger approach to Europe have been not only confirmed but triumphantly reasserted. The limited role of Europe in America's global policy, indeed the merely instrumental or supplemental role of Europe, is more evident than ever. First there is now the grand strategy toward OPEC: here Europe's role merely consists in joining the common consumer front, so that OPEC countries may not play divide-and-rule, while the United States tries to regain the initiative which OPEC moves have taken away. Second, there is the new general approach to the developing nations; here, switching (once the IEA was in place) from "confrontation" to "conciliation," Kissinger let the preparatory conference requested by the French fail, and immediately after that failure (which had exposed once more the Europeans' own divisions), he made the concessions that would have ensured its success—thus proving that only the United States, not Europe, retains the key to a bargain with the nations of the Third and Fourth worlds. Third, there is America's mediation of the Arab-Israeli dispute (not exactly unconnected with the oil problem), but since Kissinger here cannot count on Europe's support, he shuts the allies out (and tells them to shut up), putting on his door the sign: Do not disturb. In this way (and by changing America's objectives in that part of the world), he has so far retained the initiative. Finally, there is détente, in which Europe's role is minimal so far as he is concerned.

Kissinger is trying to keep his tracks separate—in good divide-and-rule fashion. The USSR is relegated to the fourth track; Europe to the first two; the Arab countries are functionally split between the first three. But Kissinger maneuvers all four. This shows that the other implication of his earlier policy toward Europe—the desire to control its development and policies—is still of capital importance. Only it is done now, not through demands for consultations and concessions, but through demands for alignment; not by insisting that the EEC open itself up, so to speak, to American goods and preferences, but by requesting that it close ranks and be tugged behind the American vessel. The questions this policy raises are obvious: is this "demotion" of Europe wise, and insofar as Kissinger has reestablished control, what will he do with it? Where is the vessel going?

b. If America's policy has the same meaning in a new context, Western Europe's represents a major shift, all of whose implications are not yet clear. It can be summed up as follows. For years the EEC had hesitated between an "Atlantic" and a "European" Europe. It had dodged a clear-cut choice and usually been divided whenever pressed to make one. (The one exception was the year 1973 before the oil price hike, as we have stated before; but even then the "tilt" toward the French conception, in reaction against U.S. postures and pressures, was not strong enough to overcome internal sluggishness and discord.) In 1974, eight of the Nine chose an "Atlantic" Europe, by accepting the IEA and Kissinger's strategy. The ninth—France—with no other effective avenue of activity but Europe, resigned itself to "alignment," with the hope that this conciliatory attitude would allow the Nine to resume their Sisyphean march toward a "European Europe," now that a major factor of paralysis, the Franco-American discord, was removed from the EEC and that France had made some institutional concessions to its associates. We have seen that Pompidou, in his friendliness to the United States in 1969-72, had made the same calculation. But a policy that seemed justified in the years of "benign neglect" by the United States and had to be dropped when the United States itself began showing unfriendliness makes much less sense today when the United States, both in its calls for allied solidarity and its own initiatives toward OPEC and the other developing nations, seems determined not to leave much breathing space for a distinctive West European voice. There is a false symmetry between France's nonparticipation in, yet cooperation with, NATO and her nonmembership in, yet cooperation with, the IEA. Defense was never an EEC function, whereas energy was always supposed to be within its orbit and has clear connections with issues that go to the heart of the EEC: industrial policy, trade, monetary cooperation.

In other words, the Europeans, having discovered that their economic security is endangered by OPEC, have turned *to the United States*, just as they turned to the United States when they realized that their military safety was threatened by the USSR. It was obvious, in the latter case, that liberal democracies would choose America's protection rather than appease an over-powering totalitarian Empire. But it was not obvious that Western Europe would also turn to the United States in the energy crisis. Indeed, Jobert—speaking for Pompidou—had pushed for an alternative solution: a collective European approach to OPEC, based on the idea that Europe had a great deal to offer, that its interests were not identical with America's (given the different dependence on imported oil), that the OPEC countries themselves might prefer to deal with Europe separately, and that a common consumer front might put the Western Europeans under America's political, economic, and financial dependence without necessarily saving them from OPEC. His partners and Pompidou's successor have in effect preferred a choice dictated this time, not by a felt community of political values with Washington, but by a felt community of economic systems: rather a "common front of industrial powers" than a "North-South alliance." If the threat of exploitation and blackmail comes from OPEC, a consumers' front led by the United States—whatever disadvantages *might* result for the neediest consumer nations—would at least be able to meet strength with strength. West Germany, from its own more enviable position, had made this calculation from the start.

Now this choice, in turn, raises two major questions. First, what is the domain of action left to the EEC in and of itself? What is going to be "European" that is not either being kept jealously national (such as labor relations, incomes policies, taxation) or bilateral (such as deals with separate Arab countries, or each member's *Ostpolitik*), or "neo-Atlantic" (such as energy and the payments problems connected with it or the issues of raw materials, development, and food to be discussed in "global" conferences or agencies)? In these last the industrial powers tend to form one component, with Western Europe either dividing or else following the lead of the more powerful United States. Are not the new issues in the economic realm of such global magnitude (by contrast with the old intra-European issues or the purely "bilateral" U.S.-European ones) that the geographical framework of the Nine is irrelevant to their solution, which exceeds both the limits and the capacity of Western Europe—a sad reality that has always prevailed in the realm of military security, but now extends to so much more? Now that the EEC has a new motor (the Council of Presidents, no longer tied to the notion of unanimity) and the promise of a better transmission (an Assembly to be elected by universal suffrage), will it—if one may use this metaphor—still have any fuel to go anywhere? Will it not become a mere subcontractor of America's global schemes? At best, will it not just be the forum in which joint positions will be prepared for presentation to other, broader bodies which will actually be in charge of dealing with the issues—a forum for proposition but not for decision? Has not OPEC brought about de Gaulle's oldest nightmare—*l'Europe américaine*?

This brings me to the second question, for France: France's grudging, partly concealed, but undeniable alignment (in the realm of energy and of arms production) is undoubtedly more tactical than real; it is being rationalized as a necessary precondition for any future distinctively European policy, rather than as a change of heart. But will it allow France to prod a "de-dramatized" European Community toward genuine achievements of its own (and not merely toward recurrent promises of future achievements)? Will France's good will toward Washington allow it to put the whole Kissinger train on the rails of the kind of "North-South" policy the French seem to be aiming for, but for which some of its European partners (such as Bonn) show little enthusiasm, and which Kissinger himself seems quite determined to "preempt"? Or will the European institutions not become rather the transmission belt for Kissinger's signals and commands and a straitjacket for France? Will France not find itself a prisoner on the train it has joined? Who is hijacking whom?

Future

A. Any discussion of alternatives must either take the form of a series of scenarios covering a wide range of possibilities (cf. the Kahn-Wiener book on the year 2000)[9] or else be based on definite assumptions that limit that range by ruling out either "far out" hypotheses or (alas) more likely ones, but of a kind that make forecasting too difficult. I will adopt the second method. (The first would require a volume and still be of dubious usefulness.)

1. My first assumption is the continuing importance of Western Europe to

the United States. It is sufficiently great to justify that much overworked expression, a "special relationship." The three ranges of common interests postulated by the United States since the late 40s are still present.

a. In the realm of military security, I would argue that the interest of the United States remains in the existence of a Western Europe that is both safe from military attack or nibbling from the East, and sufficiently confident in its capacity to deter such encroachment not to be tempted to glide into "Finland-ization," i.e., into a policy of accommodation to Soviet demands (for instance, a veto of any extension of EEC activities in diplomacy or defense, always opposed by Moscow). It has been argued that the physical safety of the United States would not be threatened by the "loss" of Western Europe. But clearly the complex balance of world power, which does not consist of the nuclear strategic stalemate alone, would be imperiled (far more than it was by the Soviet move in Cuba in 1962). Besides, the main concern of a great power, after physical security, is influence. Surely this is what the massive build-up of Soviet might is aiming at: the expansion of Soviet influence and the eventual neutralization of Western Europe as an actor in world affairs. The very reason why Western Europe remains a major, if currently inaccessible, prize for Moscow, explains why it remains a crucial stake for the United States.

b. What is more, military safety and the political self-confidence it breeds are closely connected with economic orientation. A "Finlandized" Western Europe could be prosperous (Finland is). But would it remain part of the "open" international economy, would it accord shelters, springboards, and good treatment to United States investments, dollars, goods, and services? America's original interest in Western Europe's recovery has been transformed into an interest in Western Europe's prosperity and financial solvency, because of the very strength of the links of trade and financial involvement that make of the North Atlantic (if you'll pardon the expression) a coprosperity sphere. The political base of this "community" of advanced capitalism *is* the security link established in the late 40s. Quasi-instinctively, this is what NATO's European members understood when they decided to follow Kissinger's oil strategy.

c. On the new global issues that have, along with oil, come to the fore, as well as on what might be called the "old" global issues (such as East-West relations or the Arab-Israeli dispute, which is far more than a regional powder keg), it remains important for the United States to be able to count either on Western Europe's support and cooperation, or on its benevolent self-restraint. The United States would be weakened if some of its allies, owing to domestic shifts, switched to neutrality; or if the Europeans appeared as rivals on the road to Moscow (for the USSR could then prove more demanding in its dealings with Washington); or if they behaved as the last cold warriors at a time when the American strategy is to entangle the imperial bear in a fine net. In the complex relationships that will have to be established with the developing nations, even an American administration intent on "conciliation, not confrontation," to use the French cliché, has an interest in obtaining *good* terms from conciliation and therefore in presenting to these nations a reasonably coherent front. The aim would be to limit, for instance, the danger of competing bilateral deals between separate consumers and producers of oil, or the danger of financial collapses among the advanced countries due to payments crises. Nor can a new international monetary system be established without the support of the West Europeans. Nor can the world's food problems be tackled without their cooperation, given the importance of Western Europe's agriculture.

d. To conclude: America's interest is both positive (enlist support) and negative (prevent the unraveling of a network that is one of its main assets in the world struggle for influence). But this does not imply either of the two following propositions. First, it does not mean that these American interests can only be covered by the perpetuation of present policies and institutions (such as NATO). If the end is clear, the means allow for choices—and disagreements. (To take an example from the first range: if "Finlandization" is bad, would "Swedenization" threaten the American interest?) In particular, the necessity for and advantages of a *united* Western Europe—as a means to these ends—remain a subject of intense discussion.

Second, U.S.-European agreement on common interests does not mean that *all* West Europeans agree on the range and character of these common interests. There are huge variations here. If I may hazard a vast oversimplification, I would say that the consensus is greatest on security (leaving out only Western Europe's Communists), far more limited in economic matters. Thus there are many non-Communists who believe that either domestic national priorities or West European priorities, which require planning, should be given precedence over the maintenance of the "open" capitalist Atlantic economy; indeed that they entail the regulation of foreign investments, or the control of capital movements, or the building of a separate monetary bloc. Consensus is probably even more restricted regarding relations with the world outside of Europe. There support for the notion of *separate* West European interests remains strong. The questions raised above about the importance of recent developments was whether the "Atlantic" road selected by the EEC would really allow for these separate interests to be heard and heeded, but not even the most enthusiastic supporter of IEA believes that American and West European interests in the energy crisis, or indeed in the world of the developing nations, are identical.

2. My second assumption concerns precisely the West Europeans.

a. I will assume that what I have just said about the present consensus will continue, even if there are major internal political changes. In Britain (especially after the referendum on Europe), in West Germany, the Benelux countries, Denmark and Ireland, the range of foreign policy alternatives offered by competing political forces continues to be extremely narrow. There may be shifts in tone and style: a Strauss regime in Bonn would not behave like Brandt's—but neither does Schmidt's! I see no reason to expect, however, or fear more than that. This leaves us with France and Italy. Concerning the first, my own shorthand prediction is that the advent of a left-wing government would probably usher in a period of domestic turmoil, but that the tensions in Franco-American relations would not exceed those we have known in the Gaullist era. Communists and Socialists would find a common denominator in resisting American pressures and demands in the second and third realms, but the Socialists—intent on demonstrating their independence from the Communist party—would cling to "Europe" as their raft, and this would in itself limit their inclination to loosen the ties between France and the international capitalist economy, given the strength of the EEC's ties to it. In other words, the old tug-of-war between France and her partners about control of the direction of the EEC would resume, but the very need of the Socialists for an external anchor would, paradoxically, make them less likely to accept isolation and an EEC paralysis as cold-bloodedly as did de Gaulle throughout and Pompidou in his last weeks. As for military security, the Socialists keep toning down their criticism of the *force de frappe*, they stress the need for armed forces, and they show little inclination to "appease" Moscow. Indeed, here too their anti-Atlanticism and their objections to French military nationalism might find as a common denominator the idea of a West European defense system, which is anathema to both the French Communist party and to Moscow. The easiest way to resolve *that* Communist-Socialist tension would be to stick to the status quo.

On Italy, there are two answers, one serious, one flippant. The flippant one is that—short of having a government determined to expel the United States from its bases—it does not really matter: Italy has largely opted out of active politics in the world arena. The serious one is that a Left-Center coalition (the "historical compromise") would need EEC support on payments issues at least as much as the current coalition; that the Italian Communists have gone very far toward endorsing the EEC not merely as a fact of life but as a good thing; that they have shown an interest in reassuring the United States so far as NATO and "the present equilibrium of forces in Europe" are concerned; that their relations with Moscow are poor and have worsened over events in Portugal; and indeed that a coalition capable of putting order and honesty into Italy's corrupt bureaucratic-financial chaos should be welcomed by all her partners, so long as it does not rock the military boat—which the Communist party says it has no intention of rocking.

b. I will also assume that the West Europeans will keep the EEC on its present course (the question about the *substance* left to EEC remains, however). They will try to save the CAP (perhaps by revising it), to keep Britain in the Market as a full participant, to develop a regional policy, to harmonize their economic courses (which does not necessarily mean detailed coordination), to preserve the internal open market for industrial goods, capital, and labor, and to define common stands (diplomatic, economic, financial) on global problems as often as possible.

Whether this will amount to much is another matter. Everything depends on world events, on the West Europeans' own will to overcome factors of division and inertia, and on the United States. But the West European nations will keep going through the motions, even if these do not take them very far. Each one of them derives benefits, tangible or intangible but real, from the Community's existence; indeed one could almost argue that the Community is less a prelude to an entity "beyond the nation-state" than a means of reinforcing the nation-state. Each one of them needs the façade, or figleaf, of EEC too much to drop it. Naked without it, most of them need the semblance of collective power it provides, for want of the real thing. To put it differently, as long as the clothes are there, they may believe, or believe others will believe, that there is an emperor. Or else, as in Bonn's case, they need the EEC, not as a protection from the cold, but as a pole to which it is good to be tied, for this attachment preserves one, at least a bit, from the conflicting pushes and pulls of the superpowers.

In the second place, I assume that the old obstacles to the emergence of a strong entity will continue: that is, there will still be divergent domestic priorities, and vast bureaucratic and parochial systems will still resist breaking the heavy crust of their intricate patterns and busy self-involvement. Differences in resources, in national policies, and institutions will continue to make joint programs difficult and compromises laborious. Different assessments of Western Europe's ultimate interests in world affairs will also persist. Concerning these, there may (as at present) occur a temporary bowing to necessity, a muting of divergences on distant ends, while one concentrates on surviving in the near future. But I would predict that the very difficulty of defining a separate or specifically "European" interest on many of the new global issues will tend to perpetuate a subtle, or at times open, tension. On the one hand there will be statesmen concerned above all with the *issue* and intent on finding a globally acceptable outcome even if it has no specific European mark, dimension, or function; on the other, statesmen more concerned with Europe's *identity*, intent on making a distinctively European contribution to the solution. I would also predict that, for complex reasons, the former will be German and English, while the latter will be French. In any case, this will mean that the EEC, both for internal and for external reasons, remains a perpetual adolescent staggering through an identity crisis.

3. My third assumption—or rather assumptions—concern the United States.

a. I begin with a negative and very shaky one: there will be no cataclysm. By this I mean two things. No depression *à la* 1929, for should the predictions of recovery prove false and the recession deepen and drive the United States and its European clients to despair at a time when they are all pressed by OPEC and other developing countries and when the vindication of earlier predictions about the decline of capitalism could lead to a toughening of the USSR, then the United States might well find no other way out than some grand military adventure in the Middle East, undertaken on behalf (even if not with the consent) of the so-called West. I also mean no Arab-Israeli war leading to a Soviet-American military confrontation; or to a new embargo on oil or price hike that would meet Kissinger's conditions for a military intervention (it is difficult to imagine OPEC's thus triggering it without such a war, or the United States' feeling strangled otherwise, except if the recession spreads). A fifth Arab-Israeli war that did not produce a new "oil war" in its wake and was stopped by the superpowers in circumstances close to those of October 1973 would not be "cataclysmic" in this sense (although it could be for the populations and armies involved). The reason I make this assumption is not that I think such calamities impossible, alas. But these would transform the international landscape in a way that cannot be adequately forecast. (Robert W. Tucker's recent neat and reassuring sketches are no more convincing than his earlier pretty and heart-warming picture of neo-isolationism.)[10] Also, in the aftermath of such cataclysms, U.S.-European relations would not be the most interesting or important issue.

b. A positive assumption is that whatever happens in 1976, the broad outlines of American foreign policy will not disappear. To be sure, it matters enormously whether Henry Kissinger will remain the captain of the battleship or not, for many features of current U.S. policy are his own (just as many traits of French foreign policy in 1958-1969 were de Gaulle's). If Kissinger stays in charge, an exercise like this one is purely academic—both because he is not the most influenceable of men, and because his strategy is a peculiar mix of permanent thirst for uninhibited control with what the French call *disponibilité*, that is, the determination to keep all directions open, to be flexible and free to maneuver from that pinnacle of control into whatever field of action may appear promising or inescapable at a given moment. In other words, the current exercise becomes an attempt to say what should be done, but either will be done anyhow if he thinks it is the right thing at the right time, or else will be ruled out by his very personality and style of action. My main point, however, is that even if he should leave office, some important features are likely to persist, just as he has preserved some essential traits of his predecessors' policy. To be sure, both the style of the policy and the style of policy-making are too intimately tied to him to be transmissible. But a great deal is.

Concerning what might be called "posture," I would rule out any "neo-isolationism," any *drastic* voluntary curtailment of American military and economic positions abroad (this does not rule out, for instance, a reduction of the number of bases in Japan or the Philippines or of the size of our force in South Korea). That there should be some battle fatigue in the public at large with a world that we do not seem able to "manage" easily, is perfectly normal; that Congress should try to reassert its authority in foreign affairs after twenty years of docility is unsurprising. Neither phenomenon amounts to a repudiation of America's postwar stance.

On the other hand, I would "rule in" as likely, even after Kissinger, what I have called elsewhere a policy of "indirect primacy," an attempt to preserve America's eminent role by getting others to adopt favorable policies, or by creating frameworks or constraints limiting the capacity of others to adopt hostile policies and imposing high risks and penalties and frustrations if they try.[11]

Concerning not posture but policy, I will make a hedged assumption about détente. I believe work on arms control will continue between the superpowers, and I do not believe in a return to the tone of Soviet-American confrontation in the 50s. But between deep hostility and "entente and cooperation," there is a huge zone which the word détente does not help delimit. As the second half of 1975 has shown, a new chill, new tensions are perfectly possible, if only because Soviet détente policies abroad entail ideological tightening at home—hence the will to protect the regime in Moscow and in the satellite nations from the very "infiltrations" that détente breeds; and also because détente does not prevent the superpowers from backing rival factions in helpless third countries. Much will depend on America's own economic and military strength and on leadership changes in the USSR. Further collaboration—over forces in Europe, or scientific projects, or joint economic ventures—is not ruled out. But *at best*, I do not see the rivalry ending or any "convergence" of regimes.

My other assumption about policy is that "global" issues will continue to dominate the agenda—that is, all the issues that concern the foundations of economic interdependence and have, in recent years, become "high politics." These include the establishment of a new world monetary system, a new division of industrial labor in the world, the impact and control of multinational corporations, the pricing and supply of raw materials and sources of energy, tariff and nontariff barriers to trade, the problems of food and foreign aid, the management and conservation of natural resources on earth and in the oceans, etc. This means, inevitably, that the relative "demotion" of Western Europe, or of purely bilateral U.S.-European issues, in America's agenda of priorities will not be reversed: policy toward Europe will tend to be part of, dependent on, or subordinated to the global policy of the United States on a given issue.

Hence a paradox: despite the very broad assumptions of common interests by the United States, Washington's attention to Western Europe is likely to remain both less high and more instrumental than in the days of the cold war. Conversely, a Western Europe that is much *less* convinced either of the vast scope of common interests or of the identity of views on ends across the Atlantic may well be the loser in this change of American attitudes and priorities. A more "global" outlook in Washington does not ensure that Washington will always have the specific West European interest in mind. In the very long run, "globalization" may well make the United States less vital and important to the Europeans should the relative power and wealth of "non-Atlantic" nations increase without a corresponding increase in the "Soviet threat" or Soviet political influence in Western Europe. But in the foreseeable future, the dependence of Western Europe on the health of the American economy (a fact of life), on American military protection (both a fact and a choice), and on America's leadership to minimize economic insecurity vis-à-vis the developing nations (partly a fact and certainly a choice) means that "globalization" only makes the tie more important to the Europeans—at a time when Washington finds it less crucial and when many Europeans find the price to be paid for it less acceptable. Or to put it a bit differently: the absence of a world role may have bothered Europeans little in a less *mondialiste* world, to use Giscard's formula. In the new world, that absence is more likely to be felt, or rather the price of "being-in-the-world" without being able to affect it is likely to be far more painful—just when the capacity to affect it declines even further.

B. This suggests that the most critical choices are actually Western Europe's.

1. That statement may appear in flat contradiction with two points made above.

a. I have argued that there is a serious risk of evaporation of EEC's substance, a narrowing of the agenda; that the Market may be crowded out by new global institutions (IEA) or by revitalized old ones (the Organization for Economic Cooperation and Development [OECD] or the International Monetary Fund [IMF]) and enfeebled anyhow by internal failure to develop common "intra-European" policies. But a risk does not mean a necessity: this *is* an area of choice. Evaporation, which statesmen might *present* as a necessity, would be the result of a drift, that is, a lack of will, a policy by default—which is a form, indeed a very frequent form, of choice.

b. I have assumed that Western Europe is likely to "behave as it has customarily behaved" (the old Kelsen *Grundnorm*). But this was a way of ruling out either a collapse and dissolution of EEC or a leap into some harmonious millennium: between that floor and that ceiling, I am assuming struggle, a contest around options.

c. My thesis throughout this and other essays has been that the United States, out of sheer might as well as deliberate policy, can have a powerful impact on Western Europe and help it unite, or else provoke discord or "evaporation." But the United States by itself cannot "build" a West European entity any more than a South Vietnamese nation: neither exhortations to unity in the 50s and early 60s nor the less friendly pressures of the early 70s have succeeded in coalescing a European will. Could the United States actually destroy the EEC? Perhaps, and we shall have to see whether this would be in our interest; though united Europeans could make such deliberate destruction difficult or costly for us. On the other hand, if we aim, not at preserving what has been achieved, but either at strengthening and extending it or at fitting it into the new world, only the West Europeans themselves can ultimately do so.

2. Thus a normative discussion really ought to begin with Europe's own choices and most desirable course. This lies entirely outside the scope of this essay. Yet a few indications, however sketchy, are necessary to define the range.

a. At one extreme, there is still *l'Europe européenne*. To be blunt (and even though I am myself a nostalgic supporter of that chimera), it is made unlikely both by the circumstances and by its own ambiguities. The circumstances include, first, the old pattern of domestic divergences among EEC's members, plus different attitudes toward the United States which make a consensus on a "distinctive" Europe improbable. Second, there are the new realities evoked above: what is Europe's distinctiveness on the new range of issues? Or rather, is Europe-by-itself not just a community of weakness in this realm, exactly as it has been in the realm of military security? Third, the hypothesis behind de Gaulle's "European Europe" (and its various avatars) was a decline of the United States, a strengthening of Western Europe, *and* a receding or retrenching of the Soviet Union. This would allow the two halves of Europe to grow closer together, with the Western half playing the role of a magnet thanks to its rising power, prosperity, and autonomy. But Czechoslovakia in 1968 and Soviet policy since then have shown that Moscow is interested in détente as a way of consolidating, not overcoming, the European status quo. This has taken much of the dynamism and purpose out of the idea of a "European Europe." For the root of the resistance of France's partners, and even of several French politicians, to that idea has always been the conviction that Europe-by-itself would still need the American nuclear umbrella, plus some American troops, forward-based systems, and theater nuclear weapons, to make the umbrella plausible both to Moscow and to Washington; and the conviction that this dependence must inevitably restrict the meaning of Europe-by-itself and force it to pay a price. The same reasoning also applies in the matters of energy, payments for oil, and the world monetary system, as Raymond Aron points out in his essay.

As for the ambiguities, there are several "European Europes." Here we can play a game of models. In the realm of defense schemes, there is the Western European Union (WEU) model: a separate European defense scheme allied to the United States (with formidable question marks about tactical and strategic nuclear weapons and, as Aron argues, the nature of French defense policy, whose ambiguity presumes both France's perhaps illusory freedom of action and the possibility of à la carte cooperation between Paris and NATO, but postpones any genuine effort at European defense). Then there is the "Swedish model": a West European "nonaligned" defense scheme that is based on "the calculation that, sooner than see Europe overrun by the Soviet Union, NATO forces would intervene." (But how is this American interest made evident to Moscow without "a military presence substantial enough to make American intervention prompt and effective,"[12] and how can this be achieved without a formal alliance?) There is finally the idea of a West European component in a pan-European collective security scheme, with sharp arms reductions and the end of military blocs; but would not this be a big step toward collective Finlandization?

In the realm of money, a "European Europe" would mean a return to a policy of monetary unification. Quite apart, however, from the obstacles on

which the previous attempt foundered and which the new discrepancies within
EEC have worsened, divergences about the shape of the ideal *world* monetary
system would be reflected in different attitudes and schemes for intra-European
monetary unity.

In the realm of energy, does a "European Europe" mean one that defines its
own energy policy (import or consumption cuts, new technologies for substitutes, etc.) in order to bring about a common consumers' front or in order to
negotiate directly with the OPEC cartels? Does it mean one that works out its
own recycling facility—without either the United States or OPEC?

In the general realm of relations with the developing nations, is a "European
Europe" one that defines itself as a coalition of advanced countries whose
wealth, employment opportunities, and trade are threatened by the demands for
a new world economic order, or one that sees its mission as that of accommodating these demands in a gradual but systematic way? None of these question
marks means that some distinctiveness is out; only that its limits are sharp, its
purposes uncertain, and therefore its chances of rallying all the participants
minimal.

b. At the other extreme, there is, behind a façade of EEC business-as-
usual, a drift into fragmentation, competition, and what might be called
piecemeal or selective neutralism: unilateral cuts in the defense budget or (in the
British and French cases) the abandonment of efforts to modernize nuclear
forces; mutually harmful import restrictions, export subsidies, and exchange
controls to deal with payments crises and recession; unwillingness of the
relatively wealthy (Bonn) to pay for what they deem wasteful or nonessential
common programs, or to foot the bill for the needy; refusal of the latter to
cooperate in any serious way unless their demands for help are met first. The
risk of dissolution exists. But I would deem this "choice" unlikely for the reason
indicated above—each of the partners, for different motives, needs the EEC.
Britain has no other "live option," nor does France. Bonn does not want to rely
on Washington alone and needs the EEC as a kind of buffer against both
Washington and Moscow. And so on. Keeping the EEC afloat means playing the
perilous game of compromises and small package deals. The important thing is
not to fall into the abyss after pushing to the brink.

c. In between, there is a choice that could be called "more of the same":
an effort to develop simultaneously the internal cohesion of the EEC (by
extending the range of common policies or at least perpetuating the existing
ones, despite heterogeneities and strains) and cooperation with the United States
in old institutions (NATO, IMF, OECD) and new ones (IEA, etc.); cooperation
with the USSR in order to increase military safety by lowering the threat (if not
by improving the defenses) and to create a safety valve in the economic realm
(including energy: uranium imports); and cooperation with the Third World in
order to avoid the dreaded confrontation that would expose Western Europe's
fragility. Such a policy would obviously receive Japan's support. It has two great

advantages. One is external. It juggles enough balls to soften somewhat the drawbacks of dependence: greater internal cohesion may, for instance, help the European arms industries survive the current onslaught of more advanced American technologies and weaponry; good relations with the developing nations and Moscow help keep Washington a bit more at arm's length; good relations with Washington save one from being embraced too tightly by the bear or squeezed dry by OPEC; while dealing with all of these makes the failure to "deepen" European integration less conspicuous and the need to keep trying less harrowing. The other advantage is internal. By eschewing definitions of ultimate purposes, this policy *avoids* the divisive issue of choosing among "missions for Europe," which would otherwise be forced by *l'Europe européenne*'s own ambiguities. The policy of "more of the same" depends on not clarifying these.

But this points to a drawback: there always comes an event, or a man, that obliges such deliberate mists to dissolve. At this moment there has to be a choice among internal cohesion, cooperation with the United States, cooperation with the East, cooperation with the South: "instead of" replaces "and"—and choices are sources of trauma. Moreover, this policy of pleasing everyone allows the Europeans to give themselves the illusion of progress by concentrating on a favorite pastime—the institutional reenforcement of the EEC—thus mistaking better (or merely bigger) machinery for an improved output. And yet, for reasons having to do both with the world scene and with the delicate balances of domestic politics in the EEC countries, it is this ambiguous middle range which strikes me as most likely: like the Republic according to Adolphe Thiers, it is the regime that would divide the Europeans, and each polity, least.

C. America's choices will be discussed now. I have expressed earlier my belief in an important degree of continuity, should a "post-Kissinger era" begin soon. But there is room for change and there are ranges of alternatives, both because Kissinger's audacious enterprises have recently become more like astute improvisations than like a systematic creation, and because many of his policies (for instance, those concerning OPEC and the developing nations) are under sharp attack, and not only from the political opposition.

1. It follows from what was written above that the most fundamental American choices concern America's *global* policy, for these will determine to a large extent the nature of American policy toward Western Europe. This, needless to say, is not the place to unveil a Grand Global Design. But there is a point in describing ranges of alternatives. The question is not whether the United States should "exert leadership"; it will and can hardly escape from it. The question is *how* and *what for*? And this in turn can be divided into three related issues.

a. What should be the proper *framework* of American action? The politics of interdependence can always degenerate into sheer chaos because of the number of actors, all eager both to maximize their leaky power and to interfere with one another; because of the number of partly separate yet partly connected functional issues; because the name of the game is the manipulation of interdependence, that is, my exploitation of your own interest in helping me lest you be hurt, or of your interest in not hurting me too much lest you be hurt. One can distinguish analytically the politics of *interdependence*, that is, of (usually) nonzero-sum games or, at least, restrained games (resulting from economic solidarity or from nuclear solidarity) from the politics of *interaction*, of (usually) zero-sum games in situations of mutual hostility capable of destroying all restraints.[13] The latter have traditionally been structured, that is, given some semblance of logic and order, through alliances and guarantees. The new politics of interdependence desperately need structure in the form of bargaining coalitions and institutions for joint management[14] —whose durability and reliability in a system of competing sovereigns is, of course, dubious, as Hobbes well knew.

Here, the range of choices for the United States is as follows. First, will we encourage the development of reasonably stable structures of bargaining and institutions of collective management, even though they may seriously hamper freedom of maneuver either for us as a state, or for American multinational enterprises? Or will we give priority to maximizing this freedom and prefer unilateral action, bilateral deals, and *ad hoc* institutions or coalitions? Past behavior, especially in the Kissinger era, suggests a fundamental preference for the latter. Second, insofar as we acknowledge the need for "ordering structures" and institutionalized diplomacy, will we accept more broadly participatory or egalitarian ones, even though they may boost the role and magnify the scanty or limited assets of the weaker states or of states whose whole power derives from one simple component of power? Or will we prefer those coalitions and institutions that we tend naturally to dominate, partly in order to preserve the full margin of our overall superiority, partly in order to safeguard a traditional kind of international hierarchy—one in which the top countries are those with the biggest military arsenal, the highest degree of economic development, and the greatest stake, if not in the whole status quo, at least in keeping what they have achieved?

b. What should be the *style* of American action? At present, it oscillates in *tone* between an intensely pugnacious one, whether it is for the defense of a purely national interest (cf. the recent drive to sell American fighter planes to our NATO allies, or our reluctance, in recent years, to link Special Drawing Rights (SDRs) and foreign aid, or our preferential use of aid and food for the benefit of selected clients) or of that of the "community" of industrial nations, and an intensely idealistic one that stresses constructive interdependence and common tasks beyond politics. Unfortunately, the latter tone has often seemed reserved for homilies, the former for policies. But there is a range of choices here—it being understood, of course, that constructive idealism will rarely extend to self-abnegation.

Next to tone, there is *mode of operation*. Here the range goes from what

Thomas L. Hughes has called "personalism"[15] to what its chief practitioner himself calls (in the domestic context) "institutionalization." At one end of the spectrum lies the solo performance, with its great assets of flexibility, flamboyance, and confidentiality, but its drawback: fragility. For it depends too much on the relations between personalities abroad and neglects the vital domestic "turf" needed for roots to grow: congressional support and the involvement of a broad public. As a result, its chief advantage, creativity on the world scene, can easily wilt into sterility. At the other end of the spectrum lies what Kissinger used to criticize as the bureaucratic style: weighed down by problems of coordination, by the harrowing task of permanently coaxing influentials and reassuring interests; threatened by the risk of perversion inherent in the priority of domestic consensus-building, that is, the gradual shift of emphasis from the foreign policy need to the domestic politics of the issue. And yet this is a style that may have its advantages so long as it avoids this risk; for it gives to partners and opponents a sense of solidity that may help make the politics of interdependence more predictable.

c. What should U.S. policies aim for, in *substantive terms*? Here, of course, one would have to deal with a huge number of issues. But a few stand out. Insofar as interdependence based on the common interest in "nuclear survival" is concerned (an interest that implies that the logic of interaction, that is, of unrestrained or zero-sum games, be either contained or removed in those areas where it still prevails, as it does in the Arab-Israeli dispute), there is a question of scope and speed. How far do we want to go in involving the USSR in such an effort? How far do we want to go in trying to arrive at implicit or explicit agreements with Moscow and with our allies to limit the export of arms to third parties, especially in dangerous regions, and to delay and prevent the proliferation of nuclear weapons? How far do we want to go, beyond arms control, toward strategic arms reductions?

Insofar as interdependence based on economic solidarity is concerned, do we want a monetary system that will preserve, this time through greater flexibility than in the postwar era, the privileged position of the dollar, or will we accept a system that puts pressure even on the United States for the elimination of payments imbalances through domestic measures? Will we continue to try to solve the food problem of the developing nations by exporting food surpluses from the United States and other advanced countries, or will we help the former increase drastically their own food production and cut down on unstable export crops toward the industrial world, even though this change will entail large-scale social reform by regimes likely to be unfriendly to foreign enterprises? Do we want an international network of agreements on raw materials, energy sources, natural resources, trade *and* investment that aims at a gradual, unbrutal transfer of wealth, not only from the old to the new rich but from the rich to the poor, at the possible cost of a new world distribution of employment and industries, various temporary measures of industrial and trade protectionism for the developing countries, and a far greater say for them in the management of world monetary and trade institutions? Or shall we try to resist on a global scale the kind of democratization that has occurred, often brutally, and yet in far less unmanageable conditions (owing to the authority of the central government, national consensus, factor mobility, etc.) in domestic political and social systems over the past two centuries?

These are the overarching choices. If one relates them, one sees that the United States has, broadly speaking, a range of alternatives that extends from a policy of traditional hegemony—for the preservation of its own preeminence and of the present type of international capitalist economy—to a policy of initiatives toward common, "reformist" actions aimed at making the world both safer and more egalitarian. Let me make my own preference clear (if it is not already): I would like the United States to move in the latter direction, because I fear that otherwise the old model of the "state-of-war," temporarily and partly pushed aside by the new model of interdependence, would prevail again. For one can expect both chain reactions resulting from old-fashioned hostilities, and economic chaos as well as military contests resulting from the mismanagement of economic solidarity, that is, from aggressive, unguided, and unchanneled attempts at egalitarianism—revolutions from below instead of reforms planned from above.

2. Let us move back to Western Europe and discuss desirable American objectives, again in terms of alternatives.

a. A first question is a kind of preconsideration. Ought the United States define these objectives in foreign policy terms (what would we like the West Europeans to do, or what should we do together on the coming issues?), or should we try to influence their *domestic* political scene in order to have West European governments that are likely to recognize and conform to the range of common interests? To be sure, what kinds of governments would be "desirable" depends in part on our choice of foreign policy goals. My reason for putting this problem first, however, is double. In every region, both the balance of military power and what could be called the balance of influence between forces hostile to the United States and forces friendly or at least not antagonistic to us can be upset not merely by changes in military might—the loss of a battle or of a base, a drastic cut in our armed presence—but also by the effects of economic policies or trends and—above all—by changes in regimes, governments, and ruling elites. NATO, in fact, can far more easily be weakened by political developments, say, in the countries of its "southern flank," than by very unlikely military disasters. To use martial language, the home front, not the front line, is the weakest spot.

Second, for prudential and normative reasons, I believe that we should refrain from the manipulation of domestic politics and should realize that it is through our *foreign* policy behavior that we are most likely to affect our partners' (and even opponents') internal equilibrium. In prudential terms, we must by now understand that the days when American diplomats, CIA agents, labor leaders, or intellectuals could affect favorably the outcome of elections, the balance of party leaderships, the splitting or merging of unions, the tendencies of magazines are over. Indeed, any American public statement is likely to backfire: a few more declarations about Communism in Italy, and the "historical compromise" might finally have its day! Of course, some European politicians may tell us that our support would help them, or they may keep their rivals from power by telling them that, alas, *we* would not tolerate deals with them. But in most instances, this is a meaningless game in which we, not they, are the pawns. "The United States" is being used as a club by Italian Christian-Democrats determined anyhow not to let Communists embrace them, just as we are being taken for a ride by French "friends" who tell us how much they would like to be more cooperative, but cannot disregard such dire domestic constraints as the Gaullists or the Communists.

Normatively, I find many of the practices of domestic manipulation by outsiders disgraceful and disastrous, insofar as no stable world order will ever exist unless it is made of authentic (I did not say: necessarily democratic) national regimes, not puppets. A temporary gain obtained by "destabilizing" an Allende (already undermined by his economic errors) or by propping up a Thieu is, in the not-so-long run, likely to be offset by the price one has to pay later. That is also the lesson of the Greek experience. Moreover—here, too, the prudential and the normative converge—those who begin as "our boys" may end up proving to be rather tough nationalists, precisely because they have to establish their authenticity. After all, it was the CIA that put the Shah of Iran back in power in 1953.[b]

Of course, some European governments will be easier to deal with than others; some are more likely to share our view of our common interests than others. A Giscard is more pleasing than a de Gaulle. A leftist government in France or Spain, a Communist-Christian Democrat one in Italy would create problems. On the other hand, I see no way for us to prevent their coming to power if domestic developments make it inevitable, and no alternative to our trying to work with them if they do—unless we were to foment coups, a course I would condemn as repugnant. And I can imagine American statements and gestures that could make matters worse and earn us the animosity of the new rulers whom we were trying to thwart or to keep from power. There are enough links among European officials, parties, and interests across national borders for us to let the West Europeans influence one another's domestic trends—as in Portugal. We are, basically, outsiders—concerned outsiders, to be sure, but fortunate enough to be able to count on our allies' sense of self-interest when it

[b]Aron both misunderstands my position and, in practice, agrees with my recommendations. I do not believe that diplomacy can "confine itself to interstate relations" in a world in which foreign policy becomes the external projection of domestic needs and drives. But diplomacy has other ways of affecting societies than those whose moral *and* practical bankruptcy has been exposed by recent investigations.

comes to trying to affect events in, say, Spain or Italy or Greece. On the other hand, the question we ought to ask is not: how can we best intervene in order to prevent or arrest such complications, but what foreign policy should we pursue in order to minimize the difficulties which such domestic "setbacks" would raise? And so, we come back to essentials.

b. One foreign policy alternative would consist in downgrading the EEC and dealing with Western Europe in ways that dilute or deny its specificity: that is, either bilaterally, à la carte, with those governments that prove most amenable; or through multilateral agencies (such as the IEA or "recycling" facilities) in which we take the lead and try to prevent the "ganging up" of the Europeans. Insofar as bilateralism is concerned, C. Fred Bergsten has advocated that the United States establish a Washington-Bonn rather than a Washington-Brussels link, given the convergence or identity of interests on the monetary system, trade, agriculture, investments, and now, I suppose, recycling.[16]

Obviously, such a policy would be based on the calculation that European "togetherness" is at best an illusion or an unnecessary complication, and at worst a *point d'appui* for opposition to American views, a bunker for resistance. If European unity is a "poor show," if Europe's dependence is the reality, why support the appearance? And if it is a reality, but always potentially hostile, why not undermine it? Several European commentators have attributed such Machi-avellianism to Kissinger, who has acted and talked at times as if he wanted to vindicate their suspicions. Whether these are fair or not, impatience with the "myth of Europe" is often expressed by young United States officials, who do not partake of the "Monnet mystique" of the 50s and cast a very cold eye on the limited achievements and unlimited rhetoric of the West Europeans.

However justified such irritation may be, this is not a good policy choice. First, it is not desirable, because it is not at all clear that if we divide, we rule. The original blend of self-interest and idealism is still valid: an at least *somewhat* united Western Europe (I did not say *any* united Western Europe) serves our interests; a fragmented one might not. For we must count with the power of contagion. If we play favorites, or even if we merely deal with different countries over different issues, we will encourage the centrifugal trends that threaten to disrupt the tenuous network woven by the EEC, as well as by NATO, and to promote an unraveling that could lead to selective neutralism or disastrous beggar-my-neighbor policies. In particular, Mr. Bergsten's solution would incite the French to harden their opposition on monetary and economic issues, to diminish their rather wide (and widening) cooperation with NATO, to "look South"—and East—for support and deals. Moreover, it would make Bonn itself uncomfortable. For Bonn can only act as "Washington's assistant" *within* EEC or NATO. An overt "axis" would in fact isolate Bonn and make it less useful a relay for Washington than it is in the present context. Also, the "disaggregation" of Western Europe through separate deals and the "drowning" of Western Europe in large pools would risk encouraging both the development and the disruptiveness of anti-American political forces, for these would resist and resent the pressures from those pools and feel freed of any intra-European restraints by such deals. We would have bred in Europe what has been so often disastrous for us elsewhere: the fusion of nationalism and anti-Americanism.

Second, such a policy is not really feasible, even if one deems it partly desirable. There is no way in which the United States can prevent the EEC from having its own role in matters of trade negotiations (although the United States can, of course, restrict the EEC's range of policy choices). Nor can Washington prevent the Nine from trying to have something common to say in the "group of ten," or the IMF, or in tripartite conference with the "richer" and "poorer" developing nations; or eight of the Nine from consulting with France about what to do at the IEA, or even from joining France in carving out, if they so desire, a specific energy policy for the EEC; or eight of the Nine from thinking about ways to keep the United States deeply involved in NATO, while also trying to find ways to overcome France's "separatism." Bonn itself will tend to resist American blandishments, out of fear that a tendency that exists already within the EEC, that of making Germany and all-purpose cashier, would be magnified in the global schemes of Mr. Kissinger; for it is easier to resist weaker partners than Big Brother. Meanwhile the economic strength of West Germany has if anything sharpened commercial rivalry between Washington and Bonn (cf. Bonn's nuclear deal with Brazil).

c. A second policy alternative could be called more-of-the-same. We would not discourage greater European unification, and we would (as does Kissinger) point out that it is in our allies' own interest to unite in order to reach "a degree of financial solidarity, a degree of equalizing burdens, and a degree of ability to set common goals that cannot be done on a purely national basis.[17] But we would continue to give effective precedence to broader frameworks, such as NATO, or the IEA, and recycling schemes within or outside the IMF; and we would make it clear that it is through these schemes and in these frameworks that our contribution to Europe's physical and economic security will be given. This means, in effect, that we would continue to extract a double price in exchange: a price in terms of control of the substance or direction of the Europeans' own schemes and frameworks (EEC, "Eurogroup"); and a price in terms of such conditions for our support as their buying American armaments, importing American technologies for oil substitutes, accepting American requirements about the financial policies to be pursued by beneficiaries of "secondary recycling," or signing trade concessions and offset agreements, etc. If this has worked so far, why should it not work just as well tomorrow? It both preserves a useful shell, or residual basis, of European unity and allows global strategies and bargains to receive precedence. It both protects America's primacy and gives the West Europeans the satisfaction of playing at their own game, of working on their own enterprise. It has helped contain the nationalist ambitions or excesses of de Gaulle, it has groomed the new Germany, minimized the effects of Italy's drift, and given a semblance of a role to Britain without detaching it from the American leash. And yet, there are some serious drawbacks.

The biggest is psychological. It is a perfect formula for perpetuating the sense of dependence, the resignation to pettiness, the abdication from world influence of the Europeans, the very flaws Kissinger never fails to flail. For it creates among European leaders and elites the lulling conviction that Uncle Sam will "do what is right," while encouraging them to show their own distinctiveness in a string of joint regrets, warnings, laments, and whines blaming Washington alternatively for being too soft or too tough. It undermines their self-confidence by parking them in confined reserves, where their inefficacy or sluggishness is a cause for reproach. It feeds a certain self-contempt, for they are not stupid enough not to notice who commands, or to know that if *they* also benefit, it is because he who commands has an interest in *their* benefiting. And such self-contempt—in fine Sartrean fashion—feeds in turns an impotent rage against Washington.

The purely political drawback is that this indeed is a formula for permanent mutual resentment. Already one sees a tug-of-war within the IEA and the "recycling" schemes between the consumer-front approach of Kissinger and the Europeans' desire to involve the OPEC countries, partly in order not to be left alone with Washington. But one can also forecast, within whatever international bodies will deal, or be set up to deal, with the issues raised by the developing nations, European sullenness should the United States seize the initiative in and reap the advantages of bargaining with them, and American contempt for the Europeans' oscillation from *mondialiste* lingo to economic and financial jingo.

The area in which the American attempt to preserve control and predominance has already led to considerable friction is of course NATO. To summarize arguments I have developed in testimony to senatorial subcommittees:[18] the present structure of NATO, the presence of a high number of American troops and tactical nuclear weapons under that structure, is an irritant in U.S.-West European relations, directly and indirectly. Directly: because the Europeans' dependence on these forces and weapons as well as America's latest conventional armaments provides us with strong temptations of blackmail, while making them aware of their humiliating tie to the uncertainties of our domestic political process and to the self-assurance of our more advanced technology. Indirectly: U.S.-Soviet negotiations constantly provoke jitters among West Europeans, for they fear agreements that could partly "uncouple" America's strategic forces from Europe's defense or open the door to a "denuclearization" of Central Europe under superpower control. Also, they keep having misgivings about our strategic doctrine, which determines the way in which our, *and their* forces will be used. We in turn are irritated by their suspicions and recurrent demands for reassurance. And yet, one of the ways in which this sense of collective impotence, of being at the mercy of the Protector or of the "condominium," could be at least partly overcome—the gradual establishment of a West European Defense entity—remains outside the pale, so long as our allies fear that it might serve as an excuse for American withdrawal or estrangement and we confirm these fears by our own failure to encourage any change in the institutional status quo.

To sum up: *they* feel that a paternalistic protection may always end in the Protector's taking, or agreeing to, measures that *he* does not deem contrary to Western Europe's interests (in matters of oil substitutes, or of limits on separate oil deals, or on payments solidarity, or on arms, or on strategy, or on arms control), yet which may not be the best from the specific viewpoint of *Western Europe*. Yet *he* resents their misgivings because of his own conviction that he has not "knowingly" sacrificed their interests: are American planes not cheaper and better than French planes, is the Schlesinger doctrine not a rational deduction from nuclear parity, are not American-guaranteed loans more likely than intra-European mechanisms, etc?

d. Thus we come to a third course, which is a policy encouraging (and not just in words) Western Europe to unite and devise its own policies on as broad a range of issues as the Europeans themselves are capable of tackling. This is not properly a policy of "devolution," for I have no illusions (see above) about the possibility of a real European separatism in an age of global problems that severely constrain a half-continent squeezed between the superpowers, as well as between America and the developing world. Moreover, one "devolves" power to an existing entity capable of receiving it, and this simply does not exist. The EEC is currently too weak, and there is no defense system. What I suggest is a policy *aimed at making devolution possible*. It would encourage the emergence, not of an *independent* Western Europe (military and economic realities spell more dependence than independence), but of an autonomous entity, capable of devising, in cooperation with outsiders, measures that would be the Europeans' *own* contribution to problems that they cannot solve alone (instead of measures taken in the presence, under the leadership, or in reaction to the direct pressure of others), or their answer to problems which are clearly in their domain, or an attempt to diminish their dependence. This policy would see to it, on the one hand, that in the areas covered by the EEC (roughly speaking, economic and monetary issues), the Community is not asphyxiated by, drowned in, or subordinated to the wider agencies whose creation is indeed necessary; on the other hand, that in the area in which there is at present either no EEC, or barely a beginning—defense and diplomacy—a "European entity" or perhaps (this is a problem for the Europeans) distinct but overlapping European entities are made possible.

I find this alternative (to be spelled out below) desirable for negative and positive reasons. In the first place, the risks are limited. There is an "objective" *and* subjective solidarity of interests in the realm of security. The real danger of "Finlandization" would be far more effectively contained by this policy choice than by the first alternative, while the second—the status quo—always threatens to lead to it, should irritation prevail over co-operation. For the status quo by nourishing the Europeans' sense of almost irremediable inferiority, tempts them into both letting their own defense efforts slacken (as has been happening in several European members of NATO) and courting the USSR as a reassurance policy. This temptation might grow if the preponderance of the United States in NATO should lead Washington either to unilateral cutbacks or to extensive arms control deals with Moscow without sufficient European participation. On the other hand, a European defense entity, however limited or fragile, would have, so to speak, a vested interest in not letting itself be intimidated or seduced by the USSR.

In the economic realm, the mutual dependence of the European and American economies is such that a revitalized EEC would be unlikely to break it, unless anti-capitalist and anti-American majorities take over in *most* of its members—an unlikely prospect. Few politicians within the EEC would deny that there *are* common interests of oil consumers, that financial solidarity is needed to prevent selective blackmail by OPEC. Similarly, all would agree on the need for a new international monetary system.

Of course, on all these issues, there could be clashes between assertive Europeans and the United States; but these would be severe *only* if the United States had opted for what I have called a policy of global hegemony, in which case it would not have embraced this third course of devolution. There might be broad policy differences over the way in which Third World problems and demands should be met, or the Arab-Israeli conflict solved. But there are differences among the Europeans as well, and we have no reason to expect that the conception most opposed to that of Washington would always prevail. Kissinger seems to assume that on such issues the Europeans would, against their own self-interest, choose "appeasement" out of a mix of guilt feelings for past colonialism and dependence on imported oil and raw materials. But the measures he himself has proposed (the floor price for oil, the procedural concessions to the developing nations' demands) have exposed *him* to charges of appeasement by American businessmen, economists, Treasury officials, journalists, et al. And this derogatory attitude toward the Europeans, which may not be unfounded in the *present* context, becomes a self-fulfilling prophecy: the third course would help the West Europeans to overcome such inhibitions, lose the habit of counting on Washington to bail them out, and develop institutions and policies in which they simply could not afford to sacrifice Western Europe's interests.

Moreover, a certain amount of pluralism, the existence of alternative courses offered on the public stage, is a good thing: should *one* such course lead to a dead end, the others would become available. This is one of the positive advantages. The major one is partly psychological, partly political. Kissinger himself used to complain about the strain on America's mental and material resources imposed by American preponderance in the postwar world.[19] There is an art of letting go in order to be better able to influence events, orient trends,

channel initiatives, dampen conflicts, disconnect dominoes, divide and distinguish among challenges. The attempt at global control is heroic but doomed—too
much for one man, too much for one nation, however brilliant the man and
powerful the nation. Having allies whom one has to scold periodically for their
irresponsibility ought to make one find ways of making them behave responsibly—and this means letting them carry out responsibilities—or else demonstrate
once and for all that they cannot blame their futility on anyone but themselves.
If we are going to have any "stable structure of peace," it will have to be, not
just multipolar, but multifunctional, with different (yet overlapping) hierarchies
corresponding to each function or type of power. The United States, through its
resources, positions, interests, and dynamism, will be present at or near the top
of all; it does not have to try to be in control of each.

By substituting global mobility for the stolid immobilism of cold war policy,
Kissinger has astutely preserved the American hegemony which World War II had
largely created. But his own critique of it remains valid. In the specific case of
Western Europe, the more the West Europeans are left, if not to themselves (the
world will not leave them), at least with a domain of their own, the more likely
they are to recognize a broad range of common interests with us—far more than
if we always insist on defining it for them. Moreover, where they differ with us,
it may often be in *our* interest to follow their advice; thus with respect to the
"North-South" problem, if we leave aside Kissinger's astute but domestically still
unsupported switch to "conciliation," the relationship of the allies may well be
the reverse today of what it was in the days of dying colonialism. Popular-front
governments, which might exploit the tensions inherent in the other two
courses, would find in the European institutions that the third one favors both
an effective harness on their "separatist" tendencies and a buffer absorbing
whatever anti-American inclinations they might have.

However, there *are* obstacles and drawbacks. Just because the other alternatives entail tensions and costs does not mean that this one would be frictionless
and cost-free. The frictions are built-in. Since there is military and economic
dependence of western Europe on the United States, the kind of policy I suggest
might well transfer some power to the former only at the price of transferring
anxiety to the latter, for *we* will be left with ultimate responsibility, and *they*
will have a greater opportunity to force the outcome they want. The old cry of
no taxation without representation might be picked up by us. Meanwhile, given
our ultimate responsibility, nothing we can do can entirely eliminate European
anxiety about our performance. Also, in specific areas (see below) our self-restraint could result in sizable losses of the benefits currently linked to
preponderance, or in sizable opportunity costs.

All of this may make the devolution policy look far less desirable. Nor is it
clear that it is feasible. After years of dependence, and after being battered by
the reversals of 1973-74, can the Europeans overcome their Oblomovian
tendencies? Can they turn away from the subtle comforts of relying on an ally

who allows you the luxury of criticism and encourages your drift away from world responsibilities? Despite China's exhortations, are they not being pushed farther away from these anyhow, not merely by recent United States activism, but by such convergent phenomena as the harsh will of the Soviets, the superpower cooperation, the onslaught of OPEC, the claims of the Third World, the inadequacy of Western Europe as a framework for the solution of almost anything? It would be foolish not to raise these questions, after having criticized all other courses. I would only conclude, first, that the undesirable aspects strike me as less dreadful than those of the first two courses; second, that if indeed the devolution policy is unfeasible, if the wager on Europe is lost, then there will always remain—for all its failings—the second, that is, the present course. The risk of failure should merely incite both us and the Europeans not to dismantle anything that might have to be restored in the end. It should not deter us from trying to expand the specifically European institutions and policies that exist, or to create new ones.

3. If this is the desirable American objective, what are the methods and policies that should be adopted by American policymakers to reach it? The three guidelines that must be observed are: to define one's statements and one's proposals in such a way that they move toward the goal; to take into account and deal with the drawbacks which the desirable policies may have and the oppositions or risks they may create; to act in a way that leaves open, as a fall-back position, what I have called the second course, or rather an improved version of that course (see below).

a. A series of "don'ts" should be mentioned first: what is it that the United States should refrain from doing or saying, in order not to rule out the course I have described, which is both fragile and gradual?

i. The United States should avoid unilateral shocks, such as that of August 15, 1971, or the badly prepared "Year of Europe" speech, or the announcement of any "grand design" sprung on the allies without prior consultation or at least due warning. (I am thinking of the way in which the latest change in United States strategic doctrine was made in early 1974: one still is not entirely clear about its meaning.) The United States should not decide to withdraw theater nuclear weapons from Western Europe, where they are in excessive abundance, or to change their deployment, or to reduce the size of conventional forces by unilateral fiat.

ii. The United States should avoid bilateralism in issues concerning Western Europe. This means, on the one hand, that it should not deal with a single West European country on an issue that affects or concerns all of them. If there is a need for such a deal, it ought to be made, not by the United States, but by an international agency after consultation with the EEC (I am thinking of possible aid to Britain or Italy in case of a payments crisis); the aim would be to give the EEC itself a chance of playing a role, unless the country concerned objects. On the other hand, the United States should not sign, at summits or in

Mutual and Balanced Force Reduction (MBFR) negotiations, any agreements with the USSR that might be incompatible with the existence in Western Europe of a zone of autonomous military strength and political self-confidence (autonomy does not mean complete independence). For while peaceful coexistence and arms control agreements between the superpowers may serve the interests of the war-weary Europeans, and while the outcry of European officials after the Nixon-Brezhnev statement of June 1973 on the avoidance of nuclear war may have been a bit hysterical, there is a genuine issue of priorities. There have been instances where the common interests of the Big Two *appeared* greater than the common interests of Washington and the West European countries *qua* allies—as in the 1973 Middle East crisis.

Thus, in the coming MBFR discussions, we ought not to accept such drastic reductions on our forward-based tactical systems (FBS) or stock of tactical nuclear weapons (TNW)—in exchange for mere cuts in Soviet conventional forces—that two of the crucial links in the continuum of deterrence between conventional and strategic nuclear forces would be weakened. This would undermine any autonomous West European effort in defense. Nor should we accept Soviet proposals aimed at giving special treatment to Central Europe (through a nuclear-free zone, for instance), for these would introduce a Soviet *droit de regard* into affairs on this side of the iron curtain and cut Western Europe into two different zones. Nor should we endorse Soviet proposals for a ban on the transfer of nuclear technology to allies who are already nuclear powers (a transfer which the nuclear proliferation treaty [NPT] allows). Nor should we give the Warsaw Pact the right to pass on the political and military future of Western Europe by consenting to the setting-up of a "pan-European body (even if it includes us) other than symbolic.

iii. In general, the United States should avoid initiatives which, as de Gaulle used to say, would "insult the future," that is, make the development of a strong West European unity more difficult. When Washington suggests the creation of a new body (such as the IEA or the Kissinger recycling facility), it should not define its functions in such a way as to remove vital substance from the EEC or to preclude in areas such as diplomacy and defense any distinctive role for the West Europeans. In trade and monetary negotiations, the United States ought not to suggest schemes that are aimed at or would result in the dissolution without adequate compensation of any of the few cements of the EEC or the exclusion of distinctive regional features. (I am thinking, for example, of proposals for the abolition of tariffs on the trade of industrial goods without measures dealing with nontariff barriers.) We should deliberately *not* prevent the survival or inhibit the expansion of a strong European industry by asking, for instance, that European air companies reduce their flights over the Atlantic; or by insisting that the European members of NATO equip themselves predominantly with American weapons; or by making more difficult the development of enriched uranium plants in Western Europe. Of course material sacrifices are involved in such self-restraint, at a time when the United States, like other industrial nations, cannot afford to be delicate about ways of improving its balance -of-payments. But as I have said before, there are costs associated with *every* policy.

Nor should the United States discourage or dismiss foreign policy statements or initiatives by the West Europeans because these might interfere with the efforts of American diplomacy. For such an American veto can hardly be interpreted abroad as anything but an attempt at keeping control, and given its intimidating effect among the Nine, it usually paralyzes the Community. (I am thinking of the Euro-Arab dialogue, stalled for a while over the issue of the PLO, whose participation several of the Nine objected to because of American complaints that such participation would undermine Kissinger's quiet diplomacy in the Middle East. I am also thinking about Kissinger's actions, described earlier, concerning the French-sponsored preparatory conferences on energy—actions that are hard to interpret as anything but a deliberate snub of a European initiative and a reassertion of America's prerogative in global matters.)

iv. Finally, there is a "don't" relating to tone. The United States should avoid two of the tones it has used toward the Europeans over the years. First, it should abandon the tone of exasperation and contempt that has prevailed since 1973, the questioning of the political legitimacy of European governments or the criticism of their inability to solve their own problems. These remarks are not just unwise; they irresistibly remind one of people in glass houses. Second, Washington should beware of the tone of tight-lipped patience, paternal "understanding," and complacent "sympathy," which for all its surface gentleness reminds the Europeans—who are not exactly novices in matters of nuances—that we are waiting for them to grow up.

To sum up: should the United States—in order to perpetuate the past or even to "tilt" toward the first course described above—want to *discourage* West European unification, all it has to do is pursue the policy of 1973-74 and object to or make more difficult any move that puts the construction of a West European entity ahead of a "global" or "neo-Atlantic" policy. The idea is not to denounce the latter; this would be neither desirable nor possible. It is to enable a self-respecting and coherent Western Europe to take its full part in it.

b. Thus we come to the "do" suggestions: initiatives and incentives to improve prospects of intra-European cooperation and to help the West Europeans overcome their habit of excessive reliance on (and subsequent recriminations against) the United States. The key idea is that actual material and political *dependence* need not be tantamount to the loss of all *autonomy*: relations of "asymmetrical interdependence" need not be hegemonial.

i. It is in the military realm that the task is most difficult and considerable.[c] The stark reality of Western Europe's inability to provide for its

[c]The passages that follow are largely borrowed from my testimony before the Subcommittee on United States Security Agreements and Commitments Abroad of the Senate Foreign Relations Committee, March 7, 1974.

security has not changed. There is, now or in the foreseeable future, no West European strategic nuclear deterrent capable of replacing America's. At best, British and French strategic nuclear forces will be capable of deterring a Soviet direct nuclear attack on Britain and France and of increasing the deterrent value of French and eventual West European tactical nuclear forces. As for conventional forces, there is a fine irony here. When the United States pressed for their build-up, its own emphasis either on "massive retaliation" (in the early 50s) or on strategic superiority (in the early 60s) deterred the West Europeans from increasing their forces beyond a certain limit. Now that nuclear equality has replaced superiority and that a good case can be made for a European conventional effort designed to bolster Washington's attempt to restore the plausibility of nuclear deterrence by stressing limited counterforce, the combination of prohibitive defense costs and a widespread revolt against conscription makes such a case rather hopeless. Moreover, except in the search for better cooperation among armament industries aimed at promoting the production and procurement of European weapons, the "Europeanism" of Giscard does not yet extend to defense matters. France's defense policy remains a mix of independence and selective cooperation with NATO-as-it-is. A European defense effort would require French TNW's in Germany, not France, and a reform of NATO. But Giscard has categorically repudiated such moves, proclaimed Europe safe, and asserted his faith in Moscow's good intentions.

There is, however, in Western Europe a growing demand for a bigger European role in the common defense, and a more timid one for a separate West European organization within the North Atlantic Alliance. The United States should encourage such a larger European role. This would be part of a policy aimed at helping the functional expansion of the Common Market (or of those of its members who are not neutral) and, in particular, at promoting the military cooperation of France with its EEC partners. It would require a decision on our part to prolong the existence and allow the modernization of Britain's nuclear force, which will, in order to stay in business, need American technological support—even if there should be a great increase in Franco-British nuclear cooperation. We should grant similar support to France or allow Britain to provide it. We ought to provide nuclear-capable systems to those of our allies who are willing and able to produce the tactical warheads. We ought to participate in a reorganization of NATO's conventional forces aimed at allowing a better defense in depth and greater initial combat strength. We should announce our willingness to support a European Defense Organization that could deal with joint arms procurement (even if it gives priority to the manufacture and purchase of European weapons) and the coordination of defense policies, at the least. Such an American policy would have the advantage of allowing—as West European self-confidence and capabilities improve—eventual reductions in American forces and, through negotiations with the USSR, in the FBS and American tactical nuclear weapons stationed in Europe.

We may, for financial (troops) and for purely strategic (FBS, TNW) reasons[20] deem such reductions desirable in any case; but they should be made part of an overall policy of promoting an autonomous West European role. Otherwise, their effect might well be to discourage our allies rather than shock them into collective action. The arrangements suggested here would give to Western Europe the combination of *its own* conventional and nuclear forces necessary to create a credible deterrent threat. It is true that, initially and for a period that is likely to be long, only the conventional forces and arms can be "integrated." The nuclear forces—strategic and tactical—will remain national, but there should be intra-European agreements on the circumstances in which these national systems would be put at the service of the Community. The United States would facilitate such arrangements by allowing the British force to be assigned to the West European entity, once the latter is established. (The present assignment to NATO, decided in 1962 at Nassau, is a major obstacle to Franco-British nuclear cooperation.) This entity would negotiate with the United States and Canada the size, location, and use of American conventional and tactical nuclear forces in Europe; for there would remain an American military presence sufficient to reinforce the credibility of the West European deterrent threat and to ensure the involvement of the United States in any conflict between the Warsaw Pact nations and Western Europe.

To be sure, this policy would raise serious problems. First, it could complicate our relations with the USSR, which objects vigorously to any West European "defense bloc" and has proposed a ban on the transfer of nuclear technology. Second, insofar as the ultimate deterrent would remain the American strategic forces, a new "battle for control" might develop among our allies, in reverse so to speak. Given the divergences described above, *we* would want to make sure that the specific deployments decided by our allies are not provocative and that their strategic designs do not create unacceptable risks for us. Finally, a West European defense system might serve as the pretext either for drastic American troop cuts or for a formal "uncoupling" of our nuclear forces from Europe. It is fear of premature abandonment that has persuaded many Europeans, especially the Germans, against any change in the structure of NATO. Only a deliberate decision by the United States to promote such a change would have a chance of lifting these hesitations, but the European fear of American dissociation would persist, for it is in the nature of the situation. And now there would be the additional risk that American fears of European irresponsibility would compound those European misgivings.

These objections can be answered. As to the second, it would surely not be in the Europeans' interest to behave in a way that could provoke the withdrawals and "uncoupling" they fear. Indeed, West European sluggishness or appeasement in the face of provocation might be more to be feared—except that the very setting up of a West European defense system is likely to stiffen the common resolve and to weaken the temptation of competitive "Finlandization." As to the first objection, insofar as the Soviets' resistance is based on a legitimate fear of attack, their arguments can be met both by avoiding the emergence of a purely West German nuclear force and by agreeing on relatively low ceilings for the Western *and* for the Warsaw Pact forces in Europe. The composition of the Western forces, as between American and West European ones, would be a matter of U.S.-West European, not of East-West, negotiation. The existence of MFR talks might actually become an asset for the Western Alliance: those who, in Western Europe, see military reorganization as an obstacle to détente are likely to be less reluctant if such efforts are linked to mutual reductions. Insofar as the Soviet opposition is aimed, not at defense, but at preventing the rise of a Western European actor in world politics, it should be made clear to the USSR that the Soviets' acceptance of such a "reality" is a precondition for, or at least a corollary of, many of the things the USSR professes to desire, such as increased economic cooperation and mutual force reductions.

As to the third objection, we really have no better choice. The only alternatives would be either, in the absence of such reorganization, a perpetuation of a status quo that is increasingly humiliating to the West Europeans as well as politically fragile in the United States; or else reductions negotiated between us and the Soviets that would leave Western Europe psychologically demoralized and perhaps also militarily less safe, and therefore politically less solid, than it is now.

ii. In monetary affairs, the task is of a very different nature. The return to monetary unification in Western Europe, and in particular the possibility for the pound and the lira to join, depend above all on the ability of those countries with huge payments problems to return to equilibrium. Otherwise a "European serpent" would be a Deutsche Mark zone (or a Deutsche Mark-and-franc zone), from which Bonn itself would recoil in horror, since German reserves would have to keep the weak and laggard afloat. Moreover, the experience of 1972-73 has shown the limits of the purely "monetarist" approach to economic unification.

In this area, the contribution of the United States can only be indirect, but it is of enormous importance in three respects. First, Washington should not delay an agreement on a new international monetary system until after all the economic turbulence of recent years has been removed. Floating rates may have helped absorb some of this turbulence; but they contribute to it also, both by maintaining monetary uncertainty and by contributing to, or at least not combating, inflation.

If agreements could be reached on the rules for price-setting of raw materials (including oil), for the modalities of transfers between rich and poor countries, the ways of financing the payments imbalances of deficit countries, then the restoration of a world monetary order would be both the cause and the effect of the reestablishment of world economic order. It is as futile to wait until the latter has been achieved before one reestablishes global monetary order as it is to present European monetary unification as the last step of economic union. . . . Order must be put back everywhere at once.[21]

Second, there must indeed be sensible agreements on oil consumption, oil supplies, oil prices, and recycling, so as to help the deficit countries eliminate or reduce these deficits; and the role of the United States in this respect is vital (see below).[22] Third, and perhaps most importantly, the United States must curtail its recession; for should it last and keep spreading abroad to countries that are hard pressed financially, these will be tempted to try to increase or at least uphold their exports by competitive devaluations and trade controls; and that would make any monetary stability impossible.

iii. The realm of energy is crucial, because it involves nothing less, politically, than "North-South" (not merely "industrial-OPEC") relations in coming years; and economically, the future of industrial development, trade patterns, and economic policies and payments for the United States and its various partners. I have neither the expertise nor the space to deal with all the dimensions of the drama. But here again, if we keep our objective in mind, there is a triple international role for the United States. This is over and above the important domestic need for a consistent energy policy, aimed at reducing America's own demand for OPEC oil without raising the prices of substitutes or domestic oil so high as to provide, in effect, price support for OPEC. First, insofar as the members of OPEC are moved by very different interests—thus, the Iranian economic interest in high prices for maximum power expansion while Iran's limited oil reserves last and the Saudi political interest in putting pressure on the industrial nations for a settlement of the Arab-Israeli conflict—the quickest way to break OPEC's common front or to make it possible for Saudi Arabia to exert pressure toward a lower price that would allow an increase in its production, is to resolve that conflict.

In this respect, whatever the merits of the step-by-step approach of Kissinger, it is clear that sooner or later the USSR will have to be brought into the process. But the Europeans should also be encouraged to play a role; for their own links with the Arab countries—which we profess to find irritating and meddling, at the same time as we bolster our own—ought to allow them to prod these countries toward moderation, just as it is the strength of our own link with Israel that allows us to pressure Israel for concessions. To be sure, Israel is utterly dependent on us, whereas in the European-Arab connection it is the Europeans who are economically dependent. But the Arabs do receive technology and weapons from Europe—precisely because they do not want, in this respect, to depend only on us or only on the Soviets—and seek diplomatic support; so that the Europeans are not without some leverage.

Second, we must try to preserve a separate West European breathing space in our attempts to organize a common front of consumers capable, in the long run, of bringing about the demise of OPEC through the development of non-OPEC sources of oil and energy. On the one hand, we ought to allow the EEC to define its own common energy policy and *then* have the eight EEC members who are also in the IEA coordinate it with their other IEA partners, instead of having the

IEA adopt a joint policy, which its European members then coordinate with France's. More is involved than just preserving a semblance of an autonomous role for EEC. The Europeans must be given a chance to develop their own technologies for substitutes for oil and to look for "non-OPEC oil" on their own, rather than be snowed or preempted by the United States. Indeed, this is the only way the EEC has of resolving the ambiguity of Britain's energy policy, which aims both at independence and at obtaining Community support for the exploitation of North Sea oil, in the direction of European solidarity, not British separatism.

Similarly, among those recycling schemes that involve only the industrial powers, there ought to be room for purely EEC arrangements; and in those which involve the Europeans and the other industrial powers, the conditions of "aid to the needy" and the voting arrangements should not be such as to amount to American dictation. Again, the EEC countries ought to present plans of their own, and the loans ought to be, whenever possible, administered through Community organs. In other words, despite the separation between France and the IEA, or the role to be played by the IMF and OECD, Washington ought in these matters to deal with Brussels rather than either with larger collective institutions or single countries.

Third, and perhaps in the long run most important, instead of insisting on an ironclad common front of consumer countries that would inevitably be led by us and would have to have us as its chief representative in dealing with OPEC (just as we are the leader of NATO in MBFR talks), we ought to encourage the EEC to play a role of its own in tripartite discussions with oil-producing nations and with oil-poor developing countries. There is a risk: the EEC, given its dependence on OPEC oil, might seek direct OPEC loans or OPEC investments in their own industries, or opportunities for investments in OPEC countries, that we would consider dangerous, both because they could increase OPEC's hold on Western Europe and because they would strengthen countries whose friendliness and intentions we deeply distrust. As I have stressed before, however, we can expect the EEC to have Europe's self-interest in mind—do they really need to be told by us that they should not become their suppliers' captives?—and a role for the EEC would at least dampen the tendencies of separate European countries to make such deals on their own—a tendency that might grow if we dominated the consumer front too tightly. As for the reinforcement of OPEC countries, Kissinger's floor-price proposal was cooly received in continental Europe (including France) precisely because our partners, attracted by his long-term strategy of breaking the stranglehold of OPEC, found the promise of a long-term price for oil to the cartel both contradictory and contrary to the European interest—since some dependence on OPEC oil would remain part of Europe's condition, even if Britain became self-sufficient and the United States succeeded in "Project Independence." In other words, when it comes to OPEC, neither the United States nor the West Europeans are paragons of consistency: they have not reconciled a "soft" rhetoric and very pressing interests; whereas we still tend to talk tough even though we can afford to be, in effect, more conciliatory. In any case, we ought to remember both that the economic development of OPEC nations is preferable to arming them (and yet it is the latter we have been promoting most), and that economic growth is likely to multiply the ties with the industrial nations and therefore the restraints on OPEC "aggressivity." Western Europe is particularly keen on including the countries of OPEC in the recycling schemes—after all, it is *their* (newly acquired) money *we* recycle, and if we leave them out, they have ways of bringing down the columns of the financial temple. Such an inclusion, not merely in borrowing facilities but even more in joint investment ventures, would help the creation of bonds (hence restraints) of reciprocal interests.

iv. In diplomacy, the acquisition of a voice by Western Europe should also be encouraged. I have already referred to the Arab-Israeli conflict: should—in Geneva or elsewhere—a settlement become possible, the European Community ought to have a role in the necessary network of peace-keeping forces and territorial guarantees. Several European states have expressed their willingness or eagerness to play such a role. It is not in our interest to be sole guarantors, or to share this responsibility only with Moscow.

The Community is also well placed to play a useful role in the coming negotiations (not only in energy matters) between the industrial nations and the countries, "rich" or poor, of the Third World. It has accumulated considerable experience through its association agreements, including the recent pact of Lomé, and through its members' foreign aid programs. It has in the past shown greater understanding than the United States for demands made by the developing countries at the United Nations Conference on Trade and Development (UNCTAD) or at the UN. If we want to prevent the politics of interdependence from becoming a series of rhetorical confrontations, we will need an agency such as the EEC. A league of primarily industrial powers, it is not likely to sacrifice their interests and those of Europe's workers and consumers to demands for an immediate and drastic redistribution of the world's wealth. But its members, many of whom have mixed economies and strong Socialist components, are less easily shocked than the American elites, business community, and media by the language and the claims of the developing countries. More used to the fierce battles for equality of results (not only of opportunity) and to the ideological politics of redistribution at home, they are psychologically less unprepared than most Americans to face such issues on the world scene. To be sure, the United States—as Kissinger has hinted—will have to come to terms with these issues and grievances on its own. But the existence of a strong EEC can make our process of adjustment less painful and ease global strains while this process goes on. The EEC's importance in world trade gives it an enormous stake in making international economic relations more stable and predictable. Its own involvement in the developing world should allow it to play a major role in preparing the kinds of collective aid programs that both the industrial and the newly rich states will have to take part in. Its agriculture will be essential in helping the developing countries cope with the food shortages that seem unavoidable so long as these nations have not given priority to the increase of their own food supply and to the economic and social reforms that would make such an increase possible.

Another diplomatic realm where Western Europe ought to be encouraged to raise its voice is the field of East-West relations in Europe. The West Europeans have no interest in "destabilizing" Eastern Europe, for they know that this would only lead the Soviets to reassert their control decisively. But they have an interest in multiplying economic and cultural links between themselves and their neighbors, in promoting a sense of *Europeanness* that could give to these countries, if not a modicum of autonomy, at least a flavor of distinctiveness, and thereby a minimum of leeway from their domineering Protector. An end to the recession and a curbing of inflation are essential in this respect also, for the longer they last, the less Eastern Europe is able to pay for its imports from Western Europe with exports toward it and the more threatened the development of East-West trade will be.

However important the détente with Moscow appears to us, and it is just as important to our European allies, who preceded us in this respect, we ought not deem it incompatible with this subtle promotion, which only the West Europeans can perform. We should have shown greater support for the proposals of the Nine at the CSCE on the "basket" of human rights and cultural exchanges as well as on advance notification of war games and military moves. Even if the Conference was above all an exercise in symbols and images, the insistence and solidarity of the Nine—for once—obtained some results from a Soviet Union impatient to bring to a spectacular close a process that had proved to be a rather mixed blessing for Moscow. The Community can hardly be a "magnet-for-satellites"; it can become the kind of constant *interlocuteur* whose concerns and inventiveness, tied to its own good relations with Moscow, bring some benefits, some breathing space, some fresh air, to Moscow's dependents.

As I have said before, the United States can only create the *conditions* of a European autonomy, and we should do so because what we fear and resent—a European "inward-turning" pettiness—is partly the result of that lack of autonomy. But the impulse has to come from the other side. With such an American policy, one European alibi for discord would vanish: the split between those Europeans who prefer to resist the United States and those who prefer to cooperate with Washington. For reasons of internal inertia or discord, however— because the habit of dependence is not easily given up and because the interests of nations in very different economic circumstances necessarily diverge—it may well be that no will-to-unite manifests itself in Western Europe, and the policies advocated here do not succeed. This essay has not dealt with the measures which the West Europeans would have to take in matters of policy and procedure in order to make of what I have called the Third Course a reality. At present, despite some progress out of the abyss of early 1974—the end of Britain's agony of indecision, France's softer stand on joint institutions, the Lomé convention, the modest beginning of a regional policy, the promise of at least the beginning of an energy policy—formidable obstacles persist. Bonn's fear of being "soaked," France's delicate balance of political forces, Britain's economic plight, Italy's political and financial headaches, the continuing impact of the new agenda and new agencies on the substance of European cooperation, the persistent "separatism" of the national bureaucracies, the handicaps created by institutional splits between France and her partners in defense and energy matters or by institutional sluggishness in Brussels—none of these factors allows for great optimism.

Moreover, America's own ability to take the measures recommended here is in doubt. This is so, not so much because of the recent (and, in my opinion, temporary) turmoil created by Watergate and Vietnam, but because the pursuit of a coherent course goes against two major and disastrous trends: the unmanageability of the new international system, in which traditional contests and the new tugs-of-war of interdependence make power both more explosive and more elusive, more incalculable and less predictable; and the inconsistency of policy-making given the diversity of interests a democracy must reconcile—the welter of issues, the weight of short-run pressures, the profusion of agencies, the confusion of the publics. If we assume that these two trends are irresistible, no exercise about critical choices makes any sense at all. So we must be modest in our expectations.

Should the course I have suggested here prove impossible or fail because of all these obstacles, we would then still have NATO and the IEA, and IMF and OECD. We still ought to try to establish tripartite institutions on energy or other world economic problems. We would still have the "second course" to fall back on. I would hope that we could do so in a way that would not just be "more of the past." The *spirit* of the third course should be observed. The series of "don'ts" would still be justified. Even within this second course, moreover, there is room for a subtle shift from American hegemony to a less imperious kind of leadership. I refer back to the three dimensions of American global policy: framework, style, and substance; even continuity leaves room, in all three respects, for a broad range of new possibilities. The third course, which I prefer, would be part of an attempt to make United States global policy more "institution-oriented," more universalistic in style, more "reformist" in substance. The same trends could still be followed if Western Europe defects, so to speak, as an actor in world politics. But this would be the subject of another, far more ambitious study.

Notes

1. Stanley Hoffmann, "No Trumps, No Luck, No Will," in James Chace and Earl Ravenal (eds.), *Atlantis Lost* (forthcoming).

2. Robert E. Osgood, *Ideals & Self-interest in America's Foreign Relations; the Great Transformation of the Twentieth Century* (Chicago: University of Chicago Press, 1953).

3. Jean Jacques Servan-Schreiber, *The American Challenge*, first edition (New York: Atheneum, 1968) [*Le Défi américain* (Paris: Denoël, 1967)].

4. See Stanley Hoffmann, "Europe's Identity Crisis," *Daedalus*, Fall 1964.

5. On much of the above, see Pierre Hassner, *Europe in the Age of Negotiation* (The Washington Papers, Vol. I, No. 8) (Beverly Hills and London: Sage Publications, 1973).

6. Stanley Hoffmann, "Toward a Common European Foreign Policy?" in Wolfram Hanrieder (ed.), *The United States and Western Europe* (Cambridge, Mass.: Winthrop Publishers, 1974), pp. 79-105.

7. Cf. Michel Jobert, *Mémoires d'avenir* (Paris: Bernard Grasset, 1974).

8. David A. Walker, "Some Underlying Problems for International Monetary Reform," in Hanrieder (ed.), *The United States and Western Europe*, p. 185.

9. Herman Kahn and Anthony J. Wiener, *The Year 2000: A Framework for Speculation on the Next Thirty-Three Years* (New York: Macmillan, 1967).

10. Cf. Robert W. Tucker, "Oil: the Issues of American Intervention," *Commentary*, January 1975, pp. 21 ff.; "Israel and the United States: From Dependence to Nuclear Weapons," ibid., Nov. 1975, pp. 29 ff.; and his book, *A New Isolationism: Threat or Promise?* (New York: Universe, 1972).

11. Cf. Stanley Hoffmann, "Choices," *Foreign Policy*, no. 12 (Fall 1973): 3-42.

12. Michael Howard, "NATO and the Year of Europe," *Survival*, January-February 1974, pp. 23-24.

13. See my "Notes on the Elusiveness of Modern Power," *International Journal*, Spring 1975.

14. See Miriam Camps, *The Management of Interdependence* (New York: Council on Foreign Relations, 1974).

15. See Thomas L. Hughes, "Foreign Policy: Men or Measures," *Atlantic*, October 1974, pp. 48 ff.

16. Joint Hearings before the Subcommittee on Europe and the Subcommittee on Foreign Economic Policy of the Committee on Foreign Affairs, House of Representatives, 93d Congress, *American Interest in the European Community* November 8, 1973, pp. 89 ff.

17. Interview of Kissinger by James Reston, *State Department Bulletin*, no. 1846, November 11, 1974, p. 634.

18. See especially my testimony before the Subcommittee on Arms Control of the Senate Foreign Relations Committee, July 27, 1973.

19. See, *inter alia*, Henry Kissinger, *The Necessity for Choice* (New York: Harper & Row, 1961) and *The Troubled Partnership: A Re-appraisal of the Atlantic Alliance* (New York: McGraw-Hill, 1965).

20. Cf. Laurence Martin, "Theatre Nuclear Weapons and Europe," *Survival*, November-December 1974, pp. 268 ff.; and Jeffrey Record, U.S. Nuclear Weapons in Europe (Washington: Brookings, 1974); my Chapter 12 in

Decline or Renewal? (Viking, 1974); and the essays mentioned in notes 1 and 11 above.

21. Thierry de Moutbrial, *Le Désordre économique mondial* (Paris, 1974), pp. 40-41.

22. Cf. K. Farmanfarmaian, A. Gutowski, S. Okita, R.V. Roosa, and C.L. Wilson, "How Can the World Afford OPEC Oil?" *Foreign Affairs* 53, 2 (January 1975): 201-22.

IV Britain's Future in the International System

Andrew Shonfield

During most of the postwar period the pursuit of national economic interests has been intermittently a major element in British policy-making; but it has not dominated it absolutely. That has now changed. Economic considerations have an unchallenged priority that they have not had before.

In the late 1940s and during the 1950s British governments were deeply concerned with the Anglo-American alliance and most especially with its use in maintaining a stable balance of international power between the West and the Soviet Bloc, in the context of a policy of progressive decolonization aimed at securing the orderly transfer of power with the minimum of bloodshed. These objectives continued to have a high priority in British policy-making into the early 1960s. Then, concurrently with the dismantling of the last substantial bits of the British colonial empire, the question of Britain's future political relationship with continental Western Europe became the salient issue. It absorbed a large part of the energies of British governments, Labour as well as Conservative, until the accession of Britain to the European Community. But it has since been downgraded, subordinated like everything else to the overriding question how to manage British national interests in such a way as to produce the maximum strictly economic gain.

It may be thought that in the circumstances, the unchallenged priority accorded to economic policy is no more than the belated recognition of the obvious. It could nevertheless have significant consequences for the management of the international system. Whether it does will depend first on how long-lasting the new order of priorities is likely to be—which again poses the question of the probable effectiveness of any remedial action; and second, on how far the attachment to the economic imperative is felt by British people and governments

111

to justify a narrow and exclusive pursuit of short-term national interests. The range of possibilities can be illustrated by reference to the behavior of other medium-sized Western powers. Britain might for example become like Italy— extremely difficult to govern and at the same time obsessed by the poverty of its own resources. Or it might retreat into an isolationist type of nationalism, reminiscent of the mood of France in the 1960s. Alternatively it might shift into a posture of conscious passivity, like Japan during the last two decades, marked by an absence of any will to contribute to the international order. There are many other possibilities. This essay is an attempt to explore some of the factors which will determine where in this wide range of options the British response is most likely to occur.

To begin with there is the question of time: how long is the process of British adjustment likely to take? I believe that even if one makes favorable assumptions about the course of remedial action, the process will take a number of years and will probably have to continue well into the second half of the 1980s. The reason derives from the evidence that the weakness in the British economy is deep-seated and that Britain is not well equipped, as a result of a long period of neglect of its productive apparatus, to respond to the changed conditions of supply and demand that the Western world is likely to face during the period ahead.

It has been argued by some commentators that if we are entering on a period of slower growth of output and incomes, Britain with its established slow rate of growth will be less of an "odd man out."[1] This is not plausible. If the reason for a slowdown in economic growth is that the advanced industrial countries will have to adapt their whole system of production to a new set of conditions, for example, to the use of smaller amounts of energy and raw materials, then countries with a high level of investment and an economic structure that responds rapidly to changing conditions of demand will continue to have a marked advantage. Flexible response will pay more than ever. If the slowdown is expected to result from some protracted recession in demand for industrial goods, especially in international trade, then in the conditions of greatly sharpened competition it will once again be the high-investment economies with an established capacity to respond sensitively to changing circumstances which are likely to suffer least.

It is a misleading analogy to go back to the Great Depression of the 1930s and use this as a guide to the probable outcome in the future. It is true that in the 1930s Britain fared relatively less badly than other nations with more dynamic economies. But that was due in large part to Britain's ability to mobilize the special assets that it possessed at that time, notably its political advantage as the center of a discriminatory trading system based on imperial preference, an advantage that it no longer commands.

Historical Background

It may be asked why, if the British economic problem is both deep-seated and of long standing, it has only recently come to be seen as acute. The reason in part is that the fortuitous combination of circumstances that followed in the wake of the worldwide inflationary crisis of the early 1970s brought matters to a head. It was not that at that stage the inflation of prices in Britain was noticeably worse than in a number of other countries. Thus consumer prices during 1973 and 1974 rose faster in Japan and Italy than they did in Britain, and only a little less fast in France. True, the massive deficit which had opened up in Britain's balance of payments, nearly $10 billion on current account, amounted to over 5 per cent of the gross national product in 1974. But it was the sudden and spectacular deterioration in Britain's terms of trade, rather than any adverse movement in the volume of exports or imports, which was responsible for this yawning gap. In the two years from mid-1972 to mid-1974, the purchasing power of British exports measured in terms of imports fell by one quarter; the effect of this extraordinary movement can be seen by recalculating the value of the goods actually exported and imported in 1974 at 1972 prices. On that basis the British balance of payments would have come out with a modest surplus on current account in 1974—as it had done in 1972.

The purpose of making such calculations is merely to establish the point that the British economic crisis of the early 1970s was not the result of any sudden loss of control over the country's domestic situation. What has given this crisis an overwhelming political significance is the fact that it is itself the climax of a series of economic crises that have progressively demonstrated that the margin of resources available to Britain is too slim to allow it to cope with almost any accident. The country is seen to be so underinsured against bad luck that it is no longer, in any sense that counts, master of its own fate.

It is important to recognize that it is not the British economic problem itself that has become acute but rather its perception in political terms. There has been a tendency among some foreign observers of Britain to talk as if the real income earned by its citizens were declining; or alternatively, if that is not so, to argue that the nation itself is not paying its way and that the rise in living standards has not been truly *earned*. Yet this was certainly not true during the decade uo to 1972; and from 1973 onwards almost everyone in the Western world began living on borrowed money. No, what distinguishes Britain's case is a long history of *relative* decline: its neighbors and competitors in the industrial world have moved ahead faster pretty consistently over an extended period of time.

It is the nature of this particular experience that has to be understood if the probable political outcome is to be realistically assessed. The facile analogies that have on occasion been brought to bear on the problem—whether the economic decline of Italy in the seventeenth century from its earlier position of leadership in Europe or the long decay of the Spanish empire during the seventeenth and eighteenth centuries—miss the essential point. British production has been growing since the war faster than at any time in this century; British exports have risen much faster; and British living standards have, by any measure, improved very substantially indeed. It is possible to conclude that it will not matter to the British that other nations do these things more and better than they do.

That is essentially the view underlying the prognosis of Herman Kahn for Britain in the year 2000.[2] It must be said that the *prima facie* evidence is in favor of such a conclusion. The most compelling piece of evidence is that Britain's relative economic decline has proceeded for a very long time and yet no one has done anything serious about it. The trend line showing Britain with a lower rate of economic growth than most of the other Western industrial countries was certainly well established before the First World War, and it has continued uninterruptedly lower throughout this century. Of course in the earlier stages the diverging trends could be, and were, dismissed as part of the natural process of "catching up" by latecomers to the industrial revolution. The British, as the first in the field, felt that it was proper to make some allowance for this. Then, during the first half of the twentieth century, the underlying economic forces were obscured by two world wars and a worldwide economic depression, the more so as Britain's *comparative* performance during these disasters was notably better than in the years of prosperity.[3] There were few of the latter between the two world wars.

One recalls the prophetic remark of the German businessman commenting on the Anglo-German commercial rivalry before the First World War: "*Wenn wir noch hundert Jahre Frieden haben, werden wir England tot gemacht haben*" ("Give us a hundred years of peace, and we shall have killed England stone dead").[4] In the event it took rather fewer peacetime years for Britain's lead in production to be overtaken not only by Germany but by most of the other industrial countries of Western Europe. In 1938 British output per head was still the highest in Europe, though only by a modest margin; by 1965 Germany was some 30 per cent ahead, Belgium nearly 20 per cent, and France 10 per cent ahead.[5]

Britain's relative position has deteriorated further since then; its output per head by the early 1970s probably surpassed only that of Italy among the Western industrial countries. It would be wrong, however, to equate these measures of relative productive performance with differences in the living standards of wage earners. It has to be remembered that large parts of the real income of consumers escapes these statistical measures. Thus a country like Britain, which has been relatively rich for a very long time, possesses a large stock of social capital—notably housing—which its citizens enjoy. When it is recalled that residential construction in Britain has accounted in recent years for about one quarter of the annual value of net fixed investment, it will be appreciated that the accumulation of wealth from the past must significantly affect any realistic appraisal of changes in living standards. The same applies to the stock of such personal amenities as telephones and washing machines, which are widely owned in Britain. The recent report of the Hudson Institute, *The United Kingdom in 1980*, reaches the conclusion that the living standard of the average Briton in the early 1970s was 25 per cent below that of his French contemporary only by ignoring these elements of the comparative level of real affluence. It is indeed deeply misleading to think of the British as a people who have missed out on the great surge of affluence that was experienced by Western societies in the second half of the twentieth century. There is no evidence of a widely felt sense of deprivation.

That in itself makes more problematical the conduct of any thoroughgoing program of economic reform aimed at decisively increasing the rate of growth. A sense of failure is widely felt among the elites; but in the rest of society the events of the early 1970s, and most especially the ferocious inflation of 1973-75, have given rise only to a diffuse anxiety about the future, with little sign of a general desire for radical change in the management of the economy. If in spite of this contrast I anticipate that the issue of economic reform will dominate British politics during the period ahead, it is partly because I anticipate that political leadership will continue to be exercised by the elites, who have by now convinced themselves of the overriding priority of this problem. A further reason is that the prospective changes in the economic environment from the mid-1970s onwards will make it more difficult to secure even a modest rise in British living standards without some drastic adaptations of economic policy. I shall discuss the prospect for these adaptations in the succeeding sections.

The most obvious as well as consistent feature of the long period of relative decline of the British economy is the comparatively low level of industrial investment at home. It was remarked upon from the 1900s onwards. Capital seemed to be available for urban development, for roads, for shops, and for bold business ventures overseas; but putting money into the productive equipment of British industry at home did not seem to have the same attraction. The imperial syndrome undoubtedly affected British entrepreneurship as well as British government during the early years of this century. The export of British capital abroad during a number of these years actually exceeded net domestic investment of all kinds.[6]

The explanation for the poor record of industrial investment at that time is therefore not to be found in any lack of venturesomeness among British entrepreneurs. Nor can it be attributed, either then or later, to the failure of the spirit of innovation—not, at any rate, if the latter is to be judged by the output of inventions and new ideas coming from British sources. In this respect Britain has continued during the twentieth century as one of the leading centers in the production of new scientific ideas and technology.[7] It is simply that the technological take-up was slower in British industry than it was abroad.

It is worth stressing the point that the tendency to lag in this respect was well established in the early years of this century. Observers noted that the British were slower to develop the important new industries of that epoch, in chemicals and in electrical engineering, than their competitors abroad, notably the Germans, and that there was a resistance to the introduction of new methods of production in established industries. The dating of this process has some importance because of certain mythology about the decline of the British spirit of innovation in the course of the twentieth century. There is, however, no truth in the notion that British industrial vigor marched together with British imperial assertion and was enfeebled with the end of empire. The taking of international initiatives in the style to which Britain had become accustomed required a confidence born of the possession of wealth; there had at any rate to be a belief in the existence of reserves to fall back on in case of need; but there was no correlation between international activism and commercial achievement at home. This was notably true of the period between the two world wars. The lag in British business investment was specially marked at that time; it has been progressively narrowed since. If we use the volume of nonresidential fixed investment as a proportion of gross national product to provide an approximate indication of comparative performance, we have the following results: during the period 1920-1938 the British proportion amounted to 60 per cent of the average for the industrial nations of Western Europe; from 1940 to 1960 it was 75 per cent and in 1960-1970 it rose to nearly 80 per cent.[8]

The important point, however, is that the lag in the proportion of national resources devoted to productive investment, although considerably narrowed, continued during the 1960s, when, as we have seen, British output per capita had become one of the lowest in Europe. British governments, which had earlier been slow to recognize the problem, did at this stage consciously address themselves to the task of raising the level of industrial investment. But their efforts coincided with the emergence of another problem in acute form—that of managing the pound sterling as an international reserve currency during a period of declining confidence.

The difficulty was a familiar one; the British had been wrestling with it intermittently since the end of World War II. What was new was that the sterling system was entering its terminal phase, while there was still a deep unwillingness to recognize the nature of the disease. The long agony of the sterling crisis lasted through most of the 1960s, and British economic policy came to concentrate obsessively first on preventing a devaluation of the pound, and subsequently, after the exchange-rate had been lowered in 1967, on making the new fixed parity impregnable against speculative pressures.

A withdrawal of international confidence on the scale that was experienced by sterling in the 1960s was in any case likely to force the British economy into a severe deflation. The devotion to the Bretton Woods regime of fixed exchange rates and the exaggerated fear, vigorously encouraged by the Americans, that a movement in the pound's parity might produce a domino effect causing a breakdown of the world currency system, made certain that the British economy would be subjected to a fierce squeeze. Economic growth was once again slowed down and the desired upsurge in British industrial investment again postponed.

I do not wish to suggest that low investment provides the whole explanation of Britain's failure to match what has become the normal pace of economic advance of the industrial countries of Western Europe. There were other contributory causes, some of them of a social character. Outstanding among these is the clumsy and inefficient system of industrial relations, which will be examined below. But what is clear is that a sharp and sustained rise in British industrial investment is a necessary, if not a sufficient, condition for achieving a significantly higher rate of growth and a more competitive British economy. The postwar years have shown repeatedly how Britain's lack of productive capacity in periods of boom and market opportunity inhibit the growth of exports.

At the same time the growth of imports of industrial goods has proceeded at a rate that is higher, though not noticeably higher, than in other West European countries. But whereas, in the rest of Western Europe, the growth of exports usually more or less matches that of imports, in Britain there is in periods of economic expansion a consistent disparity between the two. That in turn means that the upswing of each business cycle is prematurely brought to a halt by measures to close a growing deficit in the balance of payments. By the early 1970s the mood of British business had come to resemble that of a childless, philoprogenitive lady who had experienced only abortions, and an excessive number of these.

Labour and Conservative Policies

Both of the major parties in British politics had in the 1960s identified the national business mood as a major impediment to economic growth. The Labour and the Conservative parties did not differ about the need for a convincing demonstration that what had come to be known as the "stop-go cycle" had been successfully overcome. But they set about the task of feeding the flagging animal spirits of British entrepreneurs in characteristically different ways. The contrast is worth noting, since it continues to be relevant to the underlying approaches of the two parties in the mid-1970s. On the Conservative side the favored policy has had the simplicity and directness of extreme paradox: Britain should simply "spend its way out of a balance-of-payments deficit." That was the line adopted by Mr. Reginald Maudling as Chancellor of the Exchequer in 1964, and it led to the biggest balance-of-payments deficit that Britain had experienced up to that point. It was pursued again by Mr. Heath's government in 1972-73 and produced a new record deficit.

Underlying the paradox of spending one's way out of the crisis is the entirely sensible notion that the early stages of a boom often have an exaggerated effect on the balance of payments. Thus the process of restocking pulls in large amounts of additional imports, while the spate of urgent new orders for capital equipment at home tends to reduce exports in the crucial sector of engineering. After some time, so the theory runs, both demand and the capacity to satisfy it will stabilize at a higher level—or at any rate the pressure on domestic resources will diminish, and so the external balance will improve again. In the meanwhile the government needs to have very good nerves and must be ready to spend its currency reserves, and beg or borrow whatever else it needs, in order to close the gap in its balance of payments.

In this sense, it will be seen, the approach fitted readily into the traditional Tory ideal of high leadership and calculated risk-taking. It also had the attraction of maintaining the government in a noninterventionist stance. It allowed growth to occur and individual spending to proceed without exhortation or controls, confident that the natural forces would reassert themselves and produce the required balance at a higher level—if only there were patience and determination enough. What the last experiment in the early 1970s seemed to indicate, however, was that the patience required for any such experiment had become very long indeed. That does not necessarily mean that the method would have failed if it had been fully tried out, with all the devices that Mr. Heath applied to it, at an earlier stage of the postwar era. These devices included quite sharp devaluations of the currency, through the medium of a downward floating exchange rate, and the acceptance of large additional debts abroad. But by the early 1970s the evidence indicated that the process of adapting the British economy to a higher growth rate and its necessary concomitant, a sustained level of greatly increased investment, would entail very heavy balance-of-payments deficits over an extended period of time. In order to secure the desired end, it would be necessary to persuade the international community to meet the cost of British imports not covered by foreign-exchange earnings.

It is possible that if a British government had adopted a policy of this kind during the 1950s, at the same time as France was acquiring the capacity for a higher rate of economic growth it would have been able to bring it off successfully—assuming that it was prepared to mobilize all the resources at its disposal for the purpose. It might even have done so in the early 1960s. Such a decision would have implied, however, among other things, a quite different approach by Britain to its international commitments. It is fairly easy to show that the British balance of payments on current account would have been healthily in surplus in almost every year up to the mid-1960s if the country had not been involved in any military expenditure abroad. As it was, successive British governments accepted as part of the nation's destiny that it had a worldwide role, of which these substantial expenditures on military forces and bases overseas were an integral part. These payments made the difference between easy external solvency and the constant threat of a balance-of-payments crisis. The amounts were not large when measured against the total value of exports of goods and services: defense spending overseas during the sterling crisis of the mid-60s absorbed no more than 3 per cent of Britain's foreign-exchange earnings. But just as the United States discovered in comparable circumstances, at a later stage, the foreign-exchange component of a peacetime military establishment abroad could, in years when the balance of payments was under pressure, significantly add to the difficulty of managing economic policy. In the British case, the effect was to constrain further the conduct of an expansionist economic policy at home.

This was precisely the opposite of the effect which the military circumstances of the postwar era produced in Germany. Between 1950 and 1970 the West German balance of payments benefited to the extent of almost $17 billion from the stationing there of American and other allied forces—while Britain had a net foreign-exchange deficit of $7 billion on military account over the same period.[9] As one historian of this period has put it: "The real cost-benefit analysis of British foreign policy would have to count the cost of government activities abroad, not merely in the hundreds of millions annually spent, but in the milliards annually lost in output and income because of the restrictions made necessary to maintain it."[10]

In any case, the policy of letting everything in the British economy rip and then building up its strength on the ruins of the balance of payments, whatever its merits might have been at an earlier stage, became less feasible as time went on.

The alternative line of policy pursued by the Labour party during its recent periods in office has been less clear-cut. Indeed it appears at times as little more than an amalgam of interventionist impulses, each designed to do some particular job better than market forces appear to be doing it. But underlying the apparent disorder are certain enduring themes. To begin with, the mixed economy, in spite of the fundamentalist socialist rhetoric, is fully accepted as the basis for national economic policy. That implies a decision to have the government collaborate with, rather than try to replace, the managements of the leading business corporations in British industry. In some ways the Labour politicians have in recent years been more concerned to cultivate a working relationship with private enterprise than the Tory politicians. The contrast was especially marked during the rather doctrinaire phase of laissez-faire politics of the Heath government in the early 1970s, when its anti-interventionism was manifest in a kind of arm's-length relationship with the City of London and with other foci of business opinion.

The Labour government's relationship with business was not only closer but more aggressive. Its intentions were deliberately discriminatory: it was going to pick and choose among enterprises on the ground of their prospective long-term contribution to the British economy. Its instrument in the 1960s was a kind of state-controlled merchant bank, the Industrial Reorganisation Corporation (IRC), whose task it was to promote the growth of promising companies, supplying them with public funds to take over control of other corporations and to finance investment programs. These activities were supposed to further the objectives set out in a five-year National Plan for accelerated economic growth, launched in 1965. The IRC was thought of as one of the tactical arms of the grand strategy. In addition the government introduced a system of regional incentives, using a combination of discriminatory tax relief and subsidies to attract businesses to areas of above-average unemployment.

Yet these praiseworthy efforts to make more productive use of labor, capital, and entrepreneurial skills had to compete with other objectives of national policy. The attempt to sustain the position of the pound sterling in the protracted balance-of-payments crisis of the second half of the 1960s has already been mentioned. Equally constraining was the task of protecting employment regardless of the efficiency of the employing firm. The issue asserted itself sharply when the Labour party returned to power at the onset of the business recession in early 1974. The politics of the intervening years of opposition had greatly strengthened the power of the big trade unions in the Labour party. And trade union pressure helped to ensure that the main emphasis of policy would be on maintaining people in their jobs, rather than on securing the more productive use of manpower.

The conflict between these two objectives of Labour policy, job security and higher productivity, was an old story. It had been evident for a long time that raising British productivity would necessarily entail a considerable redeployment of labor and changes in established work practices. But the attempt by the Labour government in the 1960s to achieve a decisive improvement in this regard as part of its National Plan made no significant headway because of the absence of support from the trade unions. A determined assault on restrictive practices would almost certainly have produced a clash with the trade union leadership. Meanwhile the other leg of the Labour government's economic program at the time, its incomes policy, depended on the cooperation of the unions in curbing wage claims. The short-term objective won out over the long-term one. In view of the overriding priority given to the maintenance of the pound sterling, it was bound to.

In the altered circumstances of the mid-1970s, however, with the exchange rate floating and the international role of sterling drastically reduced, the old motives have disappeared. On the other hand, the new, political motives which buttress the position of the trade unions in British politics make the government once again highly vulnerable to pressures from organized labor. The nature of these pressures and the way in which they are likely to operate in the period ahead require a closer examination.

The Nature of Trade Union Power

Trade union membership in Britain is substantially larger than in any other country in Western Europe, yet the effective power of the trade union organizations in the field of industrial relations is markedly less than elsewhere. This is the first paradox of British trade unionism, and it derives from the notions of grass-roots democracy that guide it.

The second paradox concerns unionism's political role. The trade union movement is an integral part of the main party of the Left and is its chief paymaster, in a fashion which is hardly known elsewhere in Western Europe; yet the trade union leadership does not generally play any significant part in politics at large, as it does in such countries as France and Italy. The Trades Union Congress has during most of the postwar period regarded itself as being, in political terms, a subsidiary of the Labour party; the parliamentary leaders of the party, who have largely determined its policies, have very rarely been heads of trade unions. Thus in spite of the theoretical ability of the trade unions to dominate Labour party policy-making through their control of overwhelming block votes at the party conferences, their positive influence on the actions of Labour governments outside the field of industrial relations has until recently been slight. There have been some negative influences, though, usually on matters where there is a traditional socialist taboo, of which certain trade union leaders like to make themselves the guardians.

These conventions have recently been subject to change, and it is possible to identify the origins of the new, activist trend with the last stages of the Labour government that went out of office in 1970. Faced with an accumulation of economic disappointments, which had together resulted in a complete failure to move towards the higher rates of economic growth boldly set out in the National Plan of 1965, the Labour leaders decided that it was time to tackle frontally one of the chief sources of national inefficiency—the chaotic state of British industrial relations. In doing so, however, they broke what had been regarded as an unwritten bargain with the party's trade union wing not to engage in any legislative tampering with this subject without its explicit say-so. The incident is worth considering in detail because of its longer-term consequences for the politics of the Left in Britain.

The issue came to a head in 1969 and centered on a white paper published by the government at the start of the year called, "In Place of Strife—A Policy for Industrial Relations" (Cmnd 3888). The legislative program set out in this document aimed to reduce the damage done to British industrial production by frequent and largely unpredictable short strikes. The Trades Union Congress argued back that these strikes, which were typically of short duration and involved relatively small numbers of people, were directly responsible for the loss of an infinitesimal proportion of total output—estimated at 1/10 of 1 per cent—in the course of a year.[11] Nevertheless the government persisted in the view that the disorderly character of British industrial relations, and in particular the absence of any authority capable of imposing a procedure for conciliation in disputes either with employers or between competing unions, seriously weakened Britain's economic effort.

A Royal Commission on the trade unions (Cmnd 3623; 1968) had in the previous year analyzed in some detail the sources of the industrial disorder and had shown that it arose largely through the action of informal workshop groups exercising effective day-to-day power and bargaining with management directly, in many cases with a minimum of control by the official trade unions. Here for the first time was a full statement of the paradox of a loss of effective industrial power by the trade unions concomitant with the growth of trade union membership. In a number of industries the trade union members used their membership cards largely as a license to conduct their purely local, workshop-centered disputes without hindrance from outsiders. The Royal Commission suggested that the road to improvement lay first in recognizing the facts of the transfer of effective power away from the center, and then in systematically building up a better relationship between workshop labor leaders and the official trade union organizations on the basis of a more decentralized system of industrial relations.

This was plainly a prescription for a long-term remedy. What the government proposed in its White Paper in 1969 was the creation immediately of a new authority, armed with legal powers to impose negotiation and arbitration procedures on the trade unions and their members. The constraints that it proposed to introduce were modest enough by the standards of other industrial countries with a legal framework for the conduct of industrial relations. But that was just the point: Britain had never recognized the need for such a legal framework; it had adopted instead, at the start of the twentieth century (in the Trade Disputes Act of 1906), the theory that trade unionism was a kind of licensed conspiracy that the courts would endeavor not to interfere with.

This theory may have had a certain legal convenience at an earlier stage, though by the second half of the twentieth century it had become a serious impediment to the assertion of the public interest. It was observed that whereas the British government had managed to introduce in the 1960s an effective code of legislative rules for the regulation of restrictive practices by business enterprises, it had not made any corresponding move to control even minimally the restrictions practiced in the name of trade unionism. For the British trade unions, however, this apparent anomaly was part of the order of nature. It was the propensity of other industrial nations to bring the authority of the law to bear on industrial bargaining and conflict that was regarded as odd. The conviction remained strong, in spite of the growing volume of evidence to the contrary, that the British could dispense with these artificial aids in managing their labor relations, simply because they were better at the job.

It is necessary to know this historical background in order to understand the fierce opposition that the Labour government's quite modest proposals aroused in the traditional trade union leadership. The leaders reacted as if they were being maltreated by a close friend who had never been given any cause for offense. The note of almost incredulous protest that emerges from the following statement of the TUC General Council in the summer of 1969, at the height of the conflict over the government's White Paper, conveys the mood: "Even if it is not moved by the fundamental opposition of all sections of the Trade Union Movement to the intrusion of punitive legislation into industrial relations, it [the government] should surely be influenced by the consideration that the controversy that its ill-judged proposals have caused will divert attention from dealing with the causes of industrial relations problems."[1][2]

Underlying the argument about principles there was of course a practical fear. This was that the introduction of standard, legally enforceable rules of procedure into industrial relations would make trade unions as organizations responsible for the activities of their members. It was this which was most especially unattractive. The British compromise on industrial relations had hitherto allowed the trade union leadership to claim political influence without industrial responsibility. The great struggle that now took place with the Labour government was chiefly about whether the British trade union leadership was to be allowed to continue in the comfortable mode of life to which it had become accustomed.

The struggle was remarkable for the energy that the Labour government put into it. By the time it lost the battle and formally abandoned any intention of legislating the reform of industrial relations, the experience had left deep marks on both sides. For the trade unions it was the start of an increasing politicization. After the defeat of the Labour party in the general election of 1970, the unions mounted an organized resistance, including systematic boycotts and defiance of courts, against the Conservative government's Industrial Relations Act, which sought to make them more responsible for the day-to-day conduct of industrial relations. The opposition to the Act was portrayed by the trade unions as a battle to sustain the democratic rights of groups of workers organized around their own work place and managing their relations with their employers as they thought best. The grass roots were being protected, it was alleged, against a right-wing conspiracy to force the imposition of trade union control from the top. This argument carried, and it proved possible to mobilize industrial workers for resistance to the Act.

In the course of the struggle, which was marked by two national strikes by the coal miners, in both of which the miners' union won its claims over government resistance, the political center of gravity of the trade union movement moved markedly left. Among other things, the movement took an unusually strong line on major issues of British foreign policy, notably against British membership in the European Economic Community. The Community was objectionable because it was seen as an incorrigibly capitalist enterprise, devoted to the use of unrestrained market forces for the enrichment of the business class at the expense of their employees.

The parliamentary leaders of the Labour party thus found on their return to office in 1974 that the trade unions had become a political force to be reckoned with as never before. The problem was further complicated by the political circumstances surrounding Labour's bare electoral victory with strong trade union support: it was accompanied by a loud chorus of contrition from Labour politicians for the party's previous conduct towards the trade unions. The party mythology had it that the earlier conflict with the trade unions was itself only an indication of how far a Labour government had allowed itself to lapse from the essential and abiding spirit of Labour party policy. In order to make amends, it was necessary to show that the trade unions were indeed being given their full weight in determining the political direction of the Labour party.

There was also a rather confused claim by the Labour government to a special kind of legitimacy because of its alliance with the trade unions—which were in turn treated, not as a sectional interest group, but as the representative of the interests of the whole of the working class, nonmembers as well as members. Thus when Mr. Harold Wilson explained to the nation his "Social Contract" with the Trades Union Congress—committing the latter to wage restraint in return for certain social and economic measures by the government (constituting the so-called social wage)—he argued that this was an agreement which in practice created an obligation for *all* employed workers. It was, he indicated, an earnest of the capacity of his government to bind substantially the whole of the "useful population" to its side. This was an attractive contention for a government that, even after the increased vote it had obtained in the second election of 1974, had still managed to attract the support of barely 40 per cent of the electorate. This was the lowest proportion polled by Labour from the end of the war until 1974. Labour had in fact only managed to take over power from the Conservatives because the greatly increased vote for the alternative parties, the Liberals and the Scottish and other Nationalist groups, had taken more from the Conservative party than from Labour. The British electorate had shown a marked swing away from them both.

It is nevertheless hard to see how the relationship between the government and organized labor could be maintained for long on the 1974 basis. At that time the problems that had led the Labour government in 1969 to defy the wishes of the trade unions had not disappeared; they had, if anything, been aggravated in the intervening five years. Business confidence, as reflected in the level of investment, was low and stubbornly refusing to revive. The volume of real investment in manufacturing industry was still below the point it had reached in 1970. Meanwhile the British record for industrial delivery and performance continued poor, and there were widespread indications that Britain was now losing business as a result. The evidence of the early 1970s pointed clearly to an inability on the part of British industry to exploit its highly competitive prices in international competition, the result of the downward float of sterling in the general realignment of currency values from 1971 onwards. The most noticeable effect of the British price advantage was that order books lengthened; there was apparently no sufficient margin of spare capacity to secure a rapid increase in deliveries to customers. This was so in spite of the fact that the level of British unemployment was now notably high by international standards. At an estimated 6.2 per cent in 1972 (using a standard measure of international comparison based on U.S. definitions),[13] it was much the highest in Western Europe.

The secondary effects of persistent low growth and low investment were beginning to make themselves seriously felt. The essential trade-off, which could no longer be evaded, was between keeping up the number of jobs and keeping down the cost of labor per unit of output. While labor costs rose at the expense of profits, there was little prospect of securing the rise in productive investment necessary for the effective functioning of the British economy. This was the point that had come home to the Labour Chancellor of the Exchequer, Mr. Denis Healey, and a number of his ministerial colleagues by the end of 1974. After a fairly extended period in which the rise in the real incomes of wage and salary earners had been sustained in part ·by the progressive reduction of the share of profits in the national income, the process had to be reversed. Positive action had to be taken to protect profits.

What this requirement implies for the *political* management of the British economy can perhaps be most readily seen by taking a brief look at the corresponding set of circumstances as they appeared in West Germany in 1974. There too there had been an erosion—though not so long or so sustained as in Britain—of the share of profit incomes in favor of wage incomes. Business investment, though still high by international standards, had slowed down and looked like slowing down further. The bargain which the German government, under the leadership of the Social Democrats, struck with the trade unions in the autumn of 1974 explicitly took account of the need for profits to rise at a faster rate than wages during the period ahead. The basic agreement was of an essentially political character: the government on its side committed itself to fiscal and monetary arrangements aimed at overcoming the business recession and securing a higher rate of economic growth, and the unions in return committed themselves to a tight curb on wage claims. The bargain was clearly understood by the Deutscher Gewerkschaftsbund (DGB: German Trade Union Federation) as a trade-off between more employment and smaller increases in real wages. The government for its part was put on notice that it was expected to achieve the promised drop in unemployment well before the end of 1975. In the event, it failed to fulfill its promise; but the agreement was nevertheless renewed for the year 1976.

This is precisely the kind of bargain the British Labour government has been hankering for but can hardly achieve unless there is a reform of the structure of the trade unions. There would be little difficulty on the government side—less difficulty, in fact, than in Germany, where the federal government does not have the same control over such critical economic variables as the money supply. On the trade union side, moreover, feelings of loyalty towards the Labour party are at least as strong as those of the DGB towards the Social Democratic party in Germany. What is missing in Britain is a locus of authority in the trade union movement capable of making such a trade-off between employment and wage claims stick. Even now, after the government was able to move in 1975 from a highly ambiguous "social contract" to a clear agreement with the major unions laying down a uniform maximum wage increase for any and all workers, the Trades Union Congress has yet to establish formal machinery for vetting individual wage claims or for forcing any deviants to fall into line.

These, then, are the reasons why it is most improbable that a confrontation between government and the trade unions can be long avoided. The problem has been made acute by the particular economic circumstances that have produced a combination of inflation with recession in the mid-1970s. But the underlying reality, which politicians of all parties have been finding increasingly unac-ceptable, is the refusal of the trade unions to accept effective responsibility for ensuring positive industrial performance, corresponding to their negative power to disrupt industry, while insisting on their full share in the political government of the country.

The conflict that is in prospect is bound to have very wide political repercussions. Only a government that visibly commands the support of an overwhelming majority of the electorate could force through a reform of labor relations after the two failed attempts, first by Labour and then by the Conservatives, in the late 1960s and early 1970s. That, in the circumstances of British politics, necessarily implies a coalition government, since single-party government under the British multiparty system almost invariably means that the governing party is sustained by less than 50 per cent of the voters. No government since the war has managed to poll as much as 50 per cent of the vote in any general election.

One reason why a government engaged in the kind of conflict envisaged here would have to be sustained by the visible support of a substantial majority of the population is that it would be faced with the need to tackle both aspects of trade union responsibility simultaneously, namely, the raising of industrial productivity and the curbing of wage increases. The second issue has taken precedence in the extreme inflationary conditions of the mid-1970s. It has also become clear—and this marks a change from the intermittent attempts to tackle the wage problem on an emergency basis in the course of the various crises since the war—that the need for severe restriction of wage earnings will last for quite a long time. That is because the level of consumption must be held down for an extended period in order to secure both the additional resources necessary to eliminate Britain's huge balance-of-payments deficit and to supply the extra investment required for a sharp increase in productive capacity. Such a transfer of resources to foreign trade and investment could only be gradual, and it would probably occupy most of the remainder of the 1970s.

It will undoubtedly be greatly eased in the later stages by the rapid growth of British oil production in the North Sea. Without this, indeed, it would be hard to feel any hope at all that the process can be accomplished. The North Sea, which will be making a large net contribution to the British balance of payments by 1980, even after allowance has been made for the servicing of the considerable sums borrowed in the interval to meet balance-of-payments deficits from 1973 onwards, offers a unique opportunity. It could make it possible for Britain to compass the changes that are needed in its economy without the trauma of actual deprivation. The open question is whether the political will is there.

The Politics of Polarization

The argument so far has been based on a number of premises. First, the political elites in Britain are by now ready for a period of radical reform designed to make the economy function more productively and efficiently. Second, the leaders of organized labor will not spontaneously make the large contribution required of them towards such a program of reform. Third, the combination of acute economic crisis and consistent failure to achieve structural changes by piecemeal measures in the recent past will probably have the effect of forcing the government into a conflict with the trade unions. The prospect is that it will have to exercise its power to determine the distribution of the national income in a sense which will be seen to be adverse to the interest of powerful groups of wage earners who occupy strategic positions in British society. Fourth, the government will only be able to meet this challenge by obtaining the visible support of the great majority of the British population by means of some form of party coalition.

Something more needs to be said about the nature of the prospective political conflict. It should be made clear that it would not be aimed—always assuming that it is rationally conducted on the government side—at smashing the power of the big trade unions. On the contrary, it would be an invitation to the leaders of these trade unions to assert their power more effectively, over their own members as well as in their relations with the rest of society. In the end a successful policy of economic reform of the kind sketched out earlier can be conducted only with the willing assent of the wage earners. The membership of the trade union movement is in any case much too large in Britain for it to be successfully challenged in a frontal assault like that attempted by the Conservative government of Mr. Heath. The problem is how to overcome the movement's inertia and the fragmentation of its power.

"One of the maddest things about our present system is that workers are confined in effect to wage bargaining. They are not allowed to know anything about investment or to discuss the future strategy of their company...."[14] The statement comes from Mr. Tony Benn, the leader of the radical Left inside the Labour government, who was minister for industry at the time (1974). He has consistently advocated active worker participation in management as a means of raising productivity. Not surprisingly, in view of the trade unions' cherished freedom from any form of contractual obligation, they have traditionally resisted the suggestion that they share responsibility for management decisions. Recently, however, there have been some signs of change. The struggle to involve the trade union leadership in the conduct of national economic policy, aimed at bringing about a new relationship between government and trade unions analogous to that which has long been established in Germany, Scandinavia, and Holland, could possibly hinge on this issue of participation in management.

Yet even if the effort to establish a new kind of responsible trade unionism in Britain were successful, the action itself would almost inevitably produce an extreme polarization of politics on the left. In this situation a Labour government would need the support of other parties to overcome the opposition of its left wing. The inhibitions to such a course of action are considerable. There is in the Labour party an intense suspicion of almost any form of coalition government, dating from the experience of the right-wing National Government formed under the premiership of the Labour party's own leader in 1931. If, as is probable in the circumstances envisaged, the Labour party were to split sharply between right and left, the resulting political alignment would be more like that of France or Italy than of Germany and Scandinavia. The split would give rise to an important independent party of the left—not necessarily Marxist, but more in the abstentionist, anti-capitalist spirit of traditional British left-wing politics— which, like the Communists in France and Italy, would be regarded as permanently excluded from government. The long-term political consequences of such a change would clearly depend on the size of the intransigent Labour Left that established itself after the split. It is perhaps worth recalling that when the Socialist party split in France after the First World War, the Communists, who were able to mobilize a majority of the votes, took over virtually everything including the Party newspaper. This gave them a head start in the long and bitter struggle for working-class support that followed. In Britain the established leaders of the Labour party would be extremely wary of any realignment of forces that left them with the support of only a minority of the Labour vote inside a coalition with the Conservatives.

There are in fact two types of political realignment which appear highly improbable. One is a coalition with a Labour minority on the 1931 model; the other is a "popular front" coalition between the intransigent left Socialists (after a Labour split) and the smaller parties, consisting of the Liberals and the regional nationalist groups. It is much more probable that in a period of extreme polarization of the kind that would accompany a program of thoroughgoing economic reform and an effective ceiling on the real incomes of wage earners, the terrain for the making of governments in Britain would lie in the center. The evidence suggests that there is a large nonideological body of supporters attached to the two main parties, Labour and Conservative, as well as most obviously to the Liberals (who have recently been polling close to one fifth of the total vote), that could in certain circumstances be readily mobilized to sustain a national program with specific aims and of limited duration addressed to a recognized emergency.

The nearest analogy that suggests itself here is that of the "Grand Coalition" of the CDU and the SPD in Germany, which was formed in 1966 when the politicians on both sides finally recognized that it was not possible to cope with the most pressing question of German foreign policy—that of relations with the Soviet bloc and with East Germany at the heart of it—without a visible manifestation of national consensus in government. In the British case there is no comparable external threat that can be used to call up a national impulse to unite. On the other hand, Britain has the advantage of not having to reckon with a powerful Communist party commanding massive working class support, whose presence in countries such as France and Italy restricts the room for maneuver of the other political parties. It is the absence of the Communist obstacle that gave Germany, and may give Britain, the opportunity to form a coalition government with the kind of exceptional authority required to compass a major change in direction of national policy.

The political drive to produce such a result may, however, prove after all to be lacking. In that case the probable outcome is not an early sharp deterioration in British domestic politics and in the nation's capacity to play a part in the international system, but rather a slow and continuous process of enfeeblement. Britain's *relative* decline could continue for some time, while the majority of its inhabitants enjoyed some modest rise in living standards.

Implicit in this scenario is a probable failure to overcome Britain's special inflationary problem, with the consequence that British prices continue to rise at a significantly higher rate than those of competing industrial countries. It is, however, wrong to suppose that inflation will by itself prevent the British economy from generating a continuing rise in real income. Constant devaluations of the currency would be used to maintain the competitive position of British goods sold abroad, while at home the government could, by an extension of the fiscal measures that it had begun to introduce in 1974-75, ensure that the broad distribution of the available resources between consumption and investment, wages and profits, and public and private expenditures was broadly maintained. There is at any rate no inherent reason why this should prove impossible.

It could be plausibly argued that in order to achieve the required result in the conditions postulated here, there would have to be increasingly vigorous and determined interference by the state and its apparatus in many of the ordinary processes of what has hitherto been regarded as private life; and that such a change could be brought about in practice only by a democratic government supported by an overwhelming popular consensus, which in British circumstances would almost inevitably mean a coalition of the main parties, or by some form of authoritarian regime. But let us assume that the British genius for muddling through—or more exactly in this instance, for muddling on—continues to assert itself, and that the party political system as we now know it is preserved, while the increase in social conflict is somehow contained without a significant realignment of political power. Is there some predictable breaking point in the process of slow national enfeeblement when the strains on people and their institutions would generate an overwhelming crisis of a kind that would compel a drastic change of policy?

It is hard to discern any such clear compulsion, in spite of the obvious sources of popular discontent. It is worth examining the latter briefly, in terms of the specific consequences of Britain's relative decline for wages and for the migration of workers. What has to be envisaged is a disparity of wage rates between Britain and its neighbors on the continent of Europe which is comparable to that which now separates southern Italy from West Germany. At the same time, it has to be assumed that the level of productive investment is insufficient in Britain to employ all the available manpower at the minimum wage rates which organized labor has effectively established. The outcome in periods of world economic prosperity would be that British workers would be drawn in considerable numbers towards neighboring European countries, where the wage level would be up to 100 per cent higher than at home. Britain's balance of payments would benefit from the remittances sent home by these migratory workers to their families—at least so long as the whole family did not emigrate to join the main wage earner abroad. But even this gain would have to be balanced against the cost incurred in the education and welfare of Britain's emigrating workers before they became productive. In periods of economic recession or merely of a slowdown in world economic expansion, Britain would tend to suffer from a higher level of unemployment than its neighbors.

Meanwhile it is to be assumed that the growing disparity of earnings between Britain and the continent of Europe in the more mobile professions would lead to a substantial outflow of highly qualified personnel in management, medicine, teaching, and so on. In this respect, the case would be less like that of southern Italy and more akin to that of India, which despite a low general standard of living produces a substantial class of professionally qualified people whose skills are in high demand abroad. There is already a sustained and considerable emigration of British medical doctors (which has hitherto been largely offset by the immigration of doctors from India and Pakistan), which in the circumstances envisaged must be expected to grow considerably and to spread to many other professions. This, together with the outward movement of young and capable industrial workers, would tend to reinforce the cycle of national decline.

Britain is especially vulnerable to such a talent drain. For one thing, it has the talent—large numbers of highly qualified people who possess the training and the skills which are in heavy demand in the industrial world. The threat that migration poses in the long run is to impoverish the society by taking away substantial numbers of its elites. For another, Britain has access to the rest of Europe owing to its membership in the European Community, which is making it increasingly easy to transfer one's place of work from one country to another with a minimum of formalities. There are also the traditional opportunities in English-speaking lands overseas.

It is of course reasonable to suppose that low British wages would also have the effect of attracting more industrial investment from abroad. This could make a useful contribution towards remedying the deficiency that was the original source of the decline. It is not to be imagined, however, that spontaneous market forces will provide a fully self-correcting mechanism for the British economy. The outcome will clearly depend on keeping British real wages low enough to offer the foreign investor a competitive return, in spite of markedly lower levels of British productivity. In practice the ready availability of alternative employment in the European Community will push British wage rates above the level that they would have reached if there had been no such ready escape available. It has to be recognized, too, that successful enterprises seeking to extend their business operations abroad are often moved in their choice of location by the prospect of being involved in rapid development. They like to feel that they are latching onto a dynamic economy. The kind of Britain that I have been describing in this alternative scenario of gradual enfeeblement, a country which is visibly losing its talented and highly qualified personnel and from which ambitious wage earners wish to escape, is hardly likely to be very attractive. Nevertheless, it must be conceded that the cushioning effects of the inward movement of foreign investment and of the outward movement of dissatisfied people who would otherwise be inclined to stir up trouble at home mean that the alternative scenario is rendered that much more possible and tolerable.

Why, then, should the hypothesis of a sharp break with existing political trends, which I adumbrated earlier, be regarded as the more probable outcome? The reason essentially is the evidence—based admittedly on past performance rather than on any identifiable features in the current situation—that there is still sufficient vigor in the British political system to take a grip on an increasingly disruptive and inefficient economic system, and to do so before the latter destroys what is still a fairly coherent and structured society. What is being postulated as the cause of the sharp exacerbation of conflict in Britain and of the polarization of politics described above is an action deliberately initiated by the political elites. There is no sudden crisis in advance that will enforce this course of action. The argument is rather that there is a high probability at some early stage of a powerful political response to the prospect sketched out in what I have called the "alternative scenario."

Such a movement would of necessity derive initially from the middle class professional and managerial groups. But its effectiveness would depend on its capacity to mobilize mass support for a program of radical change. It is important to distinguish between the kind of leadership that is envisaged for a movement of this kind and the traditional style of middle class politics in Western Europe. It would, for example, have nothing in common with the disgruntled shopkeepers' and farmers' movements that have become familiar in France and elsewhere. On the contrary, those who would set the tone in this case would typically be people who work in large organizations, including organizations like trade unions, or members of the liberal professions working in the ambience of such organizations. The number of people engaged in these managerial and quasi-managerial tasks in Britain is not small: the available data suggest that they may well amount to more than 15 per cent of the active working population.[a] These four million odd people, many of them employed in government agencies and public authorities of one kind or another, have in fact constituted the leading element in British public life for some time past, and the mood and tone of public opinion is still powerfully influenced by them. A foreigner visiting Britain for the first time is likely to be less impressed by the acknowledged decline in the status of the professional and managerial elites than by the moral authority that they still command in running the day-to-day affairs of the country. Voluntary unpaid public service is still widely given in Britain, and much of it comes from this class.

I do not want to suggest, of course, that there would be uniform support from this class for a political movement of radical change on the lines indicated. I think it is clear, however, that if such a movement materialized, it would have to depend heavily both for its initial impulse and for its sustained organization on the managerial and quasi-managerial elites to whom I have referred. That these people should organize themselves in the manner of a mass movement would be highly unusual. It is indeed assumed that such behavior would only emerge as part of a wider political impulse involving the professional and middle classes generally in unaccustomed protest activities—ranging from rent and income tax strikes to the banning of "overtime" work by hospital doctors—of which early signs are not wanting.

It would be idle to try to specify the ideology that might be expected to guide a movement of this kind. But it is worth making the point that it would almost surely not be a reaction against the underlying liberal principles of British political life—a latter-day version of fascism sponsored by a resurgent upper class. It would probably be anticorporatist in spirit. But it would aim to use the power of the state to reassert the primacy of the public interest over sectional interests that too readily escape from public control, and it would not be surprising, therefore, if its rhetoric were to develop patriotic and even authoritarian overtones. Campaigns for reform often produce such noises.

---

[a]They are identified broadly with "social classes" I and II (out of a total of five classes covering the whole population) in British census data.

What makes this kind of political scenario so elusive is that there is no simple line-up between the haves and have-nots or between other major groups with clearly opposing interests. The great debate about the proper division between private and public enterprise will have little to do with the case. Nor is the future of the welfare state conceived to be at issue. Indeed, the reforms that are likely to be proposed on behalf of the public interest will almost certainly involve the state in more active and wide-ranging intervention in many forms of economic activity. That would in any case probably be a necessary condition for obtaining the active collaboration of large numbers of British trade unionists in an extended process of economic renovation; and unless they are persuaded to collaborate, it is hard to see how the program of reform could succeed.

I should, however, emphasize that there is no presumption here of a successful mass mobilization to change the management of the British economy and society. What is being postulated is only a high probability that a major attempt to bring about the change will be made and that, whether successful or not, it will result in social and political conflict of an intensity that has not been experienced in recent British history. I have suggested where the initial political impulse might come from. If it is to proceed further, the catalyst will have to be supplied by the politicians themselves. They might in ordinary circumstances be expected to eschew such an unenviable task. The opposite expectation derives from the fact that a significant number of leading politicians in all parties had by the mid-1970s concluded, after the consistent failure of the policy of small steps to lead to major economic reform, that a large-scale and sustained effort directed over several years towards certain nationally agreed objectives was a necessary condition for the economic renovation of Britain.

Foreign Policy in the 1970s and 1980s

Given a political and economic scenario of this type, what would be the likely role of a British government in the international system? Before answering that question we need to take note of certain characteristics of the starting point: where British foreign policy had got to by the mid-1970s. Perhaps its most remarkable feature is its constancy in the postwar period. Over some thirty-five years, in the course of which Britain's position in the world has profoundly changed, the main constituent elements of British foreign policy have undergone very little modification. The primacy allotted to the American alliance, the anxiety about the assumed ever-present threat of military expansion by the Soviet Union, the presumption that it is in the national interest to play a part in shaping international relations in Africa and Asia—all these survived into the early 1970s.

The original lack of enthusiasm for British membership in the European Community derived, so far as could be judged, not from any serious questioning of the established foreign policy objectives of Britain but rather from the skepticism of a large part of the population about the need for any significant institutional change as part of a bargain with foreigners—whether Europeans or others. This was not isolationist sentiment. There was still a strong sense of being connected with distant countries overseas. The general consensus among politicians, even during the years of acute balance-of-payments difficulties, about the need to maintain the level of budgetary expenditure on foreign aid for development, without any significant popular demur, is an expression of that sentiment. What is much less readily accepted is the greatly increased dependence of the national welfare on intimate collaboration with Western neighbors—always excepting the dependence on the United States, which is regarded as a case apart. Huddling together with a lot of other West European nations was, in the popular perception, instinctively not viewed as an effective way of protecting the national interest against international disruption. Even the overwhelming support for membership of the European Community registered in the referendum of 1975 needs to be carefully interpreted as an index of popular sentiment. It was not a vote for change, it was a vote for staying in Europe, not for going in.

The decline in Britain's overseas commitments in Asia, Africa, and most recently in the Mediterranean has been such a slow and piecemeal process that it has not impinged fully on the consciousness of the British people. There is a marked lag in perception, with Britain still seen as a country which willingly shoulders the burden of a quite disproportionate international responsibility—even though stringency in the public purse may have made it necessary to drop a certain number of commitments on the way. The important point is that the decline of Britain's international role as a great power had not until the 1970s been accompanied by any popular revulsion of feeling against international involvement as such. Even when the Labour government proceeded in 1975 to carry out the promise of its general election manifesto to cut the national defense budget, it justified its action to the public by arguing that it was only adjusting British spending on defense, as a proportion of the gross national product, to the lower level that had been established by France and Germany.[b]

The anticipated sharpening of social conflict has to be set against this record of remarkable stability of political sentiment. Some might regard it merely as stolidity. In any case, it continues to manifest itself at its best in a self-conscious resistance to panic decisions—seen most recently in the low-key response to the killing of British soldiers in Northern Ireland and to the bombings by Irish terrorists in England. This kind of attitude is the other side of the entrenched tendency, which has figured so largely in the analysis of this essay, to be exceedingly slow to recognize a challenge to the basic structures of national existence for what it is. It is part of the strong preference for the piecemeal

---

[b]Its calculation was that the proposed cuts spread over a number of years would bring the proportion of GNP spent on defense down from 5-1/2 per cent to 4-1/2 per cent (the contemporary ratio in France and Germany).

response and of the propensity to believe that a tactical answer, if it is skilfully managed, will suffice to deal with most problems.

It would, however, be wrong in my view to analyze the probable international effects of Britain's changing position by extrapolating these established trends into the future. A continuation of the process of slow-motion, unruffled withdrawal from a few more international commitments seems unlikely. The reasons for that judgment are implicit in the following attempt to envisage the elements in British international policy-making in the 1970s and 1980s.

1. As regards Britain's military commitments, they have now been reduced— after the projected withdrawal of all but a token force from the Mediterranean— to a level where further economies of any significance can only be made if there is a fundamental change in British policy about the defense of the continent of Europe. We are very close to the hard core of the defense budget and of Britain's treaty obligations towards its European allies. The next step would almost of necessity raise the question whether Britain wished to have any forces whatsoever committed to military action beyond its own geographical confines—whether in fact, in an age of strategic balance between the superpowers, a medium-sized island nation was not particularly well placed to withdraw into its shell and content itself with a strictly local self-defense force after the pattern of Japan. Britain would, if it adopted this option, have the additional safeguard (not available to Japan) against possible attack by a nation which was not a superpower, of its own aging, but not insignificant, nuclear armory. The attraction of this posture, in the circumstances of economic stringency here postulated, would be that nuclear weapons, established at a given level of technology without any serious attempt to upgrade them to meet any new threats posed by improvements in the nuclear armory of the superpowers, could provide a cheap defense option.

Whether such an option is likely to be seriously contemplated by Britain will depend on a number of factors that are considered further below. It is, however, worth registering the general point at this stage that British attitudes towards the defense commitment on the continent of Europe will be closely affected by the relationship with the European Community. It is obvious that although the Community's formal treaty commitments make no mention whatsoever of defense, the political partnership which is characteristic of the Community of the 1970s—entailing the obligation to consult on all important matters and to *try* to reach concerted policies towards the rest of the world—could hardly be sustained in the face of a deliberate British decision to withdraw from its defense engagements on the continent of Europe. The crucial relationship with the German Federal Republic would suffer most particularly. One could indeed plausibly argue that from the point of view of the United States, the maintenance of an enlarged European Community with Britain inside it is in this sense a major objective of policy in the second half of the 1970s. The manner in which the United States handles any force reductions of its own in Western Europe will clearly be another important influence on British policy.

2. A major consideration in determining the direction of international policy will be the changing self-image of the British people. As I indicated earlier, this image had by the early 1970s been modified much less than the reality of Britain's altered position in the world; and this lag in perception had in turn helped stabilize foreign policy. The danger is that in the next stage the adjustment to reality may in consequence have to take place too rapidly and on too many fronts at the same time.

Any forecast of the likely shifts in something so imprecise and elusive as a nation's self-image is bound to be hazardous. Yet no serious discussion of the British prospect can altogether avoid it. There are two elements in its composition that are fairly readily identifiable and that seem to me to be especially worth noting. The first is the sense of secure national cohesion, in the simplest physical sense. For a unitary state of long standing like the United Kingdom, this is an unconsidered assumption of national life. In this Britain is one of the fortunate few in Western Europe—like France and quite unlike Germany and Italy. For a country of this type the secession of a substantial province like Northern Ireland, if it were to occur, would be a new and wholly unfamiliar experience. It is an event which is moderately probable by the end of the 1970s.

Even if separation occurred as a result of British weariness and frustration and had all the trappings of a deliberate and statesmanlike decision, it could have some traumatic quality—if it coincided with other events tending to undermine the national identity. The loss of one province in Northern Ireland would, it is reasonable to anticipate, greatly encourage the politics of separatism in Scotland. The separatists would not need to be ultimately successful in attaining all their objectives in these circumstances in order to shake the morale of the English. In that case Welsh separatism, which has hitherto been a relatively weak though vociferous movement, would tend to loom much larger at the very least in the English imagination if not in the reality of Welsh politics. It is unnecessary to pursue the detail of such a scenario. It is enough to indicate how these events could exacerbate the sense of having failed and of being isolated.

A second identifiable element in the traditional British self-image which is likely to be subject to change is that of a nation with a unique interest in the prosperity and freedom of world commerce. It has been a fixed assumption that Britain is more dependent for its welfare than any other major nation on an efficiently functioning world economy and that therefore it is sensible on occasion, even on the basis of hard-headed and selfish calculation, to sacrifice short-term national convenience to longer-term international objectives. Again, there has been some lag in perception, as other nations have increased their share of world exports at Britain's expense and have become markedly more dependent than in the past on the prosperity and buying power of foreign markets. Ask a group of moderately informed British businessmen about this, and you will find that very few of them have come to realize that Germany's national product is more dependent proportionately on merchandise exports than Britain's.

For the future, it is almost inevitable that the main effort to restore Britain's balance-of-payments to equilibrium during the 1970s will be concentrated on import saving. The two fields in which the expansion of home production to replace imports will take effect most rapidly are energy and food. The relatively efficient development of British agriculture since the war has already made Britain self-sufficient to the extent of nearly 70 per cent for its consumption of temperate-zone products. Plausible calculations of the long-term effects of the European Community's Common Agricultural Policy on the shape of British agriculture suggest that by 1980 Britain's net imports of grain and of beef could be largely eliminated.[15] It is quite possible that by then Britain's self-sufficient ratio in temperate-zone food products will be approaching 80 per cent. The outcome depends in part on the energy with which the policy of agricultural expansion is pressed. It seems highly probable that in the context of threatening food shortages, and after such unhappy experiences as the diversion of Britain's normal imports of West Indian cane sugar in 1974-75, the policy will be pressed very hard indeed.[16] It would, of course, represent a dramatic reversal of the traditional policy of cheap food and the open door for the world's agricultural exports that has been the dominant feature of British commercial ideology—though decreasingly of its practice—for a century and a quarter.

In fact a reduction of British food imports of the order of magnitude indicated above, combined with the elimination of net imports of energy by 1980, would convert Britain into a country whose dependence on foreign trade was medium to low by West European standards. The proportion of GNP derived from foreign trade, if the current forecasts of import saving were realized, would be closer to 20 per cent than to the average figure of over 25 per cent reached by the European Community of the Six at the beginning of the 1970s. The long-term significance of this outcome may be expressed by noting the fact that the British ratio of foreign trade would in these circumstances approximate to that of Italy and be markedly below that of the North European group of industrial trading countries—Scandinavia, Benelux, and West Germany.

German economic leadership in northern Europe is one result of the changing situation which is already firmly established. There is little reason to suppose that Britain's continued involvement in international financial transactions and trade in services will significantly offset the trend that appears to be in prospect. Of the traditional sources of income from services, Britain's merchant fleet no longer produces any net earnings, after allowing for the foreign-exchange cost of the transport of British imports; and the rest of the marketing and financial operations of the City of London, with the single exception of insurance, make a relatively modest contribution to the balance of payments.

The consequence of these developments for Britain's views of its own interests in the international system may perhaps be indicated by a suggestive analogy with another country, Canada. The Canadians, having assumed for a long time that their strictly national aims were best served by adopting an active internationalist posture, have shifted in recent times towards a narrower and more exclusive view of their interests. Britain, in the circumstances envisaged, would tend to respond to requests for access to its oil in the North Sea in much the same spirit as the Canadians in their dialogue with the United States, that is, by arguing that it must on no account risk its future national self-sufficiency in oil. There are also signs that the British, like the Canadians, will tend to view the seas around their shores more as a national preserve to be extended as far as possible, rather than in the traditional manner of a maritime nation for whom the freedom of the seas is a dominant concern.

Again, it is worth noting that what may be called the "Canada syndrome" will be attenuated by British membership in the European Community. It would, for example, be extremely difficult for Britain to adopt a strict, national oil conservation policy in its commercial relations with its partners in the Community, on the model of that taken by Canada towards the United States. Similarly, the issue of the limits of national jurisdiction over what have hitherto been international waters will necessarily take a different form so long as Britain is negotiating from a joint position inside the European Community.

3. Against this background, let us examine some of the specific ways in which the movement for radical economic reform postulated in the earlier analysis might impinge on Britain's international relationships. The attempt at economic reform (it is worth insisting again that all that is being predicted is an attempt, not a successful conclusion) is seen, it will be recalled, as entailing a high degree of state intervention. It will be directed simultaneously to the two sides of the economic equation: to the supply side, by means of a systematic attack on the operational practices of industry combined with a sharp increase in labor-saving investment; and to the demand side, by strict supervision and control over the distribution of real incomes. The latter would comprise unfamiliar kinds of interference with consumer spending, including severe restriction of those types of demand that would divert resources from the priority needs of investment and exports. The two characteristic features of the management of such an economy would be, first, the acceptance of an *unfamiliar* degree of austerity by consumers, and second, the exercise of an unusual degree of authority, emanating in one way or another from governments that are themselves sustained by a powerful consensus of the electorate, over the performance and rewards of both management and wage earners. Simply enumerating the conditions for the success of such a program serves to remind one of its difficulty. What I am concerned with, however, are the international consequences of making the attempt.

It is at once apparent that a political and social atmosphere of this kind would almost certainly be inimical to the liberal treatment of the export interests of other nations in the British market. It must be expected that import restrictions will probably become a normal feature of the British economy for a time. Furthermore, these restrictions are likely to be discriminatory in their effects—not because of any desire to aim them at particular countries, but because of the sharp distinction that British authorities may be expected to make between "essential" and "inessential" imports, in the light of some principle of fair shares that is believed to be acceptable to the British public. The logic of whatever principle is adopted and the consequential restriction of certain kinds of imports are not going to be immediately convincing to all outsiders. In these circumstances foreign exporters will have a lot of grievances against Britain.

These measures have to be put into the context of the more general difficulty that the industrial nations face in maintaining the momentum of the liberal trade policies established, through the GATT and other international institutions, during the quarter of a century following World War II. It is not only that the British government will be inclined to make quantitative import restrictions an integral part of the management of the national economy. In approaching the new generation of international issues, it will tend to adopt an extremely cautious attitude in which short-term national interests will predominate.

To sum up, in the negotiations of the second half of the 1970s, which will be concerned with the management of increasing interdependence in the Western world, Britain is highly unlikely to play a positive role. In a world in which the forces making for economic nationalism and autarky may well be stronger than they were during the 1950s and 1960s, British policies will tend to be especially inward-looking. Moreover, there will be good and cogent reasons for such a posture: an open British economy would run particularly large risks in the circumstances envisaged. A systematic effort to suppress consumer demand at home, while keeping production expanding at a fast rate, would inevitably cause strains of a type that could most readily be relieved by additional imports, but at the price of a larger deficit of the balance-of-payments. The rationing of imports may thus come to be regarded as almost a necessary condition of an economic policy that aims simultaneously at a massive increase in industrial investment and at an improvement in the balance of payments.

The evidence of recent years suggests in any case that the British propensity to import, in relation to a given increase in domestic incomes, is exceptionally high by European standards.[17] This is another manifestation of the general sluggishness of British industry in responding to market opportunities, whether at home or abroad. It is arguable that until British industry has reequipped and reorganized itself in ways that make its productive capacity grow faster, it will not be possible to finance the full cost of the sharp increase in consumer import demand that must be expected to occur during a period of rapid economic expansion. The argument is a variation on one usually applied to less developed countries in the early stages of industrial growth, when import restrictions (in the context of limited export capacity) are a necessary condition for achieving full employment.

In the British case there may well be persuasive arguments pointing the other way. No matter; the policy outcome is likely to be determined on political grounds. In the conditions postulated, where there is a severe incomes policy that holds down wages as a trade-off for maintaining full employment, the case for import controls as part of the armory of austerity is likely to appear overwhelming. The question then is how the international community at large would respond to a highly restrictive British trade policy. Perhaps the very diminution of Britain's importance as a market for world trade—in the late 1970s it will almost certainly rank below France in the league table of importing countries—may in this instance produce some offsetting benefits. It should at any rate be easier to restrain the impulse of injured parties to engage in retaliation than it would have been in the past. The risk of disruption of the international trading system could in that case be contained.

The odds in favor of containment will be greater with Britain inside the European Community, with a firm long-term commitment to an open trading policy towards its partners. It is to be assumed, for example, that they would insist on the right of surveillance over the operation of British import controls as part of the bargain allowing Britain to retain its free access to their markets as a member of the customs union. In these circumstances a liberal, and self-denying, attitude on the part of the United States, whose export interests would almost inevitably be subject to some discrimination by Britain in the process, would be required. The argument for adopting such an attitude would be that the essential framework of rules sustaining the international trading system would be best safeguarded by treating Britain as a special case while it was trying to carry through its program of radical economic reform—in the same spirit as the United States treated Europe as a whole during the period of postwar recovery, when Europe was given a temporary and supervised license to discriminate against dollar goods, on the promise of good behavior later on.

The European Community will in any case have problems enough in accommodating itself to a Britain that pursues a highly *étatiste* approach to the management of the national economy on the lines suggested above. Some of this is unavoidable anyway: it has for some time been clear that the European Community must face the need to adapt the laissez-faire assumptions underlying the Treaty of Rome to the changed conditions of policy-making in the 1970s and 1980s. In particular the old prejudice in favor of what was "communautaire," as opposed to intergovernmental, because the former bypassed the control of national governments, will have to be recognized as obsolescent.

Conclusions for United States Policy

The main considerations for United States policy can be summarized as follows:

Britain faces the prospect of sharply increased domestic conflict in the course of any attempt to overcome its economic weakness. This and other objective factors will make the country more inward-looking and the government less able to mobilize support for the traditional objectives of foreign policy.

Strongly interventionist government policies, combined with a decline in the relative importance accorded to international transactions, will tend to make Britain an unhelpful partner in the increasingly complicated management of international interdependence.

An important problem will probably be to contain the effects of British economic nationalism as a potential source of disorder in the international system. This may require similar diplomatic skills and patience to those which were applied to France in the 1950s and 1960s.

There is, however, no reason to anticipate that Britain will turn against the Atlantic alliance. What is more likely is that in the anticipated mood of withdrawal and national uncertainty, the British will be inclined to act more like a "free rider" on the international security system. The decisive factor will be whether Britain can be kept fully committed to the defense of the Central Front in Europe; United States decisions on the deployment of its own forces in Europe will be highly influential here.

In the incipient United States–German special relationship it will be important to watch for and anticipate British anxieties. Britain's international policies could be adversely affected—and so could Anglo-German relations—if it came to appear that Germany had not only replaced Britain as America's chief partner in Europe, but had also cut Britain out from privileged consultation with and access to the United States. It is worth making the point that any possible resurgence of German nationalist sentiment, with overtones of increased friction with the Soviet Union, will be easier to handle if there is at least one other important NATO member fully committed to the defense of Germany. It would make sense, during the period of anticipated acute strain on the British economy, for the United States to stand ready, in case of need, to provide some direct financial contribution to the British defense budget as a reinsurance against cuts in the British military establishment in Germany.

The retreat from internationalist policies (which has been sketched out with deliberate starkness in the simplified scenario reflecting the most probable development of policies in the late 1970s) is more likely to be contained and prevented from acquiring the overtones of neutralism if Britain remains an active member of the European Community. It should be a prime objective of United States policy to encourage Britain, whenever this is feasible, to maintain and if possible reinforce its European connection. The chances of Britain's continuing as a leading and effective member of the Western alliance in the 1980s probably depend chiefly on the vitality of that connection.

There will be temptations for the United States to divide the all too easily divisible members of the Community in the trade negotiations of the Tokyo Round, in the discussions on international energy policy, and on numerous other matters in which United States economic interests will be closely involved. Any tactical advantage gained from a separate bargain with Britain, say, on agricultural trade, which in any way reduces its visible solidarity with the Community should be anxiously weighed against the long-term political damage that this would be liable to cause.

Notes

1. See J. Frankel, "Britain's Changing Role," *International Affairs* 50, 4 (October 1974): 574-83.

2. Herman Kahn and Anthony J. Wiener, *The Year 2000* (New York, 1967), pp. 29 ff.

3. British productivity in fact increased at the same rate during the period of the depression of the 1930s—at 1.6 per cent per man-year of the employed population—as it had during the boom period of the 1920s, 1922-29; but during the 1920s that was by far the lowest rate of growth in the Western industrial world, whereas that of the 1930s was among the highest. See D.C. Paige, "Economic Growth: The Last Hundred Years," *NIESR Economic Review*, July 1961, p. 32.

4. Quoted in John H. Clapham, *Economic History of Modern Britain* (3 vols.; Cambridge, 1930-38), v. III, p. xv.

5. See Angus Maddison, "Comparative Productivity Levels in the Developed Countries," *Banca Nazionale del Lavoro* 83 (1967), quoted in Sidney Pollard, *The Development of the British Economy 1914-1967* (London, 1969), p. 439.

6. See W. Ashworth, *An Economic History of England 1870 to 1939* (London, 1960), p. 188.

7. See Joseph Ben-David, *The Scientist's Role in Society* (Englewood Cliffs, N.J.: Prentice-Hall, 1971), in particular his calculation that Britain consistently maintained the second place internationally as a source of scientific innovation.

8. See Angus Maddison, "Economic Policy and Performance in Europe 1913-1970," to appear in the *Fontana Economic History of Europe*, Vol. V (not yet published), Ch. x, table 17.

9. Ibid., p. 47.

10. Pollard, *The Development of the British Economy*, p. 451.

11. *Industrial Relations—A Programme for Action* (TUC General Council, 1969).

12. Ibid., p. 5.

13. See the *NIESR Economic Review*, No. 70 (Nov. 1974): 29.

14. *Financial Times*, December 23, 1974.

15. See T.K. Warley in *International Economic Relations in the Western World 1959-71* (London: Chatham House, 1976).

16. See the official White Paper, *Food from Our Own Resources* (Cmnd 6020) (London, 1975).

17. See the article by Panic, "Why the UK's Propensity to Import Is High," *Lloyd's Bank Review*, No. 115 (Jan. 1975): 4 ff., for a calculation showing a markedly high income-elasticity of demand for imports of manufactures.

V France: Autonomy in Alliance

Suzanne Berger

France has been America's most troublesome and least worrisome ally. Troublesome, for since the advent of the Fifth Republic eighteen years ago, France has been a systematic opponent of American foreign policy. In the Atlantic community, France twice opposed the entry of Britain into the Common Market; within the EEC it has refused to move toward supranational institutions. It has withdrawn its troops from the NATO military organization and turned down the nuclear cooperation that the United States proposed at Nassau in 1962. It has resisted moves to organize Western industrial states for the energy crisis. American policymakers and the American public in general have viewed these moves and others like them as both hostile and self-defeating. In the American view, they not only thwart American policies in Europe, but they also frustrate European efforts to organize a European entity that would be a strong political and economic force in the world.

Outside Europe, France has also been regarded as an irritating troublemaker. As a middle power, it is too weak to cause real problems for American designs; but as a country with historic claims to world responsibilities, France is visible enough and loud enough to attract attention from other states and to complicate American policy. In Vietnam, the Middle East, Latin America, and even closer to home in Canada, France has supported men and movements that oppose some of our fundamental interests. No other American ally has proved so resistant to American designs and so systematically willing on a global front to counter American proposals with its own.

But though French foreign policy has been a source of deep resentment and frustration to the United States, French domestic policies have made it one of the most stable and least worrisome of America's allies. No other West European country has experienced the same long, unbroken period of conservative rule. The stabilizing weight of this conservative regime in the heart of western Europe has reinforced the moderate character of the Socialist governments that in 1975 hold power in most of the other major European states. As Portugal moves left and Spain enters the first phase of a succession crisis that will almost surely increase the power of the Left in that country, the ballast function of France within Europe may acquire even more importance for American foreign policy. On the linchpin of Gaullist and neo-Gaullist rule hanges, in some measure, the stability of other European regimes.

Moreover, France's economic and social performance has been reassuring when contrasted with that of America's other allies. France has maintained higher rates of economic growth and employment than even West Germany; over the past decade the difficulties that have arisen in keeping positive trade balances and in defending the franc have yielded to government action. Until recently, all this was accompanied by acceptable rates of inflation. On the social front too, France, with the major exception of the May-June events of 1968, has been relatively calm. Indeed, one of the most remarkable facts about the May-June explosion was how rapidly the government reasserted control and, with the exception of education, how few traces now remain.

A spoiler abroad, a bastion of stability within, France of the Fifth Republic has offered both frustrations and satisfactions to Americans. In large measure, American policymakers have come to take for granted these two aspects of French politics and count on them in making decisions about Europe. For this reason, a critical reevaluation of French politics is needed at this time. In the past two years France has crossed a watershed, and neither of these two fundamental assumptions about France provides a reliable guidepost any longer to French behavior in the future.

A strange reversal seems in process, with areas for cooperation with the United States opening in the field of foreign relations at the same time as the internal stability of France seems open to question. These changes are still embryonic: too shadowy to be identified with certainty; too fragile to be certain of developing to term. Yet if it is true that ground shifts are under way in France, we may lose valuable opportunities if we do not see the new chances for cooperation on foreign policy; and we may regret not having foreseen the consequences of unsettling shifts in the structures of power within the system. The main purpose of this essay is to explore these changes in French politics and to speculate on what they may mean for France's relations with the outside world.

Domestic Stability

The Gaullist Heritage

After less than a year in office, Valéry Giscard d'Estaing has emerged as the sole heir to the Gaullist legacy. His election over Jacques Chaban-Delmas, the Union

Démocratique Républicaine (UDR) candidate, gave him the presidency, and the election as UDR party head of Jacques Chirac, Giscard's prime minister, has effectively neutralized the Gaullist opposition. Elected over the resistance of the old barons of the Gaullist movement, Chirac's victory means that the only institutional base from which a Gaullist challenge of Giscard's legitimacy could have been launched has been conquered.

The assets that Giscard has inherited can best be described under three headings: political, institutional, and economic and social. The greatest political accomplishment of sixteen years of Gaullist rule is the parliamentary majority. The UDR has dominated each of the legislatures of the Fifth Republic. In the 1968 legislature the party won a majority of seats—an unprecedented victory in French parliamentary history; but to control the other Fifth Republic legislatures, they have needed the support of minor allies. In striking contrast to the parliamentary experience of the Third and Fourth republics, however, the alliance between the UDR and its chief partner, the Independent Republicans, has been a stable one. And only once since 1958 has a government fallen because of a vote of censure; even then, the subsequent national elections returned more Gaullists. Just how significant an achievement this stable parliamentary majority is can be gauged from comparison with the past: the average life of a government under the Third and Fourth republics was eight months, while in seventeen years of the Fifth Republic there have been only six prime ministers.

Over time, the governmental majority has widened to include several of the centrist groups. Though some orthodox Gaullists have attacked this opening to the Center and Left as opportunistic, it might well be seen as the extension of one of the fundamental tenets of Gaullist belief. The Gaullists have argued that their party belongs to neither Right nor Left and that these are artificial distinctions that mask and undermine a profound national consensus among Frenchmen. In the early years of the Fifth Republic, the possibility that Gaullism might indeed overcome the deep old left-right split in French politics was plausible. There were massive defections from the left-wing parties in the first elections of the regime, and the Gaullist electorate had deep roots in all socioeconomic groups including the working class. Even in the 1968 legislative elections, the Gaullists had as much support from the working class as did the Communist party (about one third of manual workers expressed their intentions to vote for each of the two parties).

The withering away of the old issues that had given rise to the left-right split in the nineteenth century made it seem that a modernization of French politics was at last in sight. The virtual quarantine of the Communist party—during the first decade of the Fifth Republic still deeply scarred by Hungary and de-Stalinization—made it seem likely that the non-Communist Left would go the way of other Social-Democratic parties in Europe. With the Communists isolated in their ghetto and the apparent decline of old ideologies, the Radicals and Socialists would become a loyal opposition or even court a place in government in alliance with some groups of the majority.

Even today, despite the new radicalism of the Socialists, the Socialist-Communist alliance, and the decline of urban and working-class voters in the UDR, this scenario is still considered a lively possibility by some who favor it and would profit (right Socialists and various groups in the government majority) and by some who deplore it and would lose (mainly left Socialists and Communists). That the scenario seems at all plausible may testify better to a widespread sense of new political possibilities opened by the diminished intensity of old left-right conflict than to its actual probability. But whatever the chances of making the Socialists a loyal opposition or moving any of them into the majority, Giscard already enjoys the fruits of the attenuation of the left-right split in at least one tangible way: the participation in government of some parties from the old left camp.

Paradoxically, this reduction of left-right conflict may well have contributed to the third major political achievement of Gaullism: the creation of a powerful organization of the Right. Compared with the Communist or even Socialist parties, the UDR's network of local units and the strength of its central bureaucracy appear relatively weak. But for the first time in France a conservative party has developed the structures of a mass party and has enrolled a large membership (in 1973 about 200,000).

After the overwhelming defeat of its presidential candidate, the UDR fell into disarray, as rival factions quarreled over the succession and over the relationships the party should maintain with Giscard on the one hand, and with the government on the other. The UDR, "the majority within the majority," found itself facing a government in which, aside from the UDR prime minister Jacques Chirac, the most powerful members of the party had been passed over in favor of less-known and weaker figures, while important ministries were distributed to politicians from other parties. UDR spokesmen heralded a new era of autonomy for the party, but in fact, the desire of many to maintain close and privileged ties with the government ran counter to the move for distance from the government. The election of Chirac as secretary-general has at least temporarily resolved the issue and tied the party to the government. But the long-term question is whether, as Chirac argued, his victory builds up his strength relative to Giscard's in the system and hence puts the UDR in the best possible posture for the next presidential round of elections; or whether the election of Chirac reinforces Giscard's control of the political scene. Given the presidential character of the regime and the heterogeneous composition of the UDR, which seems held together more by the fruits of power than by any core doctrines, the latter seems the likelier alternative. In sum, though Giscard cannot control the party as de Gaulle or Pompidou did, he can probably count on it for the first few years of his presidency.

The second major group of assets that Giscard inherits are institutional. Here the most important accomplishment of the Fifth Republic has been to create a strong and stable executive. The executive in this mixed parliamentary-presidential regime is a double one: the president and the government. The popular election of the president has clearly strengthened this office, so that its holder, even without the charisma of de Gaulle, is the most powerful figure in the system. The power of the presidency has never been put to the ultimate test of a confrontation with a parliament of a political complexion different from the president's since throughout the regime the UDR and its allies have controlled both presidency and parliament. This last fact also explains the stability of governments. Though there has been considerable ministerial turnover in the Fifth Republic, the prime ministers have had long terms of office, and they have not had to fear falling on hostile assembly votes. Changes in government have occurred at the initiative of the president.

There have been three major consequences of the institutional development of the Fifth Republic. Except on rare occasions, the government has been able to work out policies and incorporate them into legislation without effective opposition from parliament. Power has shifted from parliament to the executive; and the locus of negotiation, compromise, and decision no longer lies in parliamentary committees but in the bureaucracy. The implications of this shift of power and of the related decline of parliament are far-reaching. They have encouraged the development of new paths to power: today's aspiring young politician finds it far more rewarding to begin his climb in the higher civil service than in the lower echelons of either local government or parties. The new distribution of power has also promoted changes in the structure and activities of interest groups, which now operate primarily in bureaucratic arenas rather than legislative. Some groups that were relatively successful in the Fourth Republic have been unable to operate effectively in this system, and their followers are among the protesters who have taken to the streets with their demands (e.g., the farmers).

Most important, the institutions of the Fifth Republic have had a deep influence on political values and attitudes toward government: the opposition parties, as well as the majority, have largely come to believe that a strong executive and stable governments, as well as the constitutional arrangements that produce them, are desirable and should be preserved even if the Left comes to power. Even in the Programme Commun, the platform of the Socialist-Communist alliance, the institutional system of the Fifth Republic and, in particular, the relations between the executive and parliament are accepted with relatively minor amendment. This consensus on institutions, in a country where traditionally the constitution has been under bitter attack, is a major stabilizing factor.

Finally, no inventory of the institutional legacy of the Gaullist period would be complete without mention of the quality of the higher civil service. Credit for this is due largely to the establishment of the Ecole Nationale d'Administration after the war and to decisions made early in the Fourth Republic about the staffing of high state posts, but the Gaullist years nonetheless contributed, by confirming and enlarging the status and power of the upper-level bureaucracy. There has been a decline in power of party politicians and elected officials and a corresponding increase in the power of bureaucrats. At the top levels of government—up to cabinet rank—sit men whose route to power has passed exclusively through, the civil service. Before 1958 only politicians held these posts. But the counterpart of the charges of rule-by-technocrats that have been leveled against the regime is that the best young men and women have been attracted into public service by the very fact that it offers a real chance for influence and power.

The economic and social achievements of the Fifth Republic are also assets on which Giscard can draw. These have been years of prosperity and growth, characterized by Raymond Aron as the "most brilliant phase of the quarter-century since the Marshall Plan, a quarter-century which itself is the most brilliant phase of the economic history of our country since the beginning of the industrial era."[1] There has been a steady increase in the incomes and purchasing power of average workers and significant improvement in the standard of living of most groups in the population.[2] France's success in navigating the transition from a closed to a more open economy swelled its reserves and built a cushion against hard times. Even in this year of deep economic troubles and social conflicts, France is in relatively good shape by comparison not only with its sick neighbors Britain and Italy, but with the United States.

The chief factor responsible for this has been the remarkable growth of national product. Even if one considers the period immediately following the economic difficulties generated by May-June 1968, the record is impressive: between 1969 and 1972 French GNP increased by 26 per cent, in contrast to 19 per cent in Germany, 15 per cent in Italy, 11 per cent in the United States, and 9 per cent in Great Britain.[3] Over this period France grew on an average of 6 per cent per year. By 1970 French *per capita* gross national product was substantially higher than the British or Italian and almost up to the German figure.

One of the major contributing factors in France's prosperity has been exports. The part of exports in national production has increased from 13 per cent to 18 per cent since the opening of the Common Market, and in the period between recovery from the 1968 events and the recent oil crisis, France ran substantial surpluses in its trade balances. Also important has been a high rate of savings and investment, plus impressive increases in the productivity of labor. Much of this gain is due to a reallocation of resources: there has been a massive transfer of population out of backward agriculture into industry and service; and within the secondary and tertiary sectors, a modernization of structures has been under way which, however uneven, has nonetheless had considerable impact. And to all these changes should be added the contribution of good management and astute fiscal, monetary, and industrial policies—though it is a hard one to measure precisely.

Finally on the social front, the accomplishments of the Fifth Republic are not insignificant. In general, the aims of social policy over the past decade have been to assist the most distressed groups in the population rather than to expand universal benefits or to narrow the very wide wage differentials.[4] Those who have gained the most in recent years from social policy have been groups such as the aged, the handicapped, and those earning the minimum wage. Even before Giscard, there was a move toward the "modernization" of state family policy, and the first steps were taken to improve the legal status of women and to legalize contraception. In education, the Fifth Republic has seen large increases of students at all levels of the school system, particularly in the universities. Indeed, the transformation of the traditional French university can probably be explained better by the impact of an almost sixfold increase in the number of students between 1945 and 1968 than by any of the Gaullist educational reforms. The contribution of the state should, however, not be overlooked, for it made it possible for an educational system conceived for a preindustrial age to absorb numbers far beyond those it had been set up to educate and to turn out people with at least some of the skills required for an industrial society and economy.

The Weaknesses and Dangers

Today the gravity of the economic situation in which France finds itself appears to menace the inheritance. Opinions differ on the causes of the economic crisis. The government blames inflation and the deteriorating balance of trade largely on the failures of the international monetary system; others assign a heavier weight to the impact of higher oil prices; and still others on the left attribute a high degree of responsibility to the economic policies of the state and, more broadly, to the capitalist structures of the economy. Whatever the underlying causes, the life-endangering symptoms are clear enough: high inflation, trade deficits, and unemployment unknown since the 1930s.

At this point no one can choose with any certainty between government's claims to have turned the tide and the opposition's charge that the policies cannot work and that the situation remains out of control. By the end of spring 1975 the government had indeed succeeded in slowing the rate of inflation from about 15 per cent (1974) to close to 11 per cent, in running trade surpluses over the first four months of the year, and in returning the franc to the "snake." But these results had been achieved at a high cost: a 65 per cent increase in the number of unemployed over a year,[5] a cut in working hours and hence in wage earnings, and a decline in industrial production. The favorable trade balances of 1975 can be attributed largely to the reduction of imports, as business cut its purchases abroad. How much more unemployment is needed, how much restriction of credit, where to put investment capital, and what growth rate to choose, remain so many questions for which the government apparently has no good answers. Even if the government did hit upon the right answers, its ability to act upon them is greatly constrained, for many of the key factors—for example, oil prices and the economic health of France's trading partners—lie beyond reach and manipulation.

It is against this background that one must evaluate the probabilities that those factors that can be identified as *weaknesses* of the system may develop into *dangers* to the internal stability of France. The success of the futurologists who have written about France is hardly encouraging for anyone seeking to predict the outcomes of current French dilemmas, and no such attempt will be made here. In analyzing societies as complex as those on both sides of the Atlantic, one has about the same range of possibilities as a seismologist who cannot predict the earthquake but can specify the fault lines along which the earth will move. "Earthquakes," such as May-June 1968, are virtually unpredictable, but one can identify the vulnerabilities of the system and, by speculating on the connections among them, pick out the likely scenarios of political and social trouble. However unforseeable acts of God and of Arab sheiks, the permanence of certain fault lines in French society does limit the range of possible political catastrophes and makes speculation about the future of French internal stability possible. Whether or not the economic crisis will produce political and social unrest sufficient to cause a major explosion, we cannot say; if it does—and to the extent it does—the forms this unrest and destabilizing of the system will take are likely to be the following.

Institutional Crisis

The principal weakness of the constitution of the Fifth Republic is that it establishes a system that will work smoothly only when the National Assembly, the government, and the presidency are controlled by the same party and fails to provide adequate remedies for when they are not. In the course of the Fifth Republic, as we have seen, the president has usually had to live with a National Assembly not controlled by his party alone; but he has rarely had trouble keeping the party's allies in line. He has never faced an assembly in which the Left had a majority.

While it is true that there are problems in the United States as well whenever the presidency and Congress are controlled by different parties, the potential for governmental breakdown as a result of institutional stand-offs is considerably higher in France. In the first place, the president names the prime minister and the members of his government, but the National Assembly can turn them out with a vote of censure. The only resort of the president, if the Assembly will not accept the governments he proposes, is to dissolve the legislature and call new elections; but if the same majority is returned, the president himself may have to yield. In sum, the treatment may be more dangerous than the disease.

At least in the next three years the second and likelier scenario of institutional trouble is conflict between the president and prime minister. The constitution itself is ambiguous on whether executive power should be wielded primarily by the president or by the prime minister; and it has been historical circumstances, rather than constitutional rules, that have answered the question in favor of the president. The circumstances were, of course, the extraordinary prestige and authority of Charles de Gaulle, who was bound to dominate his prime ministers, as well as the fact that he and then Pompidou could name prime ministers of their own party.

Critics of the constitutional system predicted from the start that the arrangement of relationships among government, parliament, and president made France vulnerable to institutional paralysis at precisely those times of political instability when a strong authority would be needed. Today for the first time in the Fifth Republic, these gloomy prognostications seem something more than wishful thinking. Giscard d'Estaing is the leader of the Independent Republicans, a small regular ally of the Gaullist UDR. Whoever Giscard chooses as prime minister, then, must be acceptable to the Gaullists, and so the relations between president and prime minister directly depend on the extent to which the UDR sees its fortunes as tied to participation in government.

While speculation whether the UDR would allow one of its own to become Giscard's prime minister was quickly ended once Chirac was nominated, there are several plausible circumstances under which the question of UDR support could once again be raised. If Giscard is unable to manage the economy and unemployment continues to rise, the UDR may find it prudent to put distance between itself and the president. If the UDR does very well—or very badly—in the 1978 legislative elections; if Giscard succeeds in wooing over the centrist parties and center electorate; if the UDR comes to believe that one of its stalwarts has a good chance of defeating Giscard in presidential elections—then conflicts may multiply between the president and the government. Neither president nor prime minister can rule without the other's consent and cooperation. And the growing restiveness of the UDR may undermine the ground rule on which the Fifth Republic has operated: that the prime minister is in all essential matters subordinate to the president.

What seems highly unlikely, however, is that the UDR would actually make it impossible for the president to name a prime minister and have him confirmed by the Assembly. The prospect of a stand-off between executive and legislature would open only if the UDR lost control of the Assembly to a left coalition. Whether the president would ever choose a prime minister and government acceptable to the Left, whether the Left would ever agree to form a government with Giscard as president—these two fundamental questions have received no clear answer from either side. No crystal ball is needed to foresee that the victory of the Left in legislative elections would open up a period of deep institutional instability. Neither parliament nor president has the constitutional resources entirely to defeat the other, but each is powerful enough to paralyze the system. And who would be the victor in a confrontation in which the president brandished parliamentary dissolution, legislative elections, and a popular referendum and the parliament returned strong enough to defeat the president's prime minister? How likely such a conflict is, depends on the political evolution of the country; discussion of this will be deferred to a later section.

Social Unrest

The postwar experience of France provides few clues to how the population will react as the economy shifts from a period of relative abundance and rapid growth into a period of relative scarcity and slow growth or stagnation. Economic dislocation itself is no new experience for Frenchmen. The extraordinary changes in the society and the economy since World War II included the displacement of much of France's agricultural work force into industry and services, the rapid urbanization of the country, and the modernization of factories and shops. This economic transformation required considerable transfers of people and resources and a massive disruption of traditional ways of life.

But despite the depth of these social and economic changes, there was relatively little protest from those whose occupations and assets were devalued. The one serious challenge to political stability in the fifties from groups threatened by economic modernization was the Poujadist movement of small shopkeepers angered by supermarket expansion and taxes. Poujadism, however, did not survive the change in regimes; and for the first decade of the Fifth Republic, the only serious protests from groups pressed by the industrialization and modernization of the country were those organized by peasants. They were unable to move beyond demonstrations and occasional road barricades to more systematic forms of challenge. As for the working class, the first decade of the Fifth Republic was so quiescent a period that many concluded that the rewards of material prosperity had finally integrated a working class whose hostility to government had been a source of latent class war since the beginning of the industrial era.

The absence of serious challenge to the system is the more striking when one considers the absence of any fundamental agreement on what French modern society should be. This point has been very well made by the authors of *1985*, a volume that spells out choices confronting France in the near future, who point out that each of the major social groups in the country perceives preservation of the status quo as more advantageous to its interests than modernization.[6] They conclude: "It is thus almost despite itself, or at least without the profound acceptance of many of its members, that French society seems to be entering into a phase of accelerated modernization. The image of an upside-down pyramid standing on its top—the weak reforming minority—suggests the fragility of the enterprise: without the support of the entire society, this minority will have trouble resolving the new problems that France's advanced development will raise."[7]

Given the extent of the social and economic disruptions and the absence of consensus on the values of the new society, one wonders why the losers have supported—or at least, have not resisted—the state that has been encouraging, inciting, and abetting these changes. Various studies of traditional elites in France suggest that as long as the economy was expanding rapidly, individuals apparently believed that their collective losses might be recouped by individual gains, that group decline need not mean individual impoverishment.[8] There were room enough and resources enough in the system to permit individuals to recover their losses in another sphere of economic activity. The substantial growth and prosperity of the economy in the postwar decades supported the virtual disappearance of Malthusian anxieties. At the same time, the state was then contributing to economic change in ways that were far less discriminatory than in subsequent years, when it has shifted from a policy of general to one of selective encouragement—from trying simply to increase output, without much concern for cost, to supporting only the most efficient firms.[9]

In the middle of the sixties, a new phase began in which concern for social unrest became a major preoccupation. Two different facts were responsible: the social and political fall-out from the new industrial policy and the political explosion of May-June 1968. Both of these, in different ways, focused on the discovery of inequality and on the role of traditional groups in the economy as major political problems.

Though the "industrial imperative" and the industrialization programs that grew out of it are policies associated with Pompidou's presidency, in fact their origins lie in the mid-sixties, when the problem of strengthening French industry for competition in the Common Market came to dominate state economic policy. The shift to selective intervention that the new industrial policy required was bound to make the state's role far more visible and open to attack. The state was now not only choosing between sectors as it had in the first two postwar decades, but within industrial branches it was helping particular firms to establish their position over others. For each "national champion" that the state brought into being, there were national losers.

This rationalization of the state's industrial policy was part of a larger process of rationalization of state action: in the welfare system, in public services, in the nationalized industries. One of the consequences has been a greatly heightened perception by various groups of the differential impact of state policy. Without reference to those changes in policy and perception, one could not explain the new salience of the "inequality" issue in France, which has figured prominently in the platforms of both the Right and the Left in recent elections. The relative lack of interest in questions of distribution and equality until recently appears thus to have been a product not only of growing affluence and optimism, but also of the kind of role the state played in the earlier phases of economic growth and modernization.

The concern with inequalities was only one of the new social tensions that were nourished—even if not wholly created—by changes in the economic role of the state in the mid-sixties. The two other sources of unrest that were exacerbated by them were ethnic nationalism on France's periphery and the revolt of traditional economic groups.

There are obviously many factors that have contributed to the increasing level of protest in France from Bretons, Corsicans, Basques, and Occitans. Not the least of these is the state's refusal to provide support for regional languages or regional power. Indeed, the state in the past has severely repressed expressions of ethnic identity and still today harasses even those individuals and groups whose ethnic demands are largely cultural.

Yet the increase in ethnic consciousness, the emergence of political groups demanding various degrees of separatism and autonomy, and the violence of some of them, cannot be explained by ethnicity alone. In fact, this protest appears at a time when the differences between minorities and other Frenchmen are at their lowest point. Rather, in France as elsewhere in Europe, ethnic nationalism is above all a way of using traditional symbols to express grievances about inequities in the relationship between a region and the central state. It is the accumulation of economic inequalities along regional lines and their increasing visibility that have sparked this ethnic protest in the last decade. At the same time, the shifts in power from parliamentary to bureaucratic arenas and from politicians to technocrats have increased the sense of impotence of groups on the periphery, for they have lost the power their numbers once gave them in parliament without acquiring any of the assets that provide leverage in the new political system. There is no reason to believe that the small regional reform of 1972 will satisfy these grievances. In ebbs and surges, ethnic protest will continue to trouble the government.

The third focus of social unrest exacerbated by the state's economic policies is the traditional economic groups: small peasants, small business, and small commerce. Here, too, the resurgence of violent forms of protest after a considerable period of calm cannot be explained only by the changes in the economic policies of the state in the mid-sixties. But it is striking how policies converged in that period to bring to the boiling point the frustration, resentment, and bitterness that had existed in latent form. To consider only the small shopkeepers: after an initial phase in the Fifth Republic when the state acted mainly to remove the barriers to the development of modern forms of distribution, a second phase followed in which state policy appeared to discriminate against small shops in favor of supermarkets. The new value-added tax system, the liberal dispensation of building permits for new large stores, the increase in the amounts that shopkeepers had to pay into social security programs—these and other policies fell with very uneven impact on traditional and modern commerce. The role of the state was not only highly visible; it was, in the eyes of the traditional groups, discriminatory and unjust. The 1962 Pisani laws on agriculture came to be seen in the same light by large parts of the peasantry; the credit policies of the state aroused similar reaction from traditional small businessmen.

Reaction was most violent from the shopkeepers. A new Poujadist-type movement led by Gérard Nicoud protested in the streets, stormed government buildings, and staged rather successful tax strikes. They swamped the more conservative elements in the National Chamber of Commerce and took over many local chambers of commerce. Despite a temporary lull in their activities, they remain a source of real trouble for the government.

The emergence of new forms of peasant protest also testifies to the radicalizing impact of government economic policies. Peasants have come to see the new agricultural laws as highly selective in the groups they favor. The growing strength of the Mouvement de Défense des Exploitations Agricoles Familiales (MODEF), a peasant organization with close links to the Communist party, shows that this group has struck a responsive chord in its defense of small peasant proprietors and its stigmatization of the modernizing agricultural policies of the state as a way of favoring the rich in the countryside over the poor. The tensions created by state agricultural policy have torn apart the National Farmers' Association (Fédération Nationale des Syndicats d'Exploitants Agricoles—FNSEA). They have also led to conflict within the countryside, where for the first time groups of peasants have battled one another over who is to profit from state interventions. Today the peasants, like the small shopkeepers, remain a volatile element in French society.

The appearance of violent forms of confrontation among traditional groups would itself have been a source of preoccupation for the government. What raised it so close to the top of the government's political agenda were two other circumstances, both of which coincided in time with the revolt of the traditional classes. The first was the May-June 1968 student rebellion and the nationwide strikes and demonstrations that ensued. The virtual impotence of the state, though it lasted only a brief time, created a panic among the political elites that left traumatic scars. Their first response was to return to their safest base of support, the traditional electorate. What these voters lacked in numbers, they made up in reliability; and even their numbers continue to be significant.

But the kind of support the state felt it needed from the traditional classes in the wake of May-June was not only electoral. Georges Pompidou's reflections on the crisis, written down immediately after, reveal a profound conern that, beneath the particular events of 1968, a deep crisis of civilization was opening; that "May 1968 may be a beginning and not a local accident."[10] At the origins of this crisis, he and others saw the collapse of traditional values, undermined by the loss of faith, by the materialism of a consumer society, and by the loosening of traditional restraints on individual behavior. To remedy this, Pompidou in his essay calls for civic discipline and a new social order. In practice, Pompidou and his party used the materials at hand to reconstruct that form of social order which seemed possible, namely a society that had room, alongside the modern groups that the new industrialization policies were strengthening, for those traditional groups that gave stability to the political system.

Pompidou's interest in preserving the traditional groups was strengthened by a second consideration: the shift in the bases of electoral support of his own party, the UDR. As the last legislative elections (1973) showed, the UDR has lost many of its early working-class and big-city voters and has gained strength among the rural, small-town, and traditional electorates. This change is reflected in a geographical shift of the party's bases of strength out of modern industrial France into more agricultural and backward regions. The UDR, which once might have been characterized as a catch-all party, is now beginning to look like a party based on an alliance of some of the most advanced elements (large industrialists, professional classes) with the backward economic groups.

The price of maintaining this alliance is support for the traditional economic groups. However much Pompidou and those interested in industrializing France might have wished to eradicate sources of backwardness in the economy, they came to realize that they could not do so without sapping the foundations of the regime. The forms this recognition have taken are varied: higher prices for peasants and the virtual abandonment of the modernization program in the countryside; a law on commerce that has given the right to dispense licenses for supermarkets to departmental committees in which small shopkeepers make up about half the membership; the appointment of ministers of agriculture and commerce who have returned to the old rhetoric about family enterprises.

The rapid increases in inflation, unemployment, and energy prices have ushered in a new period. Now the problems that the government appears to fear most as sources of social unrest are unemployment and inequality. There is probably no social disaster that the French fear more than unemployment, and in past years even very small increases in the numbers of those seeking work without success have been enough to trigger bitter recriminations from the unions and a generalized state of anxiety in the population at large. The acute national sensitivity to unemployment explains the government's decision to accord very liberal unemployment compensation: those who lose jobs for "economic reasons" will receive close to a full salary for a year. But as unemployment, partial and total, rises above previous postwar highs, it becomes clear that the new compensation agreements will not suffice to reassure the public. Unemployment will likely generate a tense and bitter relationship between the unions and the government and a generalized state of anxiety in the population, but it is unlikely that it will lead directly to an increase in political protest. Neither the unemployed nor those who fear they are likely to lose their jobs are good candidates for strikes; indeed the chilling effects of unemployment spread out beyond the likely victims of unemployment. The recent failure of a strike by postal workers suggests that in a depressed labor market even strikes by workers with protected employment are not likely to be successful, since the government need not fear their generalization. Under the circumstances, it is not surprising that the November 1974 general strike fizzled.

The inequality issue, too, is unlikely to generate serious levels of protest from its direct victims. What the government claims to be concerned about is that the economic sacrifices that the new high prices for energy impose will not be accepted by Frenchmen unless the distribution of the burden is equitable. Only if there is some redistribution of income toward the poorest will the overall reduction in consumption entailed by this new "tax" on production be socially acceptable in France.[11] This argument suggests the potential for political protest among those who are the principal victims of inequality, and yet it is hard to see what political forms the growing distress of groups at the bottom of the income distribution might take. More than half of the estimated eleven million poor in France are old or infirm or handicapped, and these are hardly candidates for political mobilization; in the other half are many of the least-well-organized occupations in the country.[12]

Rather the potential for political trouble seems far higher among those people who would have to give up income under most of the schemes thus far proposed for reducing inequalities. As Phillipe Herzog, a leading Communist party economist, pertinently commented in an attack on the idea that inequality is a cause of inflation and that austerity will be acceptable on condition that inequalities are reduced:

On the pretext of financing an increased aid to the "poor," the purchasing power of the great mass of Frenchmen would be sharply reduced. . . . The fundamental inequality is that which gives an oligarchy the ownership of our means of survival and gives it control over our lives and future. The cause of waste and of the crisis is that its interests run counter to the people's. The cause is not the income of managers, engineers, or of the well-to-do middle class. Does anyone think that it is by attacking these groups that the productivity of the economy can be improved or the way opened for the vast scientific and technical progress possible today?[13]

Whatever one may think of Herzog's analysis of the origins of the crisis, his argument about the consequences of trying to deal with it by income distribution is plausible.

In sum, unemployment and inequality, while they may contribute to a groundswell of fear, resentment, and tension, are unlikely by themselves to generate mass protest. What might do so would be the convergence of more organized protest groups in an attack on the state. Under such circumstances mass discontent would serve as underpinning to a negative alliance among groups who have little or nothing in common except for their opposition to the government. The two principal candidates for such an alliance are organized labor and the traditional economic groups.

Though unemployment has usually had more of a demobilizing than mobilizing impact on workers, there are nonetheless new factors at work in the French working class that might prove explosive in a deteriorating economic situation. First, the composition of the work force has changed. The entry into the labor market of a large cohort of young workers with more education than their fathers and far higher expectations about living standards and job security is one inflammable element in the labor situation, for it is precisely among these young workers that unemployment rates are highest.[a] The foreign workers, of whom there are now close to two million in France, are another new and unpredictable element. Despite the apparent vulnerability of these workers to reprisals, the level of protest among them has been rising over the past five years. Since the presence in France of most of these workers is regulated by long-term intergovernmental contracts, they cannot simply be sent home.

Another important new aspect of French labor relations is the growing radicalness of the provincial working class. The policy of encouraging industry to locate outside of the Paris region has, despite its many shortcomings, created a working class in areas of the country that until recently had had little or no industry. As the pattern of labor unrest in 1968 and in subsequent years has shown, these new workers, who typically earn lower wages and work under worse conditions than in areas where industry has been established longer, are willing to go out on strike and to hold out for long periods. When these factories are located in small towns, protest often spills over, and peasants, workers in other firms, and others in the community line up with the strikers.

Last, the union movement is in certain respects stronger than ever before in the Fifth Republic. The two principal labor confederations, the Confédération Générale du Travail (CGT) and the Confédération Française et Démocratique du Travail (CFDT), have, despite important and bitter differences, been able to plan and carry out together a number of joint actions in the past few years. The 1968 legislation on labor representation in factories has facilitated organizing at the plant level, and the number of plants with union sections has gone up steadily.[14]

On the side of the traditional economic groups, the reasons for predicting a resurgence of protest are simple: the fight against inflation will force the government to choose between some modernization of the industrial system and some economic growth on the one hand, and the policy of concessions to traditional economic groups (see above) on the other. The Pompidou solution cannot survive the increased pressures on the economic resources of the system. The government has in the past year already reneged on some of the protective legislation. And the mobilization of the traditional groups has begun.

In sum, what the government has most to fear in the next few years is a

---

[a] The young workers were in May-June 1968 the most radical in their demands and willingness to participate in broad-based political action.

convergence of protest from the modern industrial sector and the traditional economic groups. Whether industrial workers resisting a cut in their real wages and fearing unemployment and traditional producers fearing for survival have many interests in common is hardly important. Both groups may develop a common stake in fighting the anti-inflationary policies of the government, and this negative coalition could have profoundly destabilizing effects on the regime.

Changes in Party Politics

The evolution of party strength is the third major source of challenges to the stability of the political system in the next decade. The most important developments of the past few years are ones whose full significance will become clearer only in the 1978 legislative elections and the subsequent presidential elections. First, we have already noted major changes in the situation of the UDR: its sociological and geographical bases of strength have shifted, and it is now moving into a period when defining relations with its allies, one of whom controls the presidency, becomes all important for survival (see above, p. 151). Second, and perhaps more important, there has been a spectacular reversal of fortune by the Socialist party. After the disastrous showing of the Socialist candidate in the 1969 presidential elections and the party's poor showing in the 1968 legislative elections, the future of the largest party of the non-Communist Left seemed in jeopardy. This situation was dramatically reversed by the 1973 legislative elections, in which the Socialists won 100 assembly seats, in contrast to the 57 they had held in the 1968 legislature, and by the 1974 presidential election, in which the Socialist candidate François Mitterand won an unprecedented 49 per cent of the vote and 42 per cent of the electorate. These election returns demonstrate that the strength of the Socialist party within the Left is at least equal to that of the Communists and that, unlike the Communists, it can draw enough votes from the electors of other parties to be a serious challenger for the presidency. By early 1976 public opinion polls were showing that if elections were held, the Socialists would emerge as the largest party in the country.

The successes of the Socialists are due to a reform of the party, to a shift in the electorate, and to the alliance with the Communist party. The 1969 party reform not only brought new leadership to the top, but it also initiated a process of grass-roots change in party organization and procedure that has paid off in a large increase in membership and local activism. The new Socialist party has attracted support from a wide range of political associations, all of which had been within the Left camp, broadly defined, but had not been directly associated with any party. At the same time, the Socialists have begun to increase their electoral scores in areas where the Left has traditionally been very weak. The rise in Socialists votes in Catholic departments of France suggests a loosening of the conservative hold on Catholics and a potential reservoir of electors who were once the safe capital of the Right. Not only the geographic shifts in the electorate but also occupational shifts favor the Socialists, for they have increased their strength in groups such as white collar employees that are growing. Even more significant, polls carried out for the 1974 presidential elections showed that younger voters favored the Socialist candidate, as did the age groups that will be old enough to vote in the next elections. It is possible that this generational factor alone could carry the Socialists to power.

Finally, the alliance with the Communists appears to have strengthened the Socialist party. In contrast to various other postwar electoral alliances of the Communists and the non-Communist left, the June 1972 agreement went far beyond an electoral negotiation to the signing of a "common program" (Programme Commun) that the Left would implement if it came to power. The Communists have long argued that all Left parties do better when the Left is united, and they may now believe that their prophesies have been rather too well fulfilled by the Socialist electoral successes since 1972. The gains in terms of political momentum from pursuing a common political and legislative strategy based on the Programme Commun seem to have thus far outweighed the costs to the Socialists of frightening away some of the moderate electors who otherwise might vote Socialist on the second ballot.

No one of these three factors guarantees victory to the Socialist party; indeed, each one carries along with it tensions and uncertainties that may in the long run be destructive of even those successes that have been thus far achieved. The reform of the party, for example, by bringing in new members and leaders, has generated severe factional conflict. The followers of the old SFIO (Section Française de l'Internationale Ouvrière) leader Guy Mollet, the recruits from the PSU (Parti Socialiste Unifié), the radicals grouped in CERES (Centre d'Etudes, de Recherches et d'Education Socialiste), the long-time supporters of Mitterand—each of these groups is vying for hegemony in the party, and these struggles may well increase in intensity. The evolution of the electorate has brought new Socialist voters in traditionally right regions but also reduced the Socialist tally in some of their old strongholds in the Center and North, where the Gaullists are gaining.

The factor that creates the most uncertainty for the Socialist future is the alliance with the Communists. Thus far, the alliance has clearly been a source of strength for the Socialists, but will it continue to be so? Even if questions about the nature of the Communist party and its long-term aims are set aside, the Socialists would have in the short run to confront two other questions. Will alliance with the Communists make it impossible to win over the moderates the Socialists need, both to enlarge their parliamentary representation and to win the presidency the next time? The trade-offs between the political momentum the Socialists gain from the alliance on the one hand and from the support of centrist electors and collaboration with the center Left on the other have thus far appeared to weigh in favor of the alliance, but the point of diminishing returns of this strategy may fall short of the electoral majority the Socialists need.

The second issue concerns the Programme Commun. The Socialists have here committed themselves to a set of policies for reorganizing the French economy and society about which, even in the most prosperous of times, one might have felt considerable skepticism. What purpose would be served by the extensive nationalizations proposed? How would workers' control be reconciled with the technical requirements of efficient management? Or how could a high rate of growth be achieved without getting rid of "les petits" whom the program pledges to defend?—These are only a few of the questions which neither the program nor subsequent explanation of it by Socialists and Communists has answered satisfactorily. And on implementation: short of an act of faith that "a new logic" will take over, once a Left government determined to carry out the Programme Commun comes to power, how will it be able to implement such a program democratically in a society in which old attitudes, motives, and interests would surely persist?[15]

But even more difficult for the Socialists than deciding how the alliance affects their electoral chances or whether the Programme Commun provides any useful guideposts to managing and changing economy and society is deciding how to deal with their alliance partner, the Communist party.[16] At the heart of the matter is the question of how fundamental the changes in the Communist party have been: to what extent has the Party liberated itself from subordination to the Soviet Union? To what extent has the internal life of the Party been democratized? And how would the Communists behave if they participated in government?

While these questions were never far from the surface in Socialist party discussion of the alliance, they have moved to the fore because of two capital shifts in Communist behavior: the year-long offensive against the Socialists launched by the PCF at its October 1974 party congress and then, in late 1975-early 1976, the PCF's sudden embrace of positions close to those of the Italian Communists on relations with the Soviet Union and on democracy in a socialist state. The Communist attacks on the Socialists accused them of being willing to sell out the Programme Commun for a chance to come to power, of being unwilling to support Communist candidates with the same discipline that the Communists put behind Socialists, and of listening to the sirens on the right who are trying to lure the Socialists away from the Communists into a new governmental majority. By spring 1975, the attacks had abated and relations between the two parties resumed in a mode which, though far less antagonistic than during the preceding six months, remains more competitive than collaborative.

Why the Communists reversed course and how far they are prepared to return to the alliance are not at all clear. One line of explanation stresses the international situation, a general hardening of the Communist line in Europe and, in particular, a presumed change of policy in the Soviet Union. While there have been good reasons to question the autonomy of the French Communist party vis-à-vis the Soviet Union, at least with respect to the alliance with the Socialists one need not bring in the international situation or the Soviet Union to explain the Communist party's reversal in the fall of 1974. There are more plausible and compelling domestic political considerations that account for the twists in the Party line, from the cooperative relations with the Socialists that reached a peak during the 1974 Mitterand campaign, to the hostility of late 1974-early 1975, back to competitive but nonaggressive relations.

The French Communists, like the Italians, have understood that they need the support of other groups and parties in society to come to power, but that they cannot afford to pay such a price for this support as will endanger their own organization and membership. The support of others is needed, in the first instance, because the stability of the electorate in the major European powers is such that Communist parties have little hope of reaching a majority of the popular vote. Moreover, West European Communist parties have come to understand—and the lessons of Chile reinforced the message—that even winning a majority of votes and seats in elections would likely not be enough to allow them to govern: the balance of social and economic forces would still weigh against them, as would the international forces that more or less automatically or by design would be set in motion against a Communist government in a West European state. For both these reasons, the Communists see the path to power and, at very least, the early period in power as possible only in alliance with other major parties and with social classes beyond those which provide the party with its proletarian core. In France, the broadening of the Party program to include the demands of various middle-class groups and the alliance with the Socialists expressed these strategic concerns.

Yet the Communist party cannot afford to pay a very high price for this cooperation. In particular—and this has been the heart of what the Communists have been saying for the past year—it makes no sense for the Communists to help the Socialists to power on terms that allow the Socialists to ditch the Communists at the first convenient moment. Should the Socialists get too big, were they able to trade off Communist support for moderate support or abandon the Programme Commun with impunity, the Communists would have served as trampoline, with very little advantage to the Party itself. Even worse: participating in such an event may cost the Party support from some of its own, as well as lose for it those potential supporters who may well opt for the Socialists if the distinctions between Socialists and Communists become too blurred. Communist sensitivity on all these points is very high. This is why the Socialist gains and Communist losses in the fall by-elections, following upon the Mitterand campaign and successes of the spring, the renewed campaign of groups in the government majority to woo over the Socialists, and the diversity, indeed cacophony, in the Socialist party on the Programme Commun brought matters to a head. These irritants, added to the structural need of the Party to keep a certain distance between itself and the Socialists and to keep the Socialists from taking the alliance for granted, plausibly account for the recent course of the relationship.

While the Soviet Union might have reasons for wanting the French Communist party back in its ghetto of the first two postwar decades, it is difficult to see any powerful reasons why the French Communist party would wish to return there. The domestic interpretation of the alliance crisis and the return to regularized contacts and discussions suggests therefore that matters will be patched up well before the next legislative elections. But even if the Communists do not choose to break off relations with the Socialists, they may not wish to conduct them in such a way as to come to power with the Socialists in the near future. Why, indeed, come to power only to preside over a deep economic crisis that even a Socialist France could do little to change?

The Socialists have good reason to wonder whether the Communists want to come to power with them in the near future. But even if that issue could be resolved by some new turn in the current controversy, the conflict poses deeper questions that remain unanswered. The *volte-face* of the Communist party, with no audible protest from members who only yesterday were enthusiastically campaigning for Mitterand, raised the question of how the Party would act if it ever did get in power. The events of fall and winter 1974-1975 apparently showed that Party life and policy-making are still tightly controlled from the top and that once a decision has been taken, the possibility for free expression and debate within the Party ceases. This demonstration of the limited range of internal democracy in the Communist party moved another ugly issue that had fallen backstage to the front of political discussion: would a party that does not respect free expression and democracy within its own ranks be willing to preserve them in the country at large? The Communists have proffered numerous reassurances on this point in recent years. In particular they have insisted that they would leave power if elections turned them out. And when the cases of East Europe are raised, they have pointed to the "special circumstances" that distinguish those countries from France, with its long democratic tradition. But a doubt remains; and it has been sharpened in recent months. Finally, because pressure from the Soviet Union in the recent change of course cannot be altogether ruled out, the old question whether a Communist party in power would subordinate French interests to Soviet interests has once again reared its head.

Writing at a time of crisis in the Socialist-Communist alliance, it would be easy to overestimate the weight of factors of the past in the behavior of the Communist party in the present and future. There are, however, new forces at work in the Party whose influence, while difficult to assess, should not be neglected. The composition of the membership, first of all, has changed in ways that makes it difficult to believe that the Party could ever return to the ways of the Stalinist period. The presence in the Party today of far larger numbers of educated, middle class members, the generational turnover that has cleaned out many of the members socialized during the Stalinist period and brought a majority of members who have joined since the Fifth Republic, the decline in rural and other traditional members—all these factors have forced the Party itself to change. Next, on critical issues such as the role of middle class groups, the European Economic Community, the role of political opposition in socialism, and the path to power, the Party's doctrines have moved in a consistently more liberal direction. And finally, those elements in the Party that are pushing toward its integration into the political system are being reinforced by the growing acceptance by non-Communist Frenchmen of the legitimacy of Communist participation in government. An October 1974 public opinion survey found 50 per cent of those interviewed expecting that there would be Communist ministers within the next five years and a plurality judging the Party capable of managing the economy.

Perhaps the most significant changes of all were those initiated in late 1975-early 1976, in which the PCF openly attacked the Soviet Union for repressive, undemocratic treatment of its citizens and argued that liberal democratic rights must be guaranteed under Socialism, with protection both for individual liberties and for groups to organize political dissent and opposition. At the same time, Georges Marchais, the Party leader, announced that the "dictatorship of the proletariat"—a sacred phrase in Marxist-Leninist tradition— should be dropped from Party statutes. The term dictatorship, Marchais said, suggested an authoritarian regime; the proletariat no longer adequately defines the broad group of workers whose interests the PCF represents.

The triumph of those groups in the Party pushing for a strategy closer to the Italians' was first apparent in the joint declaration of the French and Italian Communist parties signed in November 1975, than in the rising level of French criticism of repression in the Soviet Union, and finally, in the Marchais declarations on socialism and democracy, with their open admission of disapproval of Soviet practices, at the February 1976 Party congress. One can only speculate on the intraparty shifts that underlie these strategic moves but at least two factors seem to have accelerated the process. First, the successes of the French Socialists, and more broadly, the expansion of the level of activity and influence of Socialists in all of Western Europe, have put "hard-line" Communist parties in increasingly difficult straits. The failure of the Portuguese Communists and the triumph of the Socialists provided a striking lesson, whose message was underscored by the fact that at the same time in Italy elections confirmed the opposite outcome: a Left victory in which the PCI reaped the lion's share. Second, the increasing level of pressure from the USSR at the meetings to prepare a conference of European Communist parties as well as the Soviet attacks in the summer of 1975 on the alliance strategies of West European

Communist parties seem to have backfired and, by forcing the PCF to choose between more submission to the Soviet Union or alignment on the Italian positions, to have pushed it into resistance.

With all the uncertainties about the future of the Socialist-Communist coalition, as well as about the extent of change within the Communist party, speculation about the Left in power would be quite futile. For Americans reflecting on this prospect, however, one factor does emerge clearly. No matter how solid the Left alliance or how changed the Communist party, the Left in power would be extraordinarily sensitive and vulnerable to international re-actions. First of all, even if it is true that, as René Andrieu put it, the Party is independent in the sense that Brezhnev cannot call up and give orders,[17] still, when the Party is forced to choose between international camps, it sees itself on the side of the Soviet Union rather than the United States.[b] The Communists, when confronted with cases like Solzhenitsyn and Czechoslovakia, may be increasingly willing to criticize the Soviet Union, but they still see the Soviet Union as more often and more systematically on the right side of international conflicts. Moreover, as Pierre Juquin, another Party leader, explained, "Socialism à la française is above all socialism . . . and the U.S.S.R., even if we criticize a part of what it does, is a socialist country. . . ."[18]

It is not only the special relationship of the Communist party to the Soviet Union but also the special relationship of France to the Atlantic Alliance that would make the Left in power far more vulnerable to the outside than other Fifth Republic governments. Although outside the NATO military organization, France has considered itself and has been considered a part of the Western alliance system, and the growing economic interdependence of Western states has reinforced this alignment. France is tied to the United States by so many strands of political, military, and economic interests, of shared experience, and of common goals that American reactions to the arrival of the Left in power would inevitably reverberate throughout the system. Even if the pressures that the United States brought to bear on a left government fell far short of the drastic Chilean scenarios that French left politicians imagine, the regime could still be severely shaken. Not only the American government, but a wide variety of American private interests could by relatively minor acts set off a chain of political responses in France that would have unforeseeable and uncontrollable consequences.

But this extreme sensitivity would be more likely to reduce American influence than to promote it. For the Socialists, as for the majority of the French population, the priority in international relations is maintaining national independence and autonomy with respect even to allies. If the United States

---

[b]As Andrieu said in the same interview: "Whether in the Spanish civil war, Munich, the 20 million victims of Hitler, colonial wars, etc., the Russians have been on the side of the oppressed. Whereas the champions of freedom, those people who reproach us for so much, accept the generals in Chile, they tolerate the colonels in Greece, and they find it normal to repress Communists in Indonesia."

attempted to bring pressure on a left government or was perceived as doing so, the very vulnerability of the regime would likely lead to efforts to resist, which might well grow far out of proportion to the triggering cause. This is due to an asymmetry in the relation of French political parties to the two world powers that in the short run at least would not work in favor of the United States. If the Left in power in France became an international issue, the Soviet Union might be able to influence strongly the French Communist party, but the United States would not easily find any major political group so open to its influence. The Gaullist opposition, in order to return to power, as much as the Socialists to stay in, would find it necessary to eschew any acts that suggested knuckling under to American pressure. In sum, were the Left to come to power, direct or indirect American intervention would probably produce the outcomes the United States fears most, and benevolent neutrality might be the policy of least risk.

France in the World

This essay has focused on the domestic forces and politics of France. In part, this is because the international role of France—in the EEC, in the international economy, in NATO, in relations with the United States—has been treated in depth in other chapters of this volume. There are, however, two other reasons for focusing on the constellation of domestic forces in considering the near future of France: first, the weight of continuity is likely to be far heavier in foreign policy than in domestic politics; and next, to the extent that change does occur, it will likely be not so much in the content of foreign policy as in its activism, scope, and salience. Both of these suggest that in the next period domestic politics is likely to become increasingly important to the government's central political projects and that foreign policy will shift out of center stage. The prospect of accommodation and cooperation with the United States depends more on this decline in the importance of foreign policy than on any essential change in its aspirations.

In Giscard's first year in office the pattern of his foreign policy has already become clear. The one great constant remains a determination to maintain national independence, understood in the Gaullist sense of keeping France free of those quarrels with its enemies or commitments to its allies that would tie its hands and reduce its autonomy in the international sphere. Alongside this continuity run three changes: a lessening of the activism of French policy, a reduction in its scope, and a decline in its centrality for the overall political designs of the regime. This pattern was in large measure set during Pompidou's presidency, and the description Stanley Hoffmann draws of the *politique de grandeur* in the hands of de Gaulle's immediate successors could stand as a sketch of the emerging lines of Giscard's foreign policy as well.[19]

When Giscard took office, Americans once again confidently expected that a new era in French-American relations was about to open, now that the Gaullists had departed from the presidency. The French refusal to step into line with Kissinger's proposals for organizing the oil-consuming industrial nations, Sauvagnargue's initiatives with the Palestine Liberation Organization (PLO), and Giscard's descent in the French nuclear submarine were as many bad surprises for Americans who had regarded Gaullist insistence on an independent foreign policy and its means (nuclear and other) as anachronistic and irrational behavior. For the Americans, the two key realities of the international scene have been the bipolar distribution of power and the growing economic interdependence of the Western world. A realistic adaptation to these core facts would, in the American view, require the French to accept American leadership and to cooperate in policies worked out under the American aegis.[20] That the French did not choose to regard the international system in this way or to assume the responsibilities which in the American view were appropriate to its situation as a middle-level power in the Western camp showed the essential irrationality of their position. For this, the Americans largely blamed de Gaulle, although they also came to consider the French themselves as chauvinistic and collectively somehow less mature than other European populations.

What Americans did not understand was that French policy was based on a different vision of the international system and of the possibilities it offers for a state determined to maintain and enhance prestige, power, and influence by protecting as much as possible its freedom of action. This vision was not peculiarly de Gaulle's, although he brought to the task of implementing it both an extraordinary ability to express dramatically its urgency for France and the political will to persist, despite failure. Gaullist ideas on foreign policy, so far from reflecting the peculiar ambition of a single individual, are in fact the most popular part of the Gaullist legacy. And they are, in the main, ideas and policies upon which both Left and Right agree. The autonomy that de Gaulle asserted with respect to the United States, his support for national independence movements all over the world, his refusal of supranational European institutions, and his approach to Eastern Europe found as much approval in the Socialist and Communist parties as in the UDR. The one remaining holdout for Atlanticism, the small Center party, has been too compromised by its desires to share in power to push with any vigor a set of ideas about foreign policy for which there is, in any event, less and less popular support. For all these reasons, the core ideas of Gaullist foreign policy have survived de Gaulle.

If Giscard seems more accommodating on occasion than his Gaullist predecessors, one cannot conclude that any major transformation of foreign policy is in the dawning. What the spirit of Martinique heralds is not a new era of French cooperativeness, but rather a period in which the importance of foreign policy within the overall program of government activity declines. While the content of foreign policy—its map of the international system, its preferred strategies, its declared objectives—remains largely unchanged, the energy, determination, and resources with which it is pursued have diminished and will continue to do so.

The signs of this were visible already in the Pompidou presidency, as domestic concerns became the primary focus of political attention. Under the new strain of domestic economic troubles, this tendency is likely to become even more pronounced. The symptoms are clear. First, the resources devoted to foreign policy have declined. For example, the expenditures on strategic nuclear forces have dropped (although those on tactical forces have increased slightly), and the proportion of French GNP devoted to aid to the developing countries has fallen. Even during de Gaulle's presidency there had been substantial public dissatisfaction with the real or imagined costs of an activist foreign policy. As Hoffmann puts it, "De Gaulle wanted prosperity for *grandeur*, the French wanted *grandeur* as a by-product of prosperity."[21] With the shift in resources to domestic projects, what the French will be getting in foreign policy will be a package of the same size with the same label, but less and less in it. Even a major improvement in the French economic situation would, however, be unlikely to reverse the shift in the priorities of the government and return foreign policy to the place it occupied on the Gaullist agenda. Foreign policy is not central to the realization of Giscard's political designs in the way it was to de Gaulle's: France's role in the world has become merely one concern among others for France's new rulers.

Paradoxically, this turning inward of French politics has been accompanied by a new analysis of the international system and a new rhetoric that stress global interdependence. The "globalist" doctrines that Giscard has expounded in the first year of his presidency are his original contribution to a foreign policy whose major lines were drawn by his predecessors. But although recognition of the weight of forces, economic and political, that lie beyond the range of manipulation of individual states and even of alliances of states like the European Common Market has led Giscard to pessimistic conclusions about the usefulness of international cooperation on anything less than a global level; the operational consequences of those conclusions are a foreign policy not very different from de Gaulle's and Pompidou's. The Gaullists from considerations of *grandeur*, Giscard from considerations focused on the domestic economy and on an economic analysis of the international system, all end up concluding that little is to be gained and something to be lost by closer cooperation with Atlantic allies or even by reinforcing the European Community.

Similarly, Giscard now wants to assume the brokerage role that de Gaulle tried to perform between the United States and the Third World—in Indochina and Latin America, for example—though with reduced resources and a less persevering political will. Whereas de Gaulle believed that room and need for this mediation derived above all from the mutual paralysis of the two superpowers, hence their inability to regulate regional conflicts, Giscard's analysis leans more heavily on the economic interdependence that makes even a nuclear superpower like the United States vulnerable to decision-making in Abu Dhabi. In both cases, the opportunity for an active French role in relations between the industrial and the developing worlds is linked to a perception of America's relative impotence in regulating a certain class of international problems. In yet another respect, the globalist doctrines end up where Gaullist policies did: since global international politics, like global energy conferences, rarely produce results, and since those international groups such as the EEC that can decide anything are too limited to deal with problems whose causes lie outside their reach, Giscard is left with bilateral deals. The fact that negotiating alone allows him to maximize French economic advantage without shouldering the economic problems of his EEC neighbors obviously makes this an attractive alternative to working within the Community or the Atlantic Alliance.

What this means for Franco-American relations already seems clear from the first year of Giscard's presidency. The Gaullist design remains the official blueprint, but the government will treat fewer and fewer of the issues that arise between the two countries as matters of principle to be resolved by reference to the grand design. Giscard's analysis of the differences between the two countries sets the tone: there is no principled ground of conflict between France and the United States. The United States does not aim at domination. Rather, differences are the result on the disparity in dimension of the two nations and, as such, resolvable on a case-by-case basis. Giscard's willingness to back down on the trilateral conference of oil producers, industrial states, and developing nations; his silence on the Kissinger statement on the use of force in the Middle East, where de Gaulle surely would have spoken out; his attitude toward French participation in NATO—all these are indications of what the policy of this government is likely to be: accommodating insofar as no old principle need be officially abandoned. Indeed Giscard has been willing to back off even in some cases in which Gaullists had perceived high stakes, notably, in his decision to allow the merger of the one remaining independent French computer firm (Compagnie Internationale pour l'Informatique) with an American-controlled firm, Honeywell-Bull, and in the decision to abandon the "*tous azimuts*" nuclear posture.[c] There is, then, new room for accommodation, but within limits that for all the reasons discussed above remain basically those of Gaullist foreign policy.

In sum, the likelihood that Giscard will be any more open to an American design for a new Atlantic partnership than were de Gaulle, Pompidou, and Jobert is extremely small. What has changed is the willingness to be conciliatory and cooperative on a case-to-case basis in a number of areas in which Franco-American relations have been tense. Whether this is possible will depend in large measure on whether the United States will be willing to pare down its ambitions with respect to general agreements on coordination of policies with

---

[c]The notion that French nuclear forces should be prepared to respond to an attack from any direction (*tous azimuts*) and not targeted only on Communist countries had in any event received little practical implementation.

European allies and focus on those areas in which substantive agreement can be reached. Decisions about given policies will perhaps matter less to the future of relations between the United States and France than the pattern of decision-making on issues in which both states have high stakes. What confronts the United States is not the need for critical choices but for critical rethinking of the relationships with old allies.

Notes

1. In preface to Antoine-Pierre Mariano, *Métamorphose de l'économie française 63-73* (Paris: Arthaud, 1973), p. 8.

2. For example, in 1963, 24 per cent of all households, and 30 per cent of working-class households, declared themselves to be living in inadequate housing; by 1970 the numbers had dropped to 16 per cent and 19 per cent respectively. Numbers here and in all following notes have been rounded off. Mariano, *Métamorphose*, p. 21.

3. Mariano, *Métamorphose*, p. 309.

4. Whether one considers wage differentials or the distribution of income, the inequalities in France are significantly larger than in other industrial countries. See Lionel Stoleru, *Vaincre la pauvreté* (Paris: Flammarion, 1974), pp. 28-46.

5. If calculated by ILO norms, the number of unemployed in France would be somewhat over a million (*Le Monde*, May 23, 1975).

6. Commissariat général du Plan, *1985: La France face au choc du futur* (Paris: Colin, 1972).

7. Ibid., p. 166.

8. This idea is explored in Suzanne Berger, Peter Gourevitch, Patrice Higonnet, and Karl Kaiser, "The Problem of Reform in France: The Ideas of Local Elites," *Political Science Quarterly*, no. 3 (September 1969).

9. See Charles Albert Michalet, "France," in *Big Business and the State*, ed. R. Vernon (Cambridge: Harvard University Press, 1974).

10. Georges Pompidou, *Le noeud gordien* (Paris: Plon, 1974), p. 174.

11. See Pierre Drouin, "Vivre avec la crise," *Le Monde*, December 6, 1974.

12. Stoleru, *Vaincre la pauvreté*, p. 52.

13. Phillipe Herzog, "Quelle crise, quels remèdes? II. L'austérité: un fléau et une escroquerie," *Le Monde*, December 25, 1974.

14. *Le Monde*, January 14, 1975.

15. On the "new logic," see the discussion by the Communist economist Philippe Herzog in A. Harris and A. Sédouy, *Voyage à l'intérieur du parti communiste.*

16. *Le Monde*, October 25, 1974.

17. Andrieu, a leading figure in the Party, was editor of *L'Humanité* at the time he was interviewed. Harris and Sédouy, *Voyage*, p. 44.

18. Harris and Sédouy, *Voyage*, p. 230.

19. See Stanley Hoffmann, "De Gaulle's Foreign Policy," in *Decline or Renewal? France Since the 1930s* (New York: Viking, 1974), pp. 320-21.

20. These points have been developed at greater length and with far greater lucidity by Stanley Hoffmann in "Perceptions and Policies: France and the United States," in Hoffmann, *Decline or Renewal?*

21. Hoffmann, *Decline or Renewal?*, p. 323.

VI

Germany: A
European and
World Power

Alfred Grosser

A Double Identity Problem

In spite of the trend toward transnational arrangements, in spite of the similarities among national patterns and developments, the different countries of Western Europe each have their own specific problems. The German Federal Republic is the only one to have as its central problem the question of its identity. It was central at any rate until the early 70s. Recent developments extrapolated into the future give reason to believe that a process of normalization is under way, that is, a more and more marked attenuation of this issue. The problem is a double one: identity as defined vis-à-vis the Germany of the past; and identity vis-à-vis the other German state.

Identity vis-à-vis the Past

Here the past is not that of the black years that immediately preceded the birth of the Federal Republic. On the contrary almost. The Germany of ruins and misery seems so distant that the economic difficulties of today are compared only with the prosperity of yesterday, and not with the cold and hunger of 1945-1948, by comparison with which the Germans of today are swimming in affluence. This is what led the president of the Republic to say on December 24, 1974, in a televised Christmas broadcast:

We should bethink ourselves tonight of how we celebrated the last wartime Christmas eve thirty years ago. Even twenty-five years ago my unforgotten

173

predecessor Professor Heuss said on the same occasion: "The catalogue of German distress and wants is endless. If I wanted to list it, it would be a chain of grey misery."

Breaking in appearance with logic by shifting from misery to the international situation, he continued: "Now, my dear fellow citizens, today our country stands there respected. A neighbor and a partner, one that can be relied upon, that has taken the trouble to learn from its past."

The theme is that of humiliation overcome. The Federal Republic no longer needs to identify itself with Germany punished, German excommunicated. But the excommunication did not come from misery; it came from the Hitlerian past. The democracy of Bonn has undertaken with courage ever since its birth a double operation of distancing and self-definition. Hitler was rejected, but the legacy of the unified Germany was insisted on; and this in turn entailed acceptance of liability for the crimes committed by the Germany that was.[1]

In 1975 one can say that on the whole the identity problem with reference to the past has been settled, thanks in part to the transition provided by the Heinemann-Brandt period. Just before these two old opponents of Hitler entered the government, there had been Heinrich Lübke in the presidency and Kurt Georg Kiesinger in the chancellery—two men of dubious political antecedents. De Gaulle is said to have remarked that he had great respect for Willy Brandt, but that he preferred dealing with Kiesinger: in case of disagreement, all he had to do was look Kiesinger in the eye and recall the past! When Chancellor Brandt knelt before the ghetto monument of Warsaw and signed a treaty with Poland in October 1970, an era was over. The past was both accepted and overcome. Brandt himself did not entirely understand this: one of the reasons for his fall was that he appeared to be and conducted himself in large measure as a postwar man, whereas the great majority of his compatriots expected of him that he not only put an end to the obsession with the past but open up new horizons. With Walter Scheel and Helmut Schmidt, this postwar period is now more or less over.

How much over? From the demographic point of view, no question: more than 45 per cent of the inhabitants of the Federal Republic have been born in the last thirty years, that is, since the war. Only about 15 per cent were twenty or older in 1933, when Hitler came to power.[2] That is a fact of life too often forgotten in other countries, where one speaks too easily of "the Germans" as though the composition of the population never changed.

Indeed, that is a first caveat to make concerning the apparent solution of the problem posed by the legacy of the past. The identification—unjustified—of the Federal Republic with Hitler's Germany or with a kind of eternal Germany forever to be feared is still present, consciously or potentially, in the minds of many people, in the United States as in Norway, as in Great Britain, as in Belgium. In France, this image revives every time some part of the population (including a good part of the so-called elite) feels itself in a position of inferiority vis-à-vis its eastern neighbor. In July and in September 1974, all it took was a minor incident—the trial of Beate Klarsfeld, accused of having tried to kidnap a former Gestapo chief and bring him to France—and then Helmut Schmidt's refusal to accept the French position in a matter of agricultural prices, for the French press to revive themes and phrases that one would have thought gone forever.

Even so, it seems likely that these revivals will become more and more rare, so long as American policy does not seem to favor the former enemy too much by comparison with the traditional ally, which could only incite some Frenchmen to nurse their resentment by invoking memories of the German past.

In the Federal Republic, the new leaders have no more complexes; or more precisely, make it a point of showing that they have no more, which is a kind of negative bond to the past. The sometimes overvigorous statements of the Minister of Finance Hans Apel are inspired in part by the desire to show that the men of his generation (he was born in 1932) do not have to apologize any more for the German past. It is probable that this new complex of wanting to appear without complexes will also pass in the near future.

On the other hand there are two things that give promise of lasting longer. The first is cultural in character and will simply be mentioned here: that is, the lack of roots in Germany because of the breach with its own history.[3] In the event of a serious crisis, this could be a source of confusion and an opportunity for political adventurism.

The second phenomenon will last even longer, since it touches directly on the second of the two identity problems, that of defining oneself vis-à-vis East Germany. Here it is a question of the rivalry for the legacy of a united Germany: which of the two successor states is the legitimate heir? The rivalry is complicated by changing attitudes in the German Democratic Republic (GDR) and by the determination to maintain the humiliating regime of dispossession established in 1944-45, in order to preserve a precious link to German unity.[4]

Identity in the Present

This determination has for some time been in contradiction with the desire to treat Berlin, not in the context of its four-power status (that is, with West Berlin under occupation by the United States, Great Britain, and France), but as a *Land* (province) like any other in the Federal Republic. Since 1972, the government has made a clear choice: it links West Berlin as much as possible to the Federal Republic and represents it internationally, but adheres to the fundamental principle expressed in point 5 of the *Gemeinsame Entschliessung* (Joint Resolution) of the Bundestag adopted by the three parties on May 17, 1972: "The rights and responsibilities of the four powers in regard to Germany as a whole and to Berlin are not affected by the treaties. The German Bundestag considers, in view of the fact that the final settlement of the German question as a whole is still pending, the maintenance of these rights and responsibilities as essential."

At Bonn, as in Washington, London, and Paris, it has been viewed as a success that the GDR has agreed to sign, as a supplement to the treaty between the two states on December 21, 1972, a letter to the Soviet government stating: "The GDR and the German Federal Republic affirm that the rights and responsibilities of the four powers and the four-power agreements, decisions, and practices that go with them are not in any way affected by this treaty."

The assent of the German Democratic Republic on this point was the more impressive in that it had done everything in its power since 1958 to suppress all references to the four-power statute of occupation. It had always been cognizant, moreover, that the frontier between the two German states is, like that between two African states, a line arbitrarily drawn by conquerors to delimit their future domains. One has only to see how, in late 1974 and early 1975, the two states were brandishing maps drawn up by the European Advisory Commission in London in September 1944 by way of arguing the question whether the frontier on the Elbe is located on the east bank, west bank, or middle of the stream!

Where the GDR differs markedly from the Federal Republic of Germany (FRG) is in its refusal to accept any thought of national unity, even as a distant hope.[5] On October 7, 1974, the revised constitution of the GDR went into effect. This defines the country, no longer as a "socialist state of a German nation," but as a "socialist state of workers and peasants." And the former beginning of the preamble ("born of the responsibility to lead the entire German nation on the path to socialism") now reads: "In pursuit of the revolutionary tradition of the German working class and founded on the liberation from fascism" the GDR is henceforth "forever and irrevocably" allied with the USSR and sees itself constitutionally as "an inseparable part of the socialist community of nations." In the face of this determination of the GDR to have its own identity, the FRG will certainly continue to speak of a German nation separated into two states. Its allies will have to respect this point of view. But even in the Republic the trend of opinion is moving unquestionably toward the idea of "two states, two nations."[6]

It is difficult to predict the consequences of this uncertainty for national identity. In the event of unexpected changes in the East, these could be significant. In any case, no other country in Western Europe has this problem, which showed up very well in a poll taken in November 1974 on the name people wanted to see the country called in the media. Some 57 per cent preferred Bundesrepublik Deutschland; 9 per cent, the acronym BRD; 22 per cent, Deutschland (but only 13 per cent of those under thirty years of age).[7]

No other country, then, has a neighbor at once so close and so distant—close by language and a shared past, distant especially because of an almost fantastic

ignorance of East German reality; both close and distant by the influence that
the GDR exercises directly or indirectly on the internal politics of the Federal
Republic. In what other European country could there have been a Guillaume
affair, conceivable only in Vietnam or in Korea? In what other Western country
is the "domestic enemy" seen so much as the agent, real or potential, of the
foreign enemy? The intensification of the witch hunt (more on this later) is not
understandable without taking into account the treaties that have been signed
with the USSR and the GDR. It is just because the FRG is still unsure of its
identity and itself—no doubt wrongly—that it is the only country in Western
Europe to have accompanied the détente without by a stiffening within. This
stiffening has been demonstrated once again in the verdict of the Federal
Constitutional Tribunal on May 22, 1975, published only in July of that year;
the Tribunal authorizes in effect a sort of McCarthyism, since every applicant for
a government job, whether as official or employee, in the postal service as well as
in teaching, is subject to a loyalty investigation testing whether he can be
counted upon to defend the free, democratic constitution in all circumstances.

Political Power and Economic Power

Yet barring an unforeseeable reversal of the present tendency, the orientation
and exercise of the institutionalized power of the Federal Republic will not
create any particular difficulty for its partners, as would, for example, the
participation of Communists in the governments of France or Italy, or even the
collapse of the political system in Belgium. That is not to say that there are not
power problems in the Federal Republic or that their evolution is without
importance for the United States.

Nature and Exercise of Political Power

More than in the United States or France, and as much as in Great Britain, it is
the parties that are at the heart of the political game in Germany. The array has
become simpler with time. There are only three that still count, and the total
percentage of votes won by the Social Democrats, Christian Democrats (CDU/
CSU) and Liberals (FDP) taken together has risen from 72.1 in 1949 to 99.1 in
1972.

This concentration has been fostered, first, by the electoral law, and second,
by the system of public aid to political parties. The 5 per cent clause, which
provides that no party benefits from the system of proportional representation
unless it receives a minimum of 5 per cent of the total vote on the national level,
has helped kill off the smaller groups. If, for example, on September 28, 1969
the National Democrats had gotten 226,000 additional votes, they would have

won, not zero seats, but twenty-five seats in the Bundestag, and the Brandt-Scheel government would have been mathematically impossible. As for the revenues of the different parties (dues and official subsidies), they were in 1972, 114 million DM for the Social Democrats, 137 million for the Christian Democrats-Christian Socialists (CDU/CSU), and 24.5 million for the Liberals.

The electoral law has had other consequences: it has both reinforced and weakened the third party, i.e., the Liberals. It has reinforced it because, thanks to proportional representation and the fact that, except for 1957, neither of the two big parties has ever obtained an absolute majority, the Liberals have held the balance of power. Contrast this with the situation in Britain, where the party of the same name, though much more important in its share of the electorate, plays no role: a majority system of representation gives it about 2 per cent of the seats in the House for about 20 per cent of the votes. Under Walter Scheel, as under his successor Hermann Genscher (elected president of the party on October 1, 1974), the Liberals have been able to exploit this position by demanding important posts and a role in government out of proportion to their electoral strength[8] and membership. (In mid-1975, the FDP had 70,800 members, as against 970,000 for the SDP and about 700,000 for the CDU/CSU.)

On the other hand, the Liberals are haunted by the terrible threshold of 5 per cent and never know whether it pays to play ball or mark their independence. If they were to disappear from the Bundestag (or, what would amount to the same thing, if the CDU/CSU were to obtain once again an absolute majority), German politics would be significantly altered, though surely not in its fundamental orientation, namely, in its concentration on wooing the voters of the center. In other words, the elimination of the FDP, whether as a parliamentary group or as arbiter, would no doubt generate a harder battle than ever between the two major parties, but this conflict would continue to be tempered, as in Great Britain and the United States, by the need not to frighten the independent voters.

What is more, this independent faction of the electorate, as in other countries, is more and more numerous, while partisan allegiances get weaker all the time.[9] This development reflects in part a rather remarkable homogenization of the electorate, with differences of sex, region, and even age playing a less and less important role.[10] That is why it is not easy to see more than a few months ahead, let alone a year. The provincial elections of 1974-75 saw the Social Democrats suffer heavy losses, particularly in Hamburg on March 9, 1974 and in Berlin on March 3, 1975, followed by a clear recovery (moderate losses in Rhineland-Palatinate on March 9, 1975, in Schleswig-Holstein on April 13, and in Nordrhein-Westfalen on May 4, and a slight gain in the Saar the same day). The Christian Democrats had their greatest success in Hamburg and in Hesse (on October 27, 1974), then returned to their old figures in the following spring. The FDP meanwhile started this period off well (spring 1974), then lost ground, only to regain confidence in the spring of 1975. In light of these fluctuations, who is to say how the independent voters will act in the decisive Federal elections of September 1976?

To be sure, this increasing mobility of a more homogeneous electorate might, in case of serious crisis, suddenly raise up a new party. But that is not likely in the near future. For that to happen, the CDU/CSU would have to be back in power, that is, no longer able to serve as a receptacle for fear-filled malcontents, while the SPD, if pushed into the opposition, would appear to those same malcontents as too "red" for their taste. The only real threat of break-up comes from the CSU of Franz-Josef Strauss. This group is annoyed enough with the "Big Brother party" [the CDU] (in particular because it nominated almost unanimously its own president Helmut Kohl as its candidate for the chancellorship without first asking the agreement of the CSU) to dissolve the merger and set up a genuine fourth party in provinces other than Bavaria. But the probability of such a step is small.

In the meantime the two major parties are obviously careful not to offend the mass of electors; and the directors of the SPD are particularly anxious about a possible slip between the doctrinal concerns of its militants and the bread-and-butter demands of the average voter. With more vigor even than his predecessor, Helmut Schmidt gave vent to these concerns before the party congress of the SPD in Hamburg:[11]

I should like to make a few critical remarks about what I heard yesterday evening and this morning. I must say that I am not very enthusiastic about it. You have only to imagine that the debate that is taking place here was broadcast live yesterday evening and this morning on both programs of German television or simply on the radio, so that everyone could hear it. You can imagine that of one hundred citizens, ninety-five would long since have shut it off, in part because they would not have understood it, in part because it would not have interested them, and because it has nothing at all to say about their material concerns!

A political party, that must fight daily to retain the confidence that is expressed in the small cross on the ballot, that must struggle daily to win those votes again and to see to it that next time perhaps two or three more people or 2, 3, or 5 per cent more will give it their votes—such a party need only continue to present itself to the public in this way if it wants to throw away the power of legislation and administration on the Federal level and in the provinces.

One can well understand Mr. Schmidt's concern when one sees what, under an SPD government, the word "socialism" represents for the voters (see Tables VI-1 and VI-2).

But can one entirely separate the manner of governing from all theoretical conceptions of the nature and purpose of power?[12] For example, what should be the field of action of governmental power?

One aspect of the answer is linked to the nature of federalism. Do not financial and social necessities impose a strong central power? In 1974 the deficit of public budgets was over 27 billion DM (as against 10 billion in 1973).

Table VI-1
Germany: Public Opinion Poll Concerning Socialism, 1970-73

Question: Would you vote for or against a government that said it wanted to introduce socialism?

	November 1970	May 1972	June 1973
		(in percentages)	
Against	53	53	63
For	1	17	16
Undecided and no opinion	23	30	21

Source: Institut fur Demoskopie Allensbach, *Jahrbuch der Oeffentlichen Meinung, 1968-73* (Allensbach, 1974), p. 331.

Table VI-2
Breakdown of Results of the Poll of June 1973
(in percentages)

	Against	For	Undecided
Overall	63	16	21
Men	64	20	16
Women	63	12	25
Age Groups:			
16-29 years	50	24	26
30-44 years	63	12	20
45-59 years	68	16	16
60 and older	67	11	22
Political Affiliation:			
SPD	50	27	23
CDU/CSU	84	3	13
FDP	64	15	21

The Federal share of this deficit is less than half (12 billion). Even if, as is the case, this deficit is not only accepted, but deliberately created as an instrument for priming the economic pump, can the central government have an economic policy when control over a large part of the public finances lies in other hands and it is obliged to make the best of whatever coordination can be arranged, reinforced by a little pressure on the provinces and the municipalities? A similar difficulty arises in scholastic and university matters, where the autonomy of the different provinces is far from an unmitigated advantage.

The second aspect is more important, especially with a government led by a party that claims in spite of everything to be socialist. Political power ought to be able to see ahead. Should it plan and then intervene to make its plan a reality? The answer given by one of Germany's best technicians, Professor Reimut Jochimsen (an economist who headed the team of planners of the governmental process in the Chancellery from 1969 to 1972 and is today secretary of state in the Ministry of Science), is nuanced:[13]

In sum, one may say that we have gone beyond the dogmatic rejection of the concept of planning, wherein criticism confounded an ideologically and historically motivated centrally planned economy and administration with anarchic, spreading state intervention, and the emergency controls of the Second World War with the central administration and planned economies of the Communist states of Eastern Europe. Today it is accepted that planning as a preparation and systematization of the decision-making process in a democratic state plays a necessary and legitimate role in fostering reform, participation, efficiency, and criticism. It comprises the fixing of competence, goals, means, methods, and information that are required if the state is to fulfill its public tasks within the context of the socio-economic development of our society. This task necessarily requires transcending privacy of decisions (or their consequences) in public as well as nonpublic spheres. In that regard it is clear that the integration of the plans of private enterprises into an officially conceived projection of social-economic development—and the same in regard to public data, activities, and achievements—will necessarily confront all participating agencies with ever more complex problems of the urgency, the possibilities, and the limits of the state's capacity for direction. . . . Such projections call for neither a fear of planning nor a mania for planning, but rather dull, step-by-step work and a systematically built structure of integrated special and cross-sectional plans. This structure is intended to improve the quality of day-to-day decisions while retaining flexibility with the guidance of a more deliberate, longer-run, more systematic preparation of decisions that takes account of interactions within the system . . .

So much subtlety is hardly popular within a party that, on the occasion of the Congress of Mannheim of November 1975, wanted to discuss and adopt a "long-range program" whose first draft (December 1974) had already stirred up a fuss because it provided for much more permanent and profound interventions of the state with a view to reorienting the economy and changing the social structure.

The debate is occurring just at a time when the economic crisis is evoking, in Germany as elsewhere, a double, contradictory reaction: blaming the government for the trouble while summoning it to intervene with more authority and in a wider sphere. The crisis is felt correctly to be international, which only makes the problem bigger: must we continue, at home as well as abroad, to rely on the supposed virtues of almost-pure liberalism?

Yes, the president of the Republic answers, in an astonishing passage of the speech delivered on the twenty-fifth anniversary of the Bundesverband der Deutschen Industrie (October 29, 1974):[14]

Our economic, social and political existence would very quickly be in question, if the world economy were to return to the conditions of the 30's. To be sure, we have learned in the meantime, we know today, what we have to do. We know that there is no alternative to a world economy based on free exchange of goods, services, and capital. Experience tells us that every effort to direct, all planning, every impediment to the free movement of goods in the world—means that much less in economic performance.

Is the answer really yes? This is the question posed by the monthly journal *Capital* (hardly a spokesman for nationalization), while pointing out how much of the German economy the oil-producing countries could buy if they wanted to and if ultraliberalism continued to prevail.[15]

It is obvious that this kind of interrogation is not all that different from that of the European trade unions when confronted by those foreign centers of power constituted by multinational enterprises. Thus the Deutsche Gewerkschaftsband, like central trade union federations in other countries, has come to envisage transnational actions as a way of confronting transnational entrepreneurs on an equal basis. In the programmatic address delivered by Heinz O. Vetter to the Tenth Ordinary Congress of the GDB, which reelected him president by 440 votes out of 462, he stressed the following: "After the poverty of the Third World, the greatest economic and social challenge facing us is the power of the Multis (*sic:* the multinationals)—and not only for the trade unions. They represent a challenge to the parliaments and governments of all industrial lands." Meanwhile advocacy of transnational measures has not stopped national federations from calling on their governments to use their powers to control foreign investment.

It is quite possible that the eventual aggravation of the crisis will stimulate this kind of demand. If that were to happen, the United States would not be able to avoid serious difficulties and tensions with the FRG unless it were prepared to change drastically its global attitude. The American government, instead of considering itself as a defender of American enterprise, would have to adopt a policy concerning these multinational firms that took account of its political relations with Western Europe, particularly Germany.

Extra-Institutional Forces

We will return later on to this question of the interrelations of domestic economy and foreign policy. In any event, the problem of the real distribution of power (especially but not exclusively that of the relations between institutionalized political power and economic power) is a live issue in the Federal Republic as in other Western democracies. It is difficult to analyze this problem—even harder to speculate about the future—without first discussing certain ideas which are currently fashionable and which specialists use according to their political-ideological loyalties (thus "ruling class(es)," "technostructure," "technocracy"). But without undertaking so difficult a task, some observations of a nonideological character are still possible.

The first is no doubt more pertinent to the Federal Republic than to other countries of that type: concentration of economic power is growing.[16] It is particularly strong if one ignores the evidence—significant in itself—on size of enterprise and distribution of shares and simply focuses on the degree of control of a very small number of banks.

The second observation is that in Germany, as in the United States, it is not easy to determine who leads whom to do what. Is it the business powers who are the real masters of the political power? Is it the political and administrative establishment that dominates the economy? Either thesis is exaggerated and simplistic. The complex relations between politics and the economy would be worth studying in detail (though it has yet to be done), particularly in regard to the links between the Bundesbank (the central bank) and the private banks. Uncertainty in this area obviously has implications for international diplomacy. Thus foreign policy decisions, especially in economic matters (whose importance has grown considerably since October 1973) rest on so complex an interplay within the country that foreign partners have no choice but to take account of a multiplicity of actors and are constantly tempted not to limit their efforts to relations with the government, but to combine these with overtures to the more powerful figures in the private sector.

It is not possible here to list these private powers, the less so since it would require a sort of table of the German economy by sector. On the other hand, we can look briefly at a few of the major forces at the interface of the economic, political, and social spheres.

The Federal Republic is today a country like others; that is, it no longer contains a powerful interest group born of its own peculiar situation. It was not always thus, and the German government long trembled before those refugee organizations that claimed the right to speak for those Germans driven in 1945 from Eastern Europe.

Statistically, the refugees number ten million persons, but only because the law counts as such the children of expellees born in the Federal Republic, (between 1949 and 1970 the number of expellees increased in this way from eight to thirteen millions!) In fact, these organizations, although generously subsidized by the Federal government and the provinces,[17] have no hold on the young. These are completely assimilated to the indigenous population thanks to a systematic and costly policy inaugurated by the Adenauer government in 1950. This policy is radically different from the one followed by the Arab countries in dealing with Palestinian refugees; and it was no doubt not until this policy could have its full effect that it was possible for the Federal government to normalize the international situation by recognizing the Oder-Neisse frontier and by signing peace treaties with Poland and Czechoslovakia.

On the other hand the power of the farming interest has not been injured by the fall in their numbers; or at any rate, not in the proportion of this decline. In 1962 there were still 3.3 million persons employed in the primary sector (agriculture, forestry, livestock, and fishing); today there are no more than 1.8 millions. But, while they do not have the influence of the American farmers' lobby, Germany cultivators have kept a good deal of their power, if only because of their electoral "clout." This influence is not confined to domestic politics, since agriculture is without a doubt the most Europeanized element in the Common Market economy, and since the relations between Europe and the United States are concerned in large part with the prices and markets of agricultural products.

But in the last analysis the Federal Republic is obviously first and foremost an industrial nation. How is the power of industry organized? If we confine ourselves to the cover federations, the central organizations, one can line up the employers on one side, the unions on the other—the sort of thing that President Scheel did in his speech to the BDI (Bundesverband der Deutschen Industrie): "A few weeks ago I said on a similar occasion—and I am sure that you noted this carefully: the German trade union federation and its members have deserved well of our state and people in the last twenty-five years. Now I say to you: we owe you, German industry and its representatives, the same thanks and the same recognition."

But in order to understand the relative forces, one has to remember that German employers are organized in two ways. They are grouped on the one hand as producers in the Bundesverband der Deutschen Industrie; on the other hand, as employers in the Bundesvereinigung der Deutschen Arbeitgeber-verbände (BDA) [National Association of German Employer Federations].[18] It is the latter that handles wage and salary discussions with the unions and brings pressure on the government in matters of pay and employment; whereas the BDI is concerned with problems of investment and production. The recent increase in unemployment thus makes the president of the BDA, Hanns-Martin Schleyer, a very important person.[19]

The two organizations nevertheless have similar attitudes toward state power and union power. In the speech cited above, President Scheel reproached them for a contradiction, while seemingly unable to surmount his own liberal contradiction between the will to act politically in order to influence events and trends, and the conviction that one should not do anything to hamper the "free play of forces."

Ladies and gentlemen, the shifting of losses to the state necessarily raises the question where the profits belong. The market economy cannot be simply a fair-weather organization. Whoever tries to transfer to the state responsibility for automobile or housing stocks necessarily gives up his right to free entrepreneurial decision-making.

The market economy does not guarantee profits. The market economy demands continuous foresight, continuous adaptation to new conditions. To be sure, not every shift in structure is foreseeable and assessable in advance. But this much is sure: through timely action, crises can and must in most cases be avoided.

Indeed anyone who gives currency to the false notion that severe structural crises of entire economic sectors are unavoidable implicitly poses the question: should investment decisions not be planned and made elsewhere?

Ladies and gentlemen, I am surely not suspect of suggesting a general direction of investment by the state. Therefore, my thought is that the citizens of our nation must always be convinced of the superiority of the system that gives entrepreneurs freedom to make investment decisions. Anyone who wants to drag the state into the boat in bad times will have trouble keeping it from the helm in good.

So long a quotation is justified by its significance: is it not a foretaste of what is likely to arise in all Western countries in the next few years if the crisis continues and deepens, namely, the constant reinforcement of the role of the state? In the face of union power, the attitude of the employers is nuanced. They negotiate American fashion, that is, toughly but coolly, with the aim of coming to an agreement. They consent to modified comanagement, but complain of the increasing strength of the DGB.

"On Our Way to the Trade Union State? A metamorphosis from a defensive organization of the underprivileged to the strongest power in the nation?" This headline for the report of a panel conference on trade-union power that fills several pages in two successive issues of *Die Zeit*, the great weekly of the liberal left,[20] is revealing of a widespread state of mind even among people highly critical of capitalism and of the power of the great enterprises and banks.

It is true that the German trade union federation is a power—if only by its massive presence and wealth. On January 1, 1974 it counted 7.2 million members, of whom 674,000 state functionaries, slightly less than in the Deutscher Beamtenbund [Civil servants' federation], independent and conservative, with its 718,000 members. The membership is very unequally divided among sixteen federated unions, ranging from the superpowerful IG Metall, which alone has 2.5 million members, followed at a distance by the OTV (public services and transportation) with one million, to the small artists' union with 35,000 members. The system of voting in the individual enterprises is such as to give the Federation a far greater proportion of the seats in company councils than would be justified by its share of unionized labor. Thus in the council elections of 1972 in the metallurgy industries, the IG Metall won 97 per cent of the seats in the workers' college and 82 per cent of those in the white collar council.[21]

The DGB is also, directly or indirectly, a major economic power. It is a banker (the Bank für Gemeinwirtschaft is the fourth largest in the Republic); builder (the enterprise Neue Heimat, with 261,000 apartments built and an annual volume of business of almost 5 billion DM is the largest owner of real property in the country); merchant (the "Co-op" group, with more than 4,000 food stores, 144 other stores, and 22 factories, is the largest retail chain in the country); travel agency (250,000 clients a year for the GUT [Gemeinwirtschaftliches Unternehmen für Turistik]); insurer (Volksfürsorge AG is the largest life insurance company); shipowner; proprietor of a chain of book clubs; etc., etc. This impressive list, which is often used in anti-union argument, shows how the DGB, through its business enterprises (which incidentally function in very undemocratic fashion),[22] is integrated into the economic system and has consequently very little desire to change it. In addition, its financial resources and the strength of its organization allow it to be a responsible negotiator. It makes more use of the threat of strike than of the strike itself, and this has contributed in large degree to the continuity of German production. Despite lively reactions in some of the press, the DGB's new formulation of its strike rule in June 1974 does not rule out settlements by negotiation and simply grants more autonomy in these matters to the sixteen federated syndicates.[23]

On the other hand, the spread of comanagement in private enterprises poses fundamental problems in that it brings the DGB into practically all boards of directors in large and medium firms. Meanwhile, with general elections one year away, it seems that the new codetermination law, promised by the Schmidt government as it was by the Brandt government, will probably not see the light of day—or if it does, in a form so attenuated as to be without much effect. There is no doubt that the threat of increased union power is producing a certain amount of recoil even among the center left.

The response of the unions to these reservations is that they do not want either to dispossess private enterprise or direct it, but simply to keep a hand on it.[24] In contrast to French, Italian, and British unions, they have little interest in nationalization. They want simply to participate in the management of the means of production. (The preamble of the Fundamental Program adopted in November 1963 states explicitly: "The workers, that is, the vast majority of the population, are today as before still excluded from the power of disposing of the means of production.") It is not even sure that they still aspire, as in 1950 when they demanded that comanagement be extended to the entire national economy, to a share in overall economic power; or even that they want the government, in which they are heavily represented, to make full use of such a power. Chancellor Schmidt, in his speech to the DGB of October 2, 1974 on the occasion of its twenty-fifth anniversary, teased them a little on this point:[25]

Discussions about price controls and investment controls are an example of the necessity to relate to reality. Ideology is of little use here. What's more, one can not be at once opposed to wage directives—rightly, in my opinion—and at the same time for investment directives. In any case, it's obvious that there would be plenty of fighting if we tried this, and that both are tied together. Another point: the more the state tries to make policy on investments, the less room there is for co-management and the greater the risk that particular erroneous decisions will find general implementation.

In other words, the unions would be better able to use their power against employers if the state kept hands off. But is this not equivalent to abandoning the hope of orienting the economy and even more of changing the structure of power?

That is the argument of all those who attack the government and the unions from the Left, sometimes within the SPD and the DGB. One of their arguments is that many wage-earners have lost interest in union activity because they feel betrayed. The wildcat strikes of 1973 may recur and spread.

But the reverse argument also has some weight: the DGB is losing its hold on the wage-earners precisely because it appears too powerful, too omnipresent. Proof of this disaffection seems evident in the social elections of 1974 (insurance and pension funds) in which the DGB, admittedly already no more than a minority in 1968, fell from 29.2 to 17.4 per cent of the votes to the Bundesversicherungsanstalt für Angestellte, while the rival Deutsche Angestell-tengewerkschaft, though more moderate, fell from 49.9 to 25.8 per cent. The winners were those lists that kept strictly to issues concerning the management of the funds.

The DGB is in effect exposed to double pressure, from the left and the right. Its internal evolution, as well as its economic, political, and social role, will depend for one thing on the business situation: a deeper recession would considerably reduce its power, but would perhaps give it more the appearance of a defender of the workers against a possible Christian Democratic government. But it would also depend on the ideological climate of the Federal Republic as a whole, which is obviously in its turn linked to the economic situation—but not to that alone.

Ideological Challenges and Hardenings

The ideological climate changes fast. A description of the situation in the universities, in the Catholic Church, or the media made around 1970 is very much out of date in 1975. How, then, can one predict what the climate will be in 1980?

Certainly not by looking at the figures on extremists of the Right and Left that appear regularly in the reports of the Bundesamt für Verfassungsschutz [Office for protection of the constitution], the most recent of which was published in June 1975.[26] These figures show the extreme right leveling off or in decline: 119 organizations at the end of 1974 with 21,400 members, as against 129 at the end of 1972 with 21,700 members, and a total circulation of 196,700 for the rightist press against 207,500 earlier. They also show the extreme left—orthodox Communists and "New Left"—as more concentrated and growing: 302 organizations in 1974 against 365 in 1972. But none of that is very important, since the influence, direct or indirect, of the current of opinion (including reactions against it) can hardly be measured by such statistics, which are sometimes astonishing in their pretended precision. Here is a sample:

At the end of 1974 there were, so far as we know, a total of 1,467 (1973: 1,723) left extremists in public employment. Of some 3.4 million public servants, therefore, there was one left extremist per 2,302. Of the 258 of these employed by the Federal government, approximately 78 per cent (203) were employed by the railway and postal services. Of 911 in provincial service, 45.6 per cent (415) were teachers and 29.5 per cent (269) were faculty or other personnel in higher education.

The fact is that those who were thus qualified as "radicals" are not even supposed to be employed in the public service, since for fear of subversion, the Federal Republic introduced in the early 1970s a variety of procedures designed to eliminate candidates for office and functionaries considered as "verfassungsfeindlich" [hostile to the constitution]. This is a very vague notion, for the constitution itself knows only the concept of "verfassungswidrig" [anti-constitutional] and had entrusted the Constitutional Court of Karlsruhe with the task of pronouncing on the anti-constitutionality of political parties and, so far as individuals are concerned, on their loss of constitutional rights for having abused them.

The most important official text on this subject is the Decree of January 28, 1972, which enunciates the following principles in particular—not very different from certain American texts of the cold war period:[27]

1. By virtue of the civil service regulations in the republic and the provinces . . . officials are obligated to exert themselves, both within and without their functions, to uphold this fundamental law. . . .

2.1.1 A candidate who is engaged in activities hostile to the constitution will not be installed in public office.

2.1.2 Should an official belong to an organization that pursues goals hostile to the constitution, his membership would justify doubts whether he can at any time represent and act for the free and democratic fundamental order. These doubts justify as a rule the rejection of the motion for appointment.

2.2 If an official, by dealings with or membership in an organization with goals hostile to the constitution, does not fulfill the requirements of clause no. 35 of the *Beamtenrechtsrahmengesetz* [law establishing a framework of the rights and duties of public servants], by which he is obligated to acknowledge in all aspects of his behavior the free and democratic fundamental order in the sense of the Basic Law and to work to uphold it, his superior has a right to draw the logical consequences from such facts and in particular to examine whether measures should not be taken to exclude said official from office.

The number of people fired and even those not appointed, particularly in teaching, remains very small, but the very existence of these laws is revealing of a climate which also brings pressure on private organizations to purge their ranks. Thus, for example, at the Congress of the Printers' Union (IG Druck und Papier) in October 1974, the president announced that they had thus far been able to limit exclusions of left-extremist members to thirteen. Similarly in his recent address to the congress of the DGB, Hainz-Otto Vetter declared: "He who wants to bury freedom for the sake of a dogma and compel others to his own style of happiness, cannot expect tolerance! ... Democratic trade unions belong purely and simply to democrats. We will not allow our organizations to be misused, so that political sectarians may achieve indirectly what they cannot accomplish in and with their own little groups."

The definition of extremism is vague. It obviously applies to the Baader-Meinhoff gang, which had recourse to violence, even to murder, and whose leaders were jailed in November 1974, which did not put an end to the crimes. But is that a reason to establish a sort of continuity between these unconditional opponents of existing society and the anti-Soviet Communist party (the KPD), and from them to the pro-Soviet Communist party (the DKP), and from them to the various groups who claim to be battling against the injustices of this society, and from them to the left wing of the Social Democratic party, the so-called Jusos?

One of the characteristics of the new climate of 1974-75, is that this sort of amalgamation is used more and more as a weapon by the opposition, which feels itself to be already in the majority and which uses these arguments to compel the SPD to set itself off more and more markedly from those on its left so as not to incur the reproach of compromise with the "enemies of the constitution." At the same time the wave of left criticism of the 60s has had some lasting and even profound effects, often with rather contradictory results, in a wide variety of domains. Thus the system of law and justice is at once more criticized than it was ten or twenty years ago because of its indulgence for the strong and its rigor for the weak (a poll of January 1974 shows an increasing lack of confidence in the system, especially among those under forty-five years of age);[28] and at the same time, more firmly defended than ever since some lawyers became accomplices in the Baader gang. In general, though, one hears far less criticism of the legal system and profession from the judges themselves than in France.

The same paradox holds for the army. On the one hand, there is a democratization, a liberalism unknown in France and in the United States, going so far as the plan proposed by the minister of defense Georg Leber, to defuse the problem posed by conscientious objectors by allowing young people a free choice between military service and civilian replacement duty. On the other hand, there has been a decline in the ideal of the citizen-soldier and of so-called inner leadership, that is, the democratization of the system of command. A number of critics have decried a return to traditional discipline combined with a kind of witch hunt.[29]

It is the same story for the media. In the press, there has been, as in other Western countries, an increasing concentration which has brought with it the homogenization of prudence. More and more one feels an aggressive advocacy of conservative principles of law and order in a good many dailies (notably *Bild*) and weeklies. Of the latter, *Quick* leaves no stone unturned to convince its readers of the Marxist treason of the leaders of the SPD. The *Frankfurter*

Allgemeine is clearly more categorical in its rejection of social criticism than it was a decade ago. Yet at the same time, the daily press remains on the whole very conscientious in its conception of its task, and the liberal weeklies (among which the Protestant *Allgemeines Sonntagsblatt* is perhaps the most remarkable) are marked by their firmness and balance of judgment.

In the public television companies, the last two or three years have seen a fierce struggle for power, with the representatives of a conservative Christian-Democratic point of view winning out in most instances over the advocates of a very critical medium; thus, for example, the NDR in Hamburg, the Bavarian Radio in Munich, and the ZDF, a nationwide network collectively owned by the regime. Here also the balance sheet is mixed. On the one hand we have a series of broadcasts of an anti-conformist criticism of television by television; on the other hand, many series have been stopped, especially those aimed at the young and tending to promote social and ideological criticism.

Or consider the writers who have entered the political arena. Someone like Günther Grass withdraws into "pure" literature, while the Nobel prizewinner Henrich Böll calls for more understanding for the extreme left and sees his novel attacking the press magnate Axel Springer become a best seller.[30] In the fall of 1974 there was a ferocious battle within the German PEN Club, in which the extreme left gave evidence of great intolerance—one more sign of the uncertainties of our time.

One place where uncertainty is diminishing is in the universities. To be sure, the FRG is still the only country in the world where there are universities where it is almost impossible to get appointed as professor or assistant if one is not Marxist; and others where it is impossible to be appointed if one is even suspected of Marxism. Admittedly also, many programs of instruction are still redolent of the agitation of 1967-68, that is, systematically hostile to existing social and political structures, with criticism in the name of one or another variety of Marxism. But the counterwave that is now under way has already given rise to a new conservative intolerance in many places; and the new generation of students is concerned with jobs first and foremost.

On primary and secondary levels, one can sum everything up with a quip. At first, it was the students who had long hair and the teacher who wore it short; then older students and young teachers both wore their hair long; today, many teachers wear their hair long, while the students have, many of them, returned to short hair. More seriously: in the large secondary school classes, left-wing groups now have fewer members than the new Students' Union, which is very close to the Christian Democrats.[31] The return swing of the pendulum, in other words, has already carried well past the moderate Social Democratic position. Even the GEW (Gewerkschaft für Erziehung und Wissenschaft), until 1975 the most "leftist" of all unions, has begun a kind of purge of its *"Radikale."*

The fall of Professor Friedenburg, minister of education of the province of Hesse, who was expelled from the SPD/FDP government formed in December

1974, is also an ambiguous sign. In effect, the resentment of him by many parents of students—a resentment which was an important factor in the relative defeat of the SPD in the elections in Hesse in October—was due as much to the directives he issued concerning instruction in civics and German, which were characterized by a naïve Marxism, as to real change in the school system in an egalitarian direction. The fierce debate that took place at the beginning of 1975 concerning textbooks in civics in Nordrhein-Westfalen, in Lower Saxony, and in Hesse also has double meaning: on the one hand, a simple refusal to accept absurd excesses in a pseudo-Marxian presentation of history and society; and on the other, the desire to eliminate any trace of dissent from the program of instruction, any description of the society in terms of conflict.

One of the social bodies that has been marked by the most antagonism and yet been managed by tolerant and thoughtful leaders is the Protestant Church. Yet even here, one finds that it rejected, with a vigor that would astonish a Frenchman or American, a document adopted by the Liberal party calling for the separation of church and state.[32] On the other hand, there is no such ambiguity about the Catholic Church. This deserves a detailed examination, and a comparison with the French hierarchy would be very illuminating.[33] For many French bishops, for example, an employer can barely call himself a Christian, and he is still *permitted* to be a Christian without being socialist. For the German bishops, however, one may—just about—excuse those sincere Christians who vote Social Democrat. Although the hierarchy abstained from intervening in the election of 1969—for the first time—it took a position once again in 1972; and even more, with an unprecedented explicitness in Bavaria in October 1974. There the bishop issued a pastoral letter which made the attitude of the parties toward abortion the touchstone of the vote. The letter went on to assert:[34]

Even responsible members of the parties of the Federal government recognize that the democratic substance of influential groups is seriously endangered within their ranks, and that a progressive alteration of our free social system is being consciously prepared. While destructive tendencies of that kind may withdraw for tactical reasons before the election, we must not kid ourselves about their unchanged goals after as before. In opposition to such efforts, we reject the revival of an ideologically exacerbated concept of class struggle, as well as the unrealistic (*wirklichkeitsfremde*) fantasy of the unlimited feasibility of all kinds of improvements in the human condition. We expect of our representatives that they stand for right and freedom, for solidarity and the possibility of self-fulfillment for all social classes. For us it is a question of an educational policy which will maintain for coming generations what the fathers have built.

The conclusion was moderate in tone, but unambiguous:

We acknowledge: in the government and the coalition that supports it are men and women who share our concerns; a few representatives, for example, who have spoken up with conviction against the *Fristenlösung* (legalized abortion).

But they do not find the support they need within their parties. Party policy is decisive in those questions that are fundamental for the future of our society.

On balance there seems little doubt that there is taking place in the Federal Republic today a strong counter-trend to the right, a change of climate due, in the terms of Professor Kurt Sontheimer, a member of the Presidium of the Kirchentag (Protestant Church Assembly), "to a mixture of resignation and reaction."[35]

But how deep is this phenomenon and how long can we expect it to last? How does it affect today's elites and those of tomorrow? The answers depend in part on the international situation, as we will show later on—but only in part.

Which Elites?

The elites, according to the criteria established by one of the rare Germany inquiries on the subject, alas already out of date,[36] are composed of political leaders, high-ranking functionaries, university professors, business managers, the top people in the mass media, union leaders, and directors of professional organizations.

As in other Western countries, there is little mobility, and the leadership group in large measure reproduces itself from one generation to the next. But if this phenomenon is particularly marked among professors in the universities, mobility is none the less greater than in France.[37] In any case, since the majority of the so-called university rebels came from families of high social status, it is obviously necessary to separate the problem of social stratification from that of ideological orientation. Moreover, this problem is in turn complicated by the changes which affect, at different times or even at the same time, the different cohorts of each social group. The *Zeitgeist* changes; and young people change ideas as they enter professions. One example will suffice: a poll[38] shows that in the universities 26 per cent of the professors vote SPD and 33 per cent CDU/CSU; whereas, for the assistants, the figures are 47 and 16 per cent respectively. Should one infer from this that in a few years the social group of professors will be Social Democrats in majority? Or rather, that once professors, a good many of today's assistants will be more conservative and that, without necessarily changing these proportions.

Some aspects of this situation are peculiar to Germany. In the first place, the German past is such that the change of generations has more significance than elsewhere. Thus that old strategist of the SPD, Herbert Wehner, and the president of the Confederation of Industry, Hans Günther Sohl, both of them born in 1906, lived the best years of their lives under very different conditions during the Hitler period: Wehner (an old Communist) in the Soviet Union and Sweden; Sohl in Germany. Willy Brandt (born 1913) and Hans-Martin Schleyer

(1915) have both been criticized for their behavior during the war, the first for having been in Scandinavia alongside Germany's enemies, the other for having managed industry at Prague in German-annexed "Bohemia-Moravia." What can such polemics mean for someone like Hans Apel, born in 1932, only thirteen years old at the end of the war; or for the new leaders of the Christian-Democratic party such as its president, Helmut Kohl, or its secretary-general, Professor Kurt Biedenkopf, both of them born in 1930? The point is that there is a turnover of generations taking place in several important sectors, which underlines the more the importance of differences in historical experience.

On the other hand: this turnover is also limited. For one thing, a middle generation that one would have thought over the hill is hanging on. For example, it was possible to think in 1970 that Strauss, the energetic president of the CSU, had lost his chance for leadership. He had been too young around 1960 to aspire to the post of chancellor; and now he was probably too old, because people were prepared to lower drastically the age norm for high office. This lowering of the age norm has in fact occurred, above all in the universities, but to a much more limited extent than envisaged. Thus in the elections to the Bundestag in 1972, a good part of the Assembly was reelected, and only 145 out of 518 were born after 1930 and were thus under forty-two years at the time, with only 72 of these born after 1935.[39] In the Federal ministries, the 127 officials occupying high posts in October 1973 had an average age of fifty-one.[40] For some years now it has been possible to be appointed to high office around the age of forty, substantially younger than was formerly the case, but almost never before that age—in contrast to France.

Of these 127, 79 were men of law. The monopoly of public posts held by men of this profession is not so marked as in the past, but legal training remains the best route to administrative power, and this reduces considerably the influence of those ideological movements that color the social sciences in the universities; and this in turn limits the range of political, social, and economic knowledge of the administrators. These remain distinctly separate as a social group from business leaders, who remain strictly apart from the "political class." In this regard, Germany is in no way exceptional. It is the situation of France which is peculiar. There the Ecole Nationale d'Administration turns out the same type of people for leadership positions in the economy as in government and politics, with many switching back and forth. Yet in Germany those who occupy positions of influence in these three sectors share a kind of fundamental consensus, a common credo more explicit than that of the sociologically more homogeneous leadership group in France. Of course there are differences, and indeed these have assumed, ever since the great coalition of the SPD and the CDU broke down in 1969, the character of a pitiless confrontation. But it seems reasonable to say that the common credo is more basic than even this brutal confrontation, since it touches on the essential points: political liberalism and economic liberalism (the two are considered as interdependent), moderate reformism, Westernism (both thought out and visceral), a very moderate nationalism (with accent on the interests of the Federal Republic, without a desire for prestige or a clear will to influence directly the evolution of the international system).

This consensus of Germany's leaders may well be modified, either by a change in world rivalries, the more so as it was born of the rivalry of 1947-49, or by a change in the composition of the elite, in particular, by the turn of generations. It is worth saying again: prediction is difficult here because in the past the directors of the Young Socialists and Young Christian Democrats (Junge Union) have almost always lined up with their elders when acceding to positions of responsibility. Even so, the possibility of an ideological change is greater today than it was a few years ago.

To be sure, the attitudes of the Young Christian Democrats give hardly any indication of this,[41] and the dogmatic attitudes of the Neo-Marxists among the Young Socialists have done more to hurt their party than to advance their own political careers. Moreover, those who are called "young citizens" in the Federal Republic seem to share very prudent aspirations. They offer no big surprises (thus, for example, in a very interesting recent book whose authors, all of them in responsible posts in politics or the unions, average thirty-three years of age).[42]

But changes in the outside world may have substantial repercussions on the attitudes of these young elites. It is significant, for example, how much the image of the United States has changed; how much also the Near East, as well as South America, have come to be looked upon as places where things are happening that put to the test the political conceptions of those who are interested in them. In this regard, American foreign policy is, not a decisive element, but a real factor in the political-ideological evolution of these young elites. It is not a question here any more of American policy vis-à-vis the Federal Republic or even Europe, but rather American behavior in those parts of the world which the German national problem discouraged German elites from looking at too closely.

Foreign Policy

The elements of continuity in German foreign policy are linked to the above-mentioned consensus.[43] Changes and discontinuities have been due largely to the passage of time (thus the slow acceptance of the more or less irreversible situation created for Germany in 1945-47) and the transformation of the world scene. The result in 1975, insofar as it can be projected into the future on the assumption of continued peace, is well expressed in the goals of the General Plan of Foreign Cultural Policy 1973-76 (*Gesamtplan zur Auswärtigen Kulturpolitik 1973-76*):[44]

The overall plan is being developed for the specific task of foreign cultural policy. Its major goals are:

> Improved adaptation of foreign cultural policy to the long-range goals of the foreign policy of the German government, in particular pursuance of West European unification; support for the Atlantic community; an Eastern policy aimed at détente and collaboration in the context of Europe as a whole; special attention to the Mediterranean and Near East; a partnership relationship to the developing countries; . . .

> Worldwide presentation of the common cultural heritage of the Germans side by side with the GDR, along with continuing competition between the social orders of the two states.

This provision obviously constitutes a revolution in regard to the so-called Hallstein doctrine, which required Germany to break with those countries that recognized the existence of the other German state. It harks back to a common past, also evoked by Erich Honecker, secretary-general of the East German Communist party, on the occasion of the twenty-fifth anniversary of the GDR on October 7, 1974. As Honecker put it, the state that was created on that day

> . . . was the state of the workers and peasants, the state that waked to life again the best traditions and humanistic ideals of German history, took them on itself, and is raising them to their height in socialism. These are the traditions and ideals of the German peasant war that are linked to the name of Thomas Müntzer, and of the bourgeois-democratic revolution. They are the works of Johann Wolfgang Goethe and Friedrich Schiller, of Gotthold Ephraim Lessing and Heinrich Heine, of Georg Wilhelm Friedrich Hegel, Immanuel Kant and Johann Gottlieb Fichte, of the Grimm brothers, Wilhelm and Alexander Humboldt and Albert Einstein, Robert Koch and Rudolf Virchow, the work, that is, of Thomas and Heinrich Mann, Arnold Zweig, Lion Feuchtwanger, Berthold Brecht, Johannes Becher and Erich Weinert.

> All good, forward-looking and progressive ideas and deeds of German history are carefully cherished in the German Democratic Republic and are alive in the hearts of its people. We protect and cherish the great heritage, and we have, in the last twenty-five years, done everything to deal with this obligation, this legacy, in accordance with the welfare of the people and to build socialism in the German Democratic Republic.

This passage illustrates very well the striving on both sides to lay claim to the German past; but the end of Leonid Brezhnev's response on this occasion and the style of the report in *Neues Deutschland* (the official daily newspaper in East Germany) showed that this common past has only limited political consequences:

> We Soviet people lay great store by the fact that friendship with the Soviet Union has become an irrevocable component of the internationalist policy of the SED and the GDR; that it has found a place in the hearts of millions of citizens of your land. Be assured, dear comrades and friends, that the Soviet people has the same good feelings for you. (Long, persistent, stormy applause.) True to the

internationalist commands of Marx, Engels and Lenin, our party is educating the Soviet people for friendship and brotherliness with the workers of the GDR. (Applause.) Dear comrades and friends! You may be sure of this: at all times, in any circumstance, we are with you. (Long, persistent, stormy applause. Everyone rises from his place.) We stand by your side, we stand by the side of socialism, by the side of work, of peace, and the international brotherhood of the workers! (Lively applause.) Long live and prosper the German Democratic Republic! (Long, persistent, stormy applause.) May the unbreakable friendship between the Soviet Union and the GDR grow stronger! (Long, persistent, stormy applause.) Long live the great community of socialist nations—a sure bulwark of peace and progress! (Long, persistent, stormy applause.) Long live communism! (Stormy applause. No one wants to stop. The participants rise up from their places.)[45]

It would take really a complete change in the political system of the GDR for the relations between the two states to become an important element of the foreign policy of the Federal Republic. The two conversations which Chancellor Schmidt had with Erich Honecker, the real ruler of the GDR, at Helsinki, on the sideline of the conference of late July 1975, were not so spectacular in character as those of Brandt and Stoph in 1970. They seem to have shown, however, that the tension of the first half of 1975, which was marked by a number of minor incidents regarding Berlin in particular, was only a passing phase; but that on the other hand no serious progress can be expected in relations between the two Germanies for some time to come, except perhaps on minor points touching the two permanent aspects of these relations: trade and the fate of the citizens of the GDR so far as their contacts (or lack of contacts) with those of the Federal Republic are concerned.

The two aspects are linked, since the GDR is perfectly willing to accept what the USSR has refused the United States, namely, to trade travel concessions for West German visitors or permission to some of its own citizens to visit the West, for commercial or financial advantages. At the same time, the GDR will continue to proclaim its will to maintain an absolute separation between the two states, even while profiting from the advantages that it derives from the fiction, which has been accepted by the Federal Republic and its partners in the Common Market, that trade between the two states is domestic commerce and not foreign.[46] From 1973 to 1974, the increase in the value of trade was 23.0 per cent (24.6 per cent for the exports of the Federal Republic; 21.1 per cent for its imports from the GDR). (This "Intra-German Trade" is not considered part of foreign trade and it not counted in the figures of trade with the Communist countries cited in Table VI-3, p. 199.)

But even the fate of their compatriots (or former compatriots?) is hardly a source of emotion today for the citizens and leaders of the Federal Republic. When, for example, the Catholic bishops of the GDR drew up a pastoral letter presenting a dramatic balance sheet of Communist indoctrination and anticlerical persecution,[47] it found little echo in the West. And even when, in the beginning of July 1975, the vice president of the most powerful trade union in the DGB, IG-Metall, was expelled from the GDR, where he was making an official visit, for having dared to talk to ordinary workers outside the presence of "colleagues" of the East German sister union, there was no stir—only the few brief press reports.

Even so, one should not underestimate the significance of the ideological differences. The proximity of the GDR and the existence of seventeen million Germans under Communist rule maintains between the Federal Republic on the one hand, France and Italy on the other, a deep divergence in regard to the place of Communists in political life, as well as to the conception of détente and the significance of Helsinki. The final document of the Helsinki meeting was evidently received in Germany with the same skepticism as elsewhere in the West, but with much more bitterness and doubts concerning the assurances given to the USSR that its empire, including the GDR, was absolutely inviolable, whereas the same document did not provide comparable guarantees for the future of West Berlin. In the Bundestag the government made a weak defense of the Helsinki declaration because it was not very happy about it, and the opposition made a weak attack because it was perfectly well aware that if it had been in power, it too would have been obliged to sign.

This proximity will also continue to give more importance to the question of security in foreign policy in the Federal Republic, compared to France, Italy, or Great Britain, even if security is no longer, as before, the very first priority of this policy.[48] This is especially true now, when more and more leaders feel that security is first of all economic, since the principal threat is that of an economic collapse.

Note that for all this it has still been possible to normalize relations with the USSR and the other countries of Eastern Europe. Whereas the treaties of 1970-72 have not improved relations with the GDR or Poland and the USSR as much as their principal negotiator Egon Bahr had envisaged, a simple reading of the detailed agreements signed with the USSR and Poland, one in Moscow on October 30, 1974, the other in Bonn on November 1, shows the extent to which these once difficult relations have been reduced to matter-of-fact, bread-and-butter issues.[49] With one important exception: the old difficulties have a way of brusquely cropping up again at any time. So it was with the agreement with Poland announced at the end of July 1975. This was a strange package deal. The Federal Republic granted Warsaw a credit of a billion DM at 2.5 per cent interest and paid an additional 1.3 billion in retirement rights and pension claims of Polish citizens against the German social security system. In exchange Poland will allow another 125,000 Polish citizens of German origin to leave over the next four years. The point is that the Federal Republic did not have to give any compensation on behalf of the 58,000 persons of German origin who had already come from Poland by virtue of an earlier agreement of 1970. Yet their retirement and pension rights were included in the bill. Under the circumstances, one can well understand the Christian-Democratic protest against the new arrangements: in order to complete the de-Germanization of formerly German territory, the German must once again pay! But Poland is making the most here of the argument that Germany can never pay enough to compensate for the massacres and destructions of the German occupation.

In the meantime the development of trade between the Federal Republic and the East goes on without regard to the past. This development has to be seen in the context of overall foreign trade, in two ways: on the one hand, by noting that the share of this trade in aggregate trade is barely increasing (see the next-to-last line of Table VI-3); on the other, by noting that this small increase corresponds to a drop in the share of trade with Western countries.

Breaking down the trade by country, one major change compels attention: the trade with oil-producing countries increased from 7 to 13 per cent of imports from 1973 to 1974 and from 3 to 5 per cent of exports. (For other developing countries, the share of imports fell slightly from 9.5 to 9.1 per cent, and that of exports rose from 8 to 9.) The result is that exchanges with the European Economic Community, in spite of continued spectacular growth (imports up 14 per cent, exports up 23 per cent) no longer bulked so large in global trade: share of imports down from 52 to 48 per cent, and exports from 47 to 45. That is the effect of the oil price increase!

The fact remains that almost half the trade of the Federal Republic takes place with the countries of the Common Market. Leaving aside sentimental considerations, that is in itself a sufficient explanation for Europe's place at the head of the list of priorities of the Ministry of Foreign Affairs! The same holds true for the durability, in spite of repated disagreements, of the Franco-German entente: each of the two partners knows perfectly well that the economies of the two countries have reached a kind of climax of interdependence and that any recession in the one entails a serious drop in the exports of the other. Even more: Any economic policy, whether anti-inflationary or pump-priming, in either of the two countries immediately affects the internal economic situation of the other. Hence the conviction of Helmut Schmidt and Valéry Giscard d'Estaing that the two governments must coordinate their economic measures—a perfectly reasonable conviction and one altogether free of sentimentality!

Sentimentality equally absent in Bonn—and more and more absent in matters of European unification. Bonn has become more and more critical of the functioning of the institutions in Brussels, is less and less interested in supranational arrangements, and is more and more hesitant to take on financial obligations in this sphere. There have been sharp divisions within the Schmidt government regarding the negotiations of support commitments to European agricultural policy, regional policy, and scientific research programs. How much pressure is Germany prepared to exert on European Community institutions and on its European partners by means of a sort of financial blackmail? Should Germany insist on a right of scrutiny fo the policies of Brussels and its partners

Table VI-3
German Federal Republic: Development of Commodity Trade with Control Economies and Yugoslavia (Imports and Exports), 1973 and 1974

Country	Imports and Exports (Million DM)		Rate of Increase over Previous Year (Per cent)		Imports (Million DM)	
	1973	1974	1973	1974	1973	1974
GFR						
All Countries	323,814	410,153	16.6	26.7	145,417	179,698
Of which: Trade with the East	17,430	24,294	34.3	39.4	6,617	8,410
Of which: Eastern Europe	16,070	22,451	33.4	39.7	6,178	7,852
USSR	5,107	8,049	38.7	57.6	1,993	3,295
Poland	3,854	5,042	58.0	30.8	1,219	1,426
Czechoslovakia	2,478	2,818	18.4	13.7	991	1,035
Rumania	2,041	2,800	15.9	37.2	861	964
Hungary	1,886	2,674	25.3	41.8	830	908
China (People's Republic)	1,212	1,579	38.6	30.3	397	497
Bulgaria	695	1,001	25.3	44.0	279	234
North Korea	126	266	147.8	95.6	39	58
Share of Eastern Trade in Overall Trade	5.4%	59%			4.6%	4.7%
Yugoslavia	4,616	6,133	18.8	32.9	1,630	1,605

Source: *Deutschland-Archiv*, June 1975, p. 666. N.B.: Does not include trade with the GDR.

in the Community as a counterpart for its contributions to the system? Or should it say nothing for fear of being accused of playing the role of "schoolmaster of Europe"; or of wanting to transform the Community into a kind of Deutsche Mark Zone in which Germany's economic and monetary power would give it political primacy?

Whatever happens one may anticipate in the months and years to come a whole series of tensions within the Community due in large part to the unease in the Federal Republic at being fully integrated in the Community and yet incapable of finding in the Community effective remedies to economic depression, with its unforeseeable political and social consequences.

These tensions will be the greater because in Bonn, far more than in Paris, the government thinks in transatlantic terms, which makes the search for a common European action, or even a Franco-German collaboration, however necessary, more or less futile. For Helmut Schmidt, this is already true so far as the psychological climate is concerned. In the most candid statement he has perhaps made on this subject, he declared: "I say it quite consciously: the United States is the leading power—just as New York City, as the seat of the boards of administration and executives of the multinational concerns is the center from which optimism or pessimism radiates out to the entire Western world."[50]

But the problem of the relationship of the Federal Republic and of Europe on the one hand to the United States on the other is much more complex today than it was a few years ago. This is true even in regard to military security. To be sure, the France of Giscard maintains and will go on maintaining its concern for independence along with its awareness of dependence on the United States, whereas the Federal Republic remains and will remain faithful to Atlanticism. But it asks more and more questions, on the one hand, about the exact significance of the American engagement.[51] On the other hand, about the implications for the European allies of American actions in other parts of the world. On the second point, the problem posed by the possible utilization in the Middle East of American arms and soldiers stationed in Germany came to the fore in brutal fashion in October 1973 and has given rise to considerable anxiety since.

Here are some remarks on the subject by Helmut Schmidt in January 1975 from a speech to a foreign policy working group of his party:[52]

In order to maintain these good relations, we must by the way see to it that our American friends do not overestimate our economic, financial, and political possibilities and as a result make demands on us that we cannot fulfill. Such demands would only give rise to unnecessary divergences of opinion. The Atlantic alliance is the indispensable basis of our common security and defense policy. But it is not absolutely clear whether and how the Alliance will handle problems that arise from developments outside NATO. All the members are going to have to lay special emphasis on this in the months to come. We too are going to have to make our contribution to the solution of such problems.

On the first point, one can see the consequence of German anxieties in the French handling of the *Pluto* nuclear tactical missile, introduced into service in the French army in the spring of 1975. The domestic French debate on the positioning and potential use of these missiles would have been less keen if Germany had not really wanted France to take its European responsibilities more seriously by positioning the missiles in Germany rather than in France— because such a commitment would provide more security for the Federal Republic. To put it differently, the manner in which the Vietnam War ended has given rise in Bonn to a new way of thinking—which might be called "Gaullist"— about ways of compelling the United States to intervene with nuclear weapons— which would increase the credibility of such an intervention, hence European security. French nuclear arms are in this way being endowed with new virtues.

But defense is now no more than a minor aspect of the much larger problem of German-American relations. This problem derives in part from the mix of converging and conflicting interests of the United States and Western Europe in economic matters; partly from a difference in situation. In the same talk cited above, Helmut Schmidt said: "It is not surprising, that these questions [the demands of the Third World] are taken much more seriously in a country like Germany than in America. For us these are existential problems; because every fourth worker in the Federal Republic is producing for foreign markets, whereas in the United States only every nineteenth or twentieth is so employed."

Last but not least, Germany has an obligation and the ability to play an active role in world politics simply because of its great economic, monetary, and technological power. In 1965 Chancellor Erhard, then visiting Washington, agreed to sign with President Johnson a communique giving unreserved German support to the Vietnamese policy of the United States. At that time the German government had as its almost exclusive preoccupation the maintenance of the American commitment to Europe, for German foreign policy was to all intents and purposes limited to the European continent. Today, however, things have changed considerably. The German field of vision has widened considerably and will continue to do so, even if a man like Helmut Schmidt seems, in the beginning at least, to have no particular desire to play a world role, or in any event, to show it.

Some of the discussion in Bergedorf is relevant here:

WALTER JAMES LEVY (the oil economist, New York): Mr. Schmidt has touched on the problem of leadership. In my opinion, Europe cannot evade its responsibility. My fear sometimes is that America will not be able in the long run to exercise leadership. . . . when one partner can do no more, the other must take over.

HELMUT SCHMIDT: I have said that America must exercise leadership. That is, however, unfortunately possible only insofar as it conceals the fact that it is exercising it. A European would have to conceal it sevenfold.

KARL KLASEN (president of the Bundesbank): Germany, twentyfold.

There is a competition beginning to develop between the United States and Germany that seems enormously to surprise Americans, accustomed as they are to German docility. The Federal Republic can no longer permit itself to be docile, not because it wants to be anti-American, but because it is obliged by its own weight and needs, very much changed since the oil crisis and the Western economic depression, to take on a world role. The atomic agreement with Brazil may serve as an example here—and, no doubt, also as a precedent.

On May 2, 1975, the Federal Republic deposited in Washington and London the instruments of ratification of the treaty on nuclear nondissemination. At the same time, the German government published a declaration saying:

The German government . . . .

3. Declares that no provision of the Treaty can be construed as hindering the further development of European unity, in particular, the creation of a European Union with analogous powers.
4. Assumes that research development and use of nuclear energy for peaceful ends, as well as international and multinational collaboration in this domain, may not be injured by the Treaty.
5. Assumes that the application of the Treaty, including the enforcement of security measures, will not work to the disadvantage of the nuclear industry of the Federal Republic in international competition . . .

The "Agreement between the Governments of the German Federal Republic and the United States of Brazil regarding Collaboration in Peaceful Uses of Nuclear Energy," signed in Bonn on June 27, 1975, constitutes an application of these principles. Article 2 says: "The parties to the agreement declare that they acknowledge the basic principle of nonproliferation of nuclear arms," but the agreement as a whole goes very far in the direction of German aid to Brazilian nuclear development. How sincere are American fears regarding the possible diffusion of atomic arms, in spite of Article 2? Or does the negative American reaction simply reflect the shock of German competition in South America? In any case, the time has long passed when Washington could nip in the bud without difficulty any German action that it thought harmful.

My point is that the German-Brazilian agreement hints at greater difficulties in the future if the United States persists in not taking seriously the policy and global demands of the Third World, within which poor countries and rich have been surprisingly successful in sustaining and reinforcing their solidarity. Up to now, it is the French government that has been more or less isolated in its efforts to get the other Western countries to accept the notion of global negotiation on raw materials leading to control, if not fixing, of prices and, further on, of economic exchanges between industrialized countries and new countries. The Federal Republic has been closer in this matter to the United States than to France, partly because its view of past and present was less inspired by guilt then that of France. To feel the difference, one just has to recall how Helmut Schmidt, in the Bergedorf meeting, expressed indignation at the idea that there might be a cartel of raw material producers distorting a market that has up to now been free of restraint by any such coalition!

But little by little the need to arrive at negotiated agreements with raw materials producers and some new thinking about the world economic order is pushing German leaders to the idea that this order will have to be fairly profoundly transformed for it to become acceptable to the new countries—an idea that is still shocking in the United States.

In sum, the fact that the United States can no longer count on unconditional, eternal German fidelity on everything and everywhere does not in itself require a new American political decision regarding the Federal Republic and the German problem. Even the old threat of a possible abandonment of Berlin would no longer serve in the slightest to reduce the Federal Republic to submission.

The simple fact is that the globalization of German policy should lead American leaders to make critical choices, not with regard to Europe, but with regard to those countries whose demands are willy-nilly more and more accepted by the Europeans, in particular because they see there a means of avoiding the catastrophe that would result from a takeover of these countries by one of the great Communist powers.

Notes

1. I developed this idea in *Germany in Our Time* (New York: Praeger, 1971), a work brought up to date in its German version: *Geschichte Deutschlands seit 1945* (München: DTV, 1974). For the bibliography of the present essay, see the "Bibliographische Orientierung" (pp. 476-503) of the latter edition. In the notes that follow, I shall confine myself to citing only a few works of particular interest that have appeared since 1974.

2. Percentages calculated according to the figures in the *Statistisches Jahrbuch* (Stuttgart and Mainz: Kohlhammer, 1974).

3. I was able to verify the existence of this problem by the reactions aroused by the passages in which I referred to it in my speech to the Bundestag for the "Volkstrauertag" of 1974 (text in the *Bulletin* of the Federal government of November 19) and in my essay "Die neuen Deutschen" in *Der Spiegel* of December 23, 1974. Both texts in A. Grosser, *Gegen den Strom* (Munich: Hanser, 1975).

4. See particularly Jens Hacker, *Der Rechtsstatus Deutschlands aus der Sicht der DDR* (Köln: Verlag für Wissenschaft und Politik, 1974), as well as his update in the *Frankfurter Allgemeine* of 1/9/75. There is a new and excellent survey of the German problem in Ernst Nolte, *Der Kalte Krieg in Deutschland* (München: Piper, 1974); but the best general balance sheet of the Federal Republic is the collection edited by R. Loewenthal and H.P. Schwarz, *Die Zweite Republik* (Stuttgart: Seewald, 1974).

5. Cf., e.g., the controversy between the two states in the General Assembly of the UN on December 6, 1974 (complete text of the debate in *Das Parlament* of January 11, 1975).

6. See the poll results analyzed in Bundesminister für Innerdeutsche Beziehungen, *Materialien zum Bericht zur Lage der Nation 1974* (Bonn, 1974), pp. 107-16.

7. Poll by the Allensbach Institute, as reported in the *Frankfurter Allgemeine* of December 12, 1974.

8. The schema is explicitly worked in *Capital*, October 1974, p. 13.

9. See the very vivid chart in *Der Spiegel* of February 28, 1974.

10. See especially the *Statistisches Jahrbuch* 1974, p. 127, series entitled "Wahl zum 7. Deutschen Bundestag am 19 November 1972," published by the Statistisches Bundesamt; in particular no. 8; *Wahlbeteiligung und Stimmabgabe der Männer und Frauen nach dem Alter* (Mainz: Kohlhammer, Nov. 1973), as well as the commentary of Eckhard Jesse, "Schlüssel zum Wählerverhalten," *Frankfurter Hefte*, April 1974.

11. The complete text of this speech, which is exceptionally revealing of psychology and ideology, in the *Frankfurter Allgemeine* of September 25, 1974.

12. On the personality and ideas of the present chancellor before his accession to power, the best study is undoubtedly that of Helmut Wolfgang Kahn, *Helmut Schmidt: Fallstudie über einen Populären* (Hamburg: Holsten, 1973). For those who want to continue admiring his predecessor, it is better not to read too closely Willy Brandt, *Ueber den Tag hinaus: Eine Zwischenbilanz* (Hamburg: Hoffman und Campe, 1974), a book written (by whom?) immediately after his fall.

13. Extracts of the conclusions of the chapter "Staatliche Planung in der Bundesrepublik Deutschland" of R. Jochimsen and P. Treuner in Loewenthal and Schwarz, eds., *Die Zeite Republik*, p. 843. See also R. Jochimsen, "Aktive Strukturpolitik," a supplement to *Das Parlament*, October 5, 1974, pp. 3-18.

14. Complete text in the *Bulletin des Presse- und Informationsamt der Bundesregierung* of October 31, 1974.

15. "Für Oelscheichs spottbillig," *Capital*, October 1974.

16. The literature is overabundant and often poor. An overview that is already a little old, but still clear and intelligent, is provided in Norbert Koubek et al., "Wirtschaftliche Konzentration und gesellschaftliche Machtverteilung in der Bundesrepublik Deutschland," supplement to *Das Parlament* of July 8, 1972.

17. Recent figures, though only approximate, in "Teure Heimat: Die Finanzen der Vertriebenenverbände," *Capital*, November 1974.

18. A breakdown by branches of associations' members of the BDI and BDA on January 1, 1974 is to be found in the *Statistisches Jahrbuch*, pp. 154 and 156.

19. See the remarkable biographical study in *Der Stern*, December 12, 1974.

20. November 29 and December 6, 1974.

21. Statistics in IG Metall, *Textsammlung zur Mitbestimmung* (n.p., n.d. [1973]), p. 16. For two very different viewpoints on the DGB, see G. Leminsky and B. Otto, *Politik und Programmatik des DGB* (Köln: Bund Verlag, 1974), and Günter Triesch, *Gewerkschaftsstaat oder sozialer Rechtsstaat?* (Stuttgart: Seewald, 1974).

22. See, for example, the fairly nasty analysis, "DGB als Grossunternehmer," *Der Stern*, November 7, 1974.

23. The complete text of this important document (earlier directives had been issued twenty-five years before) in *Die Quelle*, July-August 1974.

24. A very good analysis of the philosophy of control by the leading theoretician of the SPD is Helmut Koeser, "Die Kontrolle der wirtschaftlichen Macht: Heinrich Deist und das Godesberg Programm," supplement to *Das Parlament* of April 6, 1974.

25. Complete text in the *Bulletin* of October 8, 1974.

26. *Das Parlament*, June 28, 1975.

27. The complete text is in H. Borgs-Maciejewski, *Radikale im Oeffentlichen Dienst: Dokumente, Debatten, Urteile* ["Godesberger Taschenbuch," vol. 5] (Bonn: 1973).

28. There is a summary of the results in the *Frankfurter Allgemeine* of April 6, 1974. See also Rudolf Wassermann, *Justiz im sozialen Rechtsstaat* (Darmstadt: Luchterhand, 1974).

29. Cf., e.g., "Im Gleichschritt marsch!" *Der Stern* of September 26, 1974. But more useful are books such as *Studiengruppe Militärpolitik, Ein Anti-Weissbuch; Materialien für eine alternative Militärpolitik* (Hamburg: Rororo, 1974); and especially E. Kloess, and H. Grossmann, *Zur Soziologie der Streitkräfte* (Frankfurt: Fischer, 1974), which is the text of a series of television programs on the army which is testimony at once to the liberalism of the military (the inquiry was in no way impeded) and the intelligent candor of German television.

30. *Die verlorene Ehre der Katharina Blum oder Wie Gewalt entstehen und wohin sie führen kann* (Köln: Kiepenheuer, 1974).

31. See, for example, the contrasting views of this phenomenon in the *Deutsches Allgemeines Sonntagsblatt* of January 5, 1975 and in the article of Ulrich Konitzer, "Viel Lärm um rechte Schülergruppen," *Frankfurter Hefte*, January 1975.

32. See the very fine declaration of the Presidium of the Lutheran Church Assembly on the occasion of the twenty-fifth anniversary of this nonclerical body ("Kirche für die Zeitgenossen"). Complete text in *Sonntagsblatt*, August 4, 1974. This text diverges from the conclusions of the large, well-known book of Gerhard Schmidtchen, *Protestanten und Katholiken: Soziologische Analyse konfessionneller Kulturen* (Bern and München: Francke Verlag, 1973).

33. See A. Grosser, "L'incompréhension franco-allemande," *Le Monde*, December 11, 1974.

34. Complete text in the *Süddeutsche Zeitung*, October 19, 1974.

35. See the remarkable article, "Zeitgeist in Bewegung," which appeared in the strongly conservative *Deutsche Zeitung* of April 26, 1974. For a more developed and divergent point of view, see the collection edited by Martin Greiffenhagen, *Der neue Konservatismus der siebziger Jahre* (Hamburg: Rororo, 1974).

36. Inquiry of 1968 at the University of Mannheim under the direction of R. Wildenmann. These materials were not published, but have been used in a number of studies and articles, the most recent and most interesting that of Edo Enke, *Oberschicht und politisches System in der Bundesrepublik Deutschland: Soziale Mobilität und Karrieremuster von 800 Inhabern von Spitzenpositionen der westdeutschen Gesellschaft* (Frankfurt: P. Lang; Bern: H. Lang, 1974). His conclusions are unfortunately in large part out of date, in particular because the inquiry was conducted before the SPD took over the government.

37. See especially the tables in Enke, *Oberschicht*, pp. 73-81.

38. See "Professoren über Professoren: wieder Elite," the first results of a sociological investigation conducted in 1974, in *Der Spiegel*, January 6, 1975.

39. There are interesting tables, broken down by age, sex, and education, in *Kürschners Volkshandbuch Deutscher Bundestag. 7. Wahlperiode 1972* (Darmstadt: Neue Darmstädter Verlagsanstalt, 1973), pp. 174-79.

40. Cf. the very solid study of F.K. Fromme, "Bei den Präsidenten ist die Welt noch in Ordnung. Die höchsten Beamten, wer sie sind und woher si kommen," *Frankfurther Allgemeine*, April 26, 1974.

41. See their monthly review *Die Entscheidung*, or perhaps the very interesting interview with their president Mathias Wissmann in the *Sonntagsblatt*, December 8, 1974.

42. Landeszentrale für politische Bildung des Landes Nordrhein-Westfalen, ed. *Was wir wünschen: Junge Bundesbürger über die Zukunft ihres Staates* (Köln: Verlag für Wissenschaft und Politik, 1974). Of the sixteen contributors, only one, Margot Brunner, a writer for *Metall*, the organ of IG Metall, uses language that would be considered in 1975 as socialistic in France or in Italy.

43. Among the most recent publications on foreign policy of the Federal Republic and its historical background, one should read or consult:
- Hans-Peter Schwarz (ed.), *Handbuch der deutschen Aussenpolitik* (München: Piper, 1975);
- Werner Weber/Werner Jahn (eds.), *Synopse zur Deutschlandpolitik 1941 bis 1973* (Göttingen: O. Schwarz, 1974);
- Gilbert Ziebura (ed.), *Grundfragen der deutschen Aussenpolitik seit 1871* (Darmstadt: Wissenschaftliche Buchgesellschaft, 1975);
- Peter H. Merkl, *German Foreign Policies, West and East: On the Threshold of a New European Era* (Santa Barbara, 1974);
- Claus Dieter Ehlermann et al., *Handelspartner DDR: Innerdeutsche Wirtschaftsbeziehungen* (Baden-Baden: Nomos, 1975);
- Alfred Grosser, *Was ist deutsche Aussenpolitik?* (Konstanz: Konstanzer Universitätsverlag, 1975).

44. Complete text of these goals in Auswärtiges Amt, Abteilung für auswärtige Kulturpolitik, *Bericht 1973* (Bonn: 1974).

45. Complete text of the long speeches of Honecker and Brezhnev in *Deutschland Archiv*, December 1974, which reprints the version in *Neues Deutschland*.

46. Results of these exchanges for the first nine months of 1974 in the *Bulletin*, December 18, 1974. For a reasonable projection and comparison of the future of the two states, see Peter Christian Ludz, *Die doppelte Zukunft: Bundesrepublik und DDR in der Welt von Morgen* (München: Hanser, 1974).

47. Complete text in the *Frankfurter Allgemeine*, November 27, 1974.

48. See for example Helga Haftendorn, *Aufrüstung und Entspannungspolitik zwischen Sicherheitsbefürchtung und Friedenssicherung in der Aussenpolitik der Bundesrepublik Deutschland, 1955-1973* (Düsseldorf: Bertelsmann Universität, 1974).

49. Complete text in the *Bulletin* of November 5 and 8, 1974.

50. In a talk given on March 24, 1975 at a meeting of the Bergedorfer Gesprächskreis entitled "Cooperation or Confrontation: Is the Economy Tumbling into a World Political Crisis?" The full text of the proceedings is available in Protokoll No. 50 of the Gesprächskreis, published in July 1975 at Hamburg-Bergedorf. See also the interesting indications, unfortunately insufficient, in the *Süddeutsche Zeitung* of November 25, 1974: "Topmanager multinationaler Konzerne stellen sich drei Tage lang den Fragen der Bonner Prominenz." The preoccupation with the domestic consequences of decisions taken in the United States shows up also in the report of the Arbeitsgemeinschaft II, "Atlantische Partnerschaft—Kooperation oder mehr?" which was delivered by the Secretary of State Heinz Ruhnau to the Foreign Policy Conference of the SPD (Bonn, January 17-19, 1975). Thus the following passage:

Under the catchword of economic cooperation, Heinz Ruhnau recalled the party congress in Hannover, which summed up the economic problems in only one sentence: "Between the European Community and the United States of America a permanent political dialogue is necessary in order to solve differences of interest and commercial tensions in a spirit of partnership and with a view to a growing world trade."

Today, according to Ruhnau, the economic-social explosive is the greatest threat to Atlantic partnership. As a result, there is a compelling necessity for close collaboration between the European Community and North America, as well as a common understanding of the strategy to be employed in combating inflation and unemployment. This is what the automobile workers in Detroit and Wolfsburg are waiting for; this is what the steelworkers in Birmingham and Toronto are waiting for.

51. The most thoughtful consideration of this question is doubtless that of Lothar Ruehl, *Macht und Friedensstrategie* (Hamburg: Hoffman und Campe, 1974).

52. Inaugural address to the Conference cited in note 50, above.

VII Italy: On the Threshold or the Brink?

Suzanne Berger

Two years of economic disaster and Left successes have led many observers of Italy to believe that its condition, long judged fatal but not serious, has suffered a turn for the worse. This represents a major change in perception. Since the early postwar years, the failures and weakness of government in Italy had come to be accepted, both at home and abroad, as a permanent condition, with negative but tolerable consequences for what mattered: economic growth and prosperity, the overall stability of the political system, and the commitment of Italy to the Atlantic alliance and to Europe. In the years of the economic miracle the poor performance of government in providing basic social services, economic infrastructure, and an equitable distribution of burdens had appeared hardly to matter, for the expansion of the economy had rapidly and massively increased individual incomes and diffused, however unevenly, a level of prosperity through the country that raised it close to that of other European countries. The successes of the economy appeared to be virtually invulnerable to the failures of politics, and as governments fell, the national product continued to climb. The impotence of governments mattered the less because alongside the paralyzed state bureaucracies had grown up powerful and autonomous state enterprises with a capacity for coherent economic action and long-term planning, tasks that elsewhere were carried out by the state directly.

As stabilizing a factor as the autonomy of the economic process was the virtual insulation of the underlying political character of the country from the factional squabbling, clashes of leaders, ministerial musical chairs, and absence of governmental direction that were the everyday stuff of politics. From the end of World War II to the summer of 1975, Italy had thirty-four governments, with an average life of less than a year and a maximum life of two years (although only two governments survived that long). Yet beneath this instability the fundamental contours of politics had until June 1975 apparently altered little. The Left won 44.1 per cent of the votes in the 1946 elections to the constituent assembly and, twenty-six years later 46.7 per cent of the 1972 legislative assembly votes; the Right won 50.1 per cent of the votes in 1946 and 51.4 per cent in 1972.[a] The Communists increased their vote from 19 per cent in 1946 to 27.2 per cent in 1972, but the strength of all the Marxist parties combined remained the same; together they received 39.7 per cent of the vote in 1946 and 40.1 per cent in 1972. Within the Right, the Christian Democrats (DC) moved from 35.2 per cent in 1946 to 38.8 per cent in 1972; while the extreme right remained stable. The persistence of the same distribution of the electorate among parties was the more remarkable for the radical changes in the economy and shifts in population that had taken place over three postwar decades. It is hardly surprising that people came to believe that a system that had weathered such extraordinary socioeconomic transformations with so little political change might well continue in its old tracks indefinitely.

The third article of belief that supported those who saw fundamental stability under the political chaos of Italian life was the idea that the Italian commitment to NATO, to the Atlantic alliance, and, in general, to American foreign policy positions was unshakable, so long as the Christian-Democrats remained the dominant party. Italian foreign policy—indeed, in many instances, the absence of an Italian foreign policy—was perceived as deriving in all essential respects from domestic political necessity. Unlike France, where General de Gaulle had virtually detached his foreign policy from the constraints of his domestic politics and could, therefore, oppose *both* Communists at home and Americans abroad, in Italy foreign policy seemed securely anchored to domestic politics. The Christian-Democrats, anti-Communist at home, would, with only occasional and purely verbal lapses, always be reliable American allies. As long as the DC remained the dominant political force in the country—and after 1948, this never seemed in doubt—Italian foreign policy could be taken for granted, since it was both more predictable and more passive than that of the other West European allies. The only threat to Italy's relationship with the United States would be Communist participation in government.

The fears and apocalyptic warnings that the economic and political shifts of the past two years have aroused both in Italy and abroad reflect, in however distorted and exaggerated form, the fact that these three pillars of Italian stability have crumbled. The autonomy of the economy, which apparently could modernize, grow, and recover from crisis by its own spontaneous impulses, without the active and efficient intervention of the state, has been revealed to be

---

[a]The Left for this calculation includes the Republicans (PRI), the Social-Democrats (PSDI), the Socialists (PSI), the left-Socialists (PSIUP), and the Communists (PCI). The Right includes the neo-Fascists (MSI), the monarchists, the Liberals (PLI), and the Christian-Democrats (DC). "Other" votes totaled 5.8 per cent in the 1946 election and 1.9 per cent in 1972.

illusory. Whereas the role of the state in the expansive and prosperous period of the "economic miracle" was a relatively limited one, in the deep economic crisis Italy now faces, the situation has entirely changed. Only the government could defend the common interest in group struggles over the division of a shrinking pie, could channel resources into activities that maintain employment and investment while keeping inflation and balance-of-payments deficits within tolerable limits, and would have sufficient authority to distribute the burdens of crisis equitably enough to prevent the massive withdrawal of commitment, effort, and capital from the system. Whether the Italian state can perform any of these tasks is open to serious doubt.

At the same time, the immutability of a political situation in which the Christian-Democrats are the permanent party of government and the Communists the permanent opposition has suddenly been called into question. The DC has suffered two major defeats: in the 1974 referendum on divorce and in the June 1975 local and regional elections, in which the Communists increased their share by 4.9 per cent over the 1972 legislative elections and the DC lost 3.2 per cent. The two parties now stand within a million votes of each other. The striking new fact is that the Communist party is now within reach of winning a plurality in the next legislative elections.

With this political prospect, the issue of Italy's commitment to the Atlantic alliance inevitably arises, for if the principal determinant of Italy's international role is the domestic dominance of the DC, then without the Christian-Democrats at the head of governments, the future appears quite uncertain. Now, for the first time, the Italian Communist party's claims of independence from the Soviet Union, of commitment to Europe, and of willingness to maintain Italy's place in the alliance must be seriously scrutinized. Far more for Italy than for France, the changes in domestic political constellations that would admit the Communists to a role in government make the continuity of foreign policy a critical issue.

Responses from abroad to these changes in Italy have been of two kinds. Some argue that the economic reverses and political shifts of the past few years are, however dangerous, reversible. It is true that the Italian economy has recovered from other serious economic crises in the postwar period, under circumstances in which the state was not appreciably more effective than it has been in the present crisis. Just as the Italian economy pulled itself out of the 1963-64 recession, there is reason to believe that it might extract itself from this cyclical depression. Those who hold this view argue that what is needed is, first, a reform of international economic relationships, of the monetary system, and of arrangements between industrial societies and producers of primary materials; and, second, recovery of the American and the West German economies and the revival of the markets they provide for Italian goods. These events, happily, depend not at all on the capabilities of Italian governments. And so it is possible to believe that the current crisis and the future of the economic system will depend no more than in the past on the specific economic capabilities of the government. As for the changes in politics, one might argue that the reversibility of the results of the past two elections (1974 and 1975) is not at all implausible. The DC has in the past recovered from electoral reverses; and the PCI may well find it difficult to consolidate the gains it has made and to extend them.

The other reaction to the changes in Italy has been to regard them as prodromes of a profound crisis of Western civilization. Italian problems in this perspective have a specific character only insofar as they represent early and acute manifestations of a general disease, whose spread can best be checked by a vigilent policy of prevention, early identification, and quarantine. In fact, in the several variants of this view, the less the specific social, political, and historical circumstances of Italian development are considered to count and the more Italy is treated simply as the poorest and weakest of the advanced industrial societies, the more gloomy the prognosis. Viewed from this perspective, Italy, Portugal, and Greece today, possibly Spain and even France tomorrow, appear as the soft Mediterranean underbelly of the industrial world, with economic and political vulnerabilities that make Communist expansion possible and probable. Paradoxically, what both the optimistic and the apocalyptic views of current Italian affairs have in common is the idea that Italian prospects at this point depend largely on developments in the outside world. In the former view, Italy's economic recovery is held to depend on external events; in the latter, it is the threat to the existing close relationship with the United States and the prospect of increasing dependence on the Soviet Union in the event of Communist participation in government that spark the acute concern about the course of Italian society in the near future.

In this respect the following interpretation of Italy's problems and prospects departs from both the optimistic and the apocalyptic perspectives. Its starting point is an assumption that the dilemmas Italy confronts today and their likely outcomes reflect, above all, circumstances, patterns of development, and actors that are specific to the Italian situation and past. Denying neither the significance of the international context within which Italy must solve its problems, nor the impact of those external forces that constrain Italy's choices, it argues nevertheless that the principal determinants of Italian politics in the next decade remain domestic. Barring the kinds of international catastrophes that West European states have not experienced in the postwar decades, Italy's responses to even those problems generated outside its frontiers will be shaped far more by its own internal forces than by the "objective" or international characteristics of the problem. To anticipate the conclusion of the analysis that follows, this emphasis on the historical and social specificity of the forces at work in Italy today suggests that the events of the past few years reflect long-term transformations and hence are unlikely to be reversed. A new era *is* opening in Italy in which the fundamental guidelines of the three postwar decades are less and less likely to be determinative. But this conclusion in no way supports the alarmism of those who believe that the collapse of the old structures opens the way for the barbarian invasions. The flexibility, adaptiveness, and even inertia of the system are far more considerable than has been appreciated. At the same time, the changes that have taken place reflect strengths and unexploited resources that have been both underestimated and misinterpreted because of fears about the uses to which they may be turned.

Economic Prospects

The End of the Miracle

More than a decade has passed since the economic miracle, the period of rapid economic growth of the late fifties and early sixties, yet it is only now becoming fully clear that the factors responsible for the economic expansion of that period can no longer be counted on for growth and prosperity in the future. In particular, three of the factors critical in that period have not changed in ways that, barring altogether unforeseeable and unlikely events, must be considered irreversible. The industrial relations system, the relation of Italy to world markets, and the roles of the private and public sectors in the economy have experienced drastic changes over the past fifteen years, and the former contribution of each to the process of economic growth cannot be recaptured but can only be replaced.

Among the factors that account for the enormous surge of the economy after the early fifties, labor supply and export markets stand out as critical. To consider labor first, Italian industry profited in this period from an abundant labor reserve, with about 10 per cent of the work force unemployed. This made possible important quantitative and qualitative changes in the composition of the work force in northern industrial centers, in particular, a massive recruitment of workers from the countryside and from the south and the expulsion from the factory of women and younger and older workers.[1] In contrast with other industrial societies, the great increases in productivity in Italy during this period were achieved more by the rationalization of work than by investment in new technology.[2] This speed-up of the work process was greatly facilitated by the virtual absence within the factory of trade union organizations, which had been broken by years of employer repression and widespread unemployment.[3] Yet another result of the weakness of working class organization in this period of the economic miracle was the relatively low wage levels that prevailed even in the most productive sectors of Italian industry. While it is true that the most dynamic element in the economy—the automobile industry and Fiat in particular—adopted policies of rather high wages, even there and in other capital-intensive sectors, productivity gains outstripped increases in wages. While the productivity of labor employed in industry increased 6.6 per cent per year in the period 1952-1961, real wages in industry rose only 1.4 per cent.[4] The organizational weakness of labor made it possible to pull out of the 1963-64 recession and confront growing international competition by the reorganization of work processes, rather than by productive investments, "by an average decline in the cost of labor everywhere, rather than by an extension of the most productive sectors."[5]

Management's ability to effect productivity gains by the reorganization of work and then to extract the lion's share of these gains collapsed with the emergence of a strong union presence within the factory. The breakdown of the old labor relations pattern had a drastic impact on the process of capital accumulation. The decisive turning point here was the "hot autumn" of 1969. Months of strikes and the virtually continuous political mobilization of the Northern industrial work force produced negotiations at both national and plant levels in which the unions, enormously strengthened by waves of spontaneous workshop agitation and by their success in channeling it into syndical organization, obtained major wage increases from employers and significant concessions on the distribution of power within the factory. The consequence was a drastic decline in profits that continued at least through 1972. At the same time, the strength of the unions within the shop now made it impossible for firms to resort to the solutions they had used in the 1964 recession.

In sum, neither changes within the workshop nor the containment of wage demands can simply be imposed any more on the industrial work force, despite the great increases in unemployment that might once have sufficed to subdue union combativity. To reduce costs and increase productivity now requires a broad measure of agreement from organized labor. The inflation rates of the past few years (10.8 per cent in 1973, 25 per cent in 1974), the balance-of-payments problems, the decline in profits, and the fall in exports are as many pieces of evidence that labor commitment cannot be bought with wage increases at the 1969-1974 rate without disastrous economic consequences. But the alternative price for labor's consent to some form of "social compact" depends more on political decision than on industry. What the state would have to guarantee in exchange for labor self-discipline and wage restraint would be, on the one hand, a greater share of power; on the other, a program of reforms that would provide collective goods—schools, housing, hospitals, transportation, social services—in lieu of increased individual incomes. The state would have to demonstrate, moreover, by such measures as a reform of fiscal inequities, that economic sacrifices are being fairly distributed and are not being made by wage earners alone. The unions and the Communists have recognized that the high cost of labor is a major contributing factor in the current crisis and have indicated considerable willingness to moderate wage demands in exchange for guarantees on employment and on public expenditures.[6] But despite the mountain of reform promises, bills voted, and sums allocated for social and economic infrastructure, the record of accomplishment of the Italian state is meager. Why this is so and what might be required to change it, will be discussed in a later section; here we need only note that where once the role of the labor force within industry was regulated more or less autonomously by industry itself, today the regulation of the industrial relations system is above all a political problem that must be handled at the level of national government. The decisions and policies that could restore productivity and competitive prices are largely in the hands of the state and no longer under the control of industry.

The second decisive change since the years of the economic miracle lies on the side of demand. The weaknesses in domestic demand, already evident in the boom years, have since become even more important. The expansion of demand has largely depended on the increase in individual incomes and consumption, and the effective demand for collective goods has been very limited. Even the recently increased budgetary allocations to stimulate the creation of social infrastructure have been largely distributed in the form of individual payments—for example, as higher pensions instead of housing. But the current problems of internal demand are old chickens coming home to roost, rather than new elements.

In the case of exports, however, Italy faces a situation fundamentally different from the one in which the economic miracle was generated. The critical contribution of exports in the halcyon days of growth was to expand the modern industrial sector at the expense of the traditional sector as well as to compensate for flagging internal demand and support a high rate of growth in the period 1963-1969, after the boom years had passed. Exports rose from 13.9 per cent of gross national product in 1963 to 17.4 per cent in 1969, and Italy increased its share of world markets. The continuation of this success was contingent on three conditions. First, the markets of Italy's customers had to hold up. Second, insofar as Italy's sales of such commodities as textiles and shoes depended on low labor costs, these costs had to remain lower than those in competitor countries. Finally, in those sectors where advantage depended on technology and innovation, an adequate rate of productive investment had to be maintained. Although the first condition depends on world economic conditions, the latter two are largely within Italian control and in both cases the situation has altered greatly to Italy's disadvantage. Italy now faces stiff competition for its labor-intensive exports from less developed countries such as Yugoslavia and Spain, where labor costs are far lower. Indeed the Italian wage bill is, in certain industries at least, higher than that in other advanced industrial societies.[7] Italy has, moreover, failed to invest adequately to increase productivity and lower costs in the medium-range technology sectors or to expand high-technology exports.[8]

In sum, even when economic conditions in Italy's principal customers improve, the situation of Italian exports may not recover or may even worsen. Again, the forms of action that would improve the competitivity of Italian exports no longer lie entirely within the hands of the industrialists but depend increasingly on the state. Only the state can dissuade labor from escalating wage demands and channel capital into productive investment rather than speculation and foreign banks. At present, the prospects of either course of action look dim. Paradoxically, while the overall Italian export picture darkens, two kinds of exports continue: the export of capital and the export of labor. The devaluation of the lira and its recovery in 1975 may have slowed capital flight but it has not stopped it; witness the difficulty containing a new collapse of the lira and renewed capital export in January 1976. And despite lay-offs in the EEC countries that employ Italian migrants, over a million and a half Italians continue to work abroad.

Industry and the State

The third fundamental change in the Italian economy since the fifties has been in the roles of the private and public sectors and their relations with the state. In the period of the economic miracle, private industry was the most dynamic and expansive part of the economy. Fiat above all, but also the thousands of firms that developed consumer durables for domestic and export markets were the motor of the system. The public enterprises in this period played a critical role, but one quite different from that of private industry. The two public sector corporations—ENI and IRI[b]—performed functions for the economy that private firms with relatively short-term profit perspectives might not have undertaken and that the state bureaucracy was quite incapable of managing.

To some extent public enterprises were needed in Italy because of specific weaknesses of Italian industry and government, and certain of the tasks that they carried out have in other countries been performed by private firms or by governmental agencies. The absence of an effective state planning office as in France, for example, created needs that in Italy the public enterprises undertook to fulfill.[9] But the rationale for the giant public corporations went far beyond the weaknesses of specifically Italian institutions to an argument that fiscal policy and monetary manipulation are inadequate to solve certain problems that emerge in virtually all industrial societies.[10] For this reason ENI and IRI came to be regarded outside Italy as models of a new pattern of state intervention that might resolve problems of structural unemployment and uneven regional development by creating new infrastructure and encouraging new industries— tasks that neither traditional nor Keynesian economic policies had been able to accomplish.

Even a decade ago, when the balance sheets of the public corporations appeared most favorable, several major failings were evident. The Mezzogiorno

[b]Ente Nazionale Idrocarburi (ENI) was developed to exploit oil and natural gas resources; Istituto per la Ricostruzione Industriale (IRI) was set up in the thirties to rescue a number of bankrupt firms in a variety of industrial sectors.

continued to suffer from unemployment, industrial underdevelopment, and lack of capital despite the implantation of several spectacular industrial complexes, for these remained "cathedrals in the desert," with little spillover into local economies. More ominous for the future, the relations between the public corporations and the state were from the outset a mix of heavy involvement in politics with virtual freedom from systematic parliamentary review and control.

In the early days at least, this political problem was kept within tolerable limits, first, because the heads of the public corporations had goals and strategies that were relatively distinct from those of the politicians and, second, because the funds used by ENI and IRI were largely obtained from reinvested profits and from sales of shares and only secondarily from direct state grants. Over the past decade, however, both of these constraints have largely disappeared. Both on the side of the politicians and on the side of the heads of the public corporations, there have been changes leading to a virtual integration of the concerns, interests, and objectives of party politics and of the managers of the economy in general and of the public corporations in particular.[11]

At the same time, the public enterprises have become more and more dependent on the state for their funds, through direct grants, subsidized loans, and state-bank-supported bond issues, and they rely far less on self-financing and sales of stocks.[12] Where once the possibilities of expansion of the public enterprises depended significantly on success in the market, hence on the economic results of their operations, today the magnitude of the funds at their disposal depends on the political skills of their managers.

In sum, the public corporations have come both to rely more on the state and to exercise greater and greater control over it. Today their influence extends into party politics, the press, and the *grands corps* of the bureaucracy. All this has happened at the same time as the economic area dominated by the public enterprises has been expanding rapidly and the private sector shrinking.[13] The results of these two convergent developments have been largely negative. Far from enhancing the possibilities of public control over the economy, the expansion of the public sector has reduced them. The political power of the heads of the public enterprises has become so great that the ministers who in theory are to direct and control their activities confess that they themselves have become little more than spokesmen for them. The power network of the public enterprises has engulfed so many of the potential points of resistance that their demands go virtually unopposed. At the same time, the expansion of that part of the economy owned by foreign firms has further weakened public leverage on the economic system.[14]

The most visible consequence of this situation has been the wave of scandals involving officials of the public corporations in influence-peddling and graft. Perhaps even more serious has been the consolidation of an alliance between politicians and managers of the public sector, an entente founded on the recognition of their mutual interest in preserving groups and activities that are unproductive drags on the modern and dynamic sectors of the economy. In part, this is the by-product of a situation in which the public corporations respond less and less to economic opportunities and incentives and increasingly to political ones. And to this, the shrinkage of the part of the economy still responsive to the market has obviously contributed. What is most striking is the shift in objectives: where once Enrico Mattei, ENI's first president, used politics to advance the economic goals of his organization, today the heads of the public corporations use the economic strength of their institutions to advance forms of control and domination that are often more political than economic. That political considerations have been given higher priority than short- or medium-term economic return is not the problem; state corporations sometimes legitimately pursue national objectives with more immediate political than economic payoffs, as IRI did when it built factories in the south, developed a shipbuilding industry, and so forth. But when the public corporations devote substantial resources to controlling parts of the press or to acquiring influence in factions of various political parties, whose political interests are being advanced? The shift in direction and loss of economic dynamism has not been so marked in IRI as in ENI, but overall, the record in 1975 suggests that the triumph of the public corporation has become a disaster for the economy.

The three long-term shifts described above—in labor, in demand, and in economic organization—have fundamentally transformed the Italian economy since the fifties. At the same time, the long-standing problems of the Italian economy have not been significantly modified. The industrial and agricultural backwardness of the Mezzogiorno, the relatively low (and declining) proportion of the population in the active work force, the heavy weight of activities of low productivity, particularly in the bureaucracy and in commerce, continue to tax the economy with burdens far heavier than those of Italy's European neighbors. If one reads the current economic statistics for Italy against this background it is hard to find reason for optimism. While it is true that by spring 1975 Italy had succeeded in slowing the rate of inflation and reducing its balance-of-payments deficit substantially, wiping out entirely that part of the deficit due to nonoil imports and making some advance into the oil-related deficit, this was achieved by cutting industrial production, which dropped by 18.7 per cent in a year (May 1974 to May 1975). Unemployment remained high—and there were no signs of reviving demand. The Italian gross national product, which grew by 6.3 per cent in 1973 and 3.4 per cent in 1974, will likely decline by 2.75 per cent in 1975.[15]

Though the specter of bankruptcy which haunted Italy—and its Western allies—in late 1974 and early 1975 has disappeared, prospects remain gloomy. The possibility of economic apocalypse was undoubtedly exaggerated; but today's rejoicing over the economic improvement in Italian fortunes is excessive. For all the reasons of domestic origin discussed above, Italy is likely to profit far less than her trading partners from an upturn in the world economy. Success in economic competition in the next decade will for all Western states depend in significant measure on how rapidly and effectively the machinery of the economy is reorganized to take account of the new high prices of raw materials. The transfers of resources and redistributions of capital and incomes that this requires will not be easily effected in any country, but for Italy, the chances of success in this effort are greatly reduced by the impotence of the state. The contradiction of a vigorous economy in a sick state has finally exploded, and it is difficult to imagine that the necessary economic reforms can be carried out without fundamental changes in governance.

Politics

Crisis of Governance

The most visible sign of change in Italy has been the spreading chaos in political and social life. Kidnappings, bombings, and terrorism have been the most spectacular aspects, but even more ordinary forms of social disorder have reached critical proportions. Despite the recession, the number of days of work lost in strikes in Italy in 1974 was higher than in any other Common Market country—five times that of France.[16] Illegal capital flight and tax evasion are apparently on the rise, and new forms of "civil disobedience" are developing: in Turin, for example, tens of thousands of citizens refused to pay the increases in public transport fares and electricity rates. The periodic collapse of the mails, the malfunctioning of the universities, the scandals in the public service, the failure of the police and courts to identify and prosecute those responsible for political crimes—all these disparate facts symbolize for Italians and for foreign observers a kind of unraveling of the social fabric.

These phenomena reflect the declining capacity of government, rather than a decline in the governability of Italian society. Though states in other industrial societies also have serious difficulties in carrying out new tasks requiring extensive intervention in society while at the same time coping with the disruptions that arise from the weakening of social controls, Italy's troubles do not seem to be merely an extreme case of a "law and order" crisis common to all industrial societies. Rather, what the diverse forms of social unrest listed above have in common is that they have been encouraged, when not actually created, by the methods of rule that have been developed in Italy over the past thirty years. These methods have had the effect, in the short run, of strengthening the ruling political parties and keeping them in power, while in the long run they have seriously weakened the state.

To consider but two examples: the inefficiency of the bureaucracy is clearly not the product of some defect in Italian "national character" but of political decisions to use the bureaucracy as a reservoir of resources to feed the clientelistic networks on which Christian Democratic power depends. The inflated wages of the public service, the overpopulation of government offices, the politicization of civil servants and their extensive collusion with the groups they should be regulating, the failure of all schemes to reform the bureaucracy— all these phenomena stem from the ways the bureaucracy is used to keep the ruling parties in power.

The second example is the failure to put a halt to political terrorism. The evident weaknesses of the Italian police and judiciary do not adequately explain why the government has been so signally deficient in capturing and trying the perpetrators of quasi-political crimes ranging from kidnappings and hold-ups to bombings and assassinations. Rather, here again, though the politicians of the major parties probably have not initiated these crimes, their efforts to exploit them in the service of their own political interests have made it impossible to pursue effectively a course of action that would have identified and prosecuted the guilty. First, some of those responsible for the initiation of the incidents are linked more or less directly to the parties in power, and so their exposure might have costs for the politicians. But even more important, the DC has hoped to use these crimes to strengthen its own fortunes by tarring them with a red brush and attributing them to left-wing militants. Since—as has subsequently been demonstrated in case after case—most of these crimes have in fact been the work of individuals and groups on the right, the DC's persistence in presenting the problem as one of the "two opposed extremes" could only interfere with a systematic campaign to put a halt to terrorism. Even if the police and judicial bureaucracy were far more efficient than they are, they would have great difficulties in proceeding in the face of the government's politically motivated pronouncements about the origins of these crimes.

The attempts of the Italian political class to increase its own power and keep itself in government have had disastrous consequences for the capabilities of the government. The instruments of rule, the confidence of the public, and the rulers' own sense of direction have been corroded by the narrow purposes to which they have been put for thirty years. As a result, in a society with severe though not unmanageable problems and with serious though not uncontrollable sources of disorder, the government has been virtually impotent. The final irony is that the short-term power-seeking of the parties in government has, in the long run, undermined them as well. Today the DC is reaping a harvest of its own sowing.

The Decline of Christian Democracy

The defeats of the Christian Democratic party in the 1974 divorce referendum and the 1975 regional elections and the party's inability to close ranks and rally after them are symptoms of an advanced state of decomposition. After thirty years of rule, the party that has dominated every Italian postwar government is losing hold of its electors and its cadres. Though the electoral disasters are recent ones, they have been long in the making. Like the other changes in the Italian political world discussed below—the shrinkage of the minor parties and the expansion of the Communist party—the DC's decline is a process that cannot easily be reversed.

The first of the factors that has weakened the DC is the erosion of the Catholic structures on which the party depends for much of its support. The results of the divorce referendum, in which even regions of strong religious belief and practice voted to maintain divorce, are the most striking evidence of the withering of traditional Catholic attitudes; but even before the election, there were many signs of the growing unwillingness of practicing Catholics to accept Church positions as the basis of political action.[17] At the same time, the Church itself has gradually withdrawn from the political sphere and is increasingly reluctant to mobilize support for the DC from the pulpit. Catholic lay institutions, too, are less and less responsive to the political needs of the DC. The two working class organizations that developed in the Catholic subculture—the Associazioni Cristiani dei Lavoratori Italiani (ACLI) and the Confederazione Italiana dei Sindicati Lavoratori (CISL)—have broken virtually all links with the party; indeed, over the past several years, the CISL has been negotiating a fusion with the Communist trade union, the Confederazione Generale Italiana del Lavoro (CGIL). In part, the CISL's break with the DC matches the distance that the CGIL has taken from the Communist party; but while the other forms of Communist working class organization have allowed the Communists to maintain a strong presence and influence in the factories even with reduced leverage on the CGIL, the DC has found no comparable institutions to replace the links to the working class that the CISL once provided.

Another fissure in the DC's base of support has been opened by the growing tensions among the middle-class electors of the DC. The heterogeneous interests that the DC kept within the same party were held together, not only by ideological support for nonclass-based politics, inspired by Catholic precepts, but primarily by the advantage, protection, and privilege that DC policies offered to very diverse groups. The political alliance within the same party of modern and traditional industry, of small shopkeepers and supermarket owners, of peasants and capitalist farmers, of *rentiers* and workers, depended on economic resources and room for political maneuver. Both commodities are in increasingly short supply, in part because of the current economic crisis, in part because the cumulative effect of DC support for unproductive sectors has reached a critical threshold level.

There is a growing public sentiment that, as figures as diverse as Giovanni Agnelli of Fiat and leaders of the PCI put it, parasitic Italy has been living off productive Italy. This perception has been heightened by scandals in the bureaucracy and perhaps even more important, by the fact that reversing economic fortunes and relative scarcity make the patterns of allocation of resources more visible to more groups. Both the economic crisis and the politics of economic crisis make it harder to maintain the alliance of increasingly divergent interests on which the power of the Christian Democrats has rested.

Finally, the DC suffers from having been in power for thirty years. The erosion of initiative, leadership, and political will that such a long reign would produce anywhere has in the Italian case been aggravated by the fact that the DC has never had to face an effective opposition. The DC's chief political problem has not been to counter the initiatives and opposition of another party or party alliance representing a plausible alternative government.[18] The only party large enough to replace the DC as the central party in a governmental coalition is the PCI, and the PCI has never been in a position to offer a governmental alternative. In fact, as the PCI has grown larger, it increasingly represents itself, not as a party that might replace the DC, but as one that might participate *with* it in government. The DC's problem, therefore, has not been to respond to the challenge of a group that might supplant it in government, but rather, to make governments by managing relations with its minor allies—on the right, groups representing about 10 per cent of the vote, on the left, groups receiving about 20 per cent—and by arranging compromises among its own factions. The product has been stagnation.

The chances that the DC will be able to carry out any significant party reforms before the next legislative elections are slim. In the wake of the June electoral disaster, three kinds of reform for the party have been discussed. The first would entail shedding the Catholic colors of the party and developing, as the German Christian Democrats before it, into a modern conservative party. This change would help the DC to pick up votes from the small center and right parties and perhaps even to absorb these groups. Second, various DC factions have proposed rebuilding the party around the progressive Catholic elements in it, thereby recovering the left Catholic electorate that has been wooed away by the PSI and the PCI. Finally, the party might maintain its present politically heterogeneous character, but clean itself up—first, by breaking the party's reliance on *sottogoverno*;[c] second, by removing from leadership positions those responsible for the debacles of the past ten years; and third, by throwing out of the party those DC figures associated with speculation, corruption, and the Mafia. Though the removal of Amintore Fanfani as party leader was a move toward the second of these goals, the progress that his successor has made on the other objectives implied by this strategy has been too limited to suggest much further advance on this front. Neither of the first two alternatives has received enough support to make it plausible that the party will move to reduce its political heterogeneity. In sum, the most likely outcome in the near future is more of the same.

---

[c]*Sottogoverno* is the web of patronage and clientelistic relations that underpins the power of the governmental parties.

The Minor Parties

The second long-term change in the Italian political scene has been the decline in the vitality of the small parties. Most important in this respect has been the transformation of the Socialist party into a group whose political practices resemble those of the DC, even when its political rhetoric retains a militantly left cast. It is difficult today to recall the wild hopes and fears generated by the Socialist entry into power in the early sixties, with the opening to the left and the first center-left governments. After a burst of energy that exhausted itself with the nationalization of electricity, the center-left governments settled into the less exhilarating but more rewarding tasks of redividing the spoils of the bureaucracy and of clientelism. While the Socialists continued to talk of reforms and—even more menacing though equally unproductive of results—of "more advanced equilibria" that would somehow include the Communists, the party proceeded to trade in its goals for the more immediate rewards that participation in the system provides. Though the Socialists have improved their electoral fortunes in the recent shifts to the left, it seems unlikely that they can do much more than to recoup—probably from the Right—the electors they lost to the Left when the Partito Socialista Italiano di Unità Proletaria (PSIUP) split off. At the level of national government, Socialists have apparently drawn the lesson from the DC losses of 1974-75 that participation in government with the DC now, with or without the other minor DC allies, would be ill-advised. At the same time, the PCI's line—that an arrangement with the DC, the *compromesso storico*, is the only path to power that does not risk disastrous outcomes of the Chilean type—effectively bars a PCI-PSI alliance at the national level. While the PSI moves out of national government, the regional elections have enlarged its power at the local level, for the Socialists have become the pivot on which either center-left or left coalitions depend. As a result, with only 12 per cent of the vote the PSI participates in municipal coalitions in 82 per cent of all towns with over five thousand inhabitants. The Socialists govern with the Communists in five regions: Emilia-Romagna, Umbria, Toscana, Liguria, and Piemonte. And in Genoa, Milan, and Venice, where the PCI won more votes, it is the PSI that holds the office of mayor.

The fate of the other small parties is far less promising. The Social Democrats (PSDI) have been moving steadily to the right, but the gains there have been inadequate to halt an accelerating process of splintering and decay. Their electoral fortunes suggest that anti-Communism and weak reformism—the two central pillars of the party—have declining appeal for the electorate left of the DC center. With little more than 5 per cent of the vote and limited space for expansion, the Social Democrats are likely to play a much less important role in the future. The Liberals have been in decline since 1963 and now have only 2.5 per cent of the vote. The Republicans, who shared power in government alone with the DC in the months before the regional elections, were not able to turn it to much electoral profit. The Fascists (MIS) apparently peaked in the 1972 elections with 8.8 per cent of the vote and fell back to 6.8 per cent in the 1975 elections. Their extralegal activities have not maintained a momentum sufficient to compensate for electoral weakness. Opportunities like the Reggio-Calabria riots cannot be manufactured at will, and the Fascists seem, indeed, incapable even of controlling and exploiting the violence carried out by self-avowed Fascists. As it becomes clear that a number of the terrorist acts originally attributed to leftists were in fact committed by Fascists, public anxieties about "law and order"—which the MSI tried to turn to its advantage—now work against the Right.

In sum, Italian political scenarios in the future will depend less on the fortunes and choices of the small parties. The political arithmetic of the system is likely to become one that counts more on elections and less on the calculus of arrangements among the minor DC allies.

The Communist Party

With the successes of the June 1975 regional elections that brought the Left into power in five regions and one third of all Italian towns, the possibility of Communist participation in national government in the next decade has become real. The Communists in the 1975 provincial and regional elections won 32.4 per cent of the vote, the DC 35.8. (In the fifteen regional elections of June, the PCI won 33.4 per cent, the DC 35.3.) For the PCI this represents a gain of 5.5 per cent over the last regional elections (1970) and of 4.9 per cent over the last legislative elections (1972); for the DC, losses of 2.6 and 3.2 per cent respectively. The processes strengthening the PCI, like those weakening the DC, reflect political and social changes that might be channeled in different directions, but are hardly likely to be arrested or reversed. Changing electoral fortunes as well as shifting balances of power in society have altered the prospects of the Communists, who had, for years it seemed, settled into a role of permanent opposition. For the first time, they have raised the question what Communist participation in government in a major West European state would mean.

The Communist party of Italy is, of all European political groups, the one that has been most scrutinized abroad, not only by scholars, but by analysts and activists of every political persuasion—all trying to find in the evolution and behavior of the PCI a model of a Communist party different from the Soviet-East European ones and from the nonruling Communist parties around the world that seem slavishly to follow Soviet directives. What has made the PCI the object of interest for those looking for "another communism" is its approach to groups and institutions within its own society and its relative independence of and opposition to the Soviet Union. Whether the originality of the PCI domestic strategies reflects conceptions different from those that motivate Communist leaders elsewhere in West Europe or, rather, the different consequences that flow from trying to apply within the Italian context a set of ideas shared also by other European Communist movements,[19] it is a fact that the practices of the Italian Communist party are significantly different from those of other West European Communist parties. Thus the PCI plays a far more important role at local and regional levels than do other nonruling Communist parties; and it now has acquired considerable experience in government and a reputation for responsible, honest rule. In those arenas in which the PCI has gained power, it has exercised it in a fashion that has by and large buttressed rather than disrupted institutions. In contrast to the French Communists, for example, the PCI has played a highly cooperative role in Parliament, where Communist support makes it possible for a high proportion of bills to be passed in committee instead of in plenary session. Three quarters of the legislation passed between 1948 and 1968 received Communist approval.[20] And in many other governmental institutions at national regional, and local levels, there is abundant evidence of PCI cooperation with Christian Democrats and other political forces.

Around the concept of a specific Italian road to socialism (*la via italiana al socialismo*) the PCI has developed policies and programs aimed at influencing and winning over broad segments of society—peasant, middle-class, white-collar, and small propertied groups as well as the working class. Communist parties elsewhere have also moved beyond the proletariat in order to extend their influence, but the Italians have moved faster and further in this direction than any other party with the possible exception of the Spanish. They have also tried to move beyond the secular, anticlerical culture that was a central pillar of Italian Marxism before the Fascist period in order to attract Catholics. Long before Enrico Berlinguer called for a *compromesso storico* with the Christian Democrats, the Party had been making appeals to Catholic groups and had scrupulously avoided the anticlericalism that elsewhere in Europe remains an important element in left ideology (with, one might add, far less reason than in Italy, where divorce, abortion, censorship, and the financial power of the Church are still burning questions).

The second originality of the PCI with respect to the other European Communist parties lies in the degree of independence the Party has asserted in its dealings with the Soviet Union. The differences in PCI behavior are striking, though the explanation of them is rather less clear, different analysts disagreeing on the weight of various elements in PCI experience: the fact that the Italian party, outlawed and underground during the Fascist regime, was not so scarred by the years of Stalinism as was, for example, the French party; the fact that Italy has less importance for Soviet foreign policy than France or Germany, hence the larger room for maneuver left to the Italians; the influence of Antonio

Gramsci, whose writings provided the PCI with an independent intellectual tradition and a map of Italian society that had not simply been traced on Soviet models; the role of Togliatti. As early as 1956, the PCI began to express positions that clearly distinguished it from the other European parties, and by 1964 its views on the autonomy of national Communist parties were quite distinctive.[21] The PCI's open and continued opposition to the Soviet invasion of Czechoslovakia and its refusal to line up behind the subsequent "normalization" of relations with the new Czech authorities was the most striking demonstration how far beyond the other European Communist parties the PCI had moved in its support for the autonomous development of each Communist party. Another early and significant development was the Italian Communist party's acceptance of the European Common Market and decision (1969) to send a delegation to the European Parliament—a line which, until recently, contrasted with the general hostility of other West European Communist parties to European political institutions. Though the other parties have by now more or less come around to the Italian position, the PCI continues to attribute greater importance to its participation in European institutions and to have a generally higher estimate of the potential political significance of the European community.

The most recent developments continue to demonstrate the PCI's will to independent judgment and expression within the international Communist movement. One clear example is the Italian party's criticism of the Portuguese Communist party—in contrast to the French Communists' full support for it, in line with Soviet policy. Another example is the leading role that the PCI played in the 1974-1975 negotiations over the agenda of a forthcoming conference of European Communist parties, where the PCI along with the Spaniards and Yugoslavs successfully defended against the East Germans and Russians the position that the conference should not in any way dictate a common political line, but should, rather, produce as a common document only a general statement of approval of détente.

Since the summer of 1975, the frequency and sharpness of Soviet criticism of the Italian party have been stepped up. The most pointed of the attacks was Zaradov's August 6, 1975 *Pravda* article, condemning the alliance strategies of "those contemporary conciliators who do not concern themselves, even in words, with the autonomy of the party of the proletariat, but wish to dissolve it in an ideologically amorphous organization, in no matter what union, created according to the formula 'unity at any price'."[22] Zaradov's piece was followed by an article in *Kommunist*, accusing the West European parties of failure to engage themselves in the battle against Maoism; and then by a *Pravda* article (October 19, 1975) urging West European Communist parties to prepare to exploit the crisis of capitalist society. There have been no signs of the PCI's bending under this pressure. *L'Unità*, the party newspaper, thoroughly criticized the Zaradov article, which was in fact too much even for the French party, whose secretary-general, Georges Marchais, responded that its policies were and would continue to be determined in Paris and not Moscow and reaffirmed the strategy of an alliance with the Socialists.[23]

Paradoxically, despite the extraordinary interest that these domestic and international developments have aroused abroad and the volumes written about them, debate about the Italian Communist party is often carried out as if its future conduct were entirely unpredictable. Among American official commentators on Italy in particular, the prevalent view appears to be that the PCI's history over the past thirty years neither provides a reliable guide to its likely behavior in the event of its participation in government nor rules out the possibility of dramatic breaks with past practices and policies. The most plausible grounds on which this case is argued underscore, first, the organizational structures of the party and the latitude they offer to party leaders; and, second, various scenarios in which the PCI responds to hostile domestic and international reactions to its role in government.

On the first point, any argument for the future unreliability of the PCI must rest heavily on the centralization of its internal decision-making. Because of this, it seems plausible to argue that once in power the Party might and could change its colors—reverse support for democratic pluralism at home and line up squarely behind the USSR on foreign policy. Even if one recognizes a certain democratization of the PCI, on the one hand, and, on the other, admits the considerable failures of democracy in other, non-Marxist Italian political parties, still the PCI seems to stand in a category by itself in two respects. In contrast to the other parties, the PCI is extraordinarily successful in mobilizing members, not only at election time, but on a sustained day-to-day basis. At the same time, PCI leaders are provided by party structures and tradition with far greater resources than leaders of other parties for suppressing dissent and resistance within the ranks.

The relative continuity that one assumes in the future behavior of other parties derives largely from the assumption that were their leaders to revise drastically any major commitments or policies, the costs in terms of support of members and activists would be unacceptable; to reverse course on issues involving fundamental questions of social order, political liberties, or economic distribution might well be fatal. If one believes that the PCI differs radically from other parties in its leaders' capacity to bring along members and cadres, no matter what the shift in policy, then the PCI does seem uniquely unpredictable and its leadership far less hamstrung by traditions and past commitments. Even recognizing that the PCI does pay some costs for changes in course, as the troubles with the old members during de-Stalinization showed, still the discipline of members and the efficiency of the party organization are so much greater than in other groups that the party leadership is far freer in its decisions. On this chain of reasoning hangs the conclusion that PCI behavior in government might differ considerably from past practices and promises.

In this line of argument, while the democratic centralism of the PCI explains how it would be possible for it to carry out *volte-face*, another order of explanation is needed to make plausible the case that the Italian party would wish, once in government, to choose a route different from the one thus far traveled. Thirty years of Communist participation in various social institutions and at various levels of government do not provide evidence that the Italian Communists themselves really desire to institute totalitarian rule or that their democratic rhetoric and practices are but covers for different long-term intentions. The argument must be, rather, that if the Communists came to power, they would confront domestic and international opposition of such magnitude that a set of authoritarian reflexes—ever available in the Marxist-Leninist repertory even if not always used—would be activated. However good the intentions of the PCI's leaders today and however sincere their protestations about maintaining democratic pluralism, once in power, the situation with which they would have to deal would provoke responses that could transform Italy into some version of an East European state. In sum, the circumstances would provide the incentive; the Marxist-Leninist tradition, the justification; and the Leninist organization structures would furnish the means for a radical change in course.

Since the above case for the metamorphosis of the PCI once it enters government denies the relevance of the PCI's past performance for predicting future behavior, it is one that is virtually impossible to refute directly. There are, however, three considerations that appear, under all foreseeable circumstances, to be far more constraining of PCI behavior than is allowed for by either that part of the case that rests on the internal structures of the PCI or the other part that hangs on the plausibility of certain scenarios of authoritarian response to opposition. First, history shows, not that Leninist parties shed their pasts and behave in entirely new ways once in power, but rather, that the practices of Communist parties out of power are continued in large once they reach government. In the East European cases power consolidated conspiratorial, authoritarian, and intolerant tendencies that were all too visible even before the groups entered government. In other words, the degree of freedom that Communist leaders can exercise with respect to their past organizational practices may be smaller than the argument suggests.

In the case of the PCI, too, there are compelling reasons to believe that its own history would weigh decisively in future choices. The history of the Party is one of resistance to authoritarian rule, of broad coalition-building across class and religious lines, of coexistence and cooperation with other forces, and of campaigns for economic and social reforms. While the Party's capacity to mobilize its membership and discipline it in service of goals flowing out of these issues is unquestionably greater than that of other Italian parties, were the PCI to try to move its members in directions radically different from those of the past, it would certainly lose much of its hold. The PCI membership has been socialized, not only by the Party's historical record and commitments, but also by the experiences of operating within the system for thirty years. The organizational traditions and reflexes that have developed over this period would make it extremely difficult, if not impossible, for the leadership to impose practices resembling those current in Eastern Europe.

The weight of the PCI past—its historical commitments, traditions, policies, and practices—is likely to be reinforced by the circumstances under which it is trying to come to power, namely, by developing a broad and diverse appeal to groups with very different interests. The kind of organization that the PCI has become in the course of trying to win a popular majority in a country in which this implies massive support from middle strata as well as from the nonproper-tied working class bears little resemblance to the Marxist-Leninist parties that came to power in the Soviet Union and East Europe. In sum, the Party is constrained not only by its own members, but also by the broad character of the support it needs to win elections and to govern.

Finally, even if the leaders of the PCI wanted to reverse their democratic course, they would be deterred by one compelling counterargument: that nothing is so likely to trigger fatal reactions from abroad. Italian Communist leaders calculate that even under the best circumstances it may be difficult for a government with Communist participation to survive the hostility of foreign governments and foreign economic interests. They cannot forget what happened in Chile; and avoiding a repetition of that debacle in Italy has become a dominant preoccupation. Without giving this full weight, it would be impossible to comprehend the PCI's insistence on coming to power with the Christian Democrats and its rejection of the alternatives of governing in alliance with other left parties or of aiming at winning "51 per cent" of the electorate and governing with that.

Pessimistic readings of the uncertainties attached to PCI participation in government depend, however, not only on the internal factors that might push the PCI to break with its democratic past, but on the international forces that might oblige the PCI to decide the question of its ultimate allegiance. While PCI leaders out of power may honestly declare, for example, that they would not remove Italy from the NATO alliance, once in power, it has been argued, the pressures that will converge on them will force them to revise earlier positions. Three types of pressure might be brought to bear on the PCI: pressure in the form of direct demands from the Soviet Union, pressure in the form of international confrontations in which Italy is obliged to choose sides, and pressure from political and economic groups based largely in the United States.

As long as the international context remains fairly stable, chances are small that direct Soviet demands on a PCI in government would be any more successful than the USSR's past efforts to get the Italian Communists to fall into line. Indeed, the PCI would be in even a stronger position and would have greater incentives to resist Soviet pressures. The situation of the East European regimes, whose lot is often predicted as the future of any country with Communists in government, differs in critical respects from the Italian: their submission to Soviet demands is assured by the proximity of Soviet troops and by the demonstrated willingness of the USSR to intervene physically in that region. The international scene would have to change so drastically for a threat of direct Soviet intervention in Western Europe to be plausible that the East European analogy seems largely irrelevant to speculation about relations between an Italian government with Communists and the USSR.

There are, however, circumstances under which the PCI would be more likely to align itself with the USSR, even if not to buckle under: for example, an international crisis—either a crisis among third parties that Italy was drawn into, or one involving relationships between Italy and her allies. In the first case, PCI presence in government might enlarge the influence of the Soviet Union even without any direct Italian involvement: where PCI sympathies coincide with those of the Soviet Union, as in the Middle East, the simple fact of Communist participation in government would shift weights in the international balance, even if Italy remained passive in the conflict.

In the second kind of crisis as in the first, the major changes in the role of Italy would derive not so much from new initiatives in Italian policy as from changes triggered by the altered perceptions and approaches of Italy's allies. For example, should the PCI participate in government, it is extremely unlikely that the Italian government would seek to modify its NATO status, but very likely that the other NATO allies, falling into line behind the United States, would make the question of Italy's continued membership in NATO an issue. With respect to multinational corporations operating in Italy, it is improbable that an Italian government including Communists would act to restrain movement of foreign capital in and out of the country, but highly likely that the simple fact of Communist entry into government would precipitate a major perturbation of international capital markets because of actions on the part of foreign firms in Italy.

It is in this kind of situation, then—one arising from a disruption in relations triggered by Italy's allies' changed behavior—that Communist presence in government might significantly affect Italy's course of action. In order to counterbalance the hostility of allies, in order to weather economic difficulties caused by international capital movements, Italy with Communists in government would be more likely to seek support outside the Atlantic alliance. There are a variety of possibilities: closer relationships with Third World countries and, in particular, bilateral contacts with the producers of raw materials; following the French model of a more activist, more nationalist, and less pro-American foreign policy; a return to protectionist policies and a retreat from Europe.[24] While each of these alternatives falls far short of a simple transfer into the Soviet camp—an altogether improbable outcome—each of them viewed from an American perspective would represent a weakening of the Atlantic alliance.

If the above line of reasoning is correct, these changes in Italian foreign policy would occur only in response to rather gross shifts in the behavior toward Italy of its own allies. Though some changes in the international role of Italy might follow inevitably from the participation of Communists in government, they would have a minor impact so long as Italy's foreign policy posture remained essentially reactive and passive. With a high degree of public apathy on foreign policy, with no major political group in the country interested in enlarging Italy's role on the world scene, with the Communists—the only party that once did advocate a fundamental reform of Italian policy—committed to maintaining Italy's current international alliances, it seems implausible that changes in Italian domestic politics would in and of themselves result in a significantly more activist foreign policy. Rather, the shifts in foreign policy most feared by Italy's allies are likely to occur only in response to changes that the allies themselves will initiate. In this respect, the prospects for Italian foreign policy, with or without the Communists, are fundamentally different from those in France, where the legacy of Gaullist foreign policy and its popularity create an altogether different structure of expectations about the role any government should play in the international arena.

To point to the critical role that foreign responses to Communist participation in government will play in determining the subsequent foreign policy choices of Italian governments is not to suggest that the situation would be entirely dominated by American decisions. No matter what the United States decided in the event of a Communist presence in the Italian government, even with no new Italian foreign policy, there would still be the effect discussed above on third parties in the Mediterranean. No matter what American policy, the responses of international corporations and banks would remain problematic for Italy. Even if the Soviet Union were far less active and influential than it has been in Portugal, it would still be an important factor in determining the direction of Italian politics. But after all these elements are considered, the decisive variable for Italian foreign policy still appears to be the American response.

To focus on Italian foreign policy in the context of a possible Communist participation in government is in one sense misleading, for it implies a greater likelihood of this event than the political situation of late 1975 suggests. Though the preceding analysis has emphasized the strengthening of Communist prospects over the past decade, one should not underestimate the powerful domestic resistances to the PCI and the serious difficulties the PCI is likely to experience in trying to consolidate and expand the gains it has made thus far. But even if a Communist role in power is far from inevitable, an examination of Italian foreign policy in this perspective is not irrelevant, for preventing such an outcome has been the principal goal of American foreign policy toward Italy.

With respect to its other major European allies—whether France, Britain, or West Germany—the United States has had a far more complex set of objectives, seeking not only to prevent certain outcomes and to maintain the status quo but, more ambitiously, to obtain a higher measure of cooperation, coordination, and commitment than has ever been sought from Italy. The single-mindedness of American policy and its low-level, negative aspect corresponded both to the relative weakness of Italy and hence its limited capacity for any major contribution to Atlantic cooperation and to Italy's ambivalent foreign policy aspirations. Pierre Hassner has characterized these attitudes toward the Atlantic alliance as a "pacifist atlanticism," "the lowest common denominator which alone has been capable of absorbing the contradictions between and within Italian political attitudes: a passive acceptance and a political utilization of NATO, compensated by a rhetorical search for peace, détente, and an over-coming the blocs, and by feet-dragging on collective obligations."[25] The result of these two converging policies has been an Italian-American relationship based on a simple commitment to maintenance of the status quo: "What the United States wants from Italy is essentially access to military bases and a non-Communist regime. What Italian elites want from the United States is essentially bilateral help and protection and a framework symbolizing and materializing the socio-political choice in favor of a Western democratic or capitalistic regime."[26]

Whether or not the Communist party ever comes into government in Italy, one may question whether the virtually exclusive focus of American policy on this issue has been a wise one. In the first place, this policy emphasis has led the United States to intervene directly in Italian domestic politics—probably more than in any other West European nation. Direct American governmental grants to the DC and other anti-Communist groups, probably including the Fascists, at least indirectly,[27] continue the practices of the early cold war era, while the pay-offs to Italian political parties from major American corporations operating in Italy and the continuing involvement of American trade-unionists in Italian union politics extend the range of American intervention in Italian internal affairs. Perhaps even more disturbing, the DC has been allowed to wield the menace of American intervention, and American statesmen have helped them do so over the years by well-placed comments before Italian elections on how the United States could not be indifferent to political outcomes in which the Left played a role in power. The cover, protection and funds we give the DC are certainly not the only factors that have allowed it to grow fat and lazy in power and have brought it to its current state, but they have counted. Had the DC not been able so easily to fall back on its threats about the possible reactions from abroad to left gains in Italy, it might itself have felt the need earlier to take new initiatives and, first of all, to reform its own party and practices.

Similarly in foreign policy, the impact of the United States has been to discourage those initiatives that might have led to a more independent Italian role. As one considers the complexity of the issues arising in the Mediterranean—whether those involving changes in the domestic political character of regimes as in Greece or in state relations as between Israel and the Arab states, Turkey and Greece, or industrial and Third World countries—it is clear that the United States will not be able to play in each case the role of *cavalier seul* that it has in the

Middle East. Though the United States has been quick to perceive that independent Italian initiatives in these problem areas might complicate the American game and tangle the wires, it has failed to realize the advantages that might be derived from defusing the confrontation by introducing more players. In many of the conflicts in the Mediterranean, American interests are not served by reducing our allies to more or less "loyal" assistants in a design of our making. But for Italy to play—on something more consequential than a rhetorical level—any other part would require both greater political will and resources in Rome than are currently available and a new American understanding of the possible contributions of Italian initiatives in foreign policy.

Postscript, June 1976

Ten days after the legislative elections of 20-21 June 1976, the emergence of a strong and stable government in the near future in Italy seems extremely unlikely. The elections, provoked by the Socialists in order to break the political stalemate that had paralyzed governmental action on the failing economy and parliamentary decision on the abortion issue, created more problems than they solved. The results strengthened both the Christian Democrats and the Communists and drastically reduced the minor parties on which the coalitions of the past three decades have depended. The DC recovered from its slump in the 1975 regional elections and regained 38.7 per cent of the electorate, repeating its 1972 score; the PCI, which had 27.1 per cent of the vote in 1972 won 34.4 per cent in 1976. The small parties that had been regular alliance partners of the DC lost 34 seats in the Chamber of Deputies, making it impossible to build a center-right governmental coalition.

The bipolarization of Italian politics, far from simplifying the task of creating a viable government, will make it more difficult. Though Italian politics now superficially resembles English and German systems, with two major parties and one important minor party, the resemblance is misleading, for in both Britain and West Germany the legitimacy of alternation in power by the two major parties is generally accepted. In Italy, in contrast, there is no consensus on the legitimacy of Communist participation in government, let alone on a Communist government, so the simplification of the party system can only contribute to its rigidification. The apparent success with which the DC stressed anti-communism in its campaign and the re-entry of the Catholic Church into the political arena with warnings to the faithful against voting for left parties all suggest that the issue of integrating the Communist party into the political system is far from resolution.

At this writing, the DC can form a government only if the Socialists agree to support it, and the Socialists refuse to enter so long as the Communists continue to be excluded from any part in government. Since the elections have given all sides good reasons to retrench behind their earlier positions—the successes of the DC confirming for it the wisdom of refusing any form of Communist participation, the losses of the PSI strengthening it in its rejection of the old center-left formulas, and the gains of the PCI reinforcing its desire to receive some political counterpart for its heretofore unacknowledged role in supporting governments— it is difficult to see how the impasse will be broken. Beyond the uncertainties of government-building in the next year loom the larger issues: of the future of the Communist Party and of the prospects for the Christian Democrats, who may well be seeing their last chance to carry out the necessary reforms to restore a disintegrating state and a failing economy.

Notes

1. Massimo Paci, *Mercato del lavoro e classi sociali in Italia* (Bologna: Il Mulino, 1973).

2. This would explain why the rate of increase of hourly productivity could continue to rise (+6.4 per cent in the period subsequent to the economic miracle, when the rate of investment remained constant (1964-1969). Paolo Sylos-Labini, *Trade Unions, Inflation, and Productivity* (Westmead, England: D.C. Heath, 1974), p. 124.

3. This argument about the critical role of changes in industrial relations in the current economic crisis owes much to Michele Salvati's *Il sistema economico italiano: analisi di una crisi* (Bologna: Il Mulino, 1975).

4. From Sylos-Labini, *Trade Unions*, table 3.1, p. 120.

5. Salvati, *Il sistema*, p. 138.

6. See, for example, the July 8, 1975 statement by Luciano Lama, head of the CGIL, the Communist trade union federation: "The goal today is to fight unemployment rather than to obtain wage increases." Or the December 11, 1974 statement by Enrico Berlinguer, head of the PCI, that in order to recover from the present economic crisis, sacrifices are necessary, that the working class is willing to make such provided that "the hard effort they are called upon to make will actually serve to achieve the goal of a better economic and social system and not somehow shore up the present one, leaving intact and even aggravating distortions, privilege, and injustice."

7. The hourly remuneration in the cotton industry in France was 2536 liras as contrasted with 3135 in Italy in January 1975. The difference was entirely due to higher social security costs in Italy. *Le Monde*, July 19, 1975.

8. Salvati, *Il sistema*, pp. 30-31, points out that in all industrial countries except Italy, investment increased in the period 1964-1969 in order to face stiffer international competition.

9. On this point, see Andrew Shonfield, "L'impresa pubblica: modello internazionale o specialità locale?," in F.L. Cavazza and S. Graubard (eds.), *Il caso italiano* (Milan: Garzanti, 1974).

10. See Stuart Holland, "State Entrepreneurship and State Intervention," in Stuart Holland (ed), *The State as Entrepreneur* (London: Weidenfeld and Nicolson, 1972).

11. These changes are analyzed in detail in Eugenio Scalfari and Giuseppe Turani, *Razza padrona* (Milan: Feltrinelli, 1974).

12. In 1968 and 1969, public corporations supplied 45 per cent of their financial needs from self-financing; by 1971 the figure had dropped to 19 per cent. Romano Prodi, *Sistema industriale e sviluppo economico in Italia* (Bologna: Il Mulino, 1973), p. 30. See also Shonfield, "L'impresa pubblica, and Scalfari and Turani, pp. 30 ff.

13. Between 1963 and 1971, the proportion of total sales realized by firms in or controlled by the public sector increased from 17.4 per cent to 31.8 per cent. Romano Prodi, "Italy," in Raymond Vernon (ed.), *Big Business and the State* (Cambridge, Mass.: Harvard University Press, 1974).

14. Prodi, *Sistema industriale*, p. 21.

15. OECD prediction reported in *Le Monde*, July 23, 1975.

16. Statistics gathered by the EEC Commission, cited in *Le Monde*, August 15, 1975. If the number of strike days per thousand workers is considered, the Italian case is even more striking: 1783, in contrast with 650 in Britain, 201 in France, and 48 in Germany.

17. On the decline of religious practice, a recent survey found a decline in church attendance from 51.6 per cent in 1969 to 40.1 per cent in 1974. Cited in Giacomo Sani, "Secular Trends and Party Realignments in Italy: The 1975 Elections," paper presented at the APSA convention, September 1975, p. 20. On the widening gap between religious belief and political practice, it is significant that whereas 67 per cent of the respondents in a 1953 survey judged that one could not be a "good Communist and a good Catholic at the same time," by 1970 this figure had dropped to 44 per cent and by 1972, to 34 per cent. Cited ibid., p. 25.

18. This argument has been developed by Giorgio Galli in a number of works. See most recently his *Dal bipartitismo imperfetto alla possibile alternativa* (Bologna: Il Mulino, 1975).

19. As Peter Lange argues in "The French and Italian Communist Parties: Postwar Strategy and Domestic Society," paper prepared for Workshop on Radicalism of the Research Institute on International Change, Columbia University, April 2, 1975. See also the chapters on the PCI in Donald L.M. Blackmer and Sidney Tarrow (eds.), *Communism in Italy and France* (Princeton: Princeton Univ. Press, 1975), in particular, Blackmer's "Continuity and Change in Postwar Italian Communism" and Tarrow's "Communism in Italy and France: Adaptation and Change."

20. Geneviève Bibes, *Le système politique italian* (Paris: Presses Universitaires de France, 1974), pp. 166-68. Recently, the rate of PCI opposition seems to be dropping further. From January 1974 to May 1975, the PCI voted against only 15 per cent of the bills. *L'Espresso*, October 26, 1975, p. 11.

21. An excellent brief account of relations between the PCI and the Soviet Union is Donald L. Blackmer, "The International Strategy of the Italian Communist Party," in D. Blackmer and A. Kriegel, *The International Role of the Communist Parties of Italy and France* (Cambridge: Center for International Affairs, Harvard University, 1975).

22. Excerpts of Zaradov's article were printed in *Le Monde*, August 9, 1975.

23. Ibid., August 10-11, 1975.

24. Christian Democratic governments have also been tempted by these alternatives and have strayed off the path of their old attachments far enough to negotiate separate deals with some of the Arab countries, to adopt positions rather different from the American on the Middle East crisis, and to retreat from EEC commitments behind protectionist barriers during the current economic crisis. These remain, however, isolated initiatives, given the lack of political will, coordination, and, above all, of a clear sense of direction. On recent Italian foreign policy, see Cesare Merlini, "Introduction to the Yearbook 'L'Italia nella politica internazionale,' " *Lo spettatore internazionale* 9, 3-4 (July-December 1974), and Pierre Hassner, "Italian Perceptions of NATO" (paper, 1975).

25. Hassner, "Italian Perceptions," p. 9.

26. Ibid., p. 8.

27. The reference here is to payment of "at least $6 million in secret cash payments to individual anti-Communist political leaders in Italy" by the Central Intelligence Agency, as reported in the *New York Times* of Jan. 7, 1976, p. 1, and the payment in 1972-73 of $800,000 by United States Ambassador Graham A. Martin to General Vito Miceli, "a prominent rightist," head of Italy's military intelligence, a man with close ties with the extraparliamentary right. The latter payments were made over the strong objections of the CIA. Ibid., Jan. 30, 1976, p. 1. On both these stories, see the excerpts *in extenso* from the report of the House Select Committee on Intelligence (the "Pike report") in the *Village Voice*, Feb. 16, 1976.

VIII

Spain and Portugal: Critical Choices

Juan J. Linz

The Passing of Two Authoritarian Regimes and the
Problem of Creating Democracies in the Middle 70s

It is no accident that, when Willy Brandt spoke in November 1974 about an "Emergency Program for Self-Defense" and "Survival of the European Community," he should have listed among six points the need for "a policy of supporting democracy on its southern borders." This is certainly a major problem for Europe and the United States. But in order to support democracy it is first necessary to create it, and that task belongs to the leaders and the people of Portugal and Spain. After all, Europe and the United States have managed to live without democracy in the Iberian Peninsula. While not happy, they were, particularly the United States, content with stable government even when it was undemocratic. The concern with democracy is really a reflection of the impossibility of stable authoritarian regimes, and the question we have to ask

A first version of this essay was written in late 1974 and revised only partially in early February 1976. It was impossible to take into account all the dramatic events of that year and unnecessary in that chronicles of those events can be found elsewhere. Some of them have confirmed my analysis, others have forced me to modify it or qualify it. Obviously, any effort to update this essay after each of those events would have led to different emphases and predictions. My choice has been to let the original text stand, deleting references to processes that now lack relevance and adding considerations on intervening events that confirm or modify the earlier analysis. With more space I would have attempted a more systematic analysis of the social and economic factors underlying the political process.

This essay has benefited from the discussions at the miniconference on Contemporary Portugal sponsored by the Council on West European Studies of Yale University and the Council for European Studies, March 28-29, 1975.

237

ourselves is: "Will stable democracies emerge from the breakdown of the Portuguese authoritarian regime and its crisis in Spain?"

The answer to that question would have been difficult even in the stable and prosperous world of the 60s. It certainly is even more difficult today, when in addition to the uncertain variables and unpredictable events in those countries, we have to add an uncertain European and world situation. There is little social science theorizing on changes of regime on which we can lean.[1] We should not forget that the more or less stable European democracies of the interwar period were already successful democracies before World War I and that others were created by outside imposition rather than by an internally generated change. Portugal and probably Spain in the near future will have to do so on their own after many years of authoritarian rule. Our discussion will focus first on some common problems in the transition phase of both Spain and Portugal, derived from some common characteristics of their regimes and the same historical context they have to face.[2] We then shall turn to some of the distinctive problems of each case, particularly the difficult question, how Spain will get out of the Franco regime. It is easy to be misled by the similarities of both countries and to be tempted to extrapolate developments in Portugal since April 1974 to Spain after the day X. The danger lies in ignoring fundamental differences in the economic and social structure of both countries and less visible but significant differences between the regimes created by Salazar and Franco. One must also remember that the breakdown of the Salazar-Caetano regime was provoked by an unsolvable problem created by its policies in Africa in the era of decoloniza-tion, which then led to the *pronunciamento* of the army, rather than a popular revolt or a change initiated by the elites of the regime.[3] The unique position of the Movimento das Forças Armadas (MFA), whose manifesto constitutes in effect the constitutional charter of the new regime, can only be understood by keeping that in mind. The more or less costly and debatable solution to the African problem is also the source of legitimacy of the new regime.

Spaniards, when confronted with the political decay of the thirty-five-year-old Franco regime and the ambiguities of its monarchical successor state, face an internal problem—very different in quality from that posed by the African possessions of Portugal. Given the costs of holding on to the colonies, the limited benefits for most Portuguese, the lack of probabilities of ultimate success, the decision to change the regime to end the war in Africa could initially build a broad consensus reflected in the mood of Lisbon in the days of the "revolution of the flowers." For most Portuguese, in those first moments of euphoria, the political implications that have today become apparent did not even come to mind.[4]

Spain in some ways faces more difficult dilemmas. The problem to solve is an internal, political one: that of dismantling institutions that are functioning more or less badly, specifically, a political system that has coincided with and perhaps contributed to a fundamental economic and to some extent social transformation of the country and that has had the enthusiastic support of a minority, positive compliance by another large segment, the acquiescence if not the support of another large fraction of the population, and the bitter hatred of another. With the memory of a civil war, even though fading with the turnover of generations, the current transition arouses the fears of many, the doubts of many more, but also many hopes. In the absence, at least for the time being, of any unsolvable problem requiring immediate action, the regime can go on and evade the pressures and desires for change. In some sense, only the Basque problem looms on the horizon as a problem that might become unsolvable within the expectations Spaniards have about how their government should and can act. Perhaps labor conflicts and other forms of economically motivated protest may become unsolvable within the limits of what people feel the government should do today. In the case of Spain the problem is fundamentally political, and the emergence of a definitive successor regime is likely to be a much slower and more complex process than in Portugal. The awareness of this fact would allow Spanish political elites to engineer the change. Possibly, but not necessarily probably, they will derive some lessons from the Portuguese experience. At the same time, the fact that the problem is an internal political one and that there is no immediate gain for everyone like that produced by the ending of a colonial war will make it more difficult to achieve initially the vague and broad consensus achieved in Portugal. We can expect in Spain a much higher level of political mobilization, of articulation of conflicting positions and, after the Portuguese experience, of the risks of transition. It is in this sense of example (or warning) that events in Portugal will have a great impact on Spain. It is not so much the similarity between the regimes and in no way a similarity in economic and social structure that justifies dealing with both cases together.

Social scientists' analyses of the conditions for stable democracy would lead us to argue that in Spain, once the succession problem is resolved, many of the conditions are more favorable than in Portugal.[5] If we consider the indicators of economic and social modernization, Spain is far ahead of Portugal—in GNP *per capita,* in its economic growth rates over the last decade, its more balanced economic structure, the lesser underemployment and dependency on emigration, the greater development of a modern welfare state, the expansion of the social and economic activities of the state, the plurality and complexity of centers of social power, the absence of a macrocephalic capital city where the fate of the country might be decided, the more international orientation of many of its elites, and even, in recent years, a more active and less repressed political life in which government, legal semiopposition, and illegal opposition have learned to live together in semi- or pseudo-freedom.[6] Meanwhile the revival of social agitation in the form of strikes and everyday political protest and violence has undermined the image of the regime as the only possible guarantor of order. The complex changes that have taken place in the Catholic Church have also reduced the saliency of the old, anticlerical struggle. Economic development, the emergence of an industrial society, the withering away of the old, unjust rural social structure have changed the nature of class conflict from an intensely personal type of conflict in 1936 into a more modern conflict about shares in the benefit of economic development.[7] In summary, Spain on all those accounts seems to be readier than in the past for a stable democracy—once it is successfully installed. The major problem I see lies in issues raised by the transformation of a centralist state conceived by most Spaniards as a nation-state into a multinational state whose very legitimacy might be questioned by some minorities.

In Portugal, on the contrary, linguistic and cultural/historical homogeneity constitutes a favorable factor. The absence of a memory of civil war cannot be ignored either. On the other hand the economic and social underdevelopment of large parts of the country poses serious problems and might contribute to the search for radical solutions. The Portuguese even more than the Spaniards are likely to think of their country as an underdeveloped Third World country requiring solutions different from those pursued in Western Europe. This is less likely in Spain. Even though anticapitalism will be an appealing issue in Spain for reasons to be developed later, the Spanish entrepreneurial class, perhaps with the exception of the big banks, is less tied to the regime and less lacking in legitimacy than its Portuguese counterpart. The integration of the economy into that of Western Europe, the linkages between business elites and the regional nationalisms, the large number of entrepreneurs and managers, the record of performance of Spanish business—all of this contrasts with the stunted performance of a small and highly concentrated capitalist elite in Portugal. To question the capitalist model of economic development in Portugal is easier than in Spain. *Servata distantia* the difference has some similarity with that between developments in Brazil and Peru.

We shall not pursue here further the differences between both countries and their recent political, economic, and social history, which in itself would constitute an interesting problem for a comparative social scientist. Before going into a discussion of the future, it will be useful to take a step back and to ask the question to what extent these two countries have a revolutionary tradition that would manifest itself again with the dismantling of authoritarian controls. Another step back we have to take is to analyze to what extent the process of transition to democracy in Portugal and Spain will be comparable to the experience in other West European countries after World War II or will be taking place in a very different historical context.

Is Revolution the Legacy of the Past?

It is tempting to think of the Iberian Peninsula as having a radical and revolutionary tradition in contrast to the evolutionary development of political institutions in other West European societies. The strength and importance of anarchism and anarcho-syndicalism in the modern history of Spain, the revolution of October 1934 in Asturias, and the dramatic events of the civil war come immediately to mind. The fact that outside of France, Spain was the only monarchical country in the nineteenth century that established for a short period a republican regime would be another sign of precocious revolutionary potential. The continued political turmoil that accompanied the overthrow of the monarchy and the course of the Portuguese republic until the Estado Novo would be another historical antecedent. In that context it seems paradoxical that neither of the two countries experienced a really successful revolution: the frequent changes of regime in the nineteenth century and the first half of the twentieth were more the result of crises of the existing regimes than of the mobilization of their opponents—more the result of a loss of power and legitimacy by the existing regime than of effective challenges from the masses. The frequent, sporadic, localized, and violent outbursts of revolutionary discontent were generally just that, with large sectors of their natural following standing by passively.[8] In fact, a comparison of levels of mobilization for radical parties and of membership in trade unions would show that Spain, and Portugal even more, lags far behind other European countries, particularly Italy—and this in spite of universal male suffrage in Spain since the nineteenth century and a reasonable degree of civil liberty. This difference in mobilization cannot be explained by Italian precedence in industrialization, since much of the membership of the Italian Socialist movement was among farmers and farm laborers in the Po Valley before the rise of Fascism. In Spain the Socialist party was able to mobilize its potential rural support only after 1931, under a republican-Socialist coalition government. Until then it had been a party of the urban and industrial working class. Philippe Schmitter has shown the even lower levels of mobilization of the Portuguese proletariat under the republic before Salazar.[9]

Nor should we forget the indifference of large sectors of the working class and the more underprivileged peasantry to revolutionary attempts by their more activist companions—to calls by anarchists and anarcho-syndicalist leaders to establish libertarian communism, and to the October 1934 uprising in Asturias. The Portuguese political revolution in the early decades of the century was largely a Lisbon phenomenon that found only limited echo in most of the country. Nor can we ignore the large-scale electoral abstention: the municipal elections of April 1931 that brought the republic had a participation rate of 67 per cent; and the heated elections of February 1936, in which two great blocs, the Popular Front and the Antirevolutionary Front, confronted each other only five months before the outbreak of the civil war, saw 27 per cent of the eligible voters stay home. Undoubtedly, the anarcho-syndicalists' abstention contributed to that rate, but we should not forget that in 1936 many followers of the Confederacion Nacional de Trabajo (CNT) turned out to vote. In the case of Spain, the level of mobilization by the left and revolutionary parties in the civil war should not obscure the fact that the candidates of the proletarian parties obtained only 19.2 per cent of the valid votes in the 1936 election and the Communists among them 2.5 per cent.[10]

When considering the potential for popular revolution we cannot forget either that, except for a short period after 1945 in very localized areas, there has been no guerilla resistance or massive uprisings whose suppression would have required large casualties of the protestors and the forces of order—not even in recent times when widespread strikes have affected most large enterprises and whole cities or industrial regions. Such strikes, because of their illegality, have political significance, but the underlying motives have generally been economic, and they have become increasingly a recognized method of collective bargaining, whereas strictly political strikes until recently have tended to be a failure. This has been even truer in the case of Portugal under the Salazar and Caetano regimes. There even the unpopular colonial wars did not produce mass protests, and the overthrow of the regime in April was not preceded by mass protests but rather was exclusively the result of a military uprising.

The history of the Iberian countries, therefore, contrary to a superficial impression, documents the failure of radical movements there to achieve a mass mobilization comparable to that in other European countries, particularly France and Italy. It might be deceptive, however, to extrapolate from that past history to the future. Great political changes in the past have in my view been more the result of the disintegration of previous regimes, their loss of legitimacy among the middle classes, shifts in loyalty of the armed forces and other institutions, and the consequent development of a power vacuum to be filled by new active minorities. If there are to be revolutionary changes in both societies, they are more likely to be the work of active minorities exploiting the basic weakness of conservative institutions, cleavages within the elite, temporarily sympathetic sponsorship of radical political changes by broad sectors of the society, than of mass movements. The potential for revolutionary transformations in the near future lies more in the weakness and loss of legitimacy of conservative institutions: such a situation is an invitation to take-over by intensely motivated groups and activists.

The Problem of Regime Change and of Consolidation of Democracy in the Mid-1970s

In the 1920s and 1930s the political, social, and economic crisis in Europe led to the establishment of a number of undemocratic regimes, particularly in those countries that had been defeated in World War I and in a number of new nations in Eastern Europe. In 1939 the stable democracies were only those that already existed before the war, minus Italy, Portugal, and Spain. In 1945, except for the countries in the Soviet sphere of influence, the democracies destroyed by the

German occupation (Norway, the Netherlands, and Belgium) were restored without major difficulty. Internal processes made possible the creation of a new democratic regime in France, and such processes combined with the decisions of the victors in Italy. In West Germany and Austria as well as Japan, defeat in the war and the allied occupation displaced totalitarian and authoritarian rule and led to the establishment of democratic regimes of considerable stability.[11] Spain and Portugal were thus the only two surviving undemocratic regimes of the 30s in Europe. The status of Spain as a nonbelligerent, despite allied pressures against the Franco government, and the pro-allied neutrality of Portugal allowed their regimes to last into the 70s. The time elapsed since the breakdown of democracy in those countries makes it impossible to restore the institutions that preceded authoritarian rule. In fact, one of the most important differences between those two countries and all other European societies with an undemocratic interlude is the long duration of their regimes. After all, Italian fascism was in power only twenty-three years, and in fact less if we consider the time it took Mussolini to establish full control and the interval between surrender and the end of World War II. Hitler was in power less than twelve years. But the Portuguese regime that was overthrown in 1974 had lasted more than forty-five years, and Franco lasted thirty-six. This means that, even if there had been no major changes in the social structure, a restoration is out of the question. Few of the democratic leaders who went into foreign or internal exile will be able to return to active political life.

Consequently, the leadership that will establish the new post-authoritarian regimes is not likely to have a personal experience of democratic politics or be able to draw on the lessons of its breakdown. They are likely to be men emerging from the illegal underground or participation in one or another capacity in the authoritarian regime, or complete newcomers to politics. This discontinuity is certainly a disadvantage for the institutionalization of democratic political institutions.

There is also a basic difference between the Iberian authoritarian regimes and Italian fascism and even more German nazism: the leaders of the Axis regimes were basically recruited from the single party; the most prominent positions were filled by old fighters, and the single party was the center of power. There was little time for a renewal of leadership within those regimes, particularly Nazi Germany. This made it relatively easy to define clearly the political elite that had been displaced by defeat and failure. This would not be possible in the Iberian regimes, where the absence of a real Fascist party in Portugal and its weakness in Spain have compelled the regimes to coopt large numbers of people lacking strong ideological commitments from the civil service, the army, academia, the professions, intellectual life, etc. The (limited) pluralism of these authoritarian regimes[12] and their tolerance and encouragement even for apoliticism have fostered a much broader involvement of the society than in the German and Italian dictatorships. In particular the recent phases of semiliberalization have drawn into the regimes people who otherwise might have been in the opposition or politically inactive.

This means that it is (in Portugal) and will be (in Spain) much more difficult to establish a clear boundary between the collaborators and the resisters. The ambiguities of pseudo- and semi-opposition might initially facilitate the transition, but they will also make possible the displacement not only of the political, but also of social and professional elites on charges of collaboration. This ambiguity is liable to promote radicalization, for it provides a basis for the proscription of potential leaders right of center and an incentive to overcome the past by joining those who can grant absolution from the past. The end result, paradoxically, will be not so much a renewal of the political elite as a questioning and transformation of social institutions.

In this context the process called by the Portuguese *saneamento* becomes a messy affair, and opportunity for skillful, purposeful parties to colonize the administration. Accusations of collaboration could be used as an instrument of intimidation against those wanting to create new center or center-right parties and their potential financial backers, while even leaders of democratic parties may be discredited by the sins of a distant past. Obviously, this process might build in the long run the basis of a radical right opposition.

1975 Is Not 1945-1949

When we attempt to compare the process of democratization in the Iberian Peninsula today and tomorrow with that of Europe after World War II, we have to take note of the important changes that have taken place in the meantime. There are five that deserve special notice:

1. The very different role that the Catholic Church will play in that process today compared to 1945;
2. The emergence of a broad non-Fascist critique of Western democracy and particularly of the United States; this was limited in Western Europe in 1945 to the Communists and muted even among them;
3. The prolonged exposure of younger elites during their student years to a radical critique of capitalist society and the role of the West;
4. The impossibility of articulating today, as after 1948, a convincing anti-Communist position: Stalinism is dead; the world is no longer divided into only two camps of "good guys and bad guys"; everyone is tired of cold war;
5. The new identification of nationalism with the Left and the growing ambivalence in the less developed countries concerning supranational organizations.

Let us analyze in some detail these important changes and their implications.

The Changed Role of the Church

The Catholic Church in 1945 could emerge in a number of countries as one of the few institutions that had opposed nazism on the ideological level if not in practice. The hostility of the Nazis had reinforced the Catholic subculture. In some countries, such as France, the Church or at least the lay Catholic leadership had established linkages with the Resistance. In contrast, in Portugal and perhaps even more in Spain, the Church hierarchy and Catholic lay organizations have long had intimate ties with the regime in power. In the late 40s, moreover, it was easy for the Church to take a clear anti-Communist stand in the face of persecution in Eastern Europe. Since then the Second Vatican Council and changed policies of the Curia have deeply altered the political role of the Church. The revival of the prophetic, critical role of Christianity in regard to the social order has made possible the emergence of a noisy left wing among the clergy and the laity. A new concern for the loss of faith of the working class combined with moral indignation about the injustices of the social order and the emergence of specialized lay movements directed to underprivileged groups has made possible a pro-left climate of opinion among an important minority of Catholics. This, combined with a Communist emphasis on good relations with progressive Catholics and the achievement of a *modus vivendi* between the Vatican and the Communist states, makes impossible today an anti-Communist campaign like that in Italy in 1948. Statements at the Vatican Council affirming the compatibility between Christianity and socialism have contributed to that shift. The presence of a left wing in the Church as well as a reactionary right wing makes it highly undesirable to involve the Church in politics, particularly since the omnipotent authority of the hierarchy is not likely to be recognized by either as it would have been in the past. A disenchantment with Catholic politicians cannot be ignored either. In the case of Spain, a strong identification of the lower clergy and the religious orders in certain regions with aspirations of dissident nationalisms, legitimized directly by the recognition of the vernacular in the Church, constitutes another problem for the hierarchy. In this changed political and religious context, the obvious response of the hierarchy is to emphasize its pastoral and to some extent prophetic-critical mission and to disengage from political commitments that would be divisive within the Church itself.

As a result, the Church can no longer mobilize the Catholic laity, or even the lay organizations sponsored by the Church, to provide the cadres and the votes for a mass Christian-Democratic party. In fact, it seems pretty clear that in Portugal and probably in Spain the hierarchy will discourage those Catholics still willing to organize a party with an ideology and program comparable to those of the Christian-Democratic parties that acted after the war as regime builders in a number of Western European countries from using the word Christian to describe themselves. As the leader of such a party, the CDS (Centro Democratico

Social), confessed to me, this represents a handicap in its efforts to reach its natural constituency in Catholic, land-owning northern provincial Portugal. The obstacles in using the Christian appeal make it difficult to create a bridge party between the center left and the center right like the Italian DC, the German postwar CDU and similar parties in Austria, Belgium, the Netherlands, and France (the MRP in the 1950s). The large aggregation of interests and votes that such parties achieved made it possible in the late 40s and 50s to counterbalance the Left. It is not easy today to find an ideological appeal, a class-heterogeneous leadership, a pragmatic program comparable to those of these parties, or anything equivalent to the subtle pressures of the hierarchy to prevent the factional splits within such a heterogeneous aggregate. In the absence of Christian-Democratic parties, any party on the center-right will have to appeal from the beginning as a conservative party and will therefore, in the climate of the late 70s, be limited in its appeal. A party like the CDS in Portugal cannot expect to have the same broad social basis as the Italian DC.

The Catholic Left, the Christians for Socialism, are probably few in number, but they provide legitimacy and in some cases devoted cadres to the parties of the Left. Since, after Vatican II, they cannot be disciplined by the hierarchy, their pronouncements cannot be disavowed and therefore make an important contribution to the climate of opinion.

In Spain, the hierarchy might have taken advantage of the religious orientation of important sections of peripheral nationalist communities, particularly in the Basque country and to some extent in Catalonia, to promote integration of regional parties into a federative national Christian-Democratic party. That possibility today seems remote, and the party system is more fragmented than ever.

The Changed Climate of Opinion toward Democracy

In the late 1940s, after the era of Fascism and with the emergence of Communist-controlled totalitarian regimes in Eastern Europe, democracy of the Western type appeared as the only alternative and for many people as a great hope. The United States, a great Western democracy, with its prosperity and other achievements, could be seen as a model. In 1975, in contrast, all the weakness and failures of pluralist Western democracy are well known and publicized. England is no longer the model of a successful polity, and the United States has lost much of its aura. It is not difficult to show the errors of the United States and with it of democratic politics, quoting the Americans themselves on their racial troubles, McCarthyism, Vietnam, corruption and crime, Watergate and Nixon, and now the CIA. The authoritarian regimes on the Iberian Peninsula have, for their own good reasons, not opposed a constant critique of the United States in the mass media, which, limited in their possibility of criticizing the government, have been only too quick to use the United States as a whipping boy. In fact, the Right and the Fascist elements share in many ways the critique of American society and politics. On the other hand, the simplistic critique of communism by the authoritarian regimes and their spokesmen could easily be discounted as interested, while more serious critical analysis of the Soviet Union did not reach the educated public because the publishing houses wanted to use their limited but growing freedom to publish works more in tune with an opposition stance towards the regime.

The emergence of Communist regimes that could not be identified with rigid Stalinist totalitarianism and that appeared socially innovative, such as Yugoslavia, Cuba, and far-away and unknown China, created a new interest in alternatives to the capitalist bourgeois democracy of the West. The fact that new types of regimes were emerging in the Third World and challenging the Western advanced industrial countries did not pass unnoticed. To be sure, those attracted by such alternatives are likely to be in the minority, but the fact is that Western-type democracy can no longer be defended as the only meaningful alternative. I guess that most people would still prefer a Western-type of democracy, but that preference is not very intensely felt and lacks at this moment a strong ideological justification.[13]

The Students and the Young

That lack of emotional and intellectual support for democracy per se is not unrelated to a basic shift in the intellectual climate in the universities over the last decade. This shift is now making itself felt as students graduate and take their place in society. It is said that students drafted for the colonial war in Africa, some of whom became reserve officers and worked in close contact with the junior officers of the regular army, have played an important role in the leftward turn of the Movimento das Forças Armadas (MFA), which was until recently the real center of power in Portugal. Similar processes go on in the professions, among the doctors of the national health service, in the professional associations, and among younger members of the bureaucracy. Intellectual ferment, based on a more or less superficial reading of New Left writings and an interest in Marxism, is obviously reflected in the mass media and is the common coin of those people who want to be à la page. Such trends may not be reflected in party membership or voting behavior but affect the climate of opinion in the society in more subtle ways. Many of the commitments derived from those positions are more verbal than real, but they are a most serious obstacle to the intelligent articulation of a democratic opposition to those ideas.

No More Political Embargo on Communism

I do not expect the Communist parties of Spain and Portugal—in spite of the many organizational advantages gained by semi-freedom in the underground—to gain more votes than their sister parties in France or Italy. The Portuguese election of April 1975 gave good evidence of the Party's limited popularity. The real difference, however, is that after 1947 and particularly 1948 in Europe, it was possible to isolate the Communist parties politically and socially, to exclude them from government coalitions, to limit the power and influence of their functional organizations, to facilitate the breakup of those organizations they controlled and the institutionalization of rival groups on the center-left. This will be much more difficult, if not impossible, today. The difference is that today even those who are fearful of the dominance of the Communists do not dare to say so clearly in public, but only in a roundabout way, by indirect allusions to the excessive ambitions of the Communist party.

This makes the articulation of the non-Communist parties on the left and even the center-left much more difficult. They are subject from outside and inside to pressures to work with the Communists; to recognize their leading role in certain sectors, for example as spokesman of the working class; to accept the "social power" of the Party as a reality that cannot be ignored, even though, electorally and at the parliamentary level, they could probably govern without the Communists. Equally important, they are liable to be forced to attack anyone raising the anti-Communist banner as antidemocratic, as a tool of capitalism, the monopolies, and multinational corporations, hence servants of the United States, if not the CIA. Even those whose objective interests do not coincide with those of the Communists cannot afford to be anti-Communist in the late 70s.

This important change in the climate of opinion is obviously a reflection of the three changes we have listed before. In the Iberian Peninsula, moreover, it is reinforced by a curious process: those who have been linked with the regime in one or another capacity now seek to legitimate their new opposition role and make themselves acceptable to the left-wing inheritors of power by arguing that the Communists should be included in any process of democratization and by decrying anti-Communism. Even those remnants of Socialist suspicion of Communism that go back to the Spanish civil war and the Stalinist purges are denounced as obsolete and illegitimate.[14]

Given the organizational resources of the Communist party, its dedicated leadership, a considerable mass base in the large urban industrial centers, its pragmatic approach, and the Socialist tendency towards sectarian fragmentation, this climate of opinion gives the Communist party a disproportionate role. To be sure, there is always the possibility that the Party leadership will overplay its cards and arouse the opposition of those competing for the same social base (as it did in Portugal in 1975). The opportunistic appeal of Communism is also likely to stir up some opposition. Even so, whatever strength the non-Communist parties may muster, the Communist parties in the Iberian democracies will undoubtedly play a greater role than did the French and Italian Communist parties in the late 40s and 50s.

Nationalism and the Left

Last but not least the political climate in the late 70s will reflect a very different response to nationalism than in the early 50s. The hypernationalism of the Fascist powers, the contribution of nationalism to the crisis of Europe in the 30s, and the outbreak of World War II discredited for a time the conventional nationalist (or chauvinist) responses and favored a variety of internationalist attitudes that crystallized in the idea if not the realities of European integration. Let us not forget that the idea was promoted initially by many of the top leaders of the Christian-Democratic parties and then more or less reluctantly accepted by the social democrats. The economic, military, and political weakness of Europe facilitated integration into the Atlantic alliance, particularly of such countries as Germany that felt threatened by the Eastern bloc.

Recent years have seen a new and strange resurgence of nationalism both of the old nations and of the cultural, national minorities in them. There was first the Gaullist response to the American hegemony, then the reemergence of such peripheral nationalisms as the Flemish, Breton, Scottish, Welsh, and, in Spain, the Basque, Catalan, and Galician.

What is more striking and not easily explained is how nationalism, which in most countries was traditionally an appeal of the Right, has now become a central theme of the Left. Many latent sentiments diffusely felt are today overtly expressed in a new nationalist stance. Sentiments that in the 20s and 30s were very often channeled by the emerging Fascist movement reappear today. The weakening of national sovereignty that has accompanied the liberalization of the world economic system and the expansion of international capitalism in the form of the multinational corporation have evoked nationalist responses logically articulated by the Left. The inter-European labor migration, in which the Iberian Peninsula, in particular Portugal, has participated, has emphasized the inequalities between capitalist nations; the fact that similar inequalities exist within the Communist world lies outside this perception. Massive tourism has also contributed to this disagreeable awareness. The economic benefits clearly derived from these relations by the masses do not diminish the resentment of the elites, who have to pay more for labor and accept a certain competition for, even democratization of, their playgrounds.

In addition, such countries as Spain and Portugal, which do not border on the Soviet bloc and were not liberated by the American army from the Germans, have far less interest in military ties to the United States. The presence of American bases, which seem to provide little or no benefit to the countries concerned, serves to stimulate a neutralist nationlism. Worse yet, the very failure of the opposition to overthrow the authoritarian regimes has found an easy excuse in the military and economic agreements made in the 50s.

In the case of Spain, moreover, exclusion from the Common Market as a sanction against the Franco regime has prevented Spaniards from developing an identification with the process of European integration. Nor are the recession-forced return of Iberian workers from northern Europe and the closing of the foreign job market likely to foster sympathy with the richer European nations. It is paradoxical but not suprising that, as Spain has become a major industrial country, the sensitivity to economic dependence has become more acute. A vague identification with the poor countries of the Third World has made its appearance just when Spain is farthest from being a Third World country. Thus, while the Hispanidad ideology sponsored by the regime in its early years left little mark, a new identification with Latin America and the struggle of its Left against the United States has found considerable echo. It is important to note that some of these changes in opinion are, to use the term coined by Theodor Geiger, *standort inadequat*; they do not correspond to the real economic interests of Spain, but they are ideologically appealing.

A Sixth Factor

In the time since we enumerated these five factors a sixth one of potentially enormous consequences has been added: the emerging split among Western Socialist parties, between Social Democrats and Socialists, between the Northern and the Southern parties.[15] This split became apparent at the Elsinore conference in January 1976, in which Schmidt and Mitterand articulated adverse positions on the issue of collaboration with the Communists as advocated by the Latin European Socialist parties. The difference, however, goes deeper than that. It also concerns the relative importance assigned to welfare state policies and socialization of the means of production; and it reflects the always latent tension between the rich advanced industrial countries and the less developed Southern tier. Ideologically the two factions assign different weights to the Marxist heritage and practically, they have a disparate experience of the political and electoral role of the Communist party.

Portugal

The unexpected, successful, and bloodless coup that ousted Caetano on April 25, 1974 became the revolution of the flowers. It seemed to open the door to a relatively easy transition to pluralist democracy. But by the end of the year the accelerated political and increasingly social revolutionary process led us to ask the question: revolution from above or from below?

In my view the transition from a right-wing authoritarian regime to some new regime, in process now in Portugal and perhaps soon in Spain, may generate a revolutionary tyranny. The very effort of right-wing elements to oppose the leftward trend may furnish the pretext for this repression. Would such a development be a genuine response to a revolutionary predisposition of the masses, or a process initiated and imposed from above by those strong enough to exploit the power vacuum of the transition period? Undoubtedly there are elements of both, but I would emphasize the second. The hesitations of the center-left between alliance and opposition and the difficulties it will encounter in organizing and defining its potential constituency will be its undoing. Inevitably there will be significant groups of extremists on the left and right that will try to polarize the situation, and these actions will be a pretext or even legitimate reason to push the revolutionary process further while claiming and perhaps intending not to push it beyond a tolerable level.

The inevitably ambiguous relationship between the Communist party and its revolutionary competitors on the extreme left and the dilemmas this creates for the non-Communist left cannot be ignored in this situation. This relationship is not fully comparable to that of the Italian Communist party with its radical competitors, since neither the Spanish nor the Portuguese Communist party is likely to be so institutionalized and controlled by the leadership as the Italian party was before dissidents appeared on its left. If we add to this situation the inevitable provocative responses from the extreme right, which particularly in Spain has been able to win some following,[a] a sequence of polarization and conflict seems possible, with a chance of a revolutionary dénouement. In my view this would not be the result of the spontaneous revolutionary actions of the masses, nor of a conscious plan of the leadership, particularly of the Communist party, but an unintended consequence of the dynamic properties of the situation and the responses of middle-level cadres to the situation. In this context the behavior of parties that are neither Maoist nor subject to a discipline like that of the Communists and at the same time reject the model of democratic socialism of the Western European type deserves to be watched attentively. I am thinking, for example, of the Portuguese Movimento Democratico Português–Comissão Democratica Eleitoral (MDP-CED), as well as splinter groups like the Movimento da Esquerda Socialista (MES)–1 and 2 and the radical faction of the Movimento das Forças Armadas (MFA); or, in the case of Spain, of the highly ideological Marxist factions within the old Socialist party, the Partido Socialista Obrero Español (the PSOE) and some of those regional Socialist parties that are not under the thumb of the Communists but nevertheless reject anything that smells of social democracy. Let us not forget the role played in the Chilean crisis by the more radicalized sections of the Socialist party.

In connection with the preceding analysis Portuguese politics since April 25 are very instructive. There is little evidence of any revolutionary outbursts or

---

[a]There is a tendency to overestimate the threat represented by militant, violent, neo-Fascist groups like the followers of Blas Piñar, Fuerza Nueva and the Guerrilleros de Cristo Rey, and other *groupuscules*. When tolerated by the police, they could act with impunity, and since then they have acquired a political role. But they do not enjoy the support or even the sympathy of many people otherwise far from opposed to the regime. They can only be one more disruptive factor but not a political alternative.

pressures coming from the masses, few signs of spontaneous class conflict in the countryside or even in the more politicized city of Lisbon. On the other hand, those opposed to the dominance of the Left were initially easily put on the defensive, and even the Socialist party and the Partido Popular Democratico (PPD) had trouble mobilizing their opposition to the demands of those further to the left, partly owing to the ambivalent position of the MFA, which was the fount of political legitimacy during the period of interregnum and was adroitly manipulated as a symbol by those to the left of the Partido Socialista (PS) and PPD. The attempt to resist these pressures, for example, the demand for trade union unity under far-left leadership (*unidad e unicidad sindical*), was used by the far left as a pretext for mass rallies and demonstrations that have on occasion intimidated their opponents and forced them to back down. The MDP-CED has been especially prominent in these operations.

A new variable we still know little about in the Portuguese case, which has only recently made its appearance on the Spanish scene, was the left-oriented group of junior army officers, supported by noncommissioned officers, with its penchant for participatory politics and a program for raising the political consciousness of the armed forces. It is obviously impossible to know the strength of this faction, its true ideological commitments, or the ties between it and the political parties. The discredit of the preceding conservative regime, the ongoing *saneamento* of the officer corps, and the popular mobilization of the base, at least in a city like Lisbon, particularly after the resignation of Spinola, make a counter-coup unlikely and probably doom it to failure. For most of 1975 it was not clear to anyone to what extent this politicized sector of the army would relinquish power to an elected government not to its liking, or would call on the support of some parties, particularly on the left, to retain a share of power. The manifesto of the armed forces and the institutional arrangements created after April 25 had given to the MFA a constitutionally privileged status, and all parties found themselves obliged constantly to restate their allegiance to the program of the MFA. This placed the MFA at the center of political change in Portugal.

What the outcome of a showdown between different tendencies in the MFA would be, no one could say. We know much too little about the linkages between the armed forces and the new political parties, hence cannot predict how much some parties would support factions in the MFA against a government that tried to limit its power; nor could we guess at the ambitions of some young MFA leaders to establish a revolutionary regime of a new type rather than "formal bourgeois democracy." There was obviously a lot of talk of Third World models such as the Peruvian. Admittedly Portugal is objectively not in the same situation, located as it is in Europe. Even so, some similarities are striking, particularly the oligarchic character of the financial-industrial establishment in both countries and its lack of legitimacy, the sudden discovery of the poverty of the masses by the officers, their lack of real knowledge of the complexities of a modern economy, and, perhaps most decisive, the possibility of cooperation between the army and some parties in promoting an authoritarian leftist solution.

The possibility just sketched of a leftist authoritarian regime seemed to become reality after March 11, 1975. Then came the elections of April, and these can be seen in retrospect as a turning of the tide. Leftist forces found themselves increasingly challenged by the democratic parties, which just hammered away at the theme that "the popular will has to be respected." Frustrated by this mobilization of a liberal-conservative opposition, confronted with growing resistance within the armed forces (thus the "Manifesto of the Nine," in which Melo Antunes questioned the aims and actions of Premier Vasco Gonçalves), the leftists finally resorted to a putsch against his successor Pinheiro de Azevedo on November 21, 1975. They failed, compromising the Communists in the process. The big loser, however, was General Otelo Saraiva de Carvalho, the would-be European Castro, who was subsequently demoted, then arrested for his part in the plot.

It is easy now to look back and say that the apparent victory of the authoritarian left was bound to fail. History is not that logical or reasonable, and in the political vacuum that followed the fall of Caetano, anything might have happened. For a while, the Communist leader Cunhal was making no secret of his satisfaction: the country was in the bag. And even in late 1975, a successful putsch would have changed everything. It probably would not have meant a complete leftist takeover. But it might well have generated a civil war between North and South and a revolutionary commune in Lisbon.

The Election and After

The election scheduled for April 1975 was a most uncertain business. In the absence of an established tradition of party politics, it was not at all clear how the people would vote, especially in the confusion, paralegal maneuvering and sporadic violence that had marked and marred the period since the revolution of a year before. Those left-wing elements of the Armed Forces Movement that held power at the time were reluctant to risk an unfavorable judgment that might revive right-wing opposition (though the more conservative parties had been banned back in September 1974), block the advance to socialism, and place the revolution as they saw it in jeopardy. Some of them would have liked to call off the vote altogether; but the commitments made in the original manifesto of the MFA, the strength of social-democratic and liberal elements at home, the illegitimacy of authoritarian rule after years of dictatorship, and the risk of serious censure and even reprisals by the nations of Western Europe and the United States made so blatant an antidemocratic measure impractical. Instead, the electoral spectrum was cropped at both ends: the Progressives, Liberals, and

Christian Democrats (Partido Democrata Cristão: PDC) were barred on the ground of contamination by the old regime; and this exclusion was balanced by the barring of *groupuscules* on the extreme left.

A condition for holding the elections was that the parties should join with the MFA in a constitutional agreement by which they committed themselves to realize the principles of the MFA and "to realize in freedom but without sterile and divisive partisan conflicts a common program." That agreement would be valid for a transition period to be fixed in the new constitution at from three to five years. The constitution itself would be worked out by the constituent assembly in collaboration with the parties signing the agreement and a committee of the MFA, and under its provisions the Council of the Revolution, the Assembly of the MFA, and the provisional government would exercise power. With so much fixed in advance, the sole function of the election was to choose a constituent assembly to draft the constitution, while the forming of the government would be the task of the president of the Republic on the advice of the prime minister and the Council of the Revolution. The ministers of defense, internal administration, and economic planning would have to have the confidence of the MFA. The president of the Republic would be elected by an Electoral College constituted by the Assembly of the MFA and the Legislative Assembly. In addition, during the whole transition period, military power would be independent of civil authority.[16]

This agreement meant that at least constitutionally the election would not determine the composition of the government or make the cabinet responsible to a popularly elected body. Only after approval of the constitution would the 250 deputies of the Legislative Assembly share power with the 240 members of the Assembly of the MFA and jointly elect the president of the Republic. The key institution in the constitutional structure was to be the Council of the Revolution, which would determine the general lines of internal and foreign policy, verify the constitutionality of the laws, and exercise legislative power in military matters and a general control over government and the legislature. The text of the agreement, whose revision is now (January 1976) being negotiated between the parties and the MFA, created on paper a regime that could be considered at best a military-civil diarchy. The later political developments have to be understood in the context of this institutional structure. In the last analysis the shifts in power that have taken place have been the result of changing alignments within the military, even when the pressures of the parties and their supporters on the streets have contributed decisively to those shifts. The strength of the Communists in 1975 derived from their full support for the MFA, whereas the other parties had only reluctantly signed that constitutional agreement.

The election returns,[17] which showed the weakness of the Communists (12.5 per cent of the vote) and their allies, the MDP (4.1 per cent), and the strength of the Socialists (37.9 per cent) and the Popular Democrats (26.4 per cent), led inevitably to a crisis. The attempt by the Communists and/or the leftists to gain increasing control by the seizure of factories, large estates, resorts, vacation homes, and even sometimes the houses built by émigré workers with their savings inevitably provoked widespread hostility. In this context the takeover of the pro-Socialist newspaper *República* and the Catholic radio station *Renascença* became symbolic issues. The result was the withdrawal of the Socialists from the cabinet of the pro-Communist Premier Vasco Gonçalves, followed by the PPD, leaving as the only civilian parties in the government the Partido Communista Portugues (PCP) and the MDP. By early August the signs were that Cunhal was within reach of his objective: the death of "bourgeois democracy." Major Melo Antunes was dismissed from the foreign ministry, and the *gauchiste* General Saraiva de Carvalho returning from Cuba proclaimed that the time seemed to have come to put counterrevolutionaries in the Lisbon bull ring. Meanwhile the Council of the Revolution had voted to establish a governing troika above the cabinet comprising Costa Gomes, Gonçalves, and Saraiva de Carvalho, who also controlled the crack COPCON (Comando Operaçional Continental) military police forces.

At that point, the armed forces were increasingly split over the Communist issue, and more and more MFA officers were quietly rallying around Melo Antunes. A tactical alliance against Gonçalves emerged after an attempt by pro-Communist captains and enlisted men to purge Colonel Jaime Neves, commander of the commando regiment at Amadora. This incensed Carvalho, who now took his distance from Cunhal. A few days later the "Manifesto of the Nine" as it became known, inspired by Melo Antunes, protested against the intent to mold Portugal into a state on the East European model while reaffirming Socialist rather than Social Democratic aspirations. This initiated a series of complex maneuvers that coincided with attacks on Communist headquarters by angry mobs, particularly in the North, made possible by the political dualism of the country and reflected in the electoral results. Let us not forget that in the district of Oporto, which includes Portugal's second largest city, the PCP, MDP, and minor leftist parties had only 9.11 per cent of the vote, and that in Aveiro and Braga, two districts with some industry, they had only little over 7 per cent. The Communists and other radicals dominated the countryside in some southern districts. But the large, heavily populated part of the country north of Lisbon offered a solid basis to the opposition, and its protests forced a more cautious policy.

Now Costa Gomes, who wanted to get rid of Gonçalves as prime minister, thought the time ripe to sidetrack him by offering to name him chief of the general staff of the armed forces. The president apparently calculated that the armed forces would never accept Gonçalves as their chief, and responding to the pressures of the troop commanders, he announced that Gonçalves had declined the nomination. On September 19, the sixth cabinet, under Admiral José Pinheiro de Azevedo, was sworn in with Melo Antunes as foreign minister, one of his associates in Education, three Socialists, two Popular Democrats, and only the ministry of Public Works going to a Communist.

After that, in a new reversal of alliances, came the attempted coup of November 25, when the Communists and the extreme left joined with the left-wing MFA leaders in supporting a coup by a left-wing regiment. The defeat of that attempt led to a partial state of siege, the disbanding of COPCON, the dismissal of Carvalho, and a purge of left wingers. The Communists, while compromised, withdrew in time from that attempt.

The Aftermath of November 25, 1975: From MFA to FAP?

After the public implication of the Communists in the aborted *putsch* of November 25, 1975 the question of the place of the PCP in the system and particularly the government became an open question. The Socialists, as the strongest party, the one that after the *República* affair had carried the struggle against the antidemocratic forces and whose leader Mário Soares had emerged as a national and international figure, had to face this problem. For a complex series of reasons they decided not to push the Communists against the wall. For one thing, they did not want to consolidate the Communists' tactical alliance with the leftist groupuscules or allow them the advantage of being in the opposition before the elections, while the government was compelled to introduce difficult austerity measures. In addition the fear of a turn to the right, even a rightist coup, was on their minds. Ultimately the ouster of the Communists would give the non-Socialist parties greater weight in the making of policies and would lead to a setback in the Socialist advances already achieved with the nationalizations of the spring. There was also the hope that the pressures of Italian and Spanish Communists might change the course of the PCP, or that at the least greater cooperation between Latin European Communist and Socialist parties would isolate and delegitimize the PCP, whose capacity for disruption was still considerable.

The question might be asked: why did the PCP opt for staying in the government under such conditions? One answer is that Moscow is interested in proving that a Communist party can be a government party in a West European country.

It remains to be seen if the PCP can stay in the government after the revelations of its implication in the November 25 coup, especially if it loses ground in the election of April 1976. As of now, the PSP, while counting on electoral success, is nevertheless ready to retain the tripartite coalition. In the meantime coalition politics have already caused a split in the PPD. Will the PPD continue to support the tripartite solution, and how would the PSP react to a refusal? Much depends on the relative gains and losses of parties in the forthcoming election and their effects on shifts of the balance of power in the armed forces (rather than the MFA, which has disintegrated), on the economic situation, and on developments in Italy and Spain. A coalition including the Communists is not unlikely, but what remains to be seen is how capable of governing and how stable it will be. The present program, which calls for a pause in socialization, a renewal of foreign economic support and investments, the restoration of confidence among Portuguese entrepreneurs, and a reimposition of legal constraints on agrarian reform, will not be easy for such a government to carry out. In this context the resolution of the debate among European Socialist parties on cooperation with the Communists acquires decisive importance.

The aftermath of the last coup was the disintegration of the MFA as a political force and the enactment of the constitutional law of December 11, 1975 regulating the Forças Armadas Portuguesas (FAP) as "the ultimate support of authority that the political power needs to lead the country on the path of a peaceful and pluralist transition to democracy and socialism." The law further affirms that the FAP and its units and members will be "strictly nonpartisan, not allowing the development within them of sectarian political activities" and that "they shall respect the objectives of the majority of the people as declared in its constitution." After that the political debate turned to such matters as the composition of future coalitions, controversial policies such as agrarian reform, the demands of the parties for the revision of the constitutional agreement with the military, and prospective candidates to the presidency. Policy disagreements within the PPD led to an internal crisis and the secession of twenty of its eighty deputies, among them cabinet members who had to be replaced. The parties started taking positions for the forthcoming election and possible postelectoral coalition-making, and started screening military leaders who might be candidates for the presidency of the Republic.

The diarchy of the civilian parties and the armed forces is not likely to disappear totally but to be revised in favor of the parties. The ultimate form of institutionalization of power will depend on the revision of the agreement with the armed forces, the constitution, and the outcome of legislative and presidential elections. It is no accident that the question whether to hold legislative or presidential elections first is one of the issues in debate. The MFA as a political-military vanguard supported by the Communists and/or the Left seems to have been shunted aside, but the successor FAP are likely to control their own internal affairs better and to exercise strong influence on a president coming from their ranks. The power of the parties will depend on their capacity to work together and create a stable coalition capable of governing effectively outside of Lisbon.

In addition to the outcome of the forthcoming legislative election and the subsequent negotiations for the formation of the government coalition, the political future of Portugal will be strongly affected by the likely adoption of a constitution patterned after that of the French Fifth Republic. In that case, the personality of the man to be elected to the presidency of the Republic will be a far from negligible factor. At present there seems to be little doubt that he will be a military man and that the choice of candidates will be affected by the preferences of different parties as well as those of the politically active and influential officers. In the French Fifth Republic the dominance of the UDR in parliament and the defeat of Mitterand have until now prevented serious conflicts between the president on the one hand and the Chamber and prime minister on the other. In Portugal, however, the different party system, reinforced as it is by proportional representation, and the probability of a military president would make such constitutional conflicts more likely. They would prove very sticky.

The clear geographic and socio-economic dualism of Portugal combined with a new and heady taste of freedom to make a leftist authoritarian regime ultimately unviable. Even so, that phase of the Portuguese revolution fundamentally changed the distribution of economic power by transferring 65 per cent of the industrial and service sector to public ownership and permitting agrarian seizures that go far beyond the legal enactments and that are unlikely to be reversed. The new public sector of the economy employs close to 20 per cent of the labor force, and the shift in the balance of power within the enterprise, combined with the emigration of 30,000 entrepreneurial and managerial personnel, will make it difficult to relaunch economic development on the basis of private investment whether foreign or national, however much the government may wish to encourage such a policy. The MFA radicals could not become a vanguard party of political and social revolution, but in the most advanced industrial sectors and parts of the agrarian south they accomplished revolutionary changes. It is a matter of debate how much these changes will cost in economic performance, in the short and in the long run. The surprising thing is that the country in 1975 could live through a basically revolutionary situation with so few casualties.

From Empire to European State

In order to understand the complex and sometimes Byzantine history of the Portuguese revolution through six governments and at least two failed coups, it has to be seen not only in terms of internal Portuguese political, economic, and social developments, but in the light of the decolonization of Portuguese possessions in Africa. The conflict between Spinola and the MFA was largely centered on his impractical conception of the future of the empire. We still do not know the extent to which the conflicts of late 1975 centered around the future of Angola. There can be little doubt that the economic interests and military strategy of foreign powers in Africa were decisive for both internal Portuguese politics and the international responses thereto. When, how, on what terms, and to whose benefit to decolonize were central questions in the political dabate.

Now that, with the exception of Macao, all parts of the empire have become independent and Portuguese influence in the new states eliminated, the saliency of the international implications of internal political development in Portugal has been reduced. To be sure, the strategic location of Portugal on the shores of the Atlantic and its control of the Azores are still very important to the Western Alliance. But the end of decolonization has for the first time in modern history made Portugal a small European nation—a far cry from the myth that Salazar, his advisors and successors, and even Spinola wanted to sustain at a cost that exceeded the capacity of the country.

Now the problem for the Portuguese is to find their place in the European political and economic system and for the Europeans to integrate Portugal into it. Paradoxically, the complex coalition politics in Portugal, the key role that "social power" has given to the Communist party, and the emergence of a largely socialist economy are now a source of debate and even political realignments in other European countries. Developments in Portugal are ultimately more important to the United States in terms of their consequences for the political future of Europe than of the Atlantic, including the southern Atlantic. Significantly, other European states and their parties have in the last year played an increasingly important role in Portuguese politics, and a leader like Soares has seen his future in Portugal in terms of future European developments. Until recently it seemed as if Portuguese politics would have a decisive impact on developments in Spain, but today it does not seem farfetched to think that the political evolution in Spain could affect indirectly developments in Portugal. The future there will depend largely on that of other Mediterranean countries, the responses of the stable democracies of Europe to those changes, and last but not least on the position of the Communist leadership in Moscow toward the future role of Communist parties in Western Europe.

In this context the actions of the United States will have to be coordinated with those of its European allies, and positions taken in purely Atlantic and strategic terms can only contribute to the European crisis and to tensions within the Alliance. Fortunately a mixture of neglect, incapacity to act, some bungling, and internal developments in Portugal prevented American intervention at a point at which it would have been motivated solely by extra-European considerations. In the meantime the United States economic presence in Portugal is not sufficiently important to justify a procapitalist and antisocialist policy, nor is it likely that Portuguese socialism as it has emerged can in any way serve as a pole of attraction for those searching for new socioeconomic formulas. Post-imperial socialist Portugal is unlikely to break its economic ties with Western Europe, and there is little reason to expect the Soviet Union to encourage any such development.

Spain

Spain after Franco: Evolution, Breakdown, or Reaction?

Beginning in the 1960s, and particularly with the passing of the press law of Fraga in 1966, the Franco regime underwent a slow process of change whose purpose was to consolidate politically the favorable situation created by economic development and a less hostile international context. Those changes which had their ups and downs, produced a limited and controlled liberalization that benefited various forms of semilegal and alegal opposition.[18] In that phase there was no plan for any effective democratization even within the structures of the regime. A referendum approved a revised version of the constitution that represented an effort to institutionalize the regime and to assure its continuity after the death or retirement of Franco. The direct election of approximately one fifth of the members of the legislature, plans for some form of internal democratization of the single party, the initial discussion of a law of political associations that would provide for an institutionalization of pluralism within the regime, some consideration of a further democratization of the official sindicatos—these were among the few initiatives that provided a dim hope for political evolution.

The vague expectations thus created were soon to be frustrated. However, those changes ultimately contributed to a modest politicization, at least of the elites. The proclamation of Juan Carlos as future king within that constitutional framework appeared as a first step in the institution of a Franco-created monarchy. The separation between the office of head of state, held by Franco, and the prime ministership, placed in the loyal hands of Luis Carrero Blanco, was intended to ensure the continuity of the authoritarian regime. Underneath, however, opposition was growing in the intellectual world and the universities, in the factories with the comisiones obreras (workers' commissions), in the regions of peripheral nationalism, and in the Church.

The actions of the terrorist Basque left-nationalist group, the ETA (Euzkadi Ta Azkatasuna), in December 1970 and the subsequent Burgos trial initiated a change in the political climate. Faced with renewed international pressure, a noisy, chauvinistic, and violent extreme Right made its appearance on the political scene. Three years later, on December 20, 1973, Carrero Blanco would be assassinated and with him would die the hopes for continuity of the regime. Surprisingly his successor Carlos Arias Navarro, on February 12, 1974, would articulate a new spirit rather than a new program, thereby creating hopes for political evolution. The term *"apertura"*—opening—entered the political language.

It is doubtful that Premier Arias and the members of his cabinet had any clear idea of what they meant, but the spirit of February 12 served to accelerate the politicization of the country and to develop an awareness that change would be inevitable after Franco. Tension developed between members of the government and Franco, and even more the camarilla surrounding him, and the process of *apertura* was arrested, but even the dismissal of three members of the government did not produce a return to the past. Franco's illness in the summer of 1974 and the temporary transfer of powers to Juan Carlos roused expectations of imminent change and led the Communists to take the initiative of creating the Junta Democrática. This attempted to present itself as a united opposition but failed to rally parties and leaders rejecting the Communist hegemony. Those opposed to the Junta including the old Spanish Socialist party, the PSOE, the Social Democrats, and some of the Christian Democrats, who constituted in their turn the Plataforma de Convergencia Democrática. After much debate the Cortes passed a law legalizing political associations to serve as a channel for political competition within the framework of the regime. Even Arias had to admit that the law did not satisfy his hopes, and even the most eminent political figures of the regime proved unwilling to create political groups within that framework. The *asociacionismo* that had been presented as an alternative to political parties was stillborn and hence was never able to serve as a roundabout device for integrating these increasingly tolerated and visible parties into the system. Yet in spite of the lack of real progress and the continuing presence of Franco in El Pardo, a cautious optimism about political developments prevailed in the spring of 1975.

Then came a hot summer. The rapid succession of terrorist acts and encounters between the police and the ETA, with casualties on both sides; the arrest, summary trial and executions in September; the international reaction to them; and the reaffirmation of support for Franco that followed—all this transformed the political atmosphere. A few weeks later the illness of Franco created a real shock, but his prolonged struggle for life allowed Spaniards to adjust to his inevitable death and pay a solemn, somber, and emotional farewell to over thirty-five years of his rule.

The Reign of Juan Carlos: Apertura, Transition, or Rupture?

The proclamation of King Juan Carlos I after the funeral furnished a relief from the tensions of the preceding weeks and, considering his statements, provided an unreal feeling of change and hope. The statement of Cardinal Tarancón in a televised ceremony articulated that public sentiment in the pastoral language of the Church, and it was reinforced by the presence of foreign leaders who only a short time before had withdrawn their ambassadors from Madrid.

The new word might be *transición* rather than *apertura*. However, those putting their hopes in the new thirty-seven-year-old king forgot the constitution that Franco had carefully devised to bind him to the power structures of the regime.[19] The king was not to inherit the powers of Franco, but to be a constitutional monarch within the framework created by Caudillo and to be dependent on the men he had placed in key positions. The Consejo del Reino (Council of the Kingdom) would have a decisive voice in key decisions, particularly in nominating to such posts as president of the Cortes and prime minister. In that Council, composed of men committed to the continuity of the regime and undistinguished placemen, José Antonio Girón, an old Falangist with a strong personality, had unusual weight. The selection of Torcuato Fernández Miranda for the presidency of the Cortes was like a cold shower on the hopes aroused a few days earlier, and the names one could expect for the prime ministership would not have been better. At that point premier Arias Navarro, who was ready to resign, agreed to head a new cabinet including as minister of interior Manuel Fraga Iribarne and José María de Areilza in Foreign Affairs. These were powerful political leaders. Yet the very weight of the cabinet made it obvious that the Consejo del Reino, the Cortes, and the constitutional provision from which they derive their power had become serious obstacles to any effective transition to democracy. How to circumvent those institutions without a break with the legality of the regime that is the key to a united and unquestioning obedience of the armed forces is one of the many problems the new government faces.

Political life in Spain since the formation of the new government has an air of unreality. A reader of the Spanish press would think that Spain was a country with political parties, trade unions, and democratic rights.[20] He reads statements to the press and in public meetings by leaders of political parties, including different Socialist parties; he learns of parties being formed, of executives meeting, officials being elected and making programmatic statements, and so on. He will not understand very well, however, why the names of these parties are preceded by the word "illegal." He also reads that the leaders of some of these illegal parties are visiting or having lunch with the minister of interior, Manuel Fraga; that they are going abroad to attend the Elsinore conference of Socialist parties and other international conferences; and that delegations of fraternal parties abroad are coming to meetings in Spain. On the same pages he sees accounts of large-scale strikes tolerated and repressed, of demonstrations for amnesty, of the release from prison of dissidents such as Marcelino Camacho, the head of the Comisiones obreras and member of the Junta Democrática, but also of the arrest of other leaders. A cartoon can show the prime minister tied by a chain to a ferocious lion guarding the building of the Cortes. A headline can reproduce a statement of the prime minister to *Newsweek* announcing that in less than two years there will be in Spain four or five political parties, but that the Communist party will be excluded as an instrument of subversion;[21] but the reader will discover a few days later that the minister did not speak of parties, but of political groups. The most distinguished survivor of the pre-civil war leadership of the Spanish Socialist party returns to Madrid to be received by sympathizers, is politely escorted to his private car by police, and is allowed the next day to state publicly his reservations about cooperation with the Communists.

The present situation, as reflected in the Spanish press, is in many ways unique and full of contradictions. The authoritarian regime created by Franco, which despite the crises of its last five years remained basically unchanged, seems to be in the process of liquidation. On the other hand, all its institutions are still in place, basically unchanged. The elite in power consists of men who in one or another capacity occupied key positions under him. The official speeches still contain praises to his statesmanship and declarations of loyalty to his legacy. It would seem as if the goal were evolution within the regime rather than a change of regime.

At the same time we can read statements by members of the cabinet that sound as if the program of the government were to institutionalize basic changes that Franco would never have tolerated and that inevitably represent a rejection of his heritage. Obviously those statements are more often made abroad and to foreign journalists than at home and in public.[b] Even so, there is little doubt that the goal is the institution of a new regime. Fraga in the Cortes said that he conceived his task like that of Cánovas and not like that of Caetano.[c] Cánovas was the great statesman who, after the fall of the republic of 1870, shaped the 1876 constitution of the restored liberal monarchy, whereas Caetano was the man who tried unsuccessfully to continue a liberalized version of the Salazar regime. However, when we look at the specific proposal made by Arias Navarro in his programmatic speech in the Cortes on January 28, 1976, there is little indication there how the danger of Caetanismo is to be avoided.[22]

The new situation is fraught with ambiguities that are well reflected in this almost untranslatable statement, which avoids the word "parties" but expresses at the same time Arias' dissatisfaction with the association formula. That particular ambiguity is presumably to be resolved in the course of a year and a half, the more so as it is doubtful whether it could be sustained within the context of political mobilization created by the death of Franco and the statements and actions of the first government of the new king.

There seems to be no commitment of the present government to the continuity of the authoritarian regime created by Franco. But its commitment to a Western type of democracy is far from clear, as the talk about a Spanish democracy in the speech of Arias reflects. To an outsider the alternatives would

[b]Our analysis is based on the reading of the statements of the leaders of the government in the Cortes and to the press. There are obvious differences in emphasis and tone between the more official and the more informal statements, between those made in and those made outside of Spain, and among those of Arias, Fraga, and the minister of foreign affairs José María de Areilza in connection with his visits to Paris and Bonn.

[c]Antonio Cánovas del Castillo (1828-1897) was the leader of the Liberal-Conservative party that engineered the restoration of the monarchy (1874) after the First Republic and shaped the 1876 constitution, which was modeled after the British. The restored liberal monarchy, which lasted until 1923, gave Spain its most stable and liberal regime (with all its limitations) in modern history.

seem simple: either continuity with the past or the introduction of democratic institutions including a free electorate; but unfortunately things are not so simple and therefore the ultimate outcome of the present situation is far from predictable. The present government may want to pursue a slow, prudent evolution to democracy. But wish and deed are two different things, and the more extreme opposition, including the Communists, will be pushing for some kind of rupture—to use their favorite word. The ultimate outcome may well fall somewhere between these two poles.

If the Spanish constitution called for the direct election of legislature and president by universal suffrage rather than an incredibly complex corporative system of representation, the transition to new forms would not be so difficult. If the parties to be allowed to compete for power were limited to a spectrum going from democratic socialists to conservatives and neo-Fascists, the problem might find a solution. There is, however, one reality in the minds of all participants: the presence of a well-organized Communist party and of the peripheral nationalist movements. A further complication is the memory of the civil war and after, the sense of accounts still to be settled, of responsibilities for bloody repression after that war and up to the present, of vested interests of those who have benefited from the regime and held power in it. Political change does not entail merely the incorporation of those who have been excluded from the political system, but the threat of displacement and even persecution of many of those who now hold power. Resistance to change and the search for guarantees against those threats are inevitable.

A Government Program Running Against Constraints and Time: Caetano or Cánovas?

No one can know, not even the leading actors themselves, the specific plan and timetable of the transformation of the regime. Several things are becoming clear, however.

1. As far as possible the present Spanish leaders intend to work within the legal framework, even when not in the spirit, of the Franco Constitution. This clearly implies a complex and slow process in which they will attempt to fill the words of the past with new meanings. It is a process that requires slow displacement of the die-hards, those who are called the "bunker," from the entrenched positions from which they will wage war against change. (The metaphor recalls Hitler's redoubt in Berlin in the final days of the Third Reich.) In this context a number of changes have already been announced: new regulations of the right of association and assembly, the transfer to the ordinary courts of jurisdiction over crimes against the state, reforms of the criminal code. More nebulous is the plan to create a bicameral legislature, with one chamber directly elected and the present Cortes turned into a second chamber. In the

absence of the power to make laws, the decree-law will be the instrument used. Ultimately, a popular referendum in the old style will have to legitimize those changes.

2. At least some of the members of the government seem to be ready to grant more than de facto toleration to some of the existing parties, under an arrangement similar to that of the *Lizenzparteien* of the allied occupation of Germany. Some still hope that this will be possible within the framework of the political associations, thereby avoiding as long as possible the word "party." The aim is to generate within this scheme parties that would not reject the Franco heritage.

It is at this point that the whole attempt might fail. If the liberals in the government were to offer all parties but the Communists and perhaps the regional nationalists a legal opportunity to participate in the political process, this would place the opposition between Scylla and Charybdis. While many of the forces in the opposition have no love for the Communists or the extreme nationalisms on the periphery, given the visible penetration of the Communists in Spanish society and European and world developments in the mid-70s, they would not be likely to find such a formula acceptable. In the best of cases, some parties might accept it as a transitory solution; but even then it would create deep internal controversies and splits within the nonlegal democratic opposition, increasing the already high level of fragmentation.

This strategy could work only if the Communist party more or less explicitly allowed the democratic opposition to play this game with the understanding that this would be a step in the direction of its ultimate legalization and effective participation in the political process. In fact, the Communists might even opt for participation in such a scheme through front organizations that could be legalized in its stead.

In this complex game everyone faces great risks depending on the actions of the other participants, and no one wants to take the first step. There is the risk of cooptation by a rejected regime: that could mean political death. There is the danger of future recriminations and purges against those participating in such a design. At the same time refusal to participate would place the liberals in the government in an impossible position.

3. The hope, then, is to carry out a process of political change while maintaining the ban on the Communist party but allowing its front organizations a certain yet fundamentally uncertain paralegal existence. This policy is fraught with difficulties and dangers, both for the transition regime and the democratic future. It would confer on the PCE the aura and prestige of continuing opposition. Meanwhile the semilegality would allow it to continue building up its front organizations, to articulate effectively a large number of specific grievances, and to gain the support of people who would not be willing to identify with the Party itself. The Communists could go on infiltrating institutions and even other parties, while exploiting the bad conscience of those

who had connived at their exclusion. The almost inevitable repressive measures against extremist *groupuscules* could be used to discredit the transition process. There are, therefore, incentives for the PCE to condone and go along with this strategy of the government and some powerful reasons for the non-Communist democratic opposition to reject it.

An additional external factor cannot be ignored: the skillful self-presentation of the PCE as an open-minded democratic party with a moderate program, a party less subservient to Moscow than any other in Europe including the Italian. The permanence of the PCP in the Portuguese government even after November 25, 1974, the Common Program in France, the *compromesso storico* and the possible entry of the PCI into the government are all part of a complex strategy of Communist legitimation. Meanwhile the desire of the Portuguese Socialists to isolate the PCP internationally and legitimate themselves as a party of the Left, along with the parallel interest of Mitterand, has posed the difficult question of cooperation between Communists and Socialists and revived the old dreams of unity of the Left. As the Elsinore conference showed, this is an issue likely to divide European Socialists, but the successful conference of southern and French Socialists and Communists, originally proposed by Soares, can only strengthen the Spanish Communists. This issue also divides the PSOE and other democratic parties in Spain, ultimately to the advantage of the PCE. In this context the anti-Communist strategy of the government, if there is such a thing, might find a favorable echo in some Western European political circles, but would also be doomed.

It is understandable that those in the regime who want democracy, or at least consider it inevitable, but at the same time want to prevent the mobilization of the "bunker" of a broader opposition to their plans, would feel compelled to maintain the exclusion of the Communists and be disappointed if the non-Communist opposition rejected their offers. The result might very well be a stalemate that ultimately would squash any hope of a transition to a Western-type of democracy within the regime.

4. In view of the difficulties that the three policy positions we have just described create, particularly in the short run, the government is likely to turn to a complex policy of liberalization and semi-democratization that is unlikely to satisfy anyone and likely to erode the conditional support many Spaniards are willing to give it for the time being. That strategy would entail more or less free local elections, perhaps some changes in the government-controlled trade union organization, and moderation in the repression of protest and demands for political change. Such a policy is tempting, since it avoids a public break with the past and postpones the most difficult decisions while presumably preparing the country for them. Under the appearance of maintaining existing controls, however, it would increase by leaps and bounds the vacuum surrounding the institutions of the regime. It is in such a vacuum that what the Communists have called the *ruptura democrática*, that is the democratic breakthrough, and with it

the breakdown of the transition regime could suddenly occur, frustrating Fraga's hope of controlling the transition process and giving an inordinate advantage to those with the most effective organization, particularly in the big cities. It is surprising that, after the failure of a similar attempt by the transition governments of the monarchy after the Primo de Rivera dictatorship in 1931, the present rulers should even consider a similar course. Municipal elections would be an excellent arena for activists mobilizing people on specific issues, the more so as the apathetic abstention of some sectors of the electorate tends to give disproportionate political significance to the vote in the largest cities. The same would be true for trade union elections. Increasing pressures for participatory democracy in a wide range of institutions would give to "nonpartisan" groups of activists, more or less identified with the PCE but not running on that identification, important positions for the moment of rupture or at least for the future. At the same time the ultimate political choices would only be postponed.

5. The timetable for the transition, as seen even by those supporting it, is undefined and slow. This is not surprising, given the difficulties entailed by the whole project—insofar as there is one. That slowness is welcomed by those who do not want any change and paradoxically may also be favored by those who want much more than a political change. A relatively prolonged period of political ambiguity combined with semifreedom might well facilitate the mobilization of protest in streets, factories, and offices and ultimately a takeover of power in the event of a massive crisis like the *huelga nacional* (general strike) advocated by the PCE. In addition a prolonged period of hyperpoliticization nourished by the mass media, the expectations created, the opportunist responses of those in power and interested in assuring their future, the uncertainties affecting the decision-making of entrepreneurs and investors—all of this could create a climate of frustration, despair, and radicalization all along the political spectrum. Even those most committed to an orderly transition to democracy might despair of the lack of support and, confronted with tensions going beyond their tolerance, turn back to authoritarian methods. As we know from Tocqueville, this is the context in which revolutions are most likely to succeed or at least to erupt. We know that failed revolutions are also the pretext and opportunity for the worst type of counterrevolution.

We have analyzed in some detail what seems to be the project of those who favor, not evolution of the regime, but evolution *out of* the regime. For them, the time for evolution within the structures of the regime is long past. Any effort to assure the continuity of the regime beyond a certain point would only be possible through a repression that would be impossible to legitimate either internally and externally—one that would lead to civil war or at least the breakdown of the evolutionary process of Spanish society within the Western European context. On the other hand the ambiguities in the political design of the present government and the constraints under which it has to act make it hazardous to predict its success. As Fraga phrased it, he wants to be a Cánovas and not a Caetano; but Cánovas came to power with a clear, internationally accepted political model—that of a liberal constitutional monarchy—and he stated it publicly and unambiguously. The speech of Arias Navarro in the Cortes on January 28 was perhaps, despite its intent, not that of a Cánovas but of a Caetano. In view of this one cannot exclude the possibility that the present interim regime may end suddenly like the Portuguese, thereby initiating a political process that *mutatis mutandis* may have many similarities with the one experienced by Portugal since April 25, 1974.

A survey based on one thousand interviews in forty sampling points by Metra Seis around December 18, that is, after the formation of the new cabinet, asked the question: "Concretely, what do you think will be the political line of the new government?"[23] This was followed by another asking, "And in reality, what would you personally wish it to be?" The answers (Table VIII-1) show that there are few people who wish no change and expect no change. There is a respectable minority that expresses a desire for change, but no adaptation to the model of Western democracies, whereas 42 per cent of those expressing an opinion would favor copying the example of democratic Western Europe. If we turn to the expectations of what will happen, 55.8 per cent expect either no change or reforms within the system and only 19 per cent a pluralist democracy.

Table VIII-1
Desires and Expectations about the Policy of the New Government in December 1975

	(1) Personal Wish	(2) Expect the policy of the government to be	(3) Difference between columns (1) and (2)
Not make any change	13.2	13.5	+.3
Exhaust the possibilities of the system, liberalizing it but without changing its essence	5.7	14.0	+8.3
Introduce some reforms, democratizing the system but without identifying it with the Western democracies	13.3	28.3	+15.0
Make the necessary changes to make our system equal to that of the democratic countries of Western Europe	42.2	19.0	−23.2
Other answers	7.5	3.6	−3.9
No answer	18.4	21.8	−3.4
	100.3	100.2	

Source: Metra Seis, as quoted in *La Región* (Orense), January 14, 1976.

At the time of the survey, therefore, over one fifth of the respondents expected their hopes for democratization to be disappointed.

The same survey, we have seen only after writing our analysis of the situation, confirms that the majority want the government to set itself a time limit for reforms, 62.8 per cent for compared to 17.4 per cent against a limit. In addition, 27.3 per cent say that the time limit should be six months and 34.4 per cent one year. Only 10.1 per cent are willing to consider three or more years, and a surprisingly small number, 8.1 per cent, have no opinion. In that context the slow schedule for reform that the prevailing constraints seem to impose on the government will certainly prove a disappointment.

Let us assume that the first government of the king or one succeeding it would finally make the decision to allow political parties including the PCE and to call for the election of a constituent assembly in a reasonable time, assuring full political freedom for the campaign proceedings. There would still remain the thorny problem of who would govern in the interim and who would supervise the election. Obviously, forces in the opposition would argue that a government ultimately deriving its power from Franco should not stay in power until after the election. On the other hand, those in power would rightly argue that they cannot turn over the control of the state to political leaders whose representativeness has not been tested. To devise a formula to avoid that impasse would require considerable ingenuity. Fortunately, the judiciary enjoys in Spain considerable public respect and might be entrusted with the control of the electoral machinery. As to the government, there is the possibility of a fusion between the most liberal leaders of the regime and men in the opposition in a provisional government of very well defined and limited powers; there is also the more difficult alternative of a government of independent nonpartisan personalities from different sectors of the society.

The transition to democracy ultimately requires a national election in which all Spaniards can choose freely and responsibly among parties without allowing anyone to take power and implement policies that could have irreversible consequences before the will of the electorate is ascertained. Neither partial democratization within the institutions of the Franco constitution nor direct democratization of the institutions carried out "spontaneously" by the base should be allowed to substitute for the popular will in a free national election.

Institutions and Social Forces in the Transition

It might sound paradoxical that until now our discussion has focused on members of the government, the legislature, and the Council of the Kingdom, and the leaders of the opposition groups and the Communist party, that is, on political actors rather than on institutions like the armed forces, the Church, and big business. Certainly our analysis does not seem to fit with the image of

Spanish politics derived from the 30s or with an orthodox Marxist analysis such as we might find in the recent book by Poulantzas (which compares unfavorably with that provided by the PCE leadership).[24]

Undoubtedly, those institutions play a role; indeed, the armed forces may yet play the decisive role. But contrary to the expectations of many, their most immediate concern seems to be to stand aside. Two reasons account for this. The involvement of both the Church and the army in the civil war and its aftermath has left painful memories and a wish to avoid responsibilities in the future. On the other hand, particularly in the Church but probably increasingly in the army, generational change and new currents of thought in the world have created tensions that threaten the unity of these institutions. Obviously, in both there are vocal minorities with strong ideological commitments. We know of the radical left and the prophetic minority in the Church ready to challenge the political and socioeconomic order. We also hear of hard-line officers on the right and of an apparently growing alienated, liberal or leftist group of junior officers. Their existence is one more reason for the legalists, who may well constitute the majority, to opt for noninvolvement and the role of bystander in a peaceful evolutionary process that would guarantee stability to the society.

Most discussions of the army tend to focus attention on individual generals, particularly those who appear to take political positions, and recently on the dissident young officers, while overlooking the institutional character of the armed forces. In this context article 37 of *Ley Orgánica* of the state, which entrusts to the armed forces not only the "unity and independence" of the nation but "the defense of the institutional order," should be kept in mind. It is not clear who can speak for the armed forces, but the law refers to a National Defense Council formed by the prime minister, the defense ministers, the chief of the Alto Estado Mayor and the chiefs of staff of the three services. On the other hand the traditional spokesmen for the armed forces have been the lieutenant generals, who are the highest ranking officers, and the heads of the military regions (largely the same persons); should a crisis develop in which the army felt that it had to intervene "institutionally," these would be the relevant actors.

The question has been raised whether the Spanish armed forces might not follow the example of the Portuguese. There are certainly changes in the social composition and status of the officer corps that might favor radicalization,[25] but there are a number of crucial differences between Spain and Portugal. The armed forces have not been involved in a colonial war, have not suffered defeat, and until now have not been involved in the maintenance of public order within Spain. In addition, the history of the Portuguese authoritarian regime was punctuated by at least eight unsuccessful military conspiracies or coup attempts before 1974, which have no parallel in Franco's Spain. In the last few years the army leadership has indirectly undermined efforts of the extreme right to mobilize for its own purposes the organization of veterans of the civil war.

Cryptic but highly significant statements by the three defense ministers on January 6, 1975, the military's New Year's day, gave expression to this unwillingness to be drawn into political alignments.

These statements can be read as directed against the extreme right for trying to manipulate military symbols; but they are also directed against the first signs of politicization on the left, which were taking the form of an underground Democratic Military Union, protests by junior officers on specific issues, and signs of sympathy with social and economic complaints of the working class.[d] The position of the three defense ministers was that "the nature of the armed forces is beyond the concrete and passing political options." This is what we may call a von Seeckt position: like that of the famous German chief of staff, it means in my view that the armed forces want to preserve their internal unity by eschewing political involvement even in the existing regime; hence that ultimately they are willing to consider the possibility that the society might make other political choices. Those who did not feel this way were invited to resign; as the minister of the army said, "It is not honest to belong to an institution that is beyond those options if one has a conviction that one can serve Spain better by promoting or encouraging a certain political attitude."[26] It is obviously not clear how far the armed forces would go in respecting the different political institutional options of Spaniards. One thing is clear, however: these statements have placed the armed forces in a waiting posture that will ultimately allow them to decide what is best for the country, perhaps independently of Franco's political legatees.

Alongside the armed forces, the Church: the growing tensions over the last years between many members of the clergy and the political authorities and the disengagement even of the hierarchy from the regime is undeniable.[27] The issue almost came to a head when Prime Minister Arias made ready to expel from the country the Bishop of Bilbao, who had made a statement that could be interpreted as sympathy with Basque nationalism. The Church does not, however, appear as a politically effective force, owing to the deep internal cleavages caused by extremists on both sides of the spectrum and the desire of many of the clergy, the laity, and the hierarchy to withdraw to a pastoral concern that would be politically neutral and thus serve to hold the institution together. As a result, an attempt to ensure the continuity of the Franco regime cannot count on clear and public support by the hierarchy with the exception of isolated members.

At the time of the proclamation of the new king, Vicente E. Cardinal Tarancón, in a sermon that reached the whole country, gave his moral support to

---

[d]There is no way to know the strength of the Union Militar Democrática (UMD), but there have been claims of 300 to 500 members and 800 to 1,000 sympathizers in an officer corps of 20,000. Even the most leftist officers, however, do not talk about noncoms and enlisted men as a political factor. In any consideration of the political role of the armed forces, it should not be forgotten that the Guardia Civil is a highly trained, well-equipped, and disciplined force of 60,000 men, with a tradition of legalism.

change, using statements of the episcopal conferences. He has succeeded in bringing practically all the Spanish bishops over to his position and seems to have the full support of the Vatican. Whatever tensions exist among the clergy and the Catholic laymen, the hierarchy can speak with a united voice and the Cardinal has gained considerable stature. Even so, it is still doubtful whether the Church can put its weight behind a united Demo-Christian party. Except for a new anticlericalism of the Right, at least in the initial stages of the transition church-and-state issues and popular anticlericalism are unlikely to play the disruptive role they did in 1931.

Rapid industrialization, the creation of large-scale manufacturing establishments, and the concentration of industry in a few metropolitan areas have fostered the emergence of a well-organized, illegal, but tacitly recognized labor movement: the comisiones obreras. This movement, much infiltrated by the PCE, yet linked with Catholic action among workers, is without doubt the best organized and most visible political force in Spain. They are able to sustain a strike rate twice that of Belgium and almost half that of Britain (according to official statistics for 1972), despite the fact that strikes are at best semilegal, if not illegal.[28] Employers prefer to bargain collectively with this organization rather than the official trade unions, and even government officials have been known to sit down and negotiate with these "illegal" leaders. On the other hand, the government has been known to act at times against these same leaders, so that their status is at best precarious.

As a result of the amnesty recently granted by the king, Marcelino Camacho, the leader of Comisiones, was released from prison and was even allowed to travel to Paris. At this moment he is undoubtedly one of the key actors on the political scene. The political changes after Franco's death and the efforts of the present government to stop inflation by a wage freeze have led to large-scale strikes not only in industry and banking but in such public services as the Madrid subway and the Post Office. Up to now the government has managed to keep key services going by conscripting workers into the armed forces; but the strikes continue, and they show the strength and discipline of organized labor.

Terror and Counterterror: An Unpredictable Variable

In the world of the 70s, unfortunately, one factor cannot be ignored: terrorism and political violence. In Spain, the actions of the ETA and the FRAP (Frente Revolucionario Antifascista Patriótico) have already had a considerable impact on the political situation. The ETA, a far-left Basque nationalist group, by generally selecting its targets carefully and operating in a region where it has tacit support, has not aroused the same disapproval as the indiscriminate actions of the FRAP. Both, however, have allowed the Franco regime to mobilize support that otherwise would have been politically passive—support based on the desire for peace and order. Even more serious has been the mobilization of the extreme right, of the Guerrilleros de Cristo Rey and other neo-Fascist groups, with the connivance of the police.[29] Right-wing extremism was getting out of the government's control in 1975, and the internal security forces, feeling themselves isolated and frustrated, were becoming increasingly radicalized and unmanageable. Terrorism and counterterrorism unfortunately can become an extremely disruptive factor in the political process. No one probably can control the extremism of the Left and regional nationalists, but it will be the task of the minister of the interior of any government, whatever its political program, not to allow police connivance at rightist extremism. In this context a disciplined police, no tolerance for torture, repression of rightist paramilitary activities, and extreme care for the legality of prosecutions of terrorists become essential to the success of the plans of the more liberal leaders in the present government. I would go as far as to say that such a policy would be advisable even for the continuity of the Franco regime. Terror and, even more, counter-terror can only polarize the society and create unsolvable problems for any government. Unfortunately the emotional reactions to terror make such a policy difficult if not impossible, and terrorists know that very well. The transition government should also know it and must find a way to control the forces of internal security by punishing their illegal acts, give them moral support, prosecute terrorists in a way that will not find international disapproval, and retain the monopoly of violence in the society. No government aware of its responsibility can afford to do otherwise. Perhaps Fraga as minister of the interior is the person best qualified to pursue such a policy. Failure to do so might make him a Caetano rather than a Cánovas as he wishes.

Revolution in Spain?

The events in Portugal after April 1974, the threat of a Communist-controlled politico-social development there, and the memories of the civil war lead to the question of the potential for a Communist takeover in Spain. The question is obviously complex, and this is not the place to analyze it in depth. Let us note, however, a few relevant factors.

First of all, Spanish social structure has changed in a direction that diminishes the potential for spontaneous revolutionary protest of the anarcho-syndicalist type that used to flare up occasionally in the countryside and some of the minor industrial centers. The initiative for a mobilization of the working class to take power would have to come from a revolutionary vanguard, which in Spain could only be the Communist party, and it is unlikely that the armed forces could ever play the role they have in Portugal. The PCE has been committed in the last few years to a nonrevolutionary tactic closer to the *via italiana* than either that of the PCP or even the PCF.[30] Its programmatic line has paid off by transforming a small and sectarian party in the 30s, with little appeal beyond the working class and no intellectual standing within the Communist movement, into one that can claim to be conscious of its own potential importance within world Communism. Its analysis of economic and social changes in Spain, of the need to neutralize the fears of institutions like the armed forces and the Church, and its sensitivity to the danger of mobilizing the opposition certainly have contributed to shaping that tactical position, which by now is likely more than tactical. The influence of the Italian model and support cannot be ignored, any more than the resentment by its present leadership of Moscow's efforts to displace it for its condemnation of the Czech invasion. While ideological formulations cannot always serve to predict the actions of a party, they cannot be dismissed as inconsequential.[31] If the Portuguese comrades had succeeded rather than failed, their model might have seemed more attractive; but since the PCE criticized them openly and has since been proved right, these positions are likely to be reinforced.

On the other hand, it would be foolish to ignore the possibility that mismanagement of the transition to democracy might create opportunities and temptations for a Communist drive to political hegemony. One such opportunity would be a collapse of the transition regime as a result of what the Communists call the *ruptura democrática*, the democratic breakthrough, thanks to a mobilization under Communist leadership for the *huelga nacional*, the general strike.[32] The prospects for such an outcome without a violent confrontation with the armed forces are still very dim, and the risks of a Chilean scenario too great. Unlike Portugal, Spain is neither disorganized by a military defeat nor driven by a deep economic crisis. The aim of the PCE, therefore, will be go gain the greatest possible share of power within a democratic framework. Given the socio-economic structure, its electoral prospects are more favorable than those of the Portuguese party; but they are not likely to match the share won by the PCI in the Italian balloting of 1974—the fruit of years of effective organizational efforts.

In Spain, however, in contrast to Portugal, the Communist presence is likely to extend to most of the country, since in every region there are major urban and industrialized centers in which the party has activist nuclei and can count on a considerable mass following. As a result, it would be more favorably placed to gain hegemony and power by intimidation of opponents. On the other hand, the memories of the civil war, the much more numerous middle classes, the hostility of some of the older leadership of the Socialist party, and the suspicion aroused by the actions of Cunhal make it likely that any move in this direction would be more quickly and vehemently countered than in Portugal—perhaps even, if we consider the national character, more violently. Furthermore the organizational nuclei for a rightist reaction would be stronger and more threatening in Spain. If we add to that the decisive fact that the penetration of the PCE in the officer corps is likely to be much less extensive than in Portugal, the PCE seems unlikely to be tempted to take an adventurist course. It will choose instead to compete democratically and by legal means with other political forces while making the most of the control and influence that its success in the underground, the devotion of its activists, its legitimation in the struggle against the Franco regime, and its tactical adroitness have given it. Only the total failure of other political forces to mobilize support at the electoral level and to define the proper place for the PCE in a democratic political system could lure it into a risky gamble to assert hegemonic power and influence.

Any such attempt would have infinitely more serious consequences in Spain than in Portugal. The complex industrial and service economy is highly vulnerable to social and economic disruption, and the urban population, having achieved a fairly high standard of living, is in no position or mood to see it fall, the less so as they cannot fall back on family ties with the countryside as in Portugal. In addition, the Spanish economy has not been based on hoarding reserves like the Portuguese, but on active participation in the Western economic system. The political consequences of the disruption of those ties cannot have escaped the attention of the PCE leadership.

Elections in Spain

What if there were elections? That is the question increasingly asked in interviews with political leaders and by public opinion polls.[33] Without freedom for the political parties to operate and woo the electorate, the polls obviously are of limited predictive value, particularly since a large number of respondents until recently were unable or unwilling to express a preference and 30 per cent of those with a preference still mentioned in 1973 the Movimiento and 8 per cent the Falange. Among them we would find the future neo-Fascists, some respondents too cautious to express another choice, and many who will opt eventually for conservative or Christian-democratic parties. For the reasons discussed earlier Christian-democracy in a totally free election might not have even the strength it had in Italy, though probably more than the CDS had in Portugal in 1975. On the assumption that the different social strata in Spain would vote like their Italian equivalents, I estimated in 1967 that 40.5 per cent of the vote in Spain would go to the Christian-Democrats.[34] In the 1973 survey, however, only 28 per cent of those with a preference were ready to vote for Christian-democracy. In that same survey 6 per cent favored a liberal party and 12 per cent social-democracy, while 10 per cent declared themselves Socialists—a choice that would include the Communists, since they were not included in the list.[35]

At present it is impossible to predict the relative strength of the various tendencies within Spanish socialism, ranging from those who declare themselves social democrats and hold a position that is not far from the PPD to the historical PSOE (Partido Socialista Obrero Español), both of them within the Plataforma de Convergencia Democrática, to the PSP (Partido Socialista Popular) led by Enrique Tierno, which participates in the Junta Democrática. Electoral success would in part depend on the merger of different groups and their links with regional socialist parties. They would have to compete with well-organized Communist cadres appealing to the larger electorate with an Italian-style program. Spanish political leaders say that the PCE would have around 10 per cent of the vote, and PCE leaders are reluctant to claim more. Considering, however, the occupational structure of Spain and the role of the PCE in the labor movement, as well as its appeal to intellectuals and professionals, I feel that the figure may be larger, though it would be difficult for the Party to reach in the immediate future the strength of the PCI in Italy today. An additional complication is the enormously complex spectrum of regional parties still unintegrated into a national party system and the relative appeal of regional nationalisms, as compared to that of the national Spanish parties, among natives and immigrants in Catalonia, the Basque Country, Galicia, and even Valencia. Nor is it possible to know the strength of dissidents from the PCE as a result of its moderate stance.

One thing is certain: the Spanish party system is likely to be a highly fractionated, polarized, centrifugal multiparty system.[36] Obviously a plurality rather than proportional-representation system could force the fusion of parties or the formation of coalitions. But it would also create a more polarized situation and make more difficult the representation of minorities in the autonomous regions. It seems very doubtful whether any single party can come out of the first election and even subsequent ones as hegemonic. Nor does it seem likely that a conservative party created by the men now in control of the transition period will be electorally successful. The hope or fear of a UDR seems unwarranted.[e]

In this discussion of the future of democracy in Spain we have more or less ignored the problem created by a monarchy of dubious legitimacy, headed by a

---

[e]Another tempting comparison would be the post-Colonels development in Greece and the consolidation in power of Caramanlis with broad electoral support (54 per cent). Why no Portuguese and no Spanish Caramanlis in sight? Several factors have to be noted. (1) The Greek Junta regime was just that—a military regime that did not have time to coopt Greek society and elites. (2) It had displaced not only the Left—Andreas Papandreou—but also the Right, overthrowing all of democratic party politics, rather than, as in Spain, defeating the Left under circumstances that alienated even the moderate Right and pushed it to accept a military solution. (3) Caramanlis was also an exile and therefore an alternative. Only José María Gil Robles Sr., the leader of the largest party in the 1933 legislature—the Catholic CEDA—seen by the Left as the Spanish Dollfuss, hated by the Falangists and rejected by the extreme Right, exiled by Franco and opponent of the regime, could claim a similar role. For a series of reasons too long and difficult to explain, he does not seem called to play the role of De Gasperi, Adenauer, or Caramanlis, but such a possibility cannot be excluded. In this context the support by Caramanlis, that is, by the Right, of the abolition of the monarchy (voted by close to 70 per cent) deprived the Left of one issue and consolidated his position. But the Greek monarchy had dilapidated much of its legitimacy and had to be restored rather than simply retained, whereas at least initially Juan Carlos I has become a symbol of hope rather than of the past. Let us not forget that in Italy even the defeated Savoyard monarchy could get 46 per cent of the vote.

young monarch who still has not shown his personality. The question of a democratic legitimation of the monarchy is still open, and a definition of the constitutional role of the king will not be easy. It is far from clear whether the persistence of monarchy will be a factor of stability or a source of conflict.[f]

Regional Politics and the Future of Spain

Even if we assume a relatively painless transition period and free elections with outcomes not very different from those of other West European countries, specifically, even if the Communist party does not win so large a vote that the government must operate with Communist participation, the new Spanish democracy will face a complex problem that has no parallel in Italy or France. Spain will inevitably have to become a more decentralized state, and any Spanish government will have to recognize the cultural and linguistic rights of at least three or four peripheral regions. Spaniards find themselves today in the unenviable position of having moved fairly early toward a high level of centralization without having been able to assimilate fully their national minorities. The persistence of these undigested minorities acquired serious political significance in the nineteenth and twentieth centuries when the legitimacy of successive regimes came into question. Most Spaniards think of Spain as a nation-state whose historical identity was shaped by Castile and whose language is Spanish, that is, Castilian. It is, therefore, hard for them to accept the fact that there are other Spaniards who would like to see Spain a multinational entity; and even harder to understand that the more extreme nationalists, particularly in the Basque country, would reject the very existence of a Spanish state.[37]

To be sure, this multinational view of Spain is not shared by all members of these minority national communities. Many have long since been assimilated into the majority culture and are integrated into the Spanish economic and social system. Moreover, the industrial development of Catalonia and the Basque

---

[f]Portugal did not face the potentially divisive question of monarchy vs. republic, nor was there need for any debate about symbols like flag and national anthem, since Salazar did not break with the republic. Whereas the Spanish republic proclaimed in 1931 and its symbols today have mostly sentimental significance for an older generation, the monarchy has no traditional legitimacy except for small minorities. To what extent can a monarchy *installed* by Franco (he deliberately and insistently rejected the idea of *restoration*) become legitimate for those who reject the Franco inheritance by disidentifying itself from it, is an open question. Such a disidentification will be seen by some as betrayal of its source of legitimacy. The added legitimacy derived from tradition, from continuity with as well as change from Franco's Constitution, and reinforced by making democracy possible, may still be insufficient to consolidate a Western-type constitutional monarchy. The obvious recourse of the parties that define themselves (like the PSOE) as republican but are willing to accept a monarchy is a plebiscitarian legitimation of the institution. The referendum, however, would surely entail a polarization, consume political energies, and probably provide a broad left coalition with a vote that might well exceed the support for a leftist political program, while giving it momentum and a dangerous overconfidence.

country have drawn into these areas a large immigration of labor from the rest of Spain. The regional communities in turn are trying, with more or less success, to assimilate this immigrant labor force to their subcultures. The Catalans in particular are sanguine of their ability to achieve this goal, though my sense is that this is not possible without some conflict. Since these peripheral regions are all bilingual, except for small pockets in the countryside that speak only the minority language, the introduction of two official languages in these areas must necessarily give an important advantage to those natives who can speak the majority tongue as well as their own.

At the same time, the economic wealth of two of these areas at least, Catalonia and the Basque country, can only complicate relations with the central government, which will not have in Spain the kind of leverage that other European nations, faced with similar autonomist claims, can exercise over more rural populations (cf. France and Brittany). This weakness of the central government will be the more marked, because opposition political parties in these peripheral autonomist regions will almost inevitably turn to the central government for support against the dominant local power, which may well be opposed to Madrid on ideological as well as cultural grounds. Clearly, even in the best circumstances, the regional problem will consume much of the energy of Spain's political leadership.

There is a good chance, moreover, that circumstances will not be of the best. In recent years, for example, a radical Basque nationalist fringe group on the extreme left has splintered off from the old Basque nationalist party Partido Nacionalista Vasco (PNV). This group has resorted to terrorism, and it is not clear that its members will return to more normal patterns of political action if their maximalist demands are not accepted. To be sure, the support for such extremism is small; but such groups can make the most of even a diffuse sympathy that hampers repression and prosecution. The measures that the government would have to take in the process would certainly divide political opinion at the regional and national levels.

What is more, these Spanish problems will almost surely spill across the border. The Basque country is adjacent to Basque-speaking areas in France, and the emerging French Basque nationalism can count on Spanish support, just as Spanish Basques have long drawn on French support. The same would be true for an expansive and self-confident Catalan nationalism, with its own counterpart on the other side of the Pyrenees. The effect of such collaboration across the border would be to create hazardous tensions between Madrid and Paris; and it is the risk of such a development that today, in contrast to earlier periods, prevents the French from encouraging these peripheral nationalisms in Spain. This kind of activity is catching, and success in one region is bound to encourage aspirations in others. The slogan of the Europe of nationalities rather than states has an obvious attraction for these groups; but such a development would certainly complicate foreign and military policy and create new demands for industrial or agricultural protection.

These movements and trends are not of major importance to United States policy, but American leaders should be aware of their existence and avoid being carried away by sympathy with so-called oppressed people and emerging nations. The kind of statement that would legitimize maximalist aspirations can only complicate relations in a large number of areas. The emergence of regional governments sensitive to their rights and standing will require on the part of the United States a new kind of diplomatic protocol. Fleet visits to Spanish harbors, for example will never be so simple again.

Implications for the United States

Spain and Portugal are going to pose in the late 70s and early 80s a serious problem for the United States and Western Europe. Neither country has received much attention in the framework of the Atlantic alliance and European Community. This neglect is now coming home to roost. It means that the United States, and even more Europe, will have little leverage on the internal political development of these countries, if only because the citizens of these countries, and their leaders as well, have come to be relatively unconcerned with the implications of their internal development for the international system.

Let us recall briefly the historical background of the present situation. Spain, owing to its loss of empire in the early nineteenth century, its persistent internal instability and economic backwardness, has not been a significant participant in the international scene for many years. Its isolation at the time of the Spanish-American War (1898) and its lack of colonial ambitions in more peaceful times have inculcated on Spanish politics a refusal of foreign entanglements. It was this, as well as the division of opinion within the country, that saved Spain from participation in World War I, reducing thereby pressures for democratization, but also the risk of Fascism. It allowed Spain to become a permanent member of the League of Nations and led to only minor shifts in its international commitments up to the civil war. The assistance of the Axis powers in the 30s led many Spaniards to hope for a more active foreign policy and the Western powers to fear such a development. But again, both internal and international factors made it possible for Spain to stay out of World War II, leaning at first toward the Axis, but then disengaging itself to become an unloved but much-courted neutral. It was in this context that Spain joined with Portugal in the so-called Iberian Pact, which is still valid and will probably be renewed in spite of Portugal's change of regime.

It was the hope of those defeated in the civil war and the fear of government supporters that the end of World War II would lead to pressure for internal political change in Spain. These hopes and fears were disappointed. The war and its aftermath nevertheless left an important imprint. In contrast to those European nations occupied by Germany, Spain has no memory of war, of foreign troops, or of liberation by the Allies. One cannot, therefore, expect the average Spaniard to have any sense of the importance of military preparedness, and it will be difficult to create support for military expenditures proportional to those of other European countries and to Spain's present level of economic development.[38] In short, it will not be easy to persuade the Spanish to join in the defense of Europe.

This means that in the future, those Spanish military who recognize these needs will be politically isolated. This is a country in which the Right, as well as the Left, has no commitment to the Western alliance. The presence of American bases in Spain should not deceive in this regard. The agreements establishing these bases were negotiated at the highest level, without popular support.[39]

The result is a special relationship that the United States finds most convenient, so that it is not clear whether the United States would really like to see Spain integrated into the larger Atlantic or European political system. The Spanish government, in turn, finding itself rebuffed or patronized by its European neighbors, in spite of noises to the contrary, has sustained and on occasion tried to reinforce that special relationship.

All of this is very pragmatic, and this explains the readiness of the Spanish government to enter into ties that the United States has not always been happy about—thus with Castro's Cuba, and in recent years, its own version of an *Ostpolitik* and recognition of China. These initiatives, it should be noted, have enjoyed a certain degree of popularity. At the same time, the international ostracism of the Franco regime led the Spaniards to seek compensation in special ties to the Arabs and sometimes Latin America.[40]

All of this has been very convenient; but it does not go very deep. It has enabled Americans and Europeans to deal with Spain without really integrating it into the larger alliance, but it has also sustained the internal political vacuum in Spain and contributed to the weakness of the democratic opposition—which weakness can only redound to the advantage of the Communists in an eventual crisis.

The above analysis implies certain probabilities for the future. One can expect, for example, that Spain's first democratic government will put high on its agenda radical renegotiation of the special relationship with the United States, particularly the agreement on military bases. The renegotiation will take place in a climate of anti-Americansim, and needless to say, those on the left will be opposed to the extension of the present arrangements. In view of Spain's long history of neutralism and, to some extent, isolationism, one must expect little enthusiasm for any involvement in grand international designs. At the same time, the memory of years of poverty and underdevelopment, a vague affinity with Latin America and hence resentment of its dependence on the United States, and confused ideas about relations with the Arabs are liable to lead certain elites to identify with the Third World in ways that do not correspond with the economic and social realities and interests of a middle-sized industrial nation. The task for both American and European policymakers will be to turn these trends, for all their negative implications and rhetorical character, into a source of strength and legitimacy. In the absence of positive foreign initiatives to integrate Spain into the Western community of nations, there will be a strong temptation for Spanish leaders to undertake independent ventures of a potentially dangerous character that would only increase the gap between the Spanish and other Western European political systems.

Though Spain's military and political ties are with the United States, her economic links are with the countries of the Common Market.[41] In 1970, 57 per cent of Spanish exports went to Europe and 52 per cent of its imports came from there, whereas the American share in its foreign trade in 1973 was only 15 per cent. Some 82 per cent of Spain's tourists came from Europe in 1971; only 4 per cent from the United States. Over the decade of the 1960s, 34 per cent of foreign investment came from the United States; the Common Market countries provided 25 per cent; and Switzerland, 21 per cent; and the American share has tended to decrease over the years. If we add to these data the importance of Europe for Spain as an outlet for surplus labor and the contribution of immigrant worker remittances to Spanish economic development, the importance of the tie to Europe becomes manifestly primary.

Given these differences between the two links—military with the United States, economic with Europe—it is our assumption that the new leadership of a democratic Spain will pursue, at least initially, a policy of coolness toward the United States. Some of this was already apparent in the last years of the Franco regime; thus Spain voted less often with the United States in the United Nations than its other European allies. In other words, the Spanish people are being prepared, even in today's relatively favorable circumstances, for an anti-American stance that can only become more marked in the tensions of a transitional regime. In that context, any mistakes in Portugal will lead to serious difficulties. On the other hand, given the strong ties between Spain and Europe, there are opportunities for American leverage by working through the states of Western Europe. This leverage will obviously depend on the economic situation: a sharp contraction of economic activity north of the Pyrenees, with consequent reduction of employment of Spanish workers and of the number of tourists coming to Spain, would probably diminish European influence. On balance, however, this seems to me the best tack to take, and the United States should be planning now with its European allies a concerted policy of sympathetic integration of a fledgling sister democracy. Such assimilation would necessarily entail the devolution on Spain of functions that it could be expected to perform, for example, that of intermediary between Western economies and multinational corporations on the one hand, and the nations of Latin America, including perhaps even Cuba, on the other.

These, however, are tasks for the future. More immediate and urgent are the responses the United States will have to make to the political jockeying and even conflict that will probably mark the break-in period of the post-Franco monarchy. It is not clear whether the United States has done much thinking about these eventualities, though the experience of Portugal will no doubt have encouraged some contingency planning. In general, it seems to me that the best approach is one of support for those moving toward democracy, with the United States exercising some or all of its influence on these democratic leaders through European intermediaries.

It would be fatal if the United States actively involved itself in attempts by Franco supporters to sustain an authoritarian regime and prevent inevitable political change. Under no circumstances should it become identified with the effort of the successor government to consolidate its power by massive coercion; neither should we have an indirect hand in any effort to overthrow the regime by force. The United States should welcome the efforts to move toward democracy, from above and without rupture, since their success may assure long-term political stability; and it should do so in spite of the risks this may entail to some of its interests.

For a long time the United States has missed opportunities to maintain contacts with the leaders of the democratic opposition, whereas European leaders, in their visits to Madrid, have made it a point to meet them. Therefore the European parties and their leaders are better placed than the United States government to provide assistance to Spain on the road to democracy and to influence the process. It seems therefore essential that the United States coordinate its policies toward Spain with Europeans. The closer ties between American and Spanish military establishments should not be allowed to interfere with political considerations, which should have primacy. In fact, our military connections should be used to support the establishment of democracy with a minimum of political and economic crisis, within a West European framework. Should the transition end in violent conflict along political and class lines, or regional lines, the situation would have serious consequences for the stability of the European system. Even a serious destabilization of the economy, not immediately corrected, would be a more serious matter than in Portugal, given Spain's size. It could be argued, of course, that such a development could be internationally isolated and ignored by the United States: let the Spaniards pay the price for their own troubles. Yet such an option does not seem feasible, since civil strife in Spain would inevitably influence developments in France and Italy. Left-wing memories of the Spanish Civil War would generate spontaneous and Communist-inspired agitation on behalf of the Spanish Left, and this would create in Italy in particular serious problems for the government. Any misstep on the part of the United States would only aggravate this tension, and we would soon be greeted by such slogans as "Spain is not Chile."

The Portuguese Revolution in an American Perspective

In their recent articles Kenneth Maxwell and particularly Tad Szulc have given accounts from different perspectives of the impact of the Portuguese revolution on American policymakers and their confused, uneven, and divided responses.[42] It seems unnecessary to review that history; nor would it make sense to argue now about the policy alternatives that might have existed in such a volatile situation.

The Portuguese experience, however, highlights some of the dilemmas and potential contradictions in the formulation of American policy that are relevant not only to the Portuguese case but also to future developments in Spain. Others, such as those derived from the decolonization process and American policy toward southern Africa, were specific to Portugal. It is difficult to know the weight that African problems had, compared to other considerations. Certainly the strategic location of Portugal on the southwest corner of Europe and the importance of its Atlantic islands must have had considerable weight in the analysis, particularly of those concerned with Western defense and Alliance strategy.

Another major consideration must have been the implications for détente and the evaluation of Soviet intentions. Communist participation in the Portuguese government and the prospects at some points of a growing influence of the Party in alliance with some sectors of the MFA confronted Americans with a problem they had not faced in Western Europe since the ouster of the Communists from the French and Italian postwar governments. President Ford formulated the problem bluntly and probably undiplomatically on May 23, 1974, on the eve of the NATO ministerial meeting in Brussels, when he said: "I don't see how you can have a Communist element significant in an organization that was put together and formed for the purpose of meeting a challenge by Communist elements from the East." Then he added: "I am concerned about the Communist element and its influence in Portugal and therefore Portugal's relationship with NATO." A related but somewhat different question was the implication of the Portuguese experience for developments in other European countries and the temptation of what Tad Szulc calls a "vaccination theory." This he defines as a policy of accepting Communism in Portugal that it may serve as a brutal warning to the Spaniards, the French, the Italians, and the Greeks: a Communist take-over could happen to them too if they allowed the party to participate in their governments. Paradoxically, the Spanish and Italian Communist party leaders, in their critique of Cunhal's hard line, gave credence to that theory and attempted to exercise their influence on the PCP to protect their own interests.[g]

Quite a different question is the response to the Portuguese revolution and its internal social and economic policies independently of its international implications. Certainly Washington would have preferred on ideological grounds a different policy, but it is not clear that its direct interests were affected to the same extent as in Cuba or Chile. This might not be true, however, for those

---

[g]An interesting question is whether there will be a change in leadership in the PCP with the rise of Alboim Inglês or Octávio Pato. Their prospects will be affected by views in Moscow on Communist policy and strategy in Western Europe. Zagladine is said to have visited Lisbon in November and was critical of Cunhal's leadership, while Cunhal may be supported by Ponomariev and Suslov.

European countries that had strong, traditional economic ties with Portugal and had participated in its recent capitalist development. The Portuguese revolutionaries were sensitive to this danger and excluded foreign investments from their nationalization policy. Also the fact that some of the countries with economic interests in Portugal had Socialist governments reduced the international implications of the turn to socialism.

A separate problem, which sometimes gets confused with the response to social and economic changes, is the question how much the United States and Europe can and should make a commitment to the establishment and consolidation of pluralist democracy against threats from the revolutionary left, the Communists, and their allies in the MFA, or from the always potentially threatening authoritarian right. In the unstable situation since April 1974, these different but highly interrelated questions could not always be separated, since alignments on these different issues in Portugal were neither consistent nor stable.

American policy was never the dominant factor in the events in Portugal. The same can be said for the Soviet Union and to a lesser degree for Western European countries. However, the support given by European Socialist parties and leaders at the time of the election and particularly after May 1975 was important in turning the tide. The isolation of Cunhal by the PCE and the PCI for their own reasons might also have contributed. American policy, which has been described as following "a tortuous and contradictory path to the point of being at times incomprehensible even to senior State Department officials to say nothing of the Portuguese," has at least not led to any disaster. A direct American intervention—support, say, for the independence of the Azores, a demonstrable involvement in a military coup, or economic sanctions—might well have had such a result. Any such attempt would not have succeeded easily, and failing, would have surely consolidated an authoritarian outcome under the leadership of the MFA. The Communists and the extreme left who would have been the main beneficiaries. Such intervention would also have dealt a heavy blow to the chances of the democratic parties that emerged victorious from the election. If the result had been a rightist takeover, it would have entailed a bloody repression that would have totally discredited the United States in Europe, created insurmountable internal difficulties in Italy and probably France, and divided today's solidly pro-Western social democrats.

The mistakes of Cunhal; the overreaching of the left wing of the MFA, which overestimated its support within the armed forces; the unpredictable but extraordinary capacity for maneuver of President Costa Gomes; the leadership provided by Mário Soares and the hostile response by important sectors of the Portuguese population to the Vasco Goncalves government—all these produced by the end of 1975 a situation that gives hope to those favoring pluralistic democracy. To the extent that that is the primary policy goal of the United States, those developments offer an opportunity for European and American cooperation. Unfortunately, the problem is not exclusively political, but social and economic. Portugal was before the revolution the poorest West European country. Between 1960 and 1971, 900,000 Portuguese emigrated seeking jobs in wealthier countries to the north and overseas. In the past two years, the loss of Angola has meant the return of 300,000 refugees, mostly destitute. The Portuguese economy is extremely vulnerable internationally, owing to its dependence on tourism, foreign remittances, and oil imports. If to its structural problems we add the impact of the revolution, the inflationary consequences of wage demands, the increased food consumption resulting initially from income redistribution, the disruption of production in industry and agriculture due to political activism and the uncertainty of entrepreneurs and investors, the emigration of 30,000 entrepreneurs and professionals, the loss of the colonial market, and so on, the magnitude of the crisis confronting a new democracy becomes apparent.

The results of the international economic crisis, the inherent structural problems delineated above, the demobilization of the armed forces (to go from 200,000 to a planned 26,000 men), and the disruption of the revolution are to be seen in the figure of 500,000 unemployed in the winter of 1975, to say nothing of underemployment, in a country with a population of 8.2 million. The economic reckoning could be postponed only thanks to the large gold and foreign currency reserves that Salazar had so avidly accumulated. They, as Kenneth Maxwell writes,

provided a cushion that helped the revolution postpone the consequences of its actions. Or at least they allowed a series of far-reaching and radical transformations to be promulgated without much apparent pain to the population at large.

This contributed to the sense of unreality which lasted well through the late summer of 1975. The reserves helped to obscure the fact that real change was occurring that would in time have to be paid for, and not merely by its immediate victims—conservative military officers, expropriated landowners, great industrialists and banking magnates. A very high degree of sacrifice, austerity and disciplined collective action were unavoidable if a socialist revolution was to be made to work. Whether or not the Portuguese people, or a sufficiently large number of them, would be prepared for that route was a question that had been largely avoided.[43]

It is an open question how the Portuguese people, the electorate in the forthcoming election and key elites including the different factions within the armed forces, will respond to this crisis. The democrats naturally put their hope in massive Western economic aid without political strings and aim at regaining the confidence of foreign investors. They also want to restore the flow of tourism and workers' remittances and stimulate the entrepreneurial initiative of the national business class. At the same time, however, there is a deep reluctance to reverse many of the anticapitalist policies instituted after March 11: the nationalization of a large part of the economy, the official and unofficial agrarian reform (including the occupation of large estates), and the total change in the position of the worker.

Stating the problem somewhat bluntly and exaggerating, the West faces the dilemma: to save the social revolution in order to save democracy; or to allow the crisis to lead to an attempt at an authoritarian solution by either Left or Right. In my view, given the mobilization that freedom has created in Portuguese society, the geographic distribution of strength between Left and Right, the ideological and personal cleavages within the armed forces, and the international context, anything but a democratic solution could not succeed without an extremely high risk of civil war. Such an outcome would be disastrous for the political stability of Western Europe and therefore is not in the interest of the United States. Confronted with that situation, the richer countries of the West have no choice but to give support to any Portuguese leadership that proposes to satisfy the basic desire of the Portuguese people for political freedom and peaceful social change. This might very well imply foreign support for a largely socialist economy without regard to possible inefficiencies. The prescription assumes that the new electoral returns will not lead to a major shift in the strength of political parties and that what is left of the MFA will continue to support, as seems likely, a democratic socialist policy. In a way, this would be better even than an electoral shift to the center, which would provide more room for a mixed economy and private enterprise but might also encounter more difficulties from organized labor.

The West, particularly West Germany and to a lesser degree the United States, seems to be ready to support Portuguese democracy. Given the stakes, this would seem to be the only feasible, even permissible, choice. Its implementation, however, will require considerable tact and forbearance. The question of Communist participation in the government, the role of Portugal in the inner circles of NATO become largely secondary in this context. Communist participation in government is ultimately a problem for Portuguese domestic politics and will have to be decided in terms of electoral results, the parliamentary strength of parties, and the calculations of their leaders. It seems to me inadvisable, at least at this point, for the United States to make support to the democratic parties in Portugal conditional on exclusion of the Communists. To be sure, it can be argued that a certain amount of discrimination over time would produce a learning effect, so that even *ex post facto* rewards and penalties would exercise some influence *ex ante*; also that this is a policy that can be defended to the American taxpayer.

Such a position is logically quite tenable, particularly if one were to consider a similar prospect in the case of a much larger and even more vulnerable economy and society such as Spain. It ignores, however, the difficulties faced by democratic politicians in postauthoritarian Iberia and the risks of an alternative policy. Consider these. The authoritarian regimes that were presumably protecting their countries from Communism created in fact unique opportunities for the emergence of Communist parties and leftist radicalism. Now profound ideological changes impose constraints that cannot be ignored without risking even more serious difficulties from the Western point of view. In today's world, even an unstable democracy and a break with the relatively successful model of economic development pursued in the last decade are preferable in Iberia to the risk of civil war and authoritarianism of either the Left or the Right. The cost, politically, for the West of any of these alternatives is too staggering to compare with the immediate economic cost of nursing inchoate democracy and less-than-optimal social experiments. It should not be impossible for the richer democratic countries of the West to carry that burden and with some luck to succeed in creating in Portugal a mixed economy integrated into the European economy, enjoying democratic freedoms, and not hostile to the West. In pursuing that goal, the United States would have to encourage its European partners to carry a large share in the effort.

The rewards of such a policy might well go far beyond the boundaries of Portugal. A successful evolution there (from the American point of view) should also contribute to a reasonable development in other southern European countries. By way of contrast, the destabilization in Portugal that would be the inevitable result of the refusal of the West to support its democratic leaders (whatever misgivings it might have regarding their policies) could only contribute to destabilization in other countries west of the Rhine and south of the Alps.

What this means, in short, is that the United States must be prepared to bet on the people, to give them the opportunity and the help to find their way to stable democracy. This will mean a gamble, for the road to stability may prove to be very rough. But it is the only road there is.

Notes

1. The dynamics of regime changes—crises, breakdown, power transfer or takeover, consolidation, reequilibration, restoration, and so on—deserve much more theorizing and research. For a theoretical essay and case studies, see Juan J. Linz and Alfred A. Stepan (eds.), *Crises and Breakdowns of Democratic Regimes* (forthcoming). Some of the essays have been published in *Rivista Italiana di Scienza Politica* 5, 1 (April 1975). Philippe Schmitter, "Liberation by Golpe: Retrospective Thoughts on the Demise of Authoritarian Rule in Portugal," *Armed Forces and Society* 2, 1 (Fall 1975):5-33, has raised the question of a model of the disintegration of authoritarian regimes and made an important contribution to the analysis of the processes involved. For an attempt at comparison, see Gianfranco Pasquino, "L'instaurazione di regimi democratici in Grecia e Portogallo," *Il Mulino*, No. 238 (March-April 1975):217-237.

2. This is not the place to provide detailed bibliographic references to social science analyses of the nature of the Spanish and Portuguese authoritarian

regimes and their evolution. See my earlier papers: Juan Linz, "An Authoritarian Regime: The Case of Spain," in Erik Allardt and S. Rokkan (eds.), *Mass Politics, Studies in Political Sociology* (New York: Free Press, 1970), first published in Erik Allardt and Yrjö Littunen (eds.), *Cleavages, Ideologies and Party Systems* (Helsinki: "Transactions of the Westermarck Society," vol. X, 1964); also "From Falange to Movimiento-Organización: The Spanish Single Party and the Franco Regime, 1936-1968," in S.P. Huntington, and Clement H. Moore (eds.), *Authoritarian Politics in Modern Societies: The Dynamics of Established One Party Systems* (New York: Basic Books, 1970), pp. 128-201; "Opposition in and under an Authoritarian Regime: The Case of Spain," in Robert Dahl (ed.), *Regimes and Oppositions* (New Haven: Yale University Press, 1972); and "Continuidad y discontinuidad en la elite política española: de la Restauración al Régimen actual," in *Homenaje a Carlos Ollero* (Madrid: Carlavilla, 1972), pp. 361-423. See also Philippe C. Schmitter, *Corporatism and Public Policy in Authoritarian Portugal* (Beverly Hills, California: Sage Publications, 1975) (Contemporary Political Sociology Series, Volume 1). In addition to the analysis of the political system it includes interesting comparisons with Greece and Eire in regard to political, economic, and social policy.

3. A basic book on the origins of the MFA is Avelino Rodrigues, Cesario Borga, and Mario Cardoso, *O movimiento das capitaes e o 25 de abril, 229 dias para derrubar o fascismo* (Lisbon: Moraes, 1974).

4. There are a number of accounts and analyses of the Portuguese revolution. See Tad Szulc, "Lisbon & Washington: Behind the Portuguese Revolution," *Foreign Policy*, No. 21 (Winter 1975-76):3-62. Also Kenneth Maxwell, "The Thorns of the Portuguese Revolution," *Foreign Affairs* 54, 2 (January 1976):250-270; "The Hidden Revolution in Portugal," *New York Review of Books*, April 17, 1975, pp. 29-35; and "Portugal under Pressure," *New York Review of Books*, May 29, 1975, pp. 20-30. George W. Grayson, "Portugal and the Armed Forces Movement," *Orbis* 19, 2 (Summer 1975):335-378, gives tables of the composition of the four first provisional governments, election returns and campaign expenditures by party, and a political profile of the PCP leadership. See also Robin Blackburn, "The Test in Portugal," *New Left Review*, No. 87-88 (September-December 1974):5-46.

For a journalistic chronicle reproducing basic documents, speeches, interviews, biographies, and so on, see the three volumes directed by Henrique Barnilaro Ruas: *A revolução das flores. I: Do 25 de abril ao governo provisorio; II: A revolução das flores, O governo de Palma Carlos; III: A revolução das flores. O governo de Vasco Gonçalves ate ao acondo de Lusaka* (Lisbon: Editorial Aster, n.d.).

5. We are thinking mainly of the analyses that link democratic stability with economic development, expansion of education, the welfare state, and so on. For a good review of the literature, see John D. May, *Of the Conditions and Measures of Democracy* (Morristown, N.J.: General Learning Press, 1973), and

Robert A. Dahl, *Polyarchy: Participation and Opposition* (New Haven: Yale University Press, 1971). The discussion was initiated by a seminal article by Seymour M. Lipset, "Some Social Requisites of Democracy: Economic Development and Political Legitimacy," *American Political Science Review* 53 (1959):69-105.

Certainly Spain since the early sixties has experienced notable economic and social change. Industrial growth has been among the highest in developing countries, and among OECD countries, Spain has ranked second after Japan. The share of industry in GDP at constant 1964 factor costs increased between 1960 and 1972 from 31 per cent to about 40 per cent. In 1961 Spanish manufacturers exported on average under 5 per cent of their output; the 1971 share was about 15 per cent. From 21 per cent of total exports in 1961, industrial exports reached 64 per cent in 1972.

A few basic facts from the World Book, *Atlas. Population, per capita Product, and Growth Rates* (Washington, 1974), should help to place Spain and Portugal in comparative perspective. In mid-1972 Spain was the seventh European country in population with 34.4 million; Portugal, the fifteenth with 9.8. Spanish GNP was $41,470 million, $1,210 per capita, and growing at 5.8 per cent per capita per year between 1960 and 1972. The comparable Portuguese figures were respectively $7,610 million, 780, and 5.4.

A measure of the size of the Spanish economy is the fact that in 1972 its GNP ($41,470 million) was only a little less than the aggregate product of Portugal, Greece, Yugoslavia, and Turkey ($46,970 million).

Those economic changes in Spain and the different level of economic development compared to Portugal are clearly reflected in the personal experiences of Spaniards at all social and regional levels as reported in numerous surveys. Data from one executed by DATA in 1968 shows that in Spain 27 per cent of adults said living conditions were much better than five years earlier, 52 per cent slightly better, 11 per cent hardly changed, 4 per cent slightly worse, and none far worse. The proportions in Portugal were respectively 14, 30, 19, 14, and 8 per cent. In Spain the difference between upper income households saying much or slightly better (84 per cent) and lower income (79 per cent) was 5 per cent; in Portugal, respectively 54 and 34, that is, a 20 per cent difference. See The Reader's Digest, *A Survey of Europe Today* (London: The Reader's Digest Association, Ltd., 1970), table 54, pp. 166-167, which includes a wealth of data on standard of living and social attitudes for the EEC and EFTA countries. The recent recession has obviously created a pessimistic climate of opinion about the state of the economy, as a recent survey by DATA shows, but even so the expectations of a better future have not waned: 40 per cent believe the future will be better, 25 per cent the same, and 25 per cent that it will worsen. The impact of the recession shows in that 37 per cent say that in the last months the economic situation of their family has worsened, 53 per cent that it has remained unchanged, while only 9 per cent say it has improved. That same economic development, however, has created a highly urbanized population more vulnerable to economic crises, inefficiencies in public services, and politically mobilizable. In this and many other respects, Spain and Portugal are very different societies. To quote just one figure, while in Spain in 1970 54 per cent of the population lived in cities of over 20,000 (slightly more than in Italy), the proportion in Portugal was only 18 per cent. (In 1910 it was 23 and 12 per cent respectively.) In 1970 43.8 per cent of the Spanish people lived in metropolitan areas with more than 100,000 inhabitants, that is, more than in France.

6. The reader is referred to my essay, "Opposition in and under an Authoritarian Regime: The Case of Spain" (n. 2, above), for a characterization of the different types of opposition and detailed bibliographic references, which we have reduced to a minimum in this essay.

7. Rural social conflicts were a major factor in the crisis of the Republic. See Edward E. Malefakis, *Agrarian Reform and Peasant Revolution in Spain: Origins of the Civil War* (New Haven: Yale University Press, 1970). In this context the change between 1950 and 1970 in the number of farm laborers from 3,068,000 (28.7 per cent of the active population) to 926,000 (7.6 per cent) is particularly significant. See Amando de Miguel, *Manual de Estructura Social de España* (Madrid: Tecnos, 1974), p. 373.

8. The basic sources are Stanley G. Payne, *The Spanish Revolution: A Study of the Social and Political Tensions that Culminated in the Civil War in Spain* (New York, Norton, 1970); and Edward E. Malefakis, "Peasants, Politics and Civil War in Spain, 1931-1939," in Robert Bezucha (ed.), *Modern European Social History* (Lexington, Mass.: Lexington Books, D.C. Heath and Company, 1972), pp. 194-227. Malefakis notes that while the Spanish peasantry had engaged in acts of rebellion, it never had launched a revolution like those in other countries. Even the large harvest strike in 1934 was proclaimed in only 1,563 villages of some 9,000 and could be enforced in only 435. Despite the prerevolutionary mobilization in 1936 in large parts of the country, much of peasant Spain supported the Nationalists. Between July and October 1936 peasants constituted 56.7 per cent of the population of the Nationalist zone, and once the rural revolution was defeated, the peasant proportion of the population in the Republican zone dropped from 57.6 per cent (July-October 1936) to 40.5 per cent (by November 1936-February 1937).

9. On this very different level of social mobilization in Spain and Portugal in the past, see Philippe C. Schmitter, *Corporatism and Public Policy in Authoritarian Portugal*, p. 64, no. 10.

10. The last free election in February 1936 has been studied by Javier Tusell, *Las elecciones del Frente Popular* (2 vols.; Madrid: Edicusa, 1971). Using his data, Jesús de Miguel and Juan J. Linz, "Otra interpretación de las elecciones de 1936 en España," *Sistema* (forthcoming), attempt to allocate the votes given to coalitions (required by the working of the electoral system) to different parties

on the ticket. Let us note that it has been a far longer time since Spaniards last voted in a free election than, say, for Germans of the Nazi era, who went sixteen years (1933 to 1949) between votes.

11. Robert A. Dahl, "Governments and Political Oppositions," in Fred I. Greenstein and Nelson W. Polsby (eds.), *Handbook of Political Science* (Reading, Mass.: Addison-Wesley, 1975), III, 115-174; see especially pp. 155-58.

12. A basic source on the "limited" pluralism of political forces and ideological tendencies is Amando de Miguel, *Sociología del Franquismo, Análisis ideológico de los Ministros del régimen* (Barcelona: Euros, 1975).

13. Of a random sample of Spanish writers who were asked: "Which of the following geopolitical entities: United States, Western Europe and the Soviet Union, do you think has in this moment (1970) the most valid moral principles?" 55 per cent said Western Europe; 21 per cent, the USSR; and 6 per cent, the United States. The figures for those under age forty were respectively 37, 40, and 5 per cent. When asked which had the most just distribution of wealth, the proportions were 38 per cent, the USSR; 22 per cent, Western Europe; and 14 per cent, the United States.

See the survey by Rubén Caba, *389 escritores españoles opinan sobre candentes cuestiones de política nacional e internacional* (Bilbao: Editorial la Gran Enciclopedia Vasca, 1971).

On the evolution of student politics, see José M. Maravall, "Political Socialization and Political Dissent (Spanish Radical Students, 1955-1970)," *Sociology*, January 1976, and "Students and Politics in Contemporary Spain," *Government and Opposition*, April 1976, with references to other sources.

14. Rodolfo Llopis, deputy of the PSOE in the Republic and secretary general of the party in exile, on his return to Madrid (January 22, 1976) said: "There are still wounds that have not healed, painful wounds. As of today the Socialists abroad feel that we cannot and do not want to go arm in arm with the Communist party. We consider the presence of the Communists as pernicious. The accounts of the things that happened at the end of the civil war and in the beginning of life in exile have still to be closed. There are dead bodies and many other things. Let everyone work on his side, even when we recognize the existence of the Communist party." *Informaciones*, January 23, 1976. These sentiments are shared by many who fought on the Republican side in the civil war, but we should not forget that they are a rapidly dwindling proportion of the population.

One wing of the PSOE reaffirmed this position in a statement published in *Informaciones* January 5, 1976: "Collaboration with all democratic forces, without any ties to those of totalitarian character."

15. In this emerging split between Northern Social Democrats and Southern Socialists, Andreas Papandreou, in the Conference held in Paris, January 24-25, 1976, was the most articulate spokesman of the latter group and sharply criticized his friend Mário Soares for making a "fatal choice in opting for the

United States." The PSP leader was deliberately absent, and two representatives of the party stated quite divergent positions on the issue of cooperation with the Communists. *Expresso*, January 31, 1976, p. 7.

16. The text of the Plataforma de Acordo Constitucional between the MFA and the parties can be found in *1975 Primeiras Eleições Livres* (Lisbon: Decibel, 1975), pp. 17-29, which also includes a sketch of the parties and their positions and the reactions of the parties to the election returns, which are given by districts.

17. For the election returns see Instituto Nacional de Estadística, *Eleição para a Assembleia Constituinte 1975*, (Lisbon: Ministério de Administração Interna, 1975), Vol. I.

18. For a detailed analysis of the various forms of opposition and the limited attempts of liberalization under Franco, see Juan J. Linz, "Opposition in and under an Authoritarian Regime" (cited n. 2).

19. The constitutional superstructure created by Franco, in which the new government has to operate, whether to transform or dismount it, is too complex to discuss here. In recent years a number of analyses, both scholarly and polemical, have been published. A good guide is the many essays in Manuel Fraga Iribarne (ed.), *La España de los años 70. El Estado y la política* (2 volumes; Madrid: Moneda y Crédito, 1974). Further references will be found in my forthcoming essay: "Legislatures in Organic Statist-Authoritarian Regimes: The Case of Spain," to be published in Joel Smith and Lloyd Musolf (eds.), *The Roles of Legislatures in Economic and Social Development.*

The legal and political context of the reinstalled monarchy is discussed by Joan Ferrando Badía, *Teoría de la Instauración Monárquica en España* (Madrid: Instituto de Estudios Políticos, 1975).

20. Neither the few and soon-dated scholarly analyses nor the accounts of foreign journalists can substitute for the reading of the press and magazines. We have found *Expresso* for Portugal and *Informaciones* for Spain invaluable.

21. The interview with Premier Arias Navarro in *Newsweek*, January 12, 1976, p. 43, in which he said: "First we will have elections for city and regional councils in which the (political) parties will gain experience in the democratic process. This phase should be completed by the end of 1976. And then the same process will take place at the national level and be completed before the end of 1977 ... So in two years, you should see the reality of four or five political parties functioning effectively in a new Spanish democracy." The last sentence became the headline in Spanish newspapers (January 6), but on January 9 Arias stated that he had not used the word political "parties" but "groups," and that the associations would be the basis of the political future. The statements of Spanish cabinet members abroad tend to be quite different from those made at home, and the difference is duly noted in the Spanish press.

22. The article by the respected editorial writer of *Informaciones*, Guillermo Medina, "Las urnas o la fuerza" (January 31, 1976) reaches a similar conclusion:

"If Fraga wants to be Cánovas and not Caetano, Arias only wants to be Arias"; and "Spaniards have the right to know the fundamental option that is being debated, to choose between only two ways to govern this country: the ballot boxes or force."

23. A very important source for the changes in political climate in Spain in the last decade is public opinion surveys by private organizations and the Instituto Español de Opinión Pública, some of them published in the *Revista Española de la Opinión Pública.* Also Rafael López Pintor and Ricardo Buceta, *Los españoles de los años 70* (Madrid: Tecnos, 1975). Recently the publication of polls in the newspapers and magazines has become another factor in the political process. They all indicate the rapidly changing attitude toward the regime, the governing class, and so on, and the growing interest in politics. For example, in 1966 "peace" was considered the most important goal for the coming years by 57 per cent of the respondents; in March 1975, by 45 per cent; and by June, by 39 per cent. While "justice," "freedom," and "democracy" in 1966 added up to 20 per cent, in March 1975 they were chosen by 33 per cent and in June by 38 per cent.

24. Nicos Poulantzas, *La crise des dictatures: Portugal, Grèce, Espagne* (Paris: François Maspero, 1975).

To understand the present position of the party the following are essential: Santiago Carillo (sic), *Demain l'Espagne: Entretiens avec Régis Debray et Max Gallo* (Paris: Seuil, 1974); the 1975 joint statement: Enrico Berlinguer and Santiago Carrillo, *Una Spagna libera in un Europea democratica* (Rome: Editori Riuniti, 1975); Partido Communista de España, Segunda Conferencia Nacional, *Manifiesto Programa del Partido Communista de España* (Paris, Ebro, 1975); and the programmatic essay by Santiago Carrillo, *Nuevos enfoques a problemas de hoy* (n.p., n.d.).

25. Julio Busquets, *El Militar de carrera en España: Estudio de sociología militar* (Barcelona: Ariel, 1971).

26. Speeches by Coloma Gallegos, minister of the army, and Pita de Veiga, minister of the navy, *ABC*, January 5, 1975. The texts quoted are the headline of the day.

27. There are a number of publications on the changes in the Spanish church and religious sociology. For a review with a bibliography, see ISPA, *El cambio religioso en España* (Barcelona: ISPA, 1975).

28. See the strike statistics published officially by the Ministerio de Trabajo, *Informe sobre conflictos colectivos de trabajo* (Madrid, 1971, 1972, 1973). In the last year the rate-per-thousand of workdays lost in strikes in Spain was 84, compared to 21.2 in the Federal Republic of Germany, 181 in France, 279 in the United Kingdom. That rate in 1971 had been 67.5; in 1972, 46.1. See also José M. Maravall, *El desarrollo económico y la clase obrera: Estudio sociológico de los conflictos obreros en España* (Barcelona: Ariel, 1970).

29. The activist and violent groups of the extreme right have grown out of or

emerged on the periphery of the single party, the Movimiento, partly as a result of its disintegration. Like other neo-Fascist groups, they are highly fragmented and ideologically confused, as the appearance of a Spanish Nazi organization shows. Volunteer reserve officers (the *Alféreces Provisionales*) of the civil war have been prominent among them. There are, on the other hand, the bureaucratized Movimiento-Órganización (which Franco created by the fusion of the Falange with other forces in his coalition); the bureaucracy of the official *sindicatos*; and the clientelistic structures in the provinces, particularly the Hermandades de Labradores y Ganaderos (farmers organization); the veterans of the civil war organizations; etc. In this respect, the vacuum on the Right might not be so great as in Portugal, where the União Nacional, later Ação Nacional, was little more than a paper organization. A man like José Antonio Girón might not have a significant constituency but rather an organizational network and some cadres. In Spain, there is room at least for a neo-Fascist minority and, in the case of a pseudo-revolutionary crisis and economic disintegration, for a not-so-small minority identifying with the past. On the Movimiento see Juan J. Linz, "From Falange to Movimiento" (n. 2, above), and Stanley G. Payne, "Spanish Fascism," in Stein Ugelk Larsen, Bernt Hagtvet, and Jan Petter Myklebust, *Who Were the Fascists?* (forthcoming).

The death of the Movimiento-Organización (the single party) is reflected in the fact that in 1969, in the last membership drive, only 27,806 joined in all Spain, 3,867 of them coming from the youth organization. The youth organization, still one of the liveliest parts of the Movimiento, organized only 1 per cent of the eligible age cohorts. Data in José María Val ¿Por que no fue posible la Falange? (Barcelona: Dopesa, 1975).

30. Except for Guy Hermet, *Les Communistes en Espagne: étude d'un mouvement politique clandestin* (Paris: Armand Colin, 1971), there are no scholarly studies of the PCE.

31. The position of the PCE on democracy is reflected in this text from the *Manifiesto Programa del PCE* (n. 24 above), p. 129, which deserves to be kept in mind and quoted in full: "The plurality of parties determines another of the characteristics of the form of socialism that we consider probable for Spain: the Socialist State will not have an official philosophy; will develop a free and open ideological struggle, even among the closely related socialist forces. The CP considers that in the multiparty and democratic experience of the Popular Front, which created in the Republican zone a new democratic regime, no longer capitalist, oriented toward socialism, there is an antecedent that cannot be copied mechanically because the times and the existing forces have changed, but that can offer an object of experience and for thought of value for the future." Even more of a concession is the following, which constitutes an implicit repudiation of the Communist record during the civil war: "We don't forget either that the option for a democratic way means to turn regularly to popular suffrage, to accept the existence of a legal opposition and alternation in power if

the majority of the people withdraws its trust from the governing parties." These assurances are qualified a few paragraphs below by an emphasis on the parallel development of "direct democracy, from below at all levels," which would "exercise a control that would contribute to the dynamism and good management of the organs of representative democracy." Ibid., p. 27.

For the very different style of Alvaro Cunhal, see the interview with Oriana Fallaci in *L'Europeo*, published in English in the *New York Times Magazine*, July 13, 1975, pp. 9 ff.

32. See "Necesidad de la Revolución: significado de la Huelga Nacional," PCE, *Manifiesto Programa del PCE*, pp. 143-145, for a definition.

33. The elections under authoritarian regimes obviously do not measure the strengths of the regime and its opposition, but are indicative of their potential sources of support. For Spain, see Guy Hermet, "Electoral Trends in Spain: An Appraisal of Polls Conducted under the Franco Regime," *Iberian Studies* 3, 2 (Autumn 1974), with seven maps; and Miguel Martínez Cuadrado "Representación, Elecciones, Referendum," in Manuel Fraga (ed.), *La España de los años 70*, 1, 1371-1439. The comparison between the opposition vote in 1969 and the 1975 returns in Portugal shows how the strength of the Communist left was prefigured in the 1969 election.

34. See Juan J. Linz, "The Party System of Spain: Past and Future," in Seymour M. Lipset and Stein Rokkan (eds.), *Party Systems and Voter Alignments* (New York: Free Press, 1967), pp. 197-282, particularly pp. 264-275, where we discuss the hypothetical behavior of a Spanish electorate, assuming that different social strata (in 1964) would vote like the Italians in the early 60s.

35. The Metra Seis survey in January 1975 of a quota sample in the seven largest cities posed the following question: "Speaking of political parties, which ones of those listed in this card do you think would have more supporters if they were allowed? Please mention two." The answers ran: Anarchists, 2 per cent; Communists, 10 per cent; Socialists, 33 per cent; Social-Democrats, 24 per cent; Republicans, 17 per cent; Demochristians, 34 per cent; Liberals, 14 per cent; Independents, 8 per cent; Monarchists, 21 per cent; None, 3 per cent; No answer, 13 per cent; total, 179 per cent. Obviously the meaning of the response is ambiguous but indicative of the capacity to envisage a party system (data in *Informaciones*, January 20, 1975).

36. To use the terminology and analysis of Giovanni Sartori, "European Political Parties: The Case of Polarized Pluralism," in Joseph LaPalombara and Myron Weiner (eds.), *Political Parties and Political Development* (Princeton: Princeton University Press, 1966), pp. 137-176.

37. On the regional nationalisms see Juan J. Linz, "Early State-Building and Late Peripheral Nationalisms against the State," in S.N. Eisenstadt and S. Rokkan (eds.), *Building States and Nations: Models, Analyses, and Data across Three Worlds* (Beverly Hills: Sage, 1973), II, 32-112; idem, "Politics in a Multilingual Society with a Dominant World Language," in Jean-Guy Savard and

Richard Vigneault (eds.), *Les états multilingues: problèmes et solutions (Multilingual States: Problems and Solutions)* (Quebec: Presses de l'Université Laval, 1975), pp. 367-444; and Stanley G. Payne, *Basque Nationalism* (Reno: University of Nevada Press, 1975). Amando de Miguel, "Estructura social e immigración en el País Vasconavarro," *Papers, Revista de Sociología*, III, 1974, 249-273, provides excellent insights into the complexities of the ethnic structure of this industrial and immigration region. A survey found 52 per cent of the population with both parents born in the region, 8 per cent with one parent born there, 12 per cent with neither parent, and 26 per cent who were themselves immigrants (and 2 per cent, no information). Official bilingualism is favored by 44 per cent of the first group and only by 13 per cent of the immigrants. Of the full-blooded Basques, 49 per cent claim to understand Basque, but only 14 per cent of the half-Basques and 13 per cent of the immigrants.

38. Spanish defense expenditures were relatively low: 18.6 dollars per capita and 2.7 per cent of GNP (in obvious contrast with Portugal, owing to its involvements overseas: 25.2 and 6.2, respectively), placing Spain in the 61st place in percentage of GNP, compared to Portugal in the 20th. Data for 1965 from the Economics Bureau of the U.S. Arms Control and Disarmament Agency, quoted by Charles Lewis Taylor and Michael C. Hudson, *World Handbook of Political and Social Indicators* (2nd edition; New Haven: Yale University Press, 1972), p. 35.

39. A survey by Consulta, published in *Actualidad Económica*, executed in May 1974, showed 16 per cent favorable to the continued presence of U.S. bases, 48 per cent against, with 36 per cent giving no opinion or no answer. As to the question, "Should Spain ask for entry into NATO," 31 per cent said yes, 16 no, and 54 had no answer.

40. For a collection of papers on Spanish politics and economy, particularly the international connections, see William T. Salisbury and James D. Theberge (eds.), *Spain in the Seventies and Beyond: Problems of Change and Transition* (New York: Praeger, forthcoming). The papers, which were presented at a conference on Iberia and the Security of the Western Alliance organized jointly by the Center for Strategic and International Studies, Georgetown University, the Institute of International Studies of the University of South Carolina and the Institute for the Study of Conflict, London, on May 1975, contain a wealth of information, particularly on the international aspects. See also Jonathan Story, "Spanish Foreign Policy 1957-1972" (Atlantic Institute for International Affairs, mimeo.; 1972)—an excellent survey.

41. Data from Banco Exterior de Comercio, *Hechos y cifras de la economía española* (Madrid, 1969), pp. 538-561.

42. See note 4, above.

43. Maxwell, "The Thorns of the Portuguese Revolution" (n. 4, above), pp. 261-62.

IX

The United States and the Security of Europe

Alastair Francis Buchan

I

In the heady days of the early 1970s—after the completion of the *Ostpolitik*, the increase in American leverage on Moscow by reason of the opening to China, and the negotiation of the first SALT and many other Soviet-American agreements, it became fashionable to talk of East-West détente as an "irreversible" process. But time and events have brought second thoughts.

It is a striking fact that of the 105 treaties and agreements that have been signed since the United States and the Soviet Union entered diplomatic relations in 1933, 58 were concluded between 1969 and the Spring of 1975. It is a comforting fact that there is a degree of consultation and mutual comprehension between Washington and Moscow that significantly diminishes the risk of, say, another Cuban missile crisis. It is a civilizing factor that there is now a marked degree of cooperation on medical, environmental, and other forms of research. It is a remarkable fact that a Soviet and an American spacecraft can successfully unite in outer space. But such isolated developments do not necessarily provide the basis of entente, or even a certain foundation for continuing détente.

In the first place, the strategic balance has now reached a point of complexity where it is not clear whether further negotiations can do more than set margins to the arms race, rather than reduce the level of the balance to one which a rising generation, one not reared in the atmosphere of the cold war, can find intelligible and so be ready to sustain. Technological innovations that in the late 1950s and early 1960s worked in favor of a stable superpower relationship, say, hardened missiles or *Polaris* submarines, now also work against it, thus multiple warheads and improved accuracies that engender mutual fears of a disarming attack. Second, since what has been achieved is simply détente and both superpowers have different aspirations that, in Secretary Kissinger's words, "do not spring from misunderstanding, or personalities, or transitory factors"[1] but are rooted in history and nourished by conflicting values, their competition for influence within the international system is only muted, not resolved. Third, such détente as has been attained, has been through a process of purely political negotiations and has almost no social and only a modest economic content. It has been a consequence of intergovernmental agreement and as such could be reversed by successor regimes. It is based, moreover, on mutual strategic deterrence with weapons of enormous destructive power, and this, though it may inhibit war between the great powers, is inherently a relationship of antagonism that would make social entente difficult even if the suspicious element in the Russian national character tolerated it. Finally, because both powers are enormous heterogeneous societies, intergovernmental agreements are vulnerable to the interplay of each other's domestic politics. The Soviet cancellation in January 1975 of the 1972 Soviet-American trade agreement by reason of the terms that Congress set upon it and the paucity of American credits by comparison with Soviet expectations, or Soviet interventions in the American grain market, are cases in point.

The maintenance of superpower détente will not be easy over the next decade, which is not to say that it is impossible. One difficulty arises from uncertainty about the nature of the American political temper, about what will be the balance between and within the parties and where the balance between congressional and executive power will come to rest, for the introversion this concern gives rise to makes for a passive conception of détente. Another is ignorance about the impending change in the leadership of the Soviet Union and what it means—whether it will pass to men like Andropov and Shepilov, whether it will pass to some younger and more adventurous figure, what the influence of the military will be. Second, the disarray of Western economic and energy relationships creates a host of uncertainties, including the possibility that a more dynamic Soviet leadership than today's might see in it that "crisis of capitalism" that would impel a challenge to the principle of coexistence, if not at the center, then on the peripheries of the Western system. Third, there is the question whether human judgment can control the dynamism of technological change, with missiles becoming more accurate and their warheads more sophisticated. If not, the superpowers, who originally acquired strategic hegemony because they alone combined great economic and scientific resources with continental size, may find themselves having to shift the bulk of their deterrent power from the land to the oceans if they are not to revive the anxieties about first-strike capabilities that bedeviled political relationships in the 1950s. Mutual uncertainty about the nature of the central strategic balance is more probable than a simple transference of strategic superiority from the United States to the Soviet Union. Finally, there is the danger that the Western industrialized powers may become involved in a confrontation with the more militant developing countries, a conflict in which not only might the Soviet Union be *tertius gaudens* but which might strike the spark of military conflict, especially in the Mediterranean.

When the "containment" policy was fashioned in the late 1940s, it was conceived as being necessary only for a limited time, until, that is, the Soviet Union recognized the limitations of revolutionary or nationalist policies and turned to other preoccupations; until other centers of power than the United States regained their strength and the international system reverted to its normal plural state. Some of the objectives of the containment policy have been attained. Insofar as ideological hostility has been a source of conflict between the Soviet Union and the capitalist world, it has been partly overlaid by practical considerations of security or welfare politics. This is not true of the rivalry between the two great Communist powers. As a result, the United States no longer shoulders the burden alone; and, ironically, in the area where the containment policy was criticized as being inapplicable, namely, in the Far East and Asia, much of the political task of containing Soviet power is exercised not by the United States but by China, so that the former is, or need only be, one party in a multiple balance.

But nearly a generation has passed since George Kennan's famous definition of the problem and the objective, and in the meantime the Soviet Union has expanded from a power of primarily regional concerns to one of global interests and has acquired the military forces and political skills to ensure influence far beyond her frontiers in the two continents that she bestrides. But it is in Europe that Soviet external military power is principally deployed, and it is in Europe and nowhere else that it has actually been employed. It is for this reason that the non-Communist states of Western and northern Europe see little alternative for the foreseeable future to the maintenance, not just of a balance of influence, but of a military balance of power there at some level, sustained by a close and highly integrated alliance with the United States and Canada. It might have been otherwise; the militarization of the Atlantic Alliance after Korea may have been a mistake, for it led to the Warsaw Pact, which is a more efficient counterpart. But it is fruitless, if one is considering policy or choices for the future, to sigh for the might-have-beens of history.

To say this is not to suggest that Europe must somehow be exempted from the improvement of relations between East and West that has been occurring to a limited extent between the superpowers. The treaties concluded in the early 1970s by the Federal Republic of Germany with the Soviet Union, Poland, and East Germany proved the converse. But amelioration is made possible only by a military balance. In the words of a contemporary German military philosopher, "Military imbalance can be a considerable handicap to the process of détente. The delicate nature of this problem can be accounted for by the experience of nations in the course of their history and the psychological aftereffects of confrontation."[2] There seems little disagreement on this fact between either the democratic European states and the United States or indeed, for that matter, the Soviet Union. It is the East European powers which suffer spiritually and politically for this clinch that has preserved peace for a generation in the world's ancient seat of war. For the other partners the argument is more about means than about ends.

The modest results of the Conference on European Security and Cooperation (CSCE) have illustrated the slow pace at which the normalization of relations between democratic and nondemocratic Europe is likely to occur unless the West can maintain diplomatic and political coherence. Though it has long been a Soviet objective, indeed for over twenty years, to hold such a conference in European terms alone, its membership was successfully widened to include the United States by a united stance of the members of the North Atlantic Alliance. Through a demonstration of political solidarity on the part of the European members of the Alliance, its agenda was also widened to include questions of interest to the West such as freedom of movement and information, and to both East and West such as technological exchanges; so that it was not just a bargaining session among international lawyers on declarations about respect for frontiers or the sovereign equality of states. Mr. Brezhnev was thus thwarted in his objective that the Conference should simply ratify the fact of Soviet primacy in Europe. He got his summit meeting on July 30, 1975 to sign the declarations of principle that had been agreed on. These have done no harm. But after two and a half years of almost continuous discussion among the thirty-five participating states, and despite many constructive suggestions—not just by Western allied countries but by neutral states as well—as to how the foundations of European security might really be strengthened and transnational communication ameliorated, the Conference wound up with quite trivial accomplishments, such as a commitment to give notification of maneuvers and promises of more sensible rules for visas.

The Soviet Union bears the principal responsibility for this largely negative outcome. But the United States must also bear a certain share of it, for it was the superpower bargain of early 1972 that took the crux of the problem of security in Europe, the level and nature of the armaments deployed there, and put it into a separate conference in Vienna on Mutual Force Reductions. The American government agreed to this largely in order to convince Senator Mansfield that it took this problem seriously; but it put little diplomatic weight behind the CSCE. The relative failure of CSCE and the fact that negotiation has not yet really begun on MFR, where the United States has a certain leverage, has an important bearing on American choices about the future.

II

It is over twenty-five years since the North Atlantic Treaty was signed, so there is a complete generation, reaching even to the upper echelons of military command, that has only an adolescent's memory of the reasons for signing it and creating an integrated command structure under American leadership. In ten years' time the majority of the voting population in all of the member countries will have only a dim memory of the cold war years. And only a minority of people in any country study the facts of relative military capabilities or even follow events closely. There is, therefore, a considerable risk, as developments in Holland and Denmark have shown, that the political public will simply lose interest in participating in the maintenance of a balance of military power in Europe. This is all the more likely if there is no crisis to disturb East-West relations there. This difficulty is compounded, partly by inflation, which makes all legislatures and governments anxious to reduce public expenditure, partly by the fact that all the European allies, including Britain, have now tailored their force structures to fulfill only their NATO obligations, instead of maintaining forces for a general range of contingencies as states historically have done. Consequently the temptation to ask, if Europe is quiet, why bother to make this contribution, is likely to remain with us and will grow more difficult to answer.

European security and the American relationship to it will also suffer from another difficulty. The European Community has never had, and does not look as if it will readily acquire, the characteristics of an independent strategic actor: powerful centralized institutions, a homogeneous technological base, an identical perception of external threats and interests among its component states. For the time being the disarray of the international monetary system has led to a tacit abandonment even of Economic and Monetary Union as the next step toward political union; and indeed there is some risk that the Community may end up primarily as an intergovernmental system like the OECD, rather than the supranationally directed Community that its founders envisaged—and this, even though the question of British membership is no longer in doubt. But as a group of states, the Nine are, independently of the Treaty of Rome and the fate of the Community institutions, gradually acquiring a greater coherence of political interest, and NATO is not the American proconsulate that it was a decade ago. This has been most evident in relations with the OPEC countries and in the monetary initiatives that were necessitated by the rise in oil prices. The rancor of 1973, Dr. Kissinger's unsuccessful Year of Europe, may have been alleviated. But the fact remains that the stability of the European balance of power depends on the maintenance of what is still largely an American-dominated military system at a time when the European members of the Alliance are not only acquiring somewhat different political and economic interests from those of the guarantor power, but also a limited ability to express them collectively. Consequently, it requires increasing diplomatic skill to sustain the political confidence needed to maintain the trans-Atlantic relationship.

There is also the more obvious problem of inflation, which, though it affects the Warsaw Pact to a certain degree, troubles the Atlantic Alliance far more. Throughout the past fifteen or twenty years, the rise in the cost of maintaining a given level of forces has accelerated faster than the rise in the general level of prices, partly because of the high proportion of research and development costs in major systems, partly because the Soviet Union has since the early 1960s become such a highly efficient and innovative military power that Western systems such as aircraft and radar have a shorter and shorter life before they must be replaced. A less competitive and more rational attitude toward innovation for its own sake has now been adopted by the governments of the Alliance, but even so, inflation is now rapidly escalating the price of those systems that must be replaced.

The effect of military inflation is, of course, felt most keenly by those countries which, by reason of their role or geographical position, must maintain the most modern aircraft, tanks, communications, and so on; and which, by reason of their social history, have abandoned conscription. The bill for military manpower in the United States for the fiscal year ending in June 1975, for instance, was $6 billion larger than it was at the peak of the Vietnam War, when the armed forces were 1,400,000 men larger than they are today. If a slowing down of procurement programs and a final withdrawal from a number of ex-imperial outposts had not recently been decided upon, the share of Britain's GNP devoted to defense would have risen from 5 per cent in 1973 to 6 per cent by the end of the decade. But the burden is heavy for all countries and its cost is rising.

However, a number of ghosts that haunted the corridors of Western power in the late 1960s and early 1970s seem to have been laid to rest. The transatlantic snarling over support costs has abated, largely because the magnitude of international monetary transactions has dwarfed the problem. Mr. James Schlesinger writes of "settling down for the long haul,"[3] and in all the post-Vietnam discussions about American overseas commitments, there seems little disposition to question the necessity of American participation in NATO and the European military balance. Senator Mansfield's amendment to the Defense Appropriations Bill calling for a major reduction in American forces overseas did not pass the Senate in 1974 and was not even introduced in 1975. The warnings of American military sociologists[4] that volunteer forces might produce a total of only about 1,750,000 (half those of the Soviet Union) have been disproved by an enlistment rate that rose throughout the early 1970s and has produced forces of well over 2,000,000; and owing to unemployment in the United States and elsewhere, recruiting should be no great problem in the years immediately ahead. The American forces in Europe are, in fact, in process of being increased, so that the American contingent will be restored to its full complement of five divisions for the first time since the height of the Vietnam War. The Jackson-Nunn amendment, which would have related the level of American forces in Europe to the American balance of payments, ran out in 1974, and Senator Nunn now seems more interested in the efficiency of the forces in Europe than their size. German fears that American volunteers in Europe would be predominantly black have been allayed by the fact that the black enlistment rate seems to have settled down at about 15 per cent of American armed forces.

At the same time, American fears of European neutralism or accusations that the Europeans are getting "a free ride" have similarly abated. A Labour government in Britain with a strong left wing has declared that "NATO is the linchpin of British security and will remain the first charge on the resources available for defense."[5] A Socialist-dominated coalition government in Germany has not reduced over the past five and a half years in office the strength of the German armed forces, though German defense expenditure has been reduced. It is true that there is no real sign of France's reentering into a formal relationship with the other fourteen countries that are members of NATO, the integrated planning and command system of the Alliance from which French forces were removed by President de Gaulle in 1966; and French defense expenditure has also declined. On the other hand, although Giscard d'Estaing's center and right-wing coalition obtained only a bare majority over M. Mitterand's Union de la Gauche in the spring of 1974, the days of flirtation with the idea of a purely European balance of power, which were evident in de Gaulle's later years, or of using the European Community and other European institutions as a stick with which to beat the Americans, seem to have passed.

There is also a much clearer recognition in American official statements of the large proportion of the total burden of defense and deterrence in Europe that is borne by the European powers themselves. In terms of ground forces, it is of the order of 90 per cent; in the terms of ships, it is 80 per cent; and in terms of aircraft, it is 75 per cent. As Mr. Schlesinger has emphasized, "in the critical central region of Europe, the United States contributes only 23 per cent of NATO's manpower—compared, for example, with the Soviet Union's share of 46 per cent of Warsaw Pact manpower."[6]

III

This does not mean that the European-American military and security relationship, which has been full of difficulties since the early cold war years, has shot suddenly beneath the bridge of discord, so evident in 1973, into calm water. It simply means that the problems are different and in some ways more difficult to solve for being diffuse in character.

Apart from the general problems of the changing climate of opinion to which I have referred, the specific security issues that are likely to beset the United States and Western Europe over the next decade seem to me in ascending order of importance: the ossification of the central institutions of the Atlantic Alliance; the structure and function of the forces, especially in the central area; the development of functional cooperation among the West European allies; the maintenance of the domestic authority of governments; the control of political irredentism and decay in southern Europe. Finally, there is the endemic problem that threats to the security of all the NATO allies may arise from developments outside NATO's agreed sphere of responsibility and common action or in areas where European and American interests are not necessarily identical.

In the early years of the Atlantic alliance, its Council, with permanent representatives and delegations and meetings twice a year at ministerial level, was envisaged as being the political cabinet of the West, just as OEEC was envisaged as its economic cabinet. There were obvious fallacies in any such conception. The very size of the Alliance, which had grown to fifteen states by 1955, since it had been originally conceived more as a collective security system than as a collective action mechanism; the disparity in the resources of the various members; and the limitations of the geographical scope of its responsibilities—all of these militated against the continuous use of the Council as the prime focus for the discussion of high policy. This was particularly true for countries that had extra-European commitments, such as the United States, Britain, and France. The Suez debacle of 1956 emphasized this fact, but in 1957 the NATO powers, largely at the insistence of Lester Pearson, the Canadian foreign minister, swore repentance. In the 1960s the problem assumed a different form, namely increasing European uneasiness, German especially, about the United States reaction to a European crisis and about the precise substance of American strategic doctrine and contingency planning. It was exacerbated by the change in American strategy to one of flexible response, which was badly and didactically explained to the European allies and seemed to them at first the abandonment of deterrence as a central function of the Alliance. The inference was that America preferred to fight a land battle in central Europe rather than risk threatening the use of nuclear weapons to deter it.

The problem was falsely diagnosed by the State Department as a desire of the nonnuclear European allies, Germany in particular, to have direct control over some part of the very large stockpile of American nuclear weapons located in or targeted on Europe and led to the abortive initiative of the Multilateral Force (MLF). When it became clear that it was not physical control of nuclear triggers that preoccupied the European allies, but a clearer understanding of American contingency planning, a Nuclear Policy Committee was constituted within the framework of the NATO Council in 1966. This was strengthened by the simultaneous creation of a more confidential Nuclear Planning Group, of which the United States, Britain, Germany, and Italy are permanent members, with a rotating membership of two to four other allies. And to this inner group the past four American secretaries of defense have been scrupulous, and to a large extent successful, in explaining their thoughts and policies. Thus Mr. Schlesinger's revival of a strategy of selective response, possibly entailing the controlled use of nuclear weapons if a European crisis should come to the point of war, in order to sustain the credibility of the American deterrent posture in Europe, has not raised anything like the same flurry of doubt in European capitals as Mr.

McNamara's advocacy of a limited counterforce strategy in 1962. There is some skepticism about the real relevance of what he has been discussing, since the whole of the NATO force structure is now seen in Europe largely in political terms, as a shield against Soviet pressure on exposed European allies, and the expectation of actual armed conflict has receded. But when Mr. Schlesinger explained that "We are acquiring selective and discriminatory options that are intended to deter another power from exercising any form of nuclear pressure,"[7] there was little European inclination to dispute his objective.

The problem of consultation and joint policy-making in the Alliance now has two new dimensions: closer European association with the development of Soviet-American negotiations, in particular those that might affect American force levels or strategy in the European theater; and the better use of the Alliance machinery for the management of crises that affect all the allies or most of them but arise on the periphery of the NATO area, especially in the Middle East.

To understand the nature of the first problem, it may be well to digress for a moment and compare the "efficient" as contrasted with the "dignified" (to use Walter Bagehot's differentiation a century ago of the constituent elements of the British constitution) techniques of Alliance consultation that have evolved over the years. Because the United States is the core power of the Atlantic Alliance, because it has a very complex system of decision-making, and because NATO is such a large, disparate (and sometimes leaky) organization, the practice evolved among the major European allies of using their embassies in Washington to discuss points of substance with the American administration, pressing their points when their prime or foreign ministers came to Washington. The Pentagon and the State Department relied primarily on the same channel. Both parties then used the NATO Council as a means of multilateralizing and ratifying the substance of agreements hammered out in Washington.

When the Strategic Arms Limitation Talks (SALT) began in 1969, the American administration candidly declared that it would use the Council to inform its allies of the substance of negotiations with the Russians and the positions it intended to adopt, but that it could not undertake to consult them either individually or collectively. By reason of the complex nature of the SALT negotiations and because they involved American weapons only (the United States having successfully resisted Soviet proposals that French and British weapons should be taken into account), this formula was generally accepted.

As the difficulties emerged, however, of obtaining a clear-cut agreement in the second round of the SALT negotiations (evidenced by the loose character of the Vladivostok agreement of November 1974, which made no reference to American nuclear weapons in Europe or Soviet weapons targeted on Western Europe), it became apparent that the problem of nuclear-force levels in Europe might have to be relegated to the Vienna negotiations on Mutual Force Reductions (MFR), which were originally conceived as applying only to conventional forces. MFR is likely to become the European aspect of SALT, but with the added difficulty that it is not a two-power but an interallied negotiation. The difficulty of achieving and sustaining agreed allied positions in an ongoing negotiation of this kind makes the older system of using Washington as the prime focus of interallied debate no longer appropriate, and it is becoming necessary to use the NATO machinery in Brussels as a day-to-day policy-making instrument. MFR requires the use of the NATO political machinery for the coordination of positions, at any rate between countries with forces in central Europe (United States, Britain, Germany, Canada, Benelux), if mutual confidence is to be sustained in negotiating with the Warsaw Pact. The strengthening of the American delegation to NATO in 1974 suggests some recognition of this new problem.

The other problem, the growing effect on European-American relations and well-being, or upon European-American confidence, of developments elsewhere in the world is, as I have said, not new. But it is becoming more insistent, both because of the scale and risk of the conflict of interests that can now occur in relations between the industrial powers and the Muslim world and because of a possible cleavage in the European and the American views of how such problems should be handled. This is not simply a product of Europe's greater dependence on Middle Eastern oil or of its greater strategic vulnerability, but represents a difference in perspective between the two sides of the Atlantic on the international system as it is emerging. To some Americans, burdened as their country still is by a vast range of international obligations, the sudden rise to power of the OPEC states is a phenomenon to be confronted and contained, if necessary by a rallying of the industrial powers to face them down, prevent embargoes, and if possible reduce the value of their prime weapon—oil. Many articulate Europeans, on the other hand, believe that those new rich must be made partners, not adversaries, and would echo Ralf Dahrendorf's belief that "The central international question for the advanced world is its relationship with the threshold countries . . . that is, those which are about to reach, or have already reached, a threshold of development which enables them to make headway without outside support . . . I believe a sensible approach by the advanced countries should be motivated by one overriding purpose: to do everything possible in order to make sure that the threshold countries become members of the Club of the Rich soon."[8] This does not imply any idea of selling Israel for oil, but it does entail trying to heighten the sense of international responsibility of the OPEC states.

The reconciliation of these views, to the extent that they may be in conflict, involves international organizations and negotiations with far wider terms of reference than NATO. But the United States has a military commitment to Israel of a kind that no European ally now has, and European suspicions that America has not abandoned the option of direct military intervention in either a fresh Arab-Israeli conflict or a showdown with OPEC states, have a foundation at least in American capabilities as well as in some official innuendoes. This means that the political machinery of NATO is becoming more important again, not only for planning negotiations with the Soviet Union but also for crisis management outside of Europe. As after the Suez crisis, so after the Yom Kippur War and the oil crisis in 1973, the allies swore at the Ottawa meeting of the NATO Council in June 1974 to mend their ways. But more than good intentions and the recognition of the NATO Council as an important diplomatic instrument may be required.

The political machinery of the Alliance and the use that is made of it thus have a direct bearing on the maintenance of European-American confidence. But NATO is also a system of contingent military planning and of central command in a crisis. Though the proposition that the Supreme Allied Commander in Europe must be an American has occasionally been questioned in the past (often by Americans), there is little disposition in Europe to suggest that he should be anyone but an American, not only by reason of the size and significance of the American military contribution to European stability, but also because of the exclusively American control over the release of nuclear weapons based in Europe. He is therefore a central figure in the spectrum of deterrence. But then, in order to maintain European respect for American military planning (and Supreme Headquarters is primarily run by American officers) and confidence in the judgment of the Supreme Commander, it is important to appoint an officer of great experience, such as Eisenhower, Norstad, Lemnitzer, or Goodpaster, rather than one such as General Haig, who has never held a senior military command.

Meanwhile a central problem is that NATO has no up-to-date and agreed set of general guidelines on how the Alliance or its Supreme Commander should act in various contingencies. An immense amount of effort was put into the drafting of the Harmel Report in 1967, which was intended to provide just such guidelines, both for the handling of contingencies in Europe itself and in areas such as the Middle East that might affect the interests or security of the Alliance. But a great deal has happened in the past eight years, including six years of an administration in Washington that has preferred autonomy to consensus, and it is felt in European capitals that a successor to the Harmel Report, covering contingencies that were not foreseeable or urgent then, is overdue.

This brings us to the second problem of the next decade, namely, whether in view of the capabilities of the Soviet and Warsaw Pact forces in central Europe and the costs of maintaining an effective countervailing force to them, there is scope for reorganizing the structure and reconsidering the size of the NATO forces, especially in Germany and the Low Countries. The shadow that Soviet military power casts across the normalization of East-West relations in Europe derives not so much from the very large amount of nuclear destruction that the Soviet Union could wreak upon the cities of Western Europe, but from the twenty Soviet divisions in East Germany (ten of them tank divisions), two tank divisions in Poland, and five divisions (two of them tank) in Czechoslovakia, supported by thirty East German, Czech, and Polish divisions and some 2,000 Soviet tactical aircraft on East European airfields. Behind this force stand the vast military resources of the Soviet Union, which include a total of 167 divisions, though many of them are skeleton and forty-five of them are now deployed in East Asia. This compares with some twenty-three divisions in central Europe of varying quality, equipment, and stocks.

It is true that Warsaw Pact divisions are about three-fifths the size of NATO ones, so that the balance of deployed manpower is less uneven than the figures for divisions suggest: 620,000 front-line NATO troops in the central area confront some 910,000 Warsaw Pact forces. It is also true historically that decisive invasions have generally been attained only by forces enjoying a superiority of about three to one. Manpower figures, however, do not tell the full story, and the troubling element is that, in the central area, Warsaw Pact forces have a superiority in tanks of nearly three to one and in aircraft of over two to one. The Warsaw Pact forces, moreover, are trained and their reinforcement system is structured for a quick and decisive battle, while the reinforcement capabilities of the NATO countries, though not negligible, would take longer to mobilize and deploy.[9]

This imbalance in the relative capabilities of each side to handle, not so much a general war, which would likely give rise to the use of strategic weapons, as a European crisis entailing a significant resort to, or threat of, force, has troubled students of the problem for some years. Warsaw Pact forces might be able to bring pressure to bear on a particular area before NATO forces could react. We are past, after all, the era of overwhelming American strategic superiority, when it could be assumed that a *pax atomica* covered the whole of Europe. At the very least such an imbalance undermines confidence, not only between the two alliances in Europe but between allies.

Various approaches to the problem have been suggested. One has been to advocate the greater use of reserves in order to free the regular forces in the central area for a more mobile role. Another has been to suggest that the American divisions in Europe, whose role is crucial by reason of the link they provide to strategic weapons, should be moved from Bavaria into the center of Germany and reorganized from five into six divisions of two brigades each, with the third brigade located in the United States but the equipment for it ready in Germany. A different approach is to argue that less effort should be put into mobilizing reserves, since the concept of a prolonged nonnuclear war is difficult to sustain, and more into enhancing the mobility and firepower of the forces already deployed in the central area.[10]

One reason why this problem has not been treated by governments with the seriousness it deserves is the sense of security provided by the existence of 7,000 American tactical nuclear weapons (TNWs) in the European theater since the early 1960s. But with the passage of time, however, such security is coming to be regarded as illusory. For one thing, the Soviet Union itself now has a large force of TNWs in central Europe, of the order of 3,500. For another, the prospect of an exchange of tactical nuclear weapons which did not escalate to higher levels is improbable, so that it is likely that both superpowers would be profoundly reluctant to permit their use. Third, their existence creates an illusion of strength that inhibits the NATO allies, in Europe especially, from considering the steps necessary to provide real flexibility for their strategic posture in central and southern Europe.[11]

A second reason why it has proved difficult to generate serious consideration of an overhaul of NATO strategy and forces has been the Conference on Mutual Force Reductions, which since its inception in January 1973 has tended to discourage interallied discussion for fear of jeopardizing the negotiations with the Warsaw Pact. However, it was clear by the spring of 1975 that these negotiations were stalled in respect of their original aim, namely, a reduction of superpower conventional forces. This was partly by reason of the disparity in American and Soviet military strength in central Europe, partly because the Soviet Union is as interested in a reduction of German as of American military strength in Europe. Moreover, so long as it still appeared possible that Senator Mansfield might successfully insist on a unilateral reduction of American forces in Europe, the American negotiating position was the weaker of the two.

It is possible, however, that the smoke of debate may now be starting to clear. The Soviet Union has made it perfectly plain in CSCE that it prefers the continued existence of two military alliances in Europe to a more radical revision of the structure of European security; the West does not dissent. What worries the NATO powers is the enormous Soviet tank and tactical air force in central Europe. And what has always worried the Soviet Union is the large number of nuclear weapons in Western Europe, especially as the aircraft and missiles that would carry them are for the most part in the hands of America's European allies, and the Soviet Union has no firm assurance that American control over the warheads and firing arrangements is foolproof. The East European countries are even more anxious on this score, for it is primarily against them that these weapons are targeted. In addition, there is rising concern everywhere that some terrorist group may hijack, steal, or even fabricate a nuclear weapon.

The Conference on Mutual Force Reductions (to which are now appended the words, "and Allied Measures") might be more profitable if it negotiated a trade-off of Soviet tanks and aircraft in central Europe for American tactical nuclear weapons. The proposition has immense difficulties. The Soviet Union must be persuaded that it does not need ten tank divisions as well as ten infantry divisions to maintain a Communist regime in East Germany. The negotiation could be fruitful only if the United States were to give it a high priority in its dealing with the Soviet Union. It would require careful explanation by the

United States to the more exposed NATO allies that in suggesting a reduction of its stock of tactical nuclear weapons in Europe, it was not in any sense "going home." It is not clear how much influence the East European countries can exert on Moscow to take such a proposition seriously. But it should be possible to convince the Soviet Union that only by a substantial reduction of offensive forces in central Europe can it achieve its own long-term objective, namely, that of preventing the Federal Republic becoming the dominant military power in Western Europe.

There is, in addition, a great deal of useful housecleaning that NATO could accomplish, independently of any agreement on a revised formula for negotiating first-stage force reductions with the Warsaw Pact. Its military command structure, for instance, dates from the period when communications were much less rapid and secure than they are today and when considerations of national prestige were more significant in eliciting contributions from the European allies. To give one instance, an order from the Supreme Commander must be filtered through five headquarters (three of them internationally staffed and therefore large consumers of manpower) before they reach a brigade commander in Germany.

The truth is that because so much else has been at stake in European-American and in East-West relations in recent years, a kind of intellectual inertia has overcome official attempts to modernize the strategy and force structure of the Alliance. But in a time of rapidly mounting equipment and manpower costs on both sides of the Atlantic, when the fourth Arab-Israeli war has shown that quite simple equipment can upset the offensive and defensive balance between tanks and infantry (or between ground forces and interceptors), a thorough overhaul of NATO's military force and equipment should not be delayed. I happen to believe that the most viable goal would be a modification of the present forward strategy, which is becoming brittle, by defense in depth: a combination of screening forces to identify a crisis and smaller regular forces than today across the main axes of communication, backed up by more powerful reserve formations than the European allies at present have available. Into such reorganization could be fitted a certain redeployment of American forces. But it is essential in terms of German confidence alone that neither the flexible-response strategy nor the forward strategy be abandoned, and since modification in any direction would take a number of years to implement, since much research is required, since there are many governments to convince, and since any change would require changes in equipment and even in training, the process cannot be started too early.

IV

Ten years ago modifications in NATO strategy emerged out of arguments among the Americans, the British, and the Germans (in the 1950s it had been the

Americans, the British, and the French). Now the problem is different, because the European allies, in helping evolve a NATO force structure that is not unduly onerous for the United States, must also ensure that it is not unduly onerous for themselves. Can the European allies, especially the core powers of the Community, develop sufficient identity of view to work out a set of proposals that would both stabilize the cost of the American contribution to European security and also make better use of the $35 billion a year that the European allies as a whole spend on defense?

In the present disarray of the Community the prospects do not look promising. Yet all its members (including the single neutral member, the Irish Republic) share a set of common assumptions: that a drastic reduction in the level of American force levels would have a serious effect on European security and would open up all kinds of temptations for the Soviet Union, possibly destroying the Community itself in the process; that such a reduction cannot be ruled out in the future unless there is evidence of European will to revise Alliance strategy and shoulder as large a proportion as possible of the common burden; that it is essential that this strategy should be one that permits Western political and military flexibility in a crisis (French views have quietly become aligned with NATO on this point); that the question of a European nuclear force is not a pressing one and would destroy any prospect of functional collaboration if it were set as an immediate objective.

Objectively the problem is simple to formulate. The institutional aspect is that the members of the Community, or the eleven European members of the Atlantic alliance, have no central body in which to argue and reconsider their views on defense questions. The planning function of Western European Union was absorbed by NATO in 1950. France has not been a member of NATO since 1966. The Euro-group of the ten European allies (of which France is not a member) can only harmonize the positions of defense ministries and not undertake original work of its own. So what is required is some form of European institution for the development of a common European conception on what is increasingly seen as a common problem. But assuming as a first step the foundation, say, of a European counterpart of the RAND Corporation, under the aegis of the new European Council (the triennial meeting of the nine heads of government) or the Council of Ministers, to formulate a coherent view on the medium-term security requirements of Europe, what should be the second step? To what specific tasks would a European defense organization of some sort address itself? Surely not to the resurrection of any counterpart of the old EDC plan or to the creation of a separate European operational force outside the integrated NATO command structure. That would make it hard for the United States to sustain its NATO commitment, while evoking the resistance of the smaller European allies.

Again to talk in terms of the ideal, the objective of a European defense system should be to maximize European defense resources and to create a certain capacity for joint European action. NATO still works to deter Soviet aggression in Europe. What works less and less well, is the attempt of eleven middle and small European powers to maintain balanced forces. There are two principal reasons for this: one is that in any national defense establishment, between 25 per cent and 40 per cent of expenditure goes to national overheads, recruiting, training establishments, research and development, logistics, administration. The second is that the unit cost of equipment is higher, the smaller the quantities in which it is ordered and the higher the national overheads in research and development that precede production (*Concorde* is the most haunting example of this). There is also the problem that the military call lack of inter-operability: the cost and military weakness incurred if the aircraft of one country cannot use the navigation or refueling system of another; or the fact that four kinds of main battle tank need more kinds of ammunition or spare parts, hence consume more manpower, than one or two.

In an important recent study prepared for the State Department, Thomas A. Callaghan has calculated that of the $36.6 billion the United States and its European allies spent in 1974 on research and procurement for conventional forces, as much as $5.5 billion may have been wasted by the development of competitive systems by different allies or by their failure to buy from one another.[12] He adds to this a similar figure for overlapping functions in the annual support costs of national forces through national logistic systems. If one accepts a figure of $17 billion as the cost to the United States of its NATO commitment (which includes not only its forces in Europe but those that would be committed there in an emergency) and adds this to the $35 billion spent annually by the European allies in defense, this means that about one dollar in five could have been saved by a more rational approach to defense procurement and by sharing the costs of European security. This figure has naturally drawn fire, but the likelihood that it represents a correct order of magnitude has been demonstrated by the increased interest now being shown in the United States and in Europe in "a two-way street" in armaments, or in treating the Atlantic alliance as a single market in matters of defense procurement. Since the problem of the eurodollar has been replaced by that of the petrodollar, since inflation is a problem that affects both sides of the Atlantic, the older American policy of trying to offset the costs of its European security commitment by demanding that Europe purchase large amounts of American arms will have to be replaced by a greater emphasis on mutual trade and by a policy of buying in the cheapest market. In 1973 the United States bought only $150 millions worth of equipment from Europe—one tenth of what it sold.

The Callaghan study also points to the historical ineffectiveness of "military cooperation without trade," that is, to the inability of NATO in the 1950s and 1960s to lay down requirements which all the member governments would follow in their procurement decisions. It points also to the relative failure of attempts to organize collaborative procurement around a single project, such as a

German-American tank, or the German-British-Italian multirole combat aircraft, since split research and production inevitably raises the cost of the project.

The study further draws attention to the fact that the most successful relationship in this field has been that between the United States and Canada. Ever since the early days of the Second World War these two countries have regularly set goals by value for the amount of defense material they will buy from each other, unhindered by tariff or nontariff barriers. The study suggests that an analogous arrangement could be developed between the United States and Western Europe, though Callaghan insists, rightly in my view, that this would only work if the Pentagon could negotiate with a single Europe entity, some kind of European Defense Procurement Agency.

But any effort to make better use of Europe's limited defense resources, or to control military inflation by operating a single trans-Atlantic market for procurement, must take account of several facts. The first is that the rationalization of European defense procurement will make little headway without parallel progress on a common industrial policy within the Community. This applies particularly to those industries that are most closely linked to defense: aerospace, engineering, and shipbuilding. As long as the reconciliation of government procurement as a whole remains outside the purview of the Commission, little progress can be made on the reorganization of the European high-technology industries; and as long as the European allies are incapable of laying down common specifications for equipment, a European Defense Procurement Agency would have difficulty achieving significant economies or acting as the European end of a "two-way street." Progress in making better use of Europe's limited defense resources or in making Europe the technological partner of the United States is inseparable from progress in the development of the Community. Failure to make progress also carries the risk that NATO governments, especially those of the United States, France, and Britain, will encourage their high-technology industries to sell arms outside the trans-Atlantic market, for instance to the Middle East.

There is no reason, moreover, why the attempt to widen the basis of European defense procurement and to promote industrial cooperation within the Community need carry any anti-American overtones. The days of fulmination about le défi américain are largely a thing of the past. The subsidiaries of the great American multinational corporations are firmly established in Europe, and the high level of American investment there is increasingly seen as an important aspect of the American political commitment to Europe. As long as these American companies in Europe were prepared to accept the direction of the Commission and to cooperate with a defense procurement agency, much of European defense production, especially in high technology, could in fact be assigned to consortia in which they would play a significant part.

A second consideration is that if the costs of manpower and equipment continue to rise as they have over the past decade—and this is the only assumption one can make at present—the economies and increased efficiency of joint procurement and a common logistics system may not be sufficient to ensure that the Alliance has adequate resources to react flexibly in an emergency. So the European allies may have to move from coordination to specialization, to abandon the effort to maintain, in greater or lesser degree, a full spectrum of ground, sea, and air forces in each country, and instead assign to each a part of the common task, according to its location and its capabilities. This posits a degree of confidence among the European states and a sense of the indissolubility of their destinies that is inseparable from the notion of political union. Thus we are back to the situation noted in other fields, that in defense too Europe is reaching the end of the strategy of indirect approach to political union. If the Community wishes to retain American confidence and a viable Atlantic Alliance in the foreseeable future, as well as a reasonable degree of control over its own external environment, it must face the task of building institutions that would have most of the characteristics of political union.

European governments will face this fact with reluctance, partly because of a popular sense, which has deep historical roots, that defense and control of armed forces lie closer to the heart of what remains of sovereignty or national autonomy than any other aspect of policy. This may be illogical, since between 1969 and 1973 they were prepared to commit themselves to monetary union, which, if it had proved attainable, would have locked them in an embrace so intimate that the level of employment in Sicily would have affected the level of prices in Scotland; but logic plays only a limited part in the argument. The question has also been confused in recent years by conflicting views about what the aims of European defense cooperation should be—to create a politically independent Europe, or to reduce the waste of resources that results from trying to handle the problem of European defense and security by national collaboration only. It is my own impression that the onset of severe inflation and the urgent need to stabilize or reduce government expenditure which it has brought in its train have for the time being made the latter a more compelling argument in Europe. This is certainly true of military leaders in Europe, who now wish, as few did in the 1960s, that their political masters had the courage to embark on the construction of effective systems of functional cooperation. They fear that otherwise the NATO system may become so eroded as to become a façade, and they will be expected to sustain obligations and execute a strategy for which they know they do not have the means.

Military men are not, however, very influential in West European societies. There may be little progress until European political leaders and their constituents accept the fact that progress towards European economic and political union is the only method, not only of meeting short-term problems, but of endowing both Europe and the United States with any choice over the longer-term future. If, in ten or twenty years time, the United States was forced, for instance, by external or internal circumstances markedly to reduce its

European commitments, it might be unable to do so if European-American relationships were still largely multilateral and the European countries were still hanging on to America's skirts.

This question has been bedeviled by the existence of the two European nuclear forces. Some feel that there is no point in discussing the evolution of Europe into a political union unless and until European, American, and Soviet attitudes to a single European nuclear force have been resolved. But as I have tried to suggest earlier, nuclear collaboration can just as well be only the final step in political and economic union, pending the development of strong European institutions and habits of intimate cooperation. It is an issue that could be left in abeyance during many years of more humdrum construction. Unfortunately, as Michel Tatu has pointed out,[13] just as any assumption about European unification that is based on independence from the United States tends to divide the Europeans, so conceptions based on a continuing American involvement tend to paralyze European action. What may resolve this dichotomy, however, is the dawning realization of European governments that the one course that might eventually precipitate serious American force reductions in Europe, would be for Europeans continually to discuss the need for a European defense identity (thus making clear their anxiety about the status quo) while doing nothing about it.

Any consideration of the possibilities of stabilizing the cost of defense and deterrence in Europe, whether by strengthening the functional capabilities of the Community or by negotiating a less onerous and risky balance of power in central Europe with the Soviet Union, or both, demands some estimate of the future of French policy. So far, there are no clear indications from Paris as to what the future may hold. France has been absent from the negotiations on Mutual Force Reductions, and President Giscard has made only marginal changes in French defense policy. No one expects that France will return as a penitent son to NATO. On the other hand, the degree of French cooperation in NATO plans and exercises is increasing. For it is acknowledged in Paris that the growing strength of the Soviet Union, both as a global and as a European military power, means that the stability of the European balance must be taken seriously, while inflation means that without close coordination of the policies of the West European powers, they risk a process of self-disarmament to which there need be no counterpart in the Warsaw Pact.

But it was from anger at American didacticism and from distrust of American motives that de Gaulle took France out of NATO in the first place, and it is the United States, of all the Atlantic powers, which has the longest agenda of questions to discuss and reconcile with France. There has been some compromise on monetary issues; and there need not be a battle to the death between the United States and the Community, goaded by France, in the impending trade negotiations. But if France and the United States both compete for Arab good will to solve their hunger for petrodollars by rampant policies of arms sales, they will defeat each other's objectives and possibly send the Middle East up in flames. By the same token, France could defeat a long-standing American policy of restraining nuclear proliferation, to which the rest of the Alliance subscribes, if such deals as the recent proposal to sell a French uranium separation plant to Iran under purely bilateral safeguards were to mature. A critical choice for Americans, therefore, is how much emphasis to place on restoring good diplomatic relations with France; until the parameters of Franco-American discord and collaboration are clearer, the other European powers will be hesitant in pursuing economic and political union with France.

V

This dialogue may have to be accelerated, for the United States may have to devolve some political initiative to the Nine by reason of the rising instability of South and Southeast Europe and the relationship between Middle Eastern problems and European security. It is not only the Yom Kippur War and its attendant European-American recriminations or the Cyprus crisis of July 1974 which has demonstrated that the relative stability of East-West relations in central and northern Europe no longer applies to the Mediterranean; nor is the stability of the Mediterranean solely a NATO problem. The struggle by Rumania to assert its autonomy within COMECON; the Warsaw Pact contention of and obscure Soviet demands for military transit rights through Rumania; and the uncertain future of Yugoslavia as a state and of its relations to the rest of Europe after Tito's death—all of these trouble the Soviet perception of its position in Europe. But NATO's problems are more specific. Twenty-five years of common membership in the Atlantic alliance have not healed the wounds of the Greco-Turkish war of 1921, and the eruption of oil in the Aegean suggests that relations between Ankara and Athens will remain tense, even though Turkey, by a crass use of force, has now asserted its dominance in Cyprus. Greece may yet follow France out of NATO, and its political future also is uncertain. Italy is economically weak and politically unstable. Portugal is in a condition of political anarchy.

The prospect of a serious crisis, whether in relations between one of the superpowers and an ally or between the two alliances, seems to be increasing rather than diminishing in this area. It is not necessarily true any longer that "when the Balkans sneeze, Europe catches a cold," and no South European crisis or confrontation need necessarily contain the seeds of World War III, for all the states of both alliances have become more prudent in the use or threat of force than they were in July 1914. The peninsulas that point southward into the Mediterranean do not, moreover, lead into the heartland of Western Europe. Judging from the behavior of the Soviet Union in the Cyprus crisis, it has an interest in cultivating rather than in threatening Turkey as it used to, and it is sufficiently aware of the connection between West European and East European ideological struggles to have no great interest in exploiting the rising power of the Italian Communist party.

The real problem is that American influence in southern Europe has, for a variety of reasons, diminished markedly, while the economic and political interests of the Community in Greece and Turkey have risen. Yet the United States, by reason of its increasing commitment to Israel, has over recent years come to regard the Mediterranean as an increasingly crucial line of communication. The problem has been made more difficult by the steady withdrawal of British military power from the Mediterranean and the failure of Franco-American entente, so that, in terms of the actual deployment of force, the Mediterranean is largely an American sea despite the presence of a Soviet naval squadron at its eastern end. Meanwhile ties of trade and labor migration between the West European powers and the Mediterranean and Middle Eastern countries are growing stronger.

A good example of the confusion that Mediterranean problems can create in European-American relations is the Cyprus crisis of July 1974. Britain has sovereign base areas on the island that relate to it by nominal commitment to CENTO (the Central Treaty Organization) and were retained when Cyprus became independent fifteen years ago. The tacit assumption then was that, if necessary, Britain would forestall Greek or Turkish intervention in Cypriot affairs. In the event, British ground forces on the island proved too small to deter Turkish intervention and British diplomacy moved too slowly. Meanwhile the United States, preoccupied with other problems, was still committed to the regime of the Greek colonels and hence unwilling to intervene against Turkey, where she has important strategic installations. The German government, which a decade ago would have been horrified at any involvement in Mediterranean politics but has long had considerable influence in Ankara, offered to use its good offices to restrain Turkish action, yet got no support from the United States. After this demonstration of the fact that the United States would neither act nor encourage its major European allies to act, Turkey invaded Cyprus.

There is another aspect of the problem, namely, that the United States is, or has been, dependent on European bases for the prosecution of a Middle Eastern policy on which it does not consult its European allies and which they do not necessarily support. The 1973 war led to the first public breach in German-American relations and an overt threat by Mr. Schlesinger to move American military equipment out of Germany, as well as to bitter American recriminations that its European allies had deserted it in its hour of need. The United States has temporarily decided to diminish its dependence on European NATO bases by relying on the use of tanker aircraft based in Spain to refuel fighter bombers and transport aircraft en route to Israel in the event of a fifth Middle Eastern war. But this is both financially and politically costly, for Spain exacts a higher and higher price for base rights every few years.

The problems that Mediterranean crises create in European-American relations and may well create in East-West relations can not, in my view, be solved
by prescriptions of increased consultation in the Atlantic Alliance, for this leads
only to confusion and inaction. The chances of preventing the Mediterranean
from seriously destabilizing the politics of Europe and the Atlantic seem to me
to lie down two other avenues. The first is to recognize that the Community has
as great a stake in preventing political chaos there, and perhaps a better prospect
of doing so, than the United States. Even the Communist party recognizes the
great value of Community membership to Italy. Greece and Turkey are associate
members of it and will eventually be full members. It has a network of trade
agreements with the rest of the littoral states (though those with the Maghreb
countries are being renegotiated) including both Israel and the Arab states.
Britain and France have long-standing ties with Greece; Britain and Germany,
with Turkey. It is true that none of the Community powers have military or
naval forces in the Mediterranean of a scale that would enable them to intervene
if there were a breakdown of civil order or an armed conflict in the East
Mediterranean, but this situation could be redressed if greater European
responsibilities were given an agreed alliance priority. Besides, the presence of
the Sixth Fleet in the Mediterranean no longer seems to give the United States
decisive leverage there, nor is NATO useful as a crisis management mechanism
for the area as it was in the 1960s. The United States would do better to expect
the Community members of NATO to bear the prime responsibility for
developing the kind of economic and social cooperation with the littoral states,
or for deploying the kind of diplomatic influence, that will reduce the risks of
internal or external conflict. It might even be desirable for them to take
responsibility for military aid to Turkey, since American aid is now blocked by
congressional hostility inspired by the Greek lobby there. Hence the significance
for East-West stability of the embryo political institutions of the Nine. Such a
devolution of initiative to the European powers is reconcilable with a particular
American responsibility for the security of Israel.

The other avenue of promise is to recognize the important role that the
United Nations has consistently played in keeping the peace in the East
Mediterranean area. The UN has come once again to the forefront of world
politics with Henry Kissinger's warning in July 1975 to the developing world as a
whole that harassing tactics in the General Assembly against the industrial
powers, let alone any attempt to drive out Israel, might force the United States
to reconsider its participation in the Assembly. I think he was right to do this,
though American neglect and implied contempt for the United Nations over
recent years have helped create the problem that he now confronts. Two days
later the European Council issued an almost equally strong statement of its
intention to promote respect for the Charter and for the rights of member states
(by which it explicitly meant Israel).

But defending the Charter from abuse is one thing; actively encouraging the secretary general to sustain a central role for UN observation and peace-keeping forces in this particular area is something different. For one thing these are functions of the Security Council and not of the General Assembly. Interestingly enough, a great many of the earlier Soviet objections to these functions of the United Nations seem to be disappearing, as are those of France. And it is not difficult to see the reasons why the major powers should be prepared to support the UN in this particular part of the world. It is the area with which it has had the closest association and the longest experience. The alliances—NATO for certain, possibly the Warsaw Pact as well—are losing their effectiveness as mechanisms for the restraint or solution of interallied conflict.

It has proved necessary to revive the UN's role on the borders of Israel, this time with Israel's concurrence. It is not difficult to envisage situations in which UN diplomacy or forces might be more readily accepted and more effective than any form of allied intervention: in forestalling a fresh debacle in Greco-Turkish relations; in helping make a confederal state in Cyprus viable; in preventing a repetition of the situation of forty years ago if Franco's demise should lead to civil war in Spain and tempt outside powers to intervene; even in containing some form of civil conflict or crisis in Yugoslavia that the Soviet Union, anxious about détente, really wanted to stay out of. Now that Germany, both Germanies, are members of the United Nations, the idea that it should have no role in European security needs reexamination. But what the UN lacks, for the most part, is the means, since it owns no real estate or bases and therefore has to improvise in every new situation. This suggests a more imaginative approach to the reinforcement of stability in southern Europe and the Middle East: the United States, instead of persuading the British that they must stay in Cyprus, might encourage the transfer of the British sovereign base areas, which have lost their original strategic function, to the jurisdiction of the UN. This would not only enhance the UN's effectiveness in the area and the speed with which it could react to a particular situation, but also make clear beyond doubt that the great powers continue to regard the UN as a central instrument for the restraint of conflict.

Let me end discussion of this aspect of the problem with a brief mention of Portugal. Portugal is not part of Western Europe in the sense that even Spain may be, and it was included in the Atlantic Alliance as what the position papers of 1948 called a "stepping stone country." Two situations may arise there in the conflict between the new Socialist or democratic parties and the Marxist military and political forces. One is that Portugal may leave the Atlantic Alliance, or NATO, or both and become a neutral state. This would be a setback for European security, since it would derange plans for major American reinforcement of Germany in the event of a serious crisis in central Europe. But, especially with French cooperation, new bases could be developed east of the Iberian peninsula. But if a Portuguese government were to invite Soviet use of the Azores and if the Soviet Union were to respond (which is less likely), then a crisis of major proportions in superpower relation must ensue if the Atlantic Alliance is still to be regarded as strategically significant. It is a sense of the risk of this that may deter any such Soviet action.

VI

One of the most haunting questions about the whole future of European security concerns the domestic authority of governments, largely because it is not susceptible of exact diagnosis or to policy prescriptions. There are two questions here. First, will social change and the increasing self-consciousness of ethnic and religious minorities lead to domestic unrest that will weaken the Alliance, while creating situations in which one country can offer only marginal assistance to another? Second, if, as many people feel in their bones, the authority of the executive arm of government is declining in democratic states and if, as I have argued, détente is reversible, do governments possess the power to demand greater sacrifices or heavier defense obligations from their peoples in darker international weather?

The importance of the first aspect can be overstressed. It is true that in Belgium relations between Walloons and Flemings have deteriorated, that Breton nationalism has become more articulate, that there are regional discontents in Italy, and that Britain presents less the appearance of a United Kingdom than at any time in the past half-century. This means that these governments may be more introverted in their preoccupations, and there may be violence. But this introversion is unlikely to affect the external perspectives and commitments of governments. Even in Northern Ireland, part of an island where violence has been endemic for over a century, the amount of death and shooting arising from terrorist activity has declined steeply since 1972, thanks to the commitment of no more than a small proportion of the British army (eighteen battalions at its peak, now thirteen battalions). A new political relationship between the Catholics and the Protestant majority, and of the province to the rest of the United Kingdom and to the Republic of Ireland, will be essential. But both communities in Northern Ireland are sick of violence; the American money and the Libyan arms are drying up; and the organization of terrorism has passed from experienced hands, since many of them have been convicted of criminal offenses, to those of young and less experienced men. A great deal remains to be done by the government at Westminster to ensure that terrorism does not again become politically effective or legitimate, to elicit consent to more equitable forms of local government than simple majority rule has been in Northern Ireland, and to sustain British public confidence that the task is worth completing. But Ulster is not Britain's Vietnam.

On the credit side, moreover, racial tension is less serious in the United States than a few years ago. The wild, unhappy generation in the universities throughout the West of the late 1960s has been replaced by a more sober one. Meanwhile the Soviet Union, interested as it is in détente on the one hand and the slow attrition of Western Europe rather than its collapse into violence, does little to encourage Communist parties to seek power in the West.

The second aspect of the question, the ability of governments to face their electorates with unpleasant choices, is simply not amenable to speculation. If Ford, Giscard, Wilson, and others seem barely adequate to their responsibilities, if Helmut Schmidt seems to be losing his domestic base, it is worth recalling that nineteen or twenty years ago the same was said of Guy Mollet, Eden, and Eisenhower, while Adenauer also seemed to be growing weaker. Yet in the space of a few years the former group gave way to the powerful and popular figures of Kennedy, de Gaulle, and Macmillan, while Adenauer's strength regenerated. What is certain, however, is that, in order to elicit sacrifices from the young, today's leadership will have to offer more explicit and cogent evidence of peril than was necessary for the generation that had grown up during the Second World War and the Korean War.

VII

I have mentioned a number of specific propositions which American policy must confront: the conversion of MFR into a serious arms control negotiation on European security, a better use of the existing Alliance institutions, encouragement of European functional cooperation, a closer dialogue with France, a more imaginative approach to the problems of Mediterranean security. But such considerations must be set in a wider framework. The international system is becoming more plural in character for several reasons: the bonds of intimacy between Europe and the United States, which were partly a product of the wartime and cold war years, are tending to slacken; new powers with a widening range of action are emerging in both the developing and the developed world. One of the beneficiaries of this increasing diversity is undoubtedly the Soviet Union, which despite its minority and other domestic problems, remains a huge unitary state and would not resist the opportunity to become the arbiter of local balances and conflicts if this role were offered to it (even though it did play a secondary role in the aftermath of the 1973 Middle Eastern crisis). The United States has quite legitimate reasons for exploring new forms of relationship with the Soviet Union; so too have Western European powers. But the concept of the central balance remains a valid one.

If this concept were discarded as an irrelevant inheritance from the past, if the United States were to claim the right to complete autonomy in its relations with its fellow superpower, then the European Community would be faced with the alternatives, not of becoming a superstate, which is beyond its power at this stage, but of either fragmenting, as its component countries made different responses to the proponderance of Soviet power on their own continent, or else of remaining merely a trading system on the periphery of an enlarged Soviet sphere of influence. We should then have a polycentric world that was not in fact based on a balance of power and had none of the stabilizing factors found in earlier multiple balances. I think this fact is clearly perceived in all the component parts of the Western system. But the right conclusion is not necessarily drawn from it, namely, that the Western system, building on the foundations of alliance, is reacquiring the characteristics of a coalition.

I say re-acquiring, because in the early days of the Atlantic Alliance and even to a certain extent of the Japanese alliance, it was regarded by all concerned as a coalition of reciprocal advantages. At that time the United States was as dependent on her European or Japanese allies for bases, and as dependent on Canada for early warning, as they were on her for the strategic support to exercise a collective strategy of deterrence. Then for a while, broadly from 1957 until the early part of this decade, the element of reciprocity became subordinated in the dominance of the United States at almost every level of power. Now we are returning to a situation of reciprocal dependence; the calculus of deterrence may have changed, but new forms of interdependence have emerged. The real challenge to American statecraft is to encourage a devolution of such responsibilities to the Community and to Japan as they are able to exercise effectively and without jeopardizing the benefits that accrue both to the United States and to its allies from the existence of a network of economic and political relationships that span two thirds of the Northern Hemisphere.

Notes

1. Statement before the Senate Foreign Relations Committee, September 19, 1974.

2. Graf Wolf von Baudissin, "The Changes in the Balance of Power," mimeo ms.; Oxford International Summer School, July 1974.

3. Annual Defense Department Report, FY'75, pp. 15-16.

4. Cf. Morris Janowitz, *The United States Forces and the Zero Draft* ["Adelphi Papers," No. 94] (London: International Institute for Strategic Studies, 1973).

5. Mr. Roy Mason, Secretary of State for Defence, in the House of Commons, December 3, 1974.

6. Annual Defense Department Report, FY'75, p. 9.

7. Ibid., p. 41.

8. In "On Difference," the fourth of his 1974 BBC Reith lectures, *The Listener*, December 5, 1974.

9. The subject is carefully explored in Richard Lawrence and Jeffrey Record, *U.S. Force Structure in NATO: An Alternative* (Washington: Brookings,

1974); and *The Military Balance 1974-1975* (London: International Institute for Strategic Studies, 1974).

10. For these three approaches, see Kenneth Hunt, *The Alliance and Europe: Part II: Defence with Fewer Men* ["Adelphi Papers," No. 98] (London: I.I.S.S., 1974); Lawrence and Record, *U.S. Force Structure*; Steven Canby, "The Wasteful Ways of NATO," *Foreign Policy*, Autumn 1972.

11. The arguments are well set out in Jeffrey Record, *U.S. Nuclear Weapons in Europe* (Washington: Brookings, 1974).

12. Thomas A. Callaghan, Jr., *U.S./European Economic Cooperation in Military and Civilian Technology* (Arlington, Va.: Ex-Im Tech. Inc., n.d.).

13. Michel Tatu, "The Devolution of Power: A Dream?" *Foreign Affairs* 53, 4 (July 1975): 668-82.

X

Trade and Monetary Relations Between the United States and Western Europe

Richard N. Cooper

In the mid-seventies it became increasingly common to ask such questions as whether there would be another Great Depression, or whether Italy would endure in anything like its present political and economic form, or whether the European Community would survive as an entity, or even whether modern democracy would survive the ravages of inflation in Western countries. These are profound and disturbing questions, far overshadowing the relatively technical problems and disagreements of the sixties and early seventies.

Europe in the mid-seventies is in a state of malaise. The malaise comes from several diverse but mutually reinforcing sources. First, the cumulative corrosive power of American involvement in Vietnam followed by the revelations of Watergate have greatly reduced European confidence in the United States as the leading Western democracy. Second, United States actions (for example, in unilaterally imposing a 10 per cent import surcharge in 1971 and in unilaterally embargoing exports of soybeans in 1973) and a new personal style of diplomacy (especially Secretary of State Kissinger's penchant for secrecy and surprise) have so reduced European trust in the United States that Europeans have become skeptical of new American initiatives and proposals and are no longer willing to examine them at face value.

Third, accelerating inflation has reopened social conflicts within Europe that were muted during nearly two decades of rapid economic growth. With unexpectedly rapid increases in prices, many segments of the public have perceived others to be gaining at their expense, and this perception has triggered attempts by all organized sectors—workers, farmers, pensioners, et al.—to catch up and to keep up with the inflation. Fourth, the oil embargo of late 1973, followed by a quadrupling of oil prices, has brought home to Europeans their acute dependence on the rest of the world for a vital material and accentuated a sense of loss of control over their own destiny. Fifth, failure of the ill-conceived experiment in monetary unification has resulted in a loss of momentum toward a united Europe and left the European Community adrift, apart from relatively low-level (but often important) technical agreements.

A further source of malaise that has not received sufficient attention is the increasing assertiveness of less-developed countries—often former European colonies—in the world arena. This combines with a European wish, deriving partly from a desire to reestablish European influence on the world scene, to cater to developing countries in a variety of ways. One result is an attempt to leave to the United States the hard line against demands pressed by developing countries in such diverse areas as tariff discrimination, international monetary reform, management of the oceans, and international commodity arrangements. There remain wide differences of opinion in each of these areas within Europe, but one can observe a general tendency for Europeans, in their search both for economic security and for a new role in foreign affairs, to be especially solicitous of less developed countries, even when those countries' demands run against traditional European interests or positions.

Perhaps the central problem of Europe is that Europeans do not know where it is going. Not only is there no consensus among Europeans on the future of Europe, even the consensus *within* several European countries—Britain, Italy, the Netherlands—seems to have diminished markedly. These difficulties are related to the thawing of the cold war and the apparent easing of external threats to Europe's security, which were of course a powerful unifying influence. "Le défi américain" was never a satisfactory substitute, despite General de Gaulle's attempts to make it one, and even that seems to have waned with subsequent United States economic difficulties.

But the loss of consensus also reflects increasing questioning of traditional institutions, questioning brought about by continued postwar prosperity, by the inevitable dilution of memories of the trauma of the Second World War, and more recently by rapid inflation, which casts a shadow of uncertainty across arrangements formerly taken for granted. Moreover, in several European countries, notably Britain and Italy, trade unions have come to play an increasingly assertive role in determining national economic policies and developments without, however, taking formal responsibility for national economic management.

Europe is thus concerned simultaneously with deep soul-searching and with efforts to cope with day-to-day exigencies. Under the circumstances, there are relatively few "critical choices" that the United States faces in its economic relations with Europe. The major issues of concern to Europe are beyond American determination or even influence, and where some influence can be exerted, it arises largely from the success of policies such as domestic economic stabilization, which the United States should be undertaking for reasons other than its relations with Europe.

United States-European relations are neither especially good nor especially bad in the mid-seventies. They remain on the whole cordial, but with an air of indifference. Whereas a few years ago there were tense disagreements between Europe and the United States on trade practices and on the international monetary system, these disagreements have been partly resolved, partly rendered obsolete by ensuing events, and partly overshadowed by the twin problems of worldwide inflation and worldwide recession. Apart from petroleum, trade issues have receded into a position of tertiary importance, while long-range international monetary questions have become secondary. Inflation and stagnation and energy are now in the limelight. Subsequent sections will take up each of these topics.

Inflation and Stagnation

Increases in the cost of living in European countries in 1974 ranged from 6 to 24 per cent, all much above those experienced only a few years before (see Table X-1). Observers disagree on apportioning responsibility for this acceleration of price increases among (1) excessive domestic credit expansion, which took place in all countries; (2) excessively rapid expansion of the American economy in 1966-68 and again in 1972-73, leading to large deficits in the United States balance of international payments; (3) excessive wage claims by organized labor in many industrial countries, especially Britain and Italy; and (4) important

Table X-1
Increases in Consumer Prices, 1965-1974
(per cent, annual rates)

	1965-69	1970-72	1973[a]	1974[a]
United States	4.3	4.5	8.8	12.2
Canada	4.1	3.6	9.1	12.4
Japan	5.2	6.1	17.2	21.5
Belgium	3.4	4.6	7.9	15.7
France	4.3	5.8	8.4	15.2
Germany (F.G.)	2.1	4.7	7.8	5.9
Italy	2.6	5.1	12.6	24.5
Netherlands	4.7	6.3	8.2	10.9
Sweden	3.7	7.0	8.0	11.1
Switzerland	3.1	5.6	11.9	7.5
United Kingdom	4.2	7.6	10.6	19.2

[a]December to December

Source: IMF, *International Financial Statistics.*

natural shortages of foodstuffs and contrived shortages of oil, which drove up sharply the prices of those goods and of goods closely dependent on them, such as fertilizers and petrochemicals.

While all of these factors contributed to inflation, there seems little doubt that the major impetus to the world inflation of the early seventies was excessive expansion in the United States in 1966-68, associated with the military build-up during the Vietnam War and the failure of the United States administration, until July 1968, to use restrictive fiscal policy to combat the excess demand. The effects of the boom on the rest of the world were at first welcome, being reflected in strong export orders for many countries, including many developing countries, and coming especially, as it did, when Britain and then Germany were undergoing a period of economic slowdown. The American trade position deteriorated steadily, from a trade surplus of $5.0 billion in 1965 to a surplus of only $0.6 billion in 1969. Capital outflows, however, continued unabated until the very tight monetary policy of 1969 induced some restraint and indeed attracted large amounts of foreign capital from abroad, resulting in a decline in official reserves in the rest of the world for the first time in many years. Then, when United States monetary policy was relaxed in 1970, the full magnitude of the payments deficit was revealed: nearly $10 billion, followed by an even larger deficit (which was augmented by extensive speculation against the dollar) in 1971. These large deficits resulted in domestic monetary expansion in many countries, because of their commitment to a fixed exchange rate between their currencies and the dollar. But domestic credit expansion in most countries exceeded what could be explained by payments surpluses alone, so there was some domestic contribution to inflation as well.

Moreover, once inflation gets started in modern industrial societies, whatever its origins, it tends to take on a momentum of its own. Those elements of the population that have found their incomes eroded by inflation, or even their expected increase in income, will take steps through industrial action or through legislated action to restore their position. Wage earners in particular will press their employers for larger increases in nominal wages, to "catch up" and keep up with the increases in prices. This process confronts the economic authorities with a serious dilemma, for if in the face of these increases in nominal wages they hold growth in monetary demand steady, they will create unemployment at the higher nominal wages; while if they step up the pace of monetary demand to avoid the unemployment, they will in effect validate the higher wages and foster the higher rate of inflation. There is little question that the monetary authorities *can* stop inflation by maintaining a sufficiently tight rein on monetary expansion. The disagreement is over how rapidly economies will adjust to the restraint—that is, how much unemployment must be endured, and for how long—and whether the benefits of slowing the rise in prices are worth the cost.

In late 1973 a number of countries—notably the United States, Germany, and Japan—adopted policies of economic contraction in order to reduce inflation. By so doing they raised anxieties in close trading partners such as Denmark and Italy and Korea that *their* already difficult economic problems would be worsened by a strong contraction of their export markets. As countries individually pursued their anti-inflation policies without taking into account the consequences for other countries, the world was driven inexorably into recession by late 1974, the worst since the Second World War. Recorded unemployment in 1975 reached a million persons each in Britain, France, Italy, and even Japan (with its system of so-called lifetime employment), and it exceeded eight million persons in the United States.

Economic conditions became as bad as they did because of the sharp increase in petroleum prices in early 1974, which simultaneously gave a fillip to world inflation, reduced purchasing power in all oil-consuming countries, and created a substantial balance-of-payments problem for many oil-consuming countries. Purchasing power was reduced because, given the strong dependence on oil by all industrial countries, the fourfold increase in oil prices required an almost proportionate increase in payments for oil, leaving less income available for purchases of other goods and services. While the oil-exporting countries had their purchasing power increased by the same amount, that increase could not be translated quickly into demand for goods and services. The net contractive impact of the increase in oil prices was far greater than most national forecasters and government policymakers foresaw, and propelled what had been a deliberate policy of economic contraction in several countries into a serious worldwide recession that threatened to get out of hand.

The increase in oil prices also aggravated the problem of world inflation, making it more difficult for countries to reduce the increase in prices through restriction of aggregate demand; or, to put the same point another way, costlier oil made it necessary to impose tighter restrictions in order to achieve the same slowdown in price increases.

These developments cast a pall over financial markets everywhere, and the collapse of the international eurocurrency market, which had grown to $200 billion from virtually nothing in the early sixties, was perceived to be a real possibility, even if not yet probable.

In these difficult circumstances no single solution was available, and while there was general appreciation that collective actions were preferable to individual ones, the absence of a clear world solution in the presence of strong public demands for action inclined governments to go their several ways. Both social preferences and the behavioral responses to given policy actions vary substantially from country to country, so that no common solution is likely to be appropriate even if available. Policies should be closely coordinated among countries in the sense that each country should be carefully informed about what other countries are doing and should take that information into account in framing its own actions, but they should not be coordinated in the sense of making them all the same. Part of the problem in 1973-74 was that leading countries did not allow adequately for the fact that other leading countries were also undertaking policies of contraction, so the worldwide contraction was greater than many policymakers either anticipated or desired.

It is often said that inflation tears the social fabric. It would be more correct to say that unexpected and unanticipated inflation tears the social fabric. If inflation is expected and is anticipated, in the sense that members of the public take adequate steps to protect themselves from its effects, then the social impact will be much diminished. Besides, high unemployment also tears the social fabric, in some countries perhaps even more than inflation. So alleged damage to the social fabric does not dictate a policy of reducing inflation at any cost: the cure may be worse than the disease.

Policy for restraining inflation without generating unemployment of labor and capital can be made easier if a country can generate increases in real income and agree on some "social contract" or incomes policy for sharing these gains, thereby avoiding the inflationary scramble for higher real incomes through administered or negotiated increases in nominal incomes. Skepticism about whether incomes policies can be made to work is beside the point; *if* they can be made to work during a period in which the authorities are trying to reduce the rate of inflation, they cost that much less. Policies to reduce inflation are like investment: they entail present costs for the sake of future benefits. Any steps that can be taken to reduce the present costs make the policy more attractive as an investment.

If the mutual distrust between labor, business, and government—or among segments of labor—is such that an incomes policy cannot be made to work, then of course the country confronts a more difficult trade-off between inflation and unemployment, at least in the short run, than if some sort of general agreement on a slowdown of increases in wages and prices could be reached.

It is an extraordinary fact, if our measurements can be trusted, that in 1973 and 1974 it was only in the United States among leading industrial countries that the real incomes of wage earners employed in manufacturing activities actually fell. In all other countries real wages rose despite the substantial increases in oil prices and, to a lesser extent (because of insulation by agricultural support programs), of food prices. Since these price increases were external to the manufacturing sector, and in the case of oil external to the oil-importing countries, it meant that the real value of profits and rental incomes declined substantially. A problem for the future will be to restore these incomes in order to promote investment, or to find new, substitute sources for the investment that has sustained industrial economies so well during the past two decades.

Germany and Japan in 1975 each had some success in slowing the increase in wages, in each case on the explicit understanding that price increases would also be substantially moderated. Italy and Britain, by contrast, enjoyed no such success. And even in Germany and Japan wage increases were higher than could be supported by increases in national productivity, so some wage inflation remains in both of those economies, though less than in most other industrial countries.

Given the dramatic and special character of the increases in prices of food (on the world market) and oil, it was to be expected that the rate of price increase in 1975 would be substantially lower than that in 1974. Nonetheless, in the more fundamental sense of rising factor costs, inflation in most industrial countries actually accelerated in 1975, leaving a strong inflationary legacy for the future. The critical choice that confronts the United States and other industrial countries is whether to combat this high rate of inflation through a combination of incomes policy and restrictive demand (with the feasible mixture varying from country to country), or acknowledge that inflation in excess of what has been traditionally acceptable will be present for many years to come. Governments are reluctant to acknowledge the latter possibility, but given the costs of bringing inflation quickly to a halt, they will gradually recognize the need to reduce the costs of continuing inflation by permitting and even encouraging members of the public to prepare for it and protect themselves against it. This will require many changes in such laws and conventions as ceilings on nominal interest rates, tax provisions fixed for long periods in nominal terms, and annuities set in nominal terms. Inflation has already badly eroded *past* savings of many families and firms while conferring windfall gains on those lucky or foresighted enough to have their assets in forms that benefited from inflation. Steps should be taken to ensure that future savings are protected so far as possible against similar incursions. It must of course be recognized in making these changes that not all future economic changes, including changes in the price level, can be insured against. A worsening of the terms of trade, such as the increase in oil prices brought to all oil-consuming nations, will reduce real income of the country as a whole (compared to what it would otherwise be); no reshuffling of income among residents can restore it.

Many countries formerly looked to their balance of payments to provide a certain discipline to the domestic economy—both to firms and to unions in setting prices and wages, and to the government in determining its level of spending and taxation. An international monetary regime of fixed exchange rates contributed to this discipline, and a certain mystique about the balance of payments was built up in the public mind. Whatever its merits in the past, this discipline has clearly been greatly and irreversibly weakened with the movement to floating exchange rates and with the realization by firms, unions, and government officials that even under a regime of fixed exchange rates the currency can be devalued without catastrophic effect. So the old discipline has been lost, and countries are now on their own in their pursuit of price stability in a world of quasi-flexible exchange rates that is likely to persist for some time, as explained below.

International Monetary Arrangements

The Bretton Woods monetary system broke down completely in 1971-73 with cessation of convertibility of the dollar into gold, followed by abandonment of fixed exchange rates between major currencies, leaving them to "float" more or less freely in response to market forces. Some claim that this breakdown was a prime cause of world inflation, but more likely it was a contributing symptom: fixed exchange rates could not easily be maintained in the world of rapid inflation varying substantially from country to country that had already started before 1973. Indeed, this variation was the main reason for the breakdown of early attempts at European monetary unification, which laid predominant emphasis on fixity of exchange rates among members of the European Community. Germany, for example, showed itself to be far more successful in keeping inflation under control than Britain or Italy even before 1973.

As noted above, large United States payments deficits concealed in 1969 by tight monetary policy became manifest in 1970 and 1971. These, combined with a resumption of domestic inflation, prompted President Nixon in August 1971 to introduce his "new economic policy," which among other things froze American prices for ninety days, declared that the dollar would no longer be convertible into gold, and imposed a surcharge of 10 percent on a broad range of imports. These actions were a strong shock to American-European relations, less because of their content (which in some circles had been expected for some time), than because of the strident tone in which they were announced and the total lack of consultation with other countries. Several months of financial turmoil followed to be quieted by the Smithsonian Agreement of December 1971, which realigned the exchange rates of many currencies and resulted in American agreement to remove the import surcharge.

Financial conditions were relatively calm during 1972, despite a record United States trade deficit of $7.0 billion (it frequently happens that trade deficits are worse immediately after devaluations than before because of delays in response to the devaluation); but the U.S. Treasury was never fully satisfied with the 8 per cent devaluation of the dollar achieved in the Smithsonian Agreement, so when a brief period of currency speculation occurred in early 1973, the United States took the occasion to devalue the dollar again, unilaterally. This move so unsettled gold and currency markets that large speculative movements of funds continued, and in March most European currencies were unpegged from the dollar and allowed to float. (Canada had already floated its currency in 1970, to avoid speculative inflows, and the British pound was floated in June 1972, to avoid speculative outflows.) Members of the European Community—with the important exceptions of Britain and Italy—succeeded in floating their currencies together in what has been called a "snake"—because it allows some movement of one European currency against another, while all move together with respect to the dollar. France had to leave the snake, though, for a period of eighteen months in the wake of the oil price increases of January 1974.

This was the first period of general exchange-rate flexibility since a brief period in 1935 and a longer period ending in 1925. There had been a protracted debate among academic and official economists for some years over the merits and the workability of a system of flexible exchange rates, with academics generally taking the position that flexibility was desirable and officials taking the position that it was not (but with important exceptions on both sides). The International Monetary Fund had issued two reports, one in 1970 and one in 1972, that argued against extensive exchange-rate flexibility, and the work of the Committee of Twenty on international monetary reform, established in 1972, proceeded on the same assumption until mid-1974.

After two years of experience with flexible exchange rates it is still difficult to issue a final verdict on their desirability, since the actual performance during this period was shaped by the exceptional size and character of the disturbances to which the international monetary system was subject as well as by the nature of the exchange rate regime itself. The monetary system was in fact put under enormous strain from accelerating and divergent rates of inflation, from a huge increase in oil prices (a 10 per cent redirection of total world trade payments in the course of only a few months, probably the largest disturbance per unit time the world economy had ever experienced), and from uncertainty about the nature and duration of the regime itself—exchange rates were floating, but we did not have a *system* of flexible exchange rates.

A tentative judgment can be made that floating exchange rates—which have not been freely floating rates, as the movements in official reserves testify—have not lived up to the full claims or hopes of their proponents, but they have nonetheless performed very well under the circumstances and most likely were far better than any regime of fixed exchange rates would have been during this period. As noted above, the world economy has been under great strain, and it has weathered the strain rather well. To be sure, floating exchange rates could do little to cushion the shock of the increase in oil prices, partly because of the strong insensitivity of demand for oil to its price, partly because of the low income-elasticity of demand for some of the imports from oil consumers. But then, fixed rates might have been worse. Besides, countless secondary adjustments will be required among oil-consuming nations, and flexible exchange rates will be most helpful in making those adjustments. Meanwhile they serve as a useful shock absorber in the face of potentially large movements of capital from one currency to another.

On the other hand, a well-functioning system of exchange rates should not experience daily movements of 2 to 3 per cent between major currencies in the absence of clear, underlying monetary circumstances; yet such movements did take place between the American dollar and the German mark during this period. While fluctuations of the dollar were not great on a trade-weighted basis (which includes a heavy component of Canada and Japan), fluctuations with respect to the German mark and the other European currencies linked directly or indirectly to the mark were substantial, entailing semiannual swings of 10 per cent and by early 1975 leaving the German mark appreciated relative to the dollar by more than 50 per cent since May 1970 (including the Smithsonian adjustments of about 17 per cent). Some substantial correction between the two currencies was necessary, but by 1975 the dollar was undoubtedly undervalued on a basis of costs of production, and this fact would impede European recovery from the world recession.

In the late sixties and early seventies there was much antagonism between the United States and certain European countries—notably France—on various issues of international monetary reform. Basic disagreement still exists on the desirable ultimate form of the international monetary system, but these disagreements have been submerged by more pressing issues, and recognition of a common plight in the face of world inflation, world recession, and vastly increased payments for oil led in June 1974 to a marked convergence of views on interim arrangements. These redefined the new international money, special drawing rights (SDRs) in terms of a "basket" of sixteen leading currencies at their market value, necessary in a regime of flexible exchange rates, and broke the link of SDRs to gold; called for coordination among countries in the management of flexible exchange rates (thus acknowledging that for the time being flexible rates are necessary, even though contrary to the desires of many countries); invited countries to pledge not to impose or intensify restrictions on imports in response to the difficulties posed by large payments for oil, thereby requiring oil-consuming countries as a group to run large trade deficits; created a new facility at the International Monetary Fund for lending to countries which find themselves in special difficulty because of payments for oil; and established a new ministerial-level committee within the IMF to monitor the world economy and propose improvements on a more regular basis. In 1975 agreement was also reached on increasing the quotas in the IMF including a doubling of the *share* of quotas (which *inter alia* determine voting rights) going to the oil-exporting countries.

Differences of view remain strong on the ultimate future role of gold in the international monetary system and on the degree to which the machinery of the monetary system should be used to transfer resources to less developed countries. Some European countries, notably France and Italy, have a strong desire to mobilize the gold in their reserves, yet fear sole reliance on sales to the private market, for that would depress gold prices and hurt a large and powerful home hoarding interest. They therefore want to reintroduce the possibility of gold transactions among central banks, necessarily at a higher price, to avoid impinging on the free market price. The United States, on the other hand, along with several other countries, would like to see the gradual elimination of any official role for gold. Up to a point, these two positions are complementary rather than conflicting, but until the role of gold is definitely settled, ambiguity will remain concerning the possible reinstitution of gold as a centerpiece of the monetary system at a much higher official price. The jockeying on interim steps to deal with gold—including French objections to United States proposals to sell IMF gold at market prices and use the capital gains to help developing countries—feeds this ambiguity and creates general uncertainty about the future of the international monetary system.

Long-run monetary reform remains on the agenda, but it is not the issue of great contention between Europe and America at the present time that it was several years ago. For the possibly prolonged interim, there is no agreement as to how best to deal with the eurocurrency market and prevent its collapse or direct its expansion. A communiqué issued from the monthly Basel meeting of the central banks in the fall of 1974 went part way, but only part way, toward clarifying the responsibilities of commercial banks and of central banks toward banks that operate in the eurocurrency market. That market returned toward normalcy, though at a slower rate of growth, after the extreme jitters of the summer of 1974—jitters that were created by higher oil prices and by a series of badly handled bank failures, notably that of the German bank Herstatt. Flows of funds into and out of the eurocurrency market remain potentially unsettling, and important philosophical differences of view remain between the United States and Germany on the one hand and a number of other European countries on the other regarding the importance of maintaining relatively free movements of capital.

The benefits as well as the problems of the eurocurrency market came through clearly during 1974, when that market was able both to absorb and to rechannel to oil-consuming nations a substantial portion of the vastly increased revenues of oil-exporting nations. By the end of 1974, the market was virtually saturated with such funds, and it became necessary to find alternative mechanisms for recycling oil revenues. At the global level oil payments are self-financing, since the oil-exporting countries themselves must invest in the capital markets of the world that part of their receipts that they do not spend for goods and services. The recycling problem is to channel unspent oil revenues to the countries that most need them, on terms that will allow these countries to use them. The United States proposed in early 1975 a "safety net" recycling scheme for the OECD countries, to be used as a last resort if other sources of funds were not available. European countries, led by Britain, resisted the safety net plan, euphemistically named the Solidarity Fund by American authorities, in favor of more extensive reliance on the International Monetary Fund. The compromise worked out in early 1975 did not deal adequately with the underlying reasons for the disagreement, in particular, the new European distrust, noted above, of American motives and behavior. The United States government ill-advisedly put forward the Solidarity Fund in a context of trying to induce or even compel European countries in need of financial resources to adopt energy conservation programs—at a time in which the United States had no such program itself.

Nonetheless, the compromise, which both increased the IMF facility to $6 billion and led to a creation of a $25 billion OECD fund (about half of which would be usable), did bolster the financial solidarity of the industrial countries in the sense of making it less probable that any of these countries would be forced to take oil-induced balance-of-payments measures really damaging to the oil-consuming nations as a group.

Recycling of oil funds merely represented a palliative, although in the short run a vital one. Ultimately, if oil prices do not fall drastically to something not far from their former levels (adjusted for inflation), oil-consuming countries will have to undertake the real as opposed merely to the financial adjustments that are necessary to accommodate to their higher oil payments. The sharp rise in oil prices will change substantially the competitiveness of particular products (e.g., petrochemicals and fertilizers) formerly produced profitably in a number of Western countries. And the global flow of long-term investments will not necessarily have the same pattern as it did when Western countries were the main source of foreign investment funds. On both counts, some countries will have to make substantial adjustments in their exchange rates and in the structure of their national economies. This will necessarily be a prolonged and somewhat painful process. One side effect will be the need for further postponement of European monetary unification, since fundamental adjustments, including exchange-rate adjustments, will have to take place among the member countries.

A task requiring extremely sensitive management over the next several years concerns the proper alignment of exchange rates. Exchange-rate flexibility has brought its own problems and certainly has not performed so well as its strongest proponents had desired. But there is little doubt that exchange-rate flexibility gives the world economy an extra degree of freedom, acting as a useful shock absorber during a period in which the world economy has been subject to the severe shocks of greatly divergent national inflation rates and sharp increases in the prices of oil, food, and fertilizer. National monetary authorities have skillfully blended a degree of exchange-rate intervention with exchange-rate flexibility during this troublesome period. The task ahead will be to permit those changes in exchange rates that will be required to bring about the long-term adjustments discussed above, while trying to discover what these changes are in the process of making them.

It is neither practicable nor desirable to allow exchange rates to float freely, without direct influence by the monetary authorities of each country. For most countries, the exchange rate is the single most important price, and so long as governments are held responsible, as they should be and are in modern industrial societies, for the stabilization and growth of the national economy, they can no more eschew concern about, and if necessary interference with, the foreign exchange market than they can eschew direct influence over monetary conditions; indeed the two are closely related. But intervention in the exchange market necessarily involves at least two countries, so some degree of coordination is called for—at a minimum to ensure that two countries are not pursuing mutually inconsistent policies with respect to the same exchange rate.

The temptation will be strong to ensure this coordination by fixing the exchange-rates once again—to eliminate the "disease" of floating exchange-rates, as French Minister of Finance Fourcade put it. But this would be vastly premature. For the reasons given above, exchange-rate adjustments will be necessary for some time to come, and they are far better undertaken in small steps and continuously than with the large, single-step adjustments of the past, which are an incitement to large-scale currency speculation. Rather, the monetary authorities should intervene cooperatively in the exchange markets to ensure that exchange-rates do not adjust too rapidly in short periods of time and to ensure, insofar as possible, that they do not overshoot the mark. Guidelines might provide for daily or weekly limits to the movement in rates and stipulate that countries whose reserves had increased or decreased by more than a certain proportionate amount would adjust their exchange rates or take other steps to correct the accumulation or the reduction.

So long as the oil-exporting countries are running large trade surpluses, it will be necessary for the rest of the world to run equally large trade deficits. Under these circumstances, it would be desirable for the United States, the European Community, and Japan, as the three largest importers of oil, to agree among themselves on a rough division of the trade deficit that they collectively must run if they are not willing to provide sufficient foreign assistance to permit the developing countries to run appropriately large trade deficits. The setting of such deficit targets involves considerable artificiality, but they would help to guide balance-of-payments adjustments during the next several years and might well avoid much controversy among the regions over exchange-rate policy. The European Community of course does not yet have a unified monetary policy, but an overall target for the Community would help prod its members to coordinate their policies and to provide mutual financial support to the extent that coordination is not feasible.

Important philosophical differences of view remain on the extent to which international capital movements are a major source of balance-of-payments disturbance and should be subject to governmental control. Libertarian societies such as the United States and Germany are willing to tolerate a high degree of capital movement even if it is a source of disturbance. But this debate too carries less conviction in the circumstances of the mid-seventies, since large amounts of footloose wealth are now in the hands of oil-exporting countries and it is much more difficult in practice to control the movement of nonresident funds than of resident funds. Moreover, with an increasing amount of world trade carrying credit, it is also more difficult than in the past to separate, for purposes of control, trade transactions from capital transactions. On both counts attempts to control capital movements are likely at best to be so imperfect as to fail as a substitute for movements in exchange rates among major currencies.

By the same token, however, shifts in oil funds could play havoc with exchange rates. This is an additional reason for smoothing intervention in exchange markets, supported in the case of large movements of oil funds by lending among the leading central banks. With the necessary coordination, both the exchange rate and the domestic monetary effects of a movement of oil funds from one currency into another can be neutralized. The only consequential consideration is how the exchange risk should be shared among the cooperating central banks, and that is not very consequential; the risk can be split evenly if no better rule can be found.

A final international monetary issue concerns the continuing international role of the U.S. dollar, once a source of great friction between the United States and France—de Gaulle once spoke of the "monumentally overprivileged position that the world has conceded to the American currency." In the meantime, however, gold, when it is not supported by the United States, has shown itself to be even more erratic in its behavior than the dollar. And the SDR is not yet ready for an exclusive position as the international reserve asset, not least because a number of important oil-exporting countries have declined to participate in the SDR arrangement. Exchange-rate flexibility, fortunately, will inhibit any great new accumulation of dollars in official reserves other than those of the oil-exporting countries (except as a by-product of central bank cooperation of the type described above). There is some joint American-European interest in trying to persuade the oil-exporting countries with large reserves to convert their dollar holdings into SDRs at the IMF and to create a consolidation fund at the IMF for that purpose. But at best that will take some time, and in the meantime the dollar must perforce retain its international role.

Retention of flexible exchange rates, even managed flexibility, will have profound implications for trade policy, discussed below. It also offers a superior route to monetary unification within the European Community, although the European Commission has not yet recognized that and indeed regards the presence of exchange-rate flexibility as a setback to its plans. It has been that for the Common Agricultural Policy, since large day-to-day movements in exchange rates seem to the officials in Brussels to call for border adjustments in agricultural prices. Psychologically, moreover, it has been an impediment to plans for monetary unification, since the Commission misguidedly linked in the public mind the ultimate goal of monetary unification with the initial step of fixing exchange rates. Now the Community can get on with the more consequential task of coordinating national monetary policies in such a way that exchange rates that in principle are free to move, in fact do not; at that point de facto monetary unification will have been achieved.

Trade Relationships

Disagreements on trade issues are even more muted than they are on monetary reform. A few years ago trade issues were extremely contentious: (1) the United States insisted on compensation for the entry of Britain and other countries into the European Community (since entry entailed abrogating tariff commitments by those countries to the United States); (2) the United States charged that the Community's Common Agricultural Policy (CAP) was working strongly to the disadvantage of American farmers; (3) the United States charged the European Community with violation of its commitments to nondiscrimination in international trade by extending preferential tariff treatment to imports from a number of developing countries, and especially, in some cases, by requiring in return preferential treatment for European goods by those same countries; and (4) a bill with wide apparent support in Congress threatened to send the United States down a strongly protectionist path, starting with woolen and synthetic textiles.

The first of these issues is now settled to mutual satisfaction. The second issue was at least temporarily overtaken by food shortages throughout the world, so the problem became assurance of supply rather than access to markets; while for the longer term it involves the problem of transferring surplus food production in North America and Europe to hungry developing countries. The third issue has been muted by the adoption of a system of generalized tariff preferences for less developed countries by Europe and Japan and soon by the United States; meanwhile the Lomé Agreement of February 1975 with former colonies of European countries eliminated the offensive provision for "reverse preferences" extended by those countries to European goods. Finally, Congress in the end passed a basically liberal trade bill (at least in the hands of a president who wants to use it in a liberalizing direction), authorizing the president to negotiate further tariff cuts and the reduction of other barriers to trade.

The increase in oil prices established a greater sense of common destiny and renewed appreciation of the importance of having a forum for discussion and resolution of trade disputes between countries, but no one is really enthusiastic about another round of tariff cuts. Nonetheless, in the area of trade policy further liberalization is usually the best defense against a reversion to protectionism. Early sparring by the negotiators has brought out a number of long-standing differences of view. Europe wants to concentrate on cutting most heavily the high tariffs, which the European Community has relatively few of, while the United States wants to get rid of the very low tariffs, which the European Community has many of and which are perceived in Brussels as the very symbol of European cooperation—a sad commentary on the lack of progress toward European unity. The Americans would like to settle trade issues, especially in the domain of nontariff influences on trade, on a piecemeal basis, making progress where progress is possible. Europe apparently prefers a complete package deal, including tariffs and as many nontariff barriers as can be negotiated as part of the package.

Agriculture

The issue of agricultural trade is relatively uncontentious so long as world grain prices are at or above the support prices of the European Community, as they were in 1973-75. But with the predictable increase in support prices and drop in world prices, the Common Agricultural Policy (CAP) will once again become the main issue of trade policy between the European Community and the principal agricultural exporting areas of the world. It will remain contentious so long as the CAP is designed to treat the rest of the world as a residual source for agricultural products in deficient supply and a dumping ground for excess European production, and so long as Europe imposes no limits on production to accompany its high support prices. The main problems concern wheat and dairy products, where the Community imposes a variable levy on all imports to ensure that the Community is fully insulated from world price and supply developments, and then subsidizes the export of any surplus production, thereby aggravating price swings on the world market.

One rough measure of the pressure of European agricultural policy on world markets is the growth of export subsidies from just under 400 million units of account in 1967 to 2.7 billion units of account in 1972 (a unit of account, calculated for the purposes of setting uniform agricultural prices throughout the Community, was the equivalent of one U.S. dollar before the Smithsonian realignment of the exchange-rate). The export subsidies fell with the substantial increase in world grain prices in 1973 and 1974 and in any case can be expected to remain at a lower level following the entry of Britain, which is a large net importer of wheat and dairy products. But the replacement of the rest of the world by Britain as a disposal area for European agricultural surpluses will not make matters easier for the traditional agricultural exporters, since the British market will gradually be closed to them. On the contrary, it will give the fiscally burdensome CAP a new lease on life, by diminishing the export subsidies that have to be paid (in effect by shifting them to the British consumer) and hence reducing the Community's awkward need for ever larger revenues.

The Community has countered American complaints about the CAP by pointing out that American exports of agricultural products to the Community have continued to grow, from $1.2 billion in 1962 to $2.1 billion in 1972. The United States has countered this by pointing out that virtually all the growth has been in noncompeting products such as soybeans and oil cake, and that United States exports subject to Europe's variable levies, mainly grains and poultry, actually fell from the mid-sixties to the early seventies, despite extraordinary growth in national economies and in world trade. The Community did respond to American protests (in part in exchange for the Smithsonian Agreement on exchange-rates) by agreeing in 1972 to stockpile some of its excess wheat production instead of selling it all on the world market at subsidized prices. But this agreement was overtaken by world grain shortages within a year.

The lack of integration of European agriculture with the rest of the world, when so many other national economies show a high degree of global interdependence, can lead to serious tensions between Europe and North America. When high world feed grain prices made it unprofitable to produce meat on the previous scale, for example, meat producers throughout the world tried to trim their herds. Europe closed its market to imports of beef from such countries as Argentina and Australia, which promptly redirected their supplies to the United States, thereby hurting American meat producers, who were suffering from the same initial affliction as meat producers in Europe. At stake here is more than just agricultural trade, since a large part of the political support within the United States for a liberal trade policy derives from the farm sector, and a weakening of that sector's advocacy of liberal trade might well tilt the United States in a protectionist direction.

The French response to problems of agricultural trade has traditionally been to call for "organizing" world markets on a product-by-product basis. This stance caters to the periodic pleas by less developed countries for higher and more stable prices for their exports of primary products, pleas which reached a new high in late 1974 and 1975. French proposals for organizing markets have been made at a very general level, with no specification how prices are to be kept above long-run costs at the global level, where dumping on an "outside" market, the basis for European market organization without production controls, would not be possible. (Indeed, subsidized European wheat sales caused the demise in 1969-1971 of the International Wheat Agreement, one of the relatively few, if not wholly successful, efforts to "organize" world markets.) These periodic appeals for organizing world markets have generally met a cool reception in the United States (and in several European nations), and the French government has thereby been spared the impossible task of specifying the details of a truly workable scheme.

In 1975 the United States announced, in the context of consumer-producer discussions on oil and of the Special Session of the United Nations General Assembly to consider the calls by many developing countries for a new economic order, that it was prepared to reconsider its traditional opposition to international commodity agreements. Whatever results from this reconsideration, international commodity agreements are not likely to work any better than they have. Either you maintain tight control over production, or you must be ready to make very large purchases for storage, selling off later when commodities are in short supply.

Moreover, very little work has been done on how effective high commodity prices really are in fostering economic development—the stated objective of developing countries. A plausible case can be made that a transfer of resources through high commodity prices is far less efficient in promoting development than alternative modes of transferring resources, such as foreign assistance linked to development programming, and indeed that in some countries it might actually impede development by worsening the distribution of income because of the strong maldistribution of ownership of the means of production of primary products.

The Lomé Agreement significantly does *not* try to stabilize commodity prices (except for sugar); rather it provides for the stabilization of export earnings from twelve primary products of importance to those developing countries, to be achieved, when required, through direct transfers from the Community to the governments of the countries in question, along with much technical assistance and guidance in the framing of development plans and projects.

Whether or not agreement on commodity arrangements is reached at the global level—the sticking point is usually the price range around which prices are to be stabilized, with producers wanting them near their historic highs and consuming countries wanting them closer to their recent lows—America and Europe (and Japan) would be well advised to build up stocks of critical materials in cooperation with each other. Producing countries would welcome purchases during a period of world recession, when prices are depressed; and the existence of the stockpiles would provide both a deterrent to cartelization by producing countries and a cushion in case of embargo or other disruption of supply. It would not even be necessary at the outset to agree on the circumstances under which the stocks would be used in other than general terms; it would be sufficient to agree on the target amounts, the prices at which they would be purchased, and the financing of the stocks.

A natural medium-term solution to the problem of temperate-zone agriculture, and especially of grains, is to provide much more assistance to the developing countries of the world in the form of food. It is a paradox of the modern world that major grain-exporting countries are squabbling over markets at the same time as numbers of their own citizens are calling for reductions in meat consumption to release the grain to relieve starvation around the world. It would be a mistake to extrapolate the grain-short year of 1974 indefinitely into the future; but projections a decade or longer ahead show, not so much an absolute shortage of grain (although the more pessimistic projections do encompass that), as a growing maldistribution between the areas of surplus (including North America and Western Europe) and those heavily populated parts of the world that are unlikely in the near future to expand their agricultural output enough to feed themselves. The U.S. Department of Agriculture, for example, projects grain export requirements from North America to grow from thirty million tons in 1974 to seventy million tons in 1985. Most of this increase must go to developing countries, and surely the European Community could satisfy some of this growth in requirements without impinging markedly on the American farmer. The problem will be to finance this increase in sales, since the export earnings of developing countries are not likely to rise enough to cover the cost. The natural solution is for the wealthy, grain-rich areas to give some of their grain to the poor, grain-deficient areas. To be sure, food assistance is not without its problems. Too heavy reliance on it can discourage needed productions in the poor areas of the world, where the potential for increased food productions is great. But in the medium run, a European program of food aid along the lines of the American PL 480 program of the 1950s and 1960s would give Europe the breathing space it needs for rationalizing its agricultural production, a process that has been occurring naturally as young people leave the farms. Aid would create a financial burden; but the Community has shown itself willing to take on a considerable financial burden for the sake of agricultural support already, and this route would combine that with foreign assistance, which it is also prepared to give.

Other Trade Issues

The United States and Europe are both agreed that "safeguards" against too rapid increases in imports must be improved; in particular, that the General Agreement on Tariffs and Trade should be revised to permit temporary restrictions of imports to be imposed in a discriminatory manner, so they can be aimed at the countries whose products are in fact causing the difficulty, instead of having to be applied, as now, in a nondiscriminatory way that gives rise to inadvertent injury to third countries. In addition, there are a wide variety of "nontariff distortions" to trade that will occupy trade negotiations for some time. Americans find especially offensive the European border tax adjustments, designed to relieve European exports of indirect taxes while imposing such taxes on imports. These adjustments are legal under GATT, although the provision that permits them was not designed to cover such broad-based taxes as the European value-added tax and was probably mistakenly applied to it. But for reasons given below this issue should disappear as a source of contention.

On their side, Europeans find offensive a host of American procedures and requirements for selling in the United States—what they perceive as arbitrary methods of classification by customs officials and unnecessary labeling requirements. Many of these should be removed, but others have a rationale that the Europeans might well consider themselves, e.g., the rules for labeling of pharmaceuticals.

Exchange Rates and Trade Policy

It is not yet widely appreciated that a regime of flexible exchange rates has profound implications for trade policy, with the general effect of eliminating some of the contentious issues altogether (e.g., border tax adjustments) and reducing the consequence of others (e.g., even agricultural policy). Floating exchange rates will adjust more readily than fixed to both the conditions affecting trade flows and to any changes in those conditions. Thus an increase in indirect tax rates, with a corresponding increase in rebates on exports, will evoke a counteracting movement in exchange rates: the value of the currency of the seller country will rise relative to that of its buyers' currencies. For this reason the incentives to undertake such measures for trade-balance or balance-of-payments reasons will be diminished, and any side effects on trade of actions taken for more strictly domestic reasons will be offset.

Even larger issues, such as the protective agricultural policy and the policy of encouraging indigenous European high-technology industries—ironically the two sectors in which the United States economy has a clear competitive advantage over Europe, so that European policy in these areas understandably leaves Americans somewhat frustrated in their trade relations with Europe—become less consequential as sources of trans-Atlantic friction under flexible exchange rates. This is in part because compensatory improvements in other areas will come quickly through adjustments in the exchange rate, but perhaps even more because strong domestic counter-pressures against these policies should develop within Europe. To the extent that Europe wants to protect these sectors, it will now do so, much more than under fixed exchange rates, at the expense of the strong export industries. Increased agricultural export subsidies, for instance, will be taken out of the profits of Volkswagen and Fiat as the exchange rate of European currencies appreciates against the dollar and currencies of other agricultural exporting countries. Under fixed exchange rates it was possible to maintain the illusion—and for a number of years even to enjoy the reality—that discrimination in favor of one sector of the economy was not at the expense of other sectors of the economy. That will no longer be possible under flexible rates.

Energy

With the Arab oil embargo on the United States and the Netherlands in October 1973 and the quadrupling of oil prices that took place in 1973-74, a new area of economic (and strategic) policy was at once transferred from the background into the limelight. The numerous political and strategic implications of these developments are discussed elsewhere in this volume, but a word should be said here about the implications for economic cooperation between America and Europe.

The actions by the Arab oil-exporting countries revealed the economic vulnerability of Europe and Japan to interruption of a vital raw material and the political vulnerability arising out of their crucial dependence on that material. American dependence on Middle Eastern oil was also growing rapidly. The task each consuming country faced (beyond coping with the payments problems resulting from the higher oil prices) was how to reduce these vulnerabilities at minimum cost to standards of living.

The immediate American response was to announce Project Independence, i.e., a program to achieve complete independence of non-Canadian external oil by 1980. The goal was as unrealistic as the European Community's goal of monetary unification by 1980, and less desirable. It had the further disadvantage of sounding as though the United States had retreated into a go-it-alone policy, ignoring the problems of Europe and Japan. American officials hastened to point out that attainment of the objective would also help Europe and Japan, by reducing pressures on world oil supplies; but this correct observation did not wholly undo the impression.

Even if total independence is not a sensible goal of policy because of the unnecessary costs entailed relative to the alternatives, major efforts to diversify sources of energy make sense for all industrial countries. Diversification requires diversifying both the types of energy, away from heavy and growing dependence on petroleum, and the geographic sources of energy, away from heavy and growing dependence on the Middle East (see Table X-2).

As Table X-2 shows, the dependence of the three industrial areas on imported oil varies greatly. There are great variations even within Europe, with Norway and the Netherlands being largely self-sufficient in energy (to be joined by Britain in 1980); while France, Germany and Italy rely heavily on imported energy.

Dependency figures for individual countries such as these make sense only on the assumption that each nation may have to depend on its own resources. Yet with a world market in oil, the same basic import price (after allowance for transport costs) will prevail everywhere, no matter who is actually selling it.

Table X-2
Total Internal Consumption and Net Imports of Fossil Fuels

	United States		European Community[a]		Japan	
	1968	1973	1968	1973	1968	1973
Total Internal Consumption (10^{21} Calories)	12.8	16.1	10.7	13.5	2.1	3.3
Net Imports as a percentage of Consumption	2	8	46	53	70	83
Petroleum Imports as a percentage of Consumption	5	10	44	51	58	71
Imports from Middle East and Africa as a percentage of Petroleum Imports	8[b]	21	77[b]	70	78[b]	75

[a]Enlarged to nine members.

[b]1970.

Source: OECD, *Statistics of Energy, 1959-1973*, Paris 1974; and OECD, *Trade Statistics*, Series B. Coal converted at 7.177 billion Calories per metric ton; petroleum converted at 9.5 billion Calories per metric ton.

Traditional customers are not likely to get favored prices (as the United States learned when Canada imposed an export tax on oil, and as East European countries learned when Russia, following OPEC, raised its prices). But they may get some prorationing of supply in the event of world shortages, induced for example by an Arab boycott on export sales. That at any rate is the stated assumption underlying the new International Energy Agency of the industrialized nations. As the United States has learned, however, allocation of an item as crucial as oil generates much friction among regions of the country differently situated with respect to energy; North Sea oil has also fostered Scottish separatism and Norwegian aloofness from Europe.

The first step toward reducing vulnerability is to constrain consumption. High oil prices will do that in the course of time after families and firms have had an opportunity to adjust their expenditures on such durable items as automobiles and buildings to the new situation. It is not clear that much more than this is needed. Gasoline should be taxed heavily for environmental reasons in any case. And countries should lay down contingency plans for cutting consumption of oil in an emergency.

The other component of a diversification program entails increasing alternative energy supplies. In early 1975 the United States vetted a plan for imposing a floor on oil prices, to be agreed on by all the major industrial countries. The rationale underlying this proposal was that the heavy and long-term investments required for development of virtually all new sources of energy required an assured level of profitability; in particular, that they required some assurance that world oil prices would not fall drastically, e.g., through the breakup of the Organization of Petroleum Exporting Countries (OPEC), to the low level that Middle East countries can produce oil at. Without such assurance, few private investors would risk their capital. With it, prevailing prices of oil—or even somewhat lower prices—would be adequate to stimulate much new investment, both in oil exploration and in development of other kinds of energy.

The United States desired all industrial countries to agree on a floor price, partly to stimulate appropriate investment in all of these countries, but partly also so that the United States would not in the future be put at a cost disadvantage in energy in comparison with its major industrial competitors, which would happen if the stimulus to new energy supplies were sufficient to break the OPEC cartel in the 1980s and induce a sharp reduction in world oil prices. Under these circumstances, American officials argued Europe and Japan would get a "free ride" on United States energy policy, with the United States bearing the costs and the other countries ultimately enjoying the benefits.

Once again, under a regime of flexible exchange rates, concern with "competitiveness" is misplaced, because the exchange rate will adjust to ensure balance in international payments regardless of the particular cost factors that obtain in different countries. What is really at issue is not competitiveness, but standard of living. Deliberately adopting a high-price oil strategy to encourage investment is tantamount to adopting a lower standard of living for the sake of reduced vulnerability to foreign suppliers. Moreover, the establishment of a high floor price is almost certain to reinforce OPEC's determination and ability to maintain high world prices, since oil-exporting countries would be put on notice, in effect, that they could not sell more oil by lowering prices. Indeed, American officials began to speak as though the floor price might also provide a basis for price discussions with the OPEC nations in 1975-76. If it went this way, the policy would thus wholly deny to industrial countries the benefits of the low-cost energy that is available in nature.

The possibilities for investment in alternative sources of energy, apart from nuclear energy, are much greater in North America than in Europe or Japan. The latter countries may therefore legitimately wonder whether a floor price, or at least a floor price remotely close to oil prices actually prevailing in 1975, is in their interest. Would it not be better, that is, less costly, to subsidize selectively the development of alternative energy sources where possible while building oil stocks against sudden reductions in supply? These actions might be combined with a rather low floor price, say, the equivalent of $6 a barrel of oil in 1974 prices.

More fundamentally, should not the choice between standard of living and vulnerability to cutbacks in foreign supplies be made by each country separately or by regional groups such as the European Community independently of the United States? Although most Europeans undoubtedly regard the United States as a more stable source of energy supplies a decade from now than they do the Middle East, some would undoubtedly feel more comfortable depending on the Middle East. All of this suggests that if the United States desires to bring Europe (and, *a fortiori*, Japan) along with its idea of a floor price, it should set one sufficiently low not to appear too costly to those countries. An internationally acceptable price would undoubtedly have to be supplemented by other incentives to investment in some of the higher-cost new energy sources.

American Support for the European Community

A continuing strand of American foreign policy during the period since the Second World War has been the promotion of European unification. This seems in direct contradiction to the old Roman principle, *divide et impera*, especially in view of the New Left perception (shared by many of the European Old Right) that the United States has been engaged during the last quarter-century in carving out an imperial role for itself. In pursuit of this aim, moreover, the United States has time and again bent its major objective of nondiscrimination in international trade, an article of faith for Roosevelt's secretary of state Cordell Hull, who believed that trade discrimination was a major source of hostility between nations, and embodied in Article I of the GATT. The United States promoted the European Payments Union of 1950, which permitted European countries to discriminate in favor of European goods relative to non-European goods (on balance-of-payments grounds); it sponsored a GATT waiver for the creation of the European Coal and Steel Community in 1951; it fostered the creation of the European Economic Community (which fell within the terms of GATT), including the extension of preferential treatment to the Associated Overseas Countries (which did not). It finally balked at the gradual extension of preferences to various countries in Africa and southern Europe, dubbed *ex post* a Mediterranean policy by the Community. But if the United States can waive the trading rules for *raison d'état*, the Community might well wonder why it cannot also.

But why did the United States engage in this seemingly inconsistent policy, especially when, on the whole, trading relationships were kept on their own track, separate and apart from general foreign policy considerations?

The historical answer, it is worth recalling, is that we did it in order to reintegrate Germany into Europe in a way that would prevent for all time the outbreak yet again of hostilities between France and Germany. It is true that the emergence of the cold war strongly conditioned this objective and, in particular, increased the urgency which the United States saw for reviving the German economy and even for rearming Germany. But Franco-German détente was the deeper and historically prior objective. This particular postwar objective of United States foreign policy could hardly have been more successful.

The more contemporary reason for encouraging European unification was to share the responsibilities and costs of world leadership. John F. Kennedy's call for an Atlantic Partnership was not mere rhetoric. It reflected a deep desire by American leaders, whether or not misplaced, to get Europe to the state where its perceptions and its abilities to act were global in scope, on the assumption that in global perspective there were enough shared values between the United States and Europe so that European initiatives and actions would on the whole also serve the interests of the United States. Moreover, this was more likely to be the case if Britain were a member of the European Community, and that explains in part America's continuing efforts to encourage Britain to join.

Finally, it must be said that there has always been a sentimental strain in American policies toward Europe. George Washington wrote to Lafayette that the formation of the United States of America might one day show Europe the way to found a United States of Europe, and that theme has been echoed by American leaders since.

But sentiment aside, should the United States continue to make concessions in its trading interests for the sake of unifying Europe? Or should it, as it seemed to be doing under President Nixon, make a much more vigorous defense of what it perceives are its economic interests, especially now that the primary postwar objective with respect to France and Germany can be judged to have been achieved? This too is a critical choice.

The first point to realize, however, is that American views and actions now have much less impact on the future course of Europe than they did in the late 1940s and 1950s. They are now quite marginal; Europe is going ahead, in its own faltering way, with European unification. The United States should simply make the best of it, making clear that it expects the European Community to behave in the economic arena according to agreed principles and to use agreed procedures for handling deviations from those principles. The United States should not snub Brussels in its dealings with Europe, but neither can it ignore national capitals so long as that is where the decisions are really made. Patience and good humor will be required for a long time to come, while Europe gradually transforms its decision-making processes.

Summary: Critical Choices

Americans unfortunately have planted seeds of distrust in Europe and elsewhere abroad by various actions during the period 1969-73: arm-twisting on textiles, "benign neglect" of our balance-of-payments position followed by unilateral imposition of a 10 per cent import surcharge in August 1971, an embargo on exports of soybeans in 1973 (also without prior consultation), and so on. Europe contributed to mutual distrust by its behavior after the imposition by OPEC countries of cutbacks in oil production in late 1973. The key tasks now are to reinstitute friendly consultation on common problems, to provide a greater sense of participation in major United States decisions affecting important interests of other countries, and to revive the use of international forums for ironing out those disputes that remain.

In mid-1975 the central economic issues between the United States and Europe—indeed for the entire world economy—concern the management of domestic economies: inflation and stagnation. These issues have a strong international component that is not fully recognized in the United States.

A critical choice for the United States is how much weight it will place, in managing its economy, on fighting inflation, and how much on combating the recession. Neither inflation nor recession in the United States is good for the world economy, and any devices it can find to combat both at the same time—for example through the use of some kind of wage guidelines—will be beneficial for other countries as well. The preferable course of action is to expand the domestic economy at a brisk pace so long as unemployment is well above 6 per cent and the rate of capacity utilization is below 80 per cent, for the inflationary effects of such expansion would be negligible. In framing its actions, the United States should take into account the interests and problems of other countries. Export controls may hold down certain prices at home, for instance, but only by raising them abroad. Similarly, import restrictions may help local employment a bit, but only by increasing unemployment in some other country.

The world now needs larger total demand, not shifts of demand from one country to another. Whatever the United States can do to stabilize its economy will provide, simply by virtue of its size and importance in international trade and finance, an anchor point for other countries. We should not expect, however, that inflation will be eliminated easily or quickly in the United States or elsewhere; unfortunately, higher-than-normal rates of inflation are now built into industrial economies for some time to come.

The United States should lead in preventing an unraveling of the relatively liberal international trade and payments system so painstakingly constructed after the Second World War. This requires in particular that it continue to take an active part in "recycling" the large flow of funds from OPEC countries, the proceeds of the oil price increases, into dollar assets. Without smooth recycling many countries will be unable to pay their high oil bills and will therefore be compelled to impose tight import and exchange controls on nonessential imports, thereby passing the burden of financing, like a hot potato, to other countries. European countries may be tempted to impose trade controls even on trade with other members of the European Community, thereby setting back progress toward European unification.

The United States will be urged to reestablish a fixed exchange rate between the dollar and other leading currencies, in the interest of the international community, and to support the new rate in the exchange markets. It should resist these urgings, on the ground that such a move would not in fact be in the interest of the international community at a time when national rates of inflation continue to be strongly divergent and when the full adjustment among industrial countries to the increase in oil prices has not yet taken place. The United States should cooperate in avoiding large and erratic movements in exchange rates, but rates should not be fixed again for a long period of time.

Another critical choice the United States faces is the stance it should take in the Tokyo Round of trade negotiations, and on trade issues more generally. The very tough, economic-interest stance taken on trade issues in 1971-73 perhaps served the useful purpose of signaling other countries that the United States was serious about those issues, although it did so at substantial cost in trust and good will and hence in receptivity to American proposals. Nonetheless, that stance is much less appropriate in a regime of floating exchange rates with a highly competitive dollar than it was at the end of a prolonged period of an overvalued dollar. The United States might therefore relax a bit its tough stance on trade issues, recognizing that a number of its earlier grievances have either been resolved or are no longer relevant. But it should press strongly for a constructive resolution to the problems of temperate agriculture, largely in the form of assistance to needy developing countries, if possible financed by OPEC countries but if necessary financed by the producing countries, including the European Community.

The United States will also confront the choice of how far to go in adhering to international commodity agreements. It should discuss the details of possible agreements open-mindedly, but in the end it should refuse to agree to unworkable arrangements for symbolic reasons—and most such arrangements are likely to be unworkable. In particular, the United States should if necessary take a very critical view of such agreements, allowing Europe and Japan, which are more dependent on foreign sources of supply, to take a more moderate stance, so long as those countries understand that they should not agree to unworkable arrangements in the face of American opposition. This arrangement of course assumes that the United States does not itself become unduly sensitive about being the persistent critic.

The United States by end-1975 had yet to define a comprehensive energy program. But if it wants to do so with European cooperation it must take European circumstances and sensibilities into account. In particular, a high floor price on oil does not seem well suited to European needs in the future. Moreover, in the area of long-run energy supply the need for close harmonization of policies among industrial countries is perhaps less compelling than at first sight.

Finally, the United States must decide to what extent it will continue to support European unification, recognizing that its leverage over such developments in Europe is very much less than it was twenty years ago. It should continue to provide such support, but no longer at the expense of other important objectives.

The position of the United States in the world economy is not what it once was, either quantitatively or in the trust and good will that Americans could draw on. But it would be a mistake to withdraw from a stance of liberal leadership, however tempting that may be to a number of Americans. In his recent book, *The World in Depression*, Charles Kindleberger blames the severity of the Great Depression in the 1930s on the failure of the United States to accept world leadership at a time when Britain was giving it up. No country was thinking and acting in terms of the system as a whole, as Britain had done before the First World War and as the United States did after the Second. There have been signs in recent years that the United States has been backing away from its global system-oriented behavior and playing for more strictly national gains. Yet no other country is ready and able to take up the role of leader. American authorities should continue to take a global view of their responsibilities, and let us hope that other leading nations will cooperate closely with them whenever, as in prevention of world depression, such cooperation is crucial.

XI Critical Choices: The Structure of Industry

Raymond Vernon

Since the beginning of the modern industrial era, relations between Europe and the United States have been violently punctuated by wars and depressions. Cataclysmic interruptions of this sort have generally been followed by some significant shift in those relations.

Today Europe and the United States are at another such juncture. The assumptions on which an earlier set of relations were fashioned, mainly as an aftermath of World War II, seem to have lost their validity. This time, however, the triggering events are not war or depression; other changes, more complex in nature, are involved. Among others, these include changes in the structure of the world's economy and of the world's industry.

The refashioning of the relationships between the United States and Western Europe will be based on many different considerations. What concerns us here is only one, a piece in a larger mosaic. Briefly, the conditions of competition, cooperation, ownership, and control in much of the world's industry have come to differ from those of two or three decades ago in ways that seem fundamental and irreversible. These changes have been both a consequence and a cause: a consequence mainly of basic changes in the technology of transportation and communication; and a cause among other things of an increased interdependence among the richer countries. Though many other factors are involved in the basic shifts that are taking place in the economic relations between the United States and Europe, the changes in industrial structure represent a strong starting point for exploring the meaning of those shifts.

Interdependence and Industrial Structure

One way of looking at the economic relations between the United States and Europe is as an Hegelian process: The increasing economic interdependence among rich industrial countries represents the thesis; the swift growth in the responsibilities of modern states, the antithesis.

Most modern states frame their economic policies on the basic assumption that the geographical limits of the state correspond with some manageable economic unit. International economic policies have been seen largely as questions of the interaction between national economies. Armed with a national currency, a national monetary and fiscal policy, a national set of industries, and a national tariff frontier, each country appears to have a set of policy instruments in its control that can be used to serve its national interests.

In reality, of course, the structure of the world's economy has never been quite that well defined. In the colonial era, the metropolitan powers had their overseas appendages and spheres of influence, not fully a part of the metropolis yet not separated from it. In all periods, businessmen of given nationalities have pursued their calling outside their home territories, while claiming the protection of their home governments. But by and large, until the 1950s or so, the assumption that the nation represented a geographically discrete set of economic interests was not very far from the observable facts.

The relevance of that assumption was buttressed, at least up to World War II, by the behavior of industry itself. On the whole, most enterprises had their business fortunes centered overwhelmingly in their home territory. There were exceptions, of course. In the extractive industries, large enterprises hunted down raw materials where they could be found, even if that meant adventuring abroad; this was especially evident in oil, copper, rubber, and aluminum. In the manufacturing industries, large enterprises followed their exports into foreign markets, eventually setting up foreign production facilities to protect a position that had been created through exports.[1] According to one survey, large American firms already had over three hundred manufacturing subsidiaries in Europe at the outbreak of World War II, mainly in branches of industry that were technologically more advanced.[2] Even so, the identification of enterprises with a single national market was generally very strong.

Until the past decade or two, therefore, national industries were separated by the frictions of space, by governmental barriers, and by perceptions of role. Operating behind their national fences, many industries in the large industrialized nations tended to be parochial and exclusive; and because national markets were small, such markets tended to operate under the domination of an outstanding national leader or two. Where that situation existed, as it did for example in chemicals, aluminum, electrical machinery, and lamps, it was generally thought to be in the nature of things that the leaders should have a first lien on their own home markets. When such leaders found themselves clashing with foreigners, there was a ready resort to international agreements among them, agreements that regulated the access each might have to the national markets of the others. Eventually agreements of this sort would lead to spectacular antitrust suits on the part of the United States, suits that would contribute to the liquidation of most of these international arrangements.[3] But by and large, until World War II, the pattern of national markets prevailed.

The system of international economic agreements that was fashioned after World War II represented a clear break with the past. In formal terms, the new system was based on a consensus among the industrialized countries; in power terms, it reflected the dominant role and philosophy of the United States. The new system, like the old, was based implicitly on the assumption that national economies would continue to be the building blocks of the international order. The tariffs, licenses, and cartels which separated the economies of the industrialized countries were regarded as contraproductive and would be curbed or eliminated through GATT and the IMF. But there was no intention or expectation that national industries would lose their close identification with the national economy. On the contrary, as national barriers were reduced, nations were more than ever concerned with the competitive position of their enterprises and their labor force.

The fact that large enterprises might continue to acquire facilities in other national jurisdictions did not go altogether unrecognized, even in the 1940s; but it was seen as a solution rather than a problem—a solution to Europe's need at the time for capital and technology. Accordingly, the issues created by foreign-owned facilities were dealt with by a loose network of bilateral treaties in which nations secured guarantees that "their" nationals would be fairly treated when doing business in the other nation's economy. One set of such treaties usually spelled out the economic and legal rights of nationals in the jurisdiction of the other signatory, while another network of treaties sorted out some of the technical problems that arose from the overlapping tax jurisdictions of the signatory states.

To be sure, even in the 1940s there were occasional premonitions of the complexities that were in store. As nations sought to define "enemy" property during and after World War II, they sometimes ran afoul of the fact that a German firm might own a Swiss subsidiary which in turn might own a branch in the United States. In such cases, was the branch to be treated as the property of a neutral or of an enemy? Ambiguities of this sort, however, could be handled as exceptions—portents, perhaps, of a general condition to come, but not of one that had arrived. That easy assumption has since been put in question by the multinationalization of business interests.

In puzzling over the policy implications of the multinationalizing trend in industry, it is important to be aware of the power of the forces that have created the trend. With the spread of the commercial aircraft and of commercial radio transmission since World War II, space has been shrinking rapidly—especially international space. One result has been the convergence of consumer tastes in the various industrialized countries. Radios, cameras, hi-fi sets, and men's suits, even wines, cheeses, and ice cream—all have tended to become standardized commodities little influenced by national characteristics. Industrial standards and industrial technologies have also tended toward international norms. Chemical plants, machine tools, earth-moving equipment, computers, commercial aircraft, and countless other types of capital equipment have become practically indistinguishable by country of manufacture. Trade names that do not identify with any particular language or nationality have become the norms of industrial image building: Unidata, Exxon, IBM, and so on.

Each of these trends has added a little to the facility of international transactions. As a consequence, in the period since World War II, trade across the international borders of the industrial countries has grown much faster than trade within their borders.[4] The same tendency for international activities to grow more rapidly than national activities can be seen in the pattern of investment in industry.

Other manifestations of the interpenetration of the industrial economies are also in evidence; the distribution of patents issued in the industrial countries has been particularly telling. The leading European countries, which already in the 1930s had been granting about half of their patents to foreign applicants, found themselves in 1972 issuing about three quarters of their patents to foreigners, a considerable portion being American. In the United States, foreign applicants increased their share of total patent grants from about 13 per cent before World War II to over 30 per cent in 1972.

With improvements in international communication and travel, and with the convergence of national tastes and industrial norms, the advantages associated with multinational enterprises increased rapidly. Knowledge, once acquired, could be used and reused in different locations with very small added outlays. Systems, once developed, could be installed in different locations without great problems of local adaptation. Trade names and credit ratings built up in one country could more easily gain currency in a second. Patent monopolies could be extended at little cost. Sources and markets could be multiplied, thus reducing the vulnerability of the enterprise to national depressions, strikes, and acts of God. And over all, the problem of accountability and control—the Achilles' heel of sprawling organizations—could be managed with reduced effort. By the early 1970s, perhaps one third of all the industrial output of the advanced countries was in the hands of large enterprises that had substantial producing interests outside their own home base. The deep involvement of national enterprises in foreign jurisdictions has meant that the idea of a national industry, responsive to a national policy, has begun to lose its force. That implication has had a powerful bearing on the relations between the United States and Europe.

Industrial Structure and International Relations

As a result of the multinationalizing process over the past few decades, most of the large industrial enterprises headquartered in the United States or Europe (as well as a few in Canada) see themselves as operating in global markets. The implications of that pattern for trans-Atlantic relations, however, differ somewhat according to the activities of the enterprise.

The Technology-Based Sectors

Take, for example, the industrial sectors that are ordinarily associated with the command of modern technologies, such as those in nuclear energy, aerospace, and computers. In such industries, enterprises with a technological lead have often become multinational as a result of their efforts to protect and enlarge a foreign market originally acquired on the basis of that lead. This phenomenon has a long history. It was seen one hundred years ago, for instance, when the U.S.-based Singer Manufacturing Company first decided to produce in Scotland. The same pattern is in evidence today as U.S.-based firms introduce their special products for manufacture in Europe, and as European firms introduce their products for manufacture in the United States.

The process that has led firms with distinctive products commonly to set up production facilities in foreign markets is by now reasonably well documented. In the early stages, such firms usually have served their foreign markets by way of exports; then, as foreign demand in the product has grown and as potential competitors have shown signs of threatening the innovating firm's lead, the innovator has often responded by setting up production facilities inside its foreign market. That tendency was especially strong among U.S.-based firms in the later 1950s and 1960s, as these firms tried to exploit the unusually strong technological leads they had developed during the war years and immediately after. The abnormally strong rush to Europe was what led to Europe's dismay over the "technology gap" in the 1960s. Predictably, however, the Europeans soon learned how to produce the electronic devices, consumer durables, chemicals, and other products that accounted for the appearance of a technology gap, and the acute concern seemed to subside.

The rise and fall of concern over the technology gap from 1950 to 1970 reemphasized some fundamental points about international technological relations. The capacity for innovation was not confined to any single country, certainly not to the United States; Europe and Japan had strong innovative capabilities as well. The capacity for effective imitation and improvement under modern conditions was widespread. Technological leads, therefore, were perishable. Though many products were introduced by multinational enterprises operating on the basis of an early technological lead, these enterprises commonly found themselves obliged in the end to share these markets with national producers.

Nevertheless, the most sensitive part of the problem of the technological gap, as seen from a political point of view, still remains. In a number of the high-technology sectors, sheer scale has proved to be a critical prerequisite for success—scale in organization, scale in financing, scale in markets. In some sectors, the cost and effort involved in creating a significant industrial advance seem to have risen at an extraordinary rate. Whereas the DC-3 was developed at a cost of about one million dollars in the 1930s, the Boeing 747 was developed at a cost of about a thousand million dollars in the 1960s. As a result, in some branches of industry, such as wide-bellied aircraft, exotic electronic devices, novel synthetic materials, antipollution devices, and improvements in energy generation and energy utilization, the scale of the enterprise has become a critical factor.[5] In the industrial use of outer space, weather control, computers, electric generation, and a number of other politically sensitive industries, the same trend seems to exist.

Firms based in the United States have found it rather easier to cope with the problem of scale than European firms. Some ascribe that fact to the size of the United States market,[6] some to the scope of government programs in the high technology fields.[7] Whatever the reason, American firms in a number of politically sensitive products have been able to create a strong technological base in the home market, then subsequently to make their way into the European market on the basis of their achievements in the United States. As a result, even as U.S.-based firms lost their lead in consumer durables and electronic products, they were developing new strengths; and some of these strengths promise to be more tension-generating than those that have been dissipated.

The repeated efforts on the part of European governments since the middle 1960s to redress the balance in the technology-based industries have done little to close the gap. Some of these efforts have been national in scope; some have entailed cooperative arrangements among groups of European enterprises, drawn from several nations.

The separate national initiatives of the different European states in the high-technology industries have not been very different from those of the United States government. As in the United States, research subsidies have been dispensed to national firms, and preferential status has been granted to national firms in sales to official and semi-official buyers. When research subsidies have been handed out, the local subsidiaries of foreign enterprises have rarely been among the recipients. When governments have been buyers, such subsidiaries have generally been used as suppliers of last resort. Some of these discriminatory practices, of course, have been in violation of the existing bilateral treaties on the treatment of foreigners, but the fact has not elicited much protest. With violation so widespread, perhaps no country has felt itself in a position to complain very much.

If the national efforts of the individual European states had proved successful, the political impact of the American technological lead might conceivably have been blunted or dissipated. But by and large, national programs have proved inadequate: in various fields, from wide-bellied aircraft to nuclear fuel enrichment, the effort that an individual European state can put out has been too small. That fact has led to a series of larger multistate European initiatives; but these on the whole have not been much more successful.

The larger European projects have had certain common characteristics that may account for their lack of responsiveness to European needs. In some cases, the network of firms making up the "European" project has included United States enterprises in a major role, simply as a matter of technological necessity. In the nuclear reactor field, for instance, the leading European consortia are linked organically to General Electric and to Westinghouse. In other cases, the European projects have performed inadequately, given their purpose. One reason for the inadequacy is that the projects have generally been cooperative rather than unitary; that is, they have linked together a number of discrete elements, each of which has retained its national identity. Projects such as *Concorde* ELDO, and Unidata, all of them representing a riposte against American technological leadership, have all been modeled on this conception. Moreover, when governments have been directly involved, projects such as these have usually been operated on the notorious principle of *le juste retour,* the principle that each nation's suppliers are entitled to sell an amount of goods and services exactly equal to the nation's financial contribution to the project. In many of these cooperative projects, it has been apparent that all the participants might benefit—and benefit more—if a less compartmentalized approach were taken; but the participants have been unwilling to assume the larger measure of risk that would be entailed thereby. As a result, most projects have been disappointing in execution, leaving the Europeans with many of their original frustrations.

Of course, if the European movement had reached the point at which Europe had acquired some sort of political personality, one might conceivably contemplate a set of European initiatives in various high-technology fields, in which the individual states gave up their decision-making powers to some European entity. Tallies of cost and benefit would be kept in European terms, not in separate national terms. Programs of governmental purchase would be pan-European, not national, in scope; *le juste retour* would be modified or abandoned. In that case, the dominance of United States technology in the fields where sheer size is critical would presumably be whittled away.

My European colleagues in this collective work, however, assure me that any expectation of such developments in Europe would be optimistic to the point of being visionary. According to them, one can anticipate intimate and continuous consultations among European governments, coordination of national action, cooperative projects on a large scale—but no significant submergence of national identity, let alone of national interest. If their judgment is correct, there are certain corollaries I am inclined to draw. European industries will surely seize the technological lead in many fields, including some fields of considerable commercial importance, just as they have in the past. But the superior scale of the United States economy will mean that the American technological lead in some especially sensitive sectors will persist; that one of its consequences will be to bolster the competitive position of U.S.-based firms operating in Europe, especially of those firms whose competitive strength is dependent on large-scale technological effort; and that this will be a source of continued friction in the future.

The Mature Large-Scale Industries

Outside of the technology-based industries, the multinationalizing trend has generated rather different patterns and has produced somewhat different consequences for relations between the United States and Europe.

In industries such as oil, aluminum, steel, copper, and bulk chemicals, the forces that have moved enterprises across international borders have not been primarily technological in character. The power of multinational enterprises in these industries appears to derive from the fact that sheer size generates certain special strengths. One such strength is production efficiency. The cost of an efficient aluminum refinery or petrochemical complex in the 1970s has to be reckoned in terms of hundreds of millions of dollars, and the output of one such facility constitutes a measurable fraction of the world market. In these industries, brute size is a condition of entry. Moreover, the advantages of geographical spread—spread in markets, spread in raw material sources—may add to the advantages of size alone. The firm with multiple sources for its raw material possesses a special buffer against interruptions in supply. The firm with multiple markets can ordinarily count on a more stable pattern of demand. In industries that are highly capital-intensive, stability is an especially important factor, since relatively small variations in output can generate large changes in unit costs of production.

Conscious of the advantages of size and spread, enterprises in these industries have frequently entered into partnerships to exploit some raw material source or to make and sell their output in some distant market. This sort of arrangement has increased the reach of each participating firm beyond its own limits. In efforts to stretch their reach, European-based enterprises have linked themselves not only with other European firms, but also with U.S.-based enterprises.

Another consideration has encouraged large enterprises in these industries to move outside their home borders. This has been the compelling need of each leader to ensure that other leaders are not gaining some special advantage overseas that will upset the equilibrium of the industry. A characteristic hedge on the part of leaders in such circumstances has been to imitate the others, thereby sharing the same strengths and bearing the same weaknesses. Leaders have implanted their facilities in some areas partly in response to the earlier initiative of other leaders or of some intruder from another industry. In a variant of this follow-the-leader behavior, firms have occasionally countered the penetration of a foreign intruder by invading the home market of the intruder.[8]

The intricate interrelations that have developed among large firms in some of these capital-intensive standardized industries have elevated problems of competition and monopoly from the national to the multinational level. More and more, the attacks and ripostes of any large firm have been made with an eye to its position in the world at large.

If nations had not previously been aware of the global character of some of their major industries, the fact was forcefully illustrated in the handling of the oil crisis of 1973-1974. It goes without saying that governments felt threatened by a reduction in crude oil supplies during the crisis and that they cast about for ways of protecting themselves. For various reasons, most countries chose a go-it-alone policy. Some tried to increase their supplies by bargaining directly with exporting countries and by commanding or coercing the oil companies that happened to come under their jurisdiction. Others, including Germany, Italy, and the United States, had more passive or more confused policies.

The differences in national policies, however, seemed to have little effect upon the outcome. As it turned out, during the period of the crisis in 1973 and 1974, most countries ended up with roughly the same degree of stringency in supplies of oil.[9] This result was produced by the policies of the international oil companies, responding to the crisis according to their own means and their own priorities. For the most part, their priorities were to keep their own distribution facilities well supplied, wherever they might be, and to head off hostile political reactions wherever they threatened. With pressures from all sides, both official and unofficial, the companies' priorities appear to have worked out in such a way that the burden of shortage was fairly well distributed among the importing countries. Governmental policies in this case seemed to matter less than the operations of the international companies.

The multinationalization of the mature industries strikes me as a potential source of considerable strife between the United States and Europe. These industries play a key role in national development: Volvo is a major element in the Swedish economy, as are ICI and Shell in Britain, Péchiney-Ugine-Kuhlmann in France, and Hoechst and BASF in Germany. Yet each of these enterprises, driven by some of the factors described earlier, finds itself expanding its stake in the oversized U.S. market as rapidly as—in some cases more rapidly than—it expands its commitment at home. The stresses created inside national governments by that situation, already visible in the oil crisis, can be detected in such other industries as automobiles and aluminum.

If the leading firms of Europe were seen as European enterprises, not as enterprises of a single European state, their stake in the United States market might not loom so large; compared to their commitments in Europe as a whole, the American investments might seem of manageable size. But that is not the European perception; and apparently it is unlikely to be the European perception for some time to come. As a result, the commitment in the United States will be measured against the commitment in the national markets and will be seen as a force confusing the identity and diluting the loyalty of the national enterprises concerned.

National Responsibilities and National Politics

The growth of interdependence among nations has had a number of profound implications. One of these has been the growth of national interests with a major stake in keeping the borders open. These interests have appeared in the newer, more dynamic, more rapidly growing sectors of the national economy, responding to the new state of transportation, communication, and techniques of production. Their interests and needs, however, represent only one powerful force in modern society. Another force, representing the antithesis of our starting paradox, is the social service state. As this concept has taken root in the industrialized world, it has entailed the assignment of new responsibilities to government: such goals as the avoidance of unemployment, the suppression of inflation, the redistribution of income, and the development of lagging regions. Yet, as public officials have confronted these tasks, they have repeatedly been brought up short by the difficulties of reconciling national management with open economic borders. How, for instance, was a country to avoid inflation in a year in which the prices of imported oil quadrupled? How was unemployment to be avoided in a year in which automobile imports increased 15 per cent?

The contradiction has been much more painful for the middle-sized European states than for the huge United States economy. States that could once think seriously of a strategy based on self-sufficiency, such as France, Italy, and Germany, find it harder today to think in those terms. The losses involved in cutting themselves off from other states are perceived as too high. Even the United States, with its huge continental market, sees significant losses in separating itself from other economies. But the United States tends to see such losses as much smaller than do most Europeans. The difference in perception is altogether realistic; and it represents an asymmetry in trans-Atlantic relations that contributes strongly to American-European tensions.

In order realistically to identify some of the critical choices of the United States over the next decade, one has to have some sense of the range of decisions that the American political process is capable of generating. My reading of recent history suggests that, on international economic issues, the range is fairly wide, much wider than that of any of the middle-sized states of Europe. With not so much to lose and not so much to gain in short-run economic terms from the international economy, the United States is somewhat freer to choose its policies on the basis of other criteria.

The policy since World War II of supporting a more or less open competitive system in world markets illustrates the somewhat greater elbow room of American leaders in framing international economic policies. There is a strand of revisionist history that argues that this policy was based on a very immediate and pragmatic goal: to establish American economic hegemony in Europe and elsewhere.[10] In fact, however, United States policymakers at the time were moved by an odd alliance of forces, some motivated by narrow economic goals, some by larger perceptions of long-term interest. The alliance included Southern agricultural interests, strongly entrenched in key positions in the United States Congress, who were responding to the historical memories of the South's exploitation by a protected industrial North; also key economic policymakers in the executive branch, who were strongly influenced by neoclassical economic assumptions as well as by the Wilsonian idea of contributing to world peace through an open economic system. Absent from the coalition, at least in its early creative stages, were United States business enterprises engaged in international expansion.

Insofar as business groups were involved in the formulation of the new policies, immediate economic interests were of course important. Some industries resisted the new trend, especially those which confronted a static national demand and were burdened with high labor costs, such as textiles and shoes. The early business supporters of the new policies, such as the newly formed Committee for Economic Development, were moved by a general ideological commitment much more than by an identification with specific business interests.[11] All told, the role of business in the shaping of the new policies was not central. Because no powerful business interests felt themselves greatly threatened by the trend, no strong disposition existed in this quarter to head it off.

The part played by the U.S. labor movement in the development of an open competitive order during the early postwar years also displayed a mixture of special interests and larger concepts. Some opposition from labor was evident, often in the static industries referred to earlier.[12] But the important role was played by key labor leaders operating at the national level, many of them not closely identified with any specific industry or locality. Labor leaders such as Walter Reuther and David McDonald, like other U.S. leaders of the time, saw themselves committed to the creation of a new international order, and many found themselves developing a considerable interest in labor organizations abroad. Missionary work in Europe, Japan, and the less developed world provided an outlet for international aspirations that were viewed as compatible with the interests of American labor. Whatever the main motivating force of the leaders might be, they could always assert to their home labor constituency that any increase in foreign labor costs would reduce the foreign threat to American labor. Accordingly, the national labor leaders of the immediate postwar period were prepared to try to hold in check the strong protectionist instincts that were found in the less dynamic sectors of the United States labor market.

The ability of the United States government to lead a general movement toward the opening up of international economic boundaries in the decades following World War II, therefore, rested on a fragile national coalition. Nevertheless, the coalition was firm enough to allow the United States to take the lead in several huge multinational tariff negotiating sessions, beginning in Geneva in 1948 and culminating in that same city with the Kennedy round of negotiations in the 1960s. These tariff-reducing sessions, together with the progressive abandonment by the industrialized countries of import licenses and foreign-exchange licenses, transformed the conditions for trade. To be sure, pockets of high duties still existed in a few sections of each country's tariff; agricultural products continued to be governed by a set of rules all their own; and government agencies continued to practice various primitive forms of protectionism in their own official purchases, epitomized in "buy-at-home" policies and practices. But barriers of this sort were of minor consequence when measured against the norms that had prevailed before 1950.[13]

Concurrently with the dismantling of trade barriers went a quickening in the propensity of United States businessmen to establish producing subsidiaries and affiliates in other countries. The four hundred or so manufacturing subsidiaries of large U.S. firms found in Europe at the end of World War II mushroomed so rapidly that by 1967 the number of subsidiaries of these same firms reached 1,438.[14] The dismantling of trade restrictions and the spread of U.S.-owned subsidiaries may not have been closely related; in fact, there is some support for the proposition that if European trade barriers had remained high, United States firms would have established themselves in Europe in even greater number.[15] In any case, it is clear that the establishment of such subsidiaries was not greatly impeded by other kinds of restrictions, such as restrictions on capital exports. The American restraints on the export of capital that were in effect during most of the 1960s simply led businessmen to borrow what they needed in European capital markets.

The ability of U.S.-based enterprises to spread into other countries despite restrictions on the export of capital showed that the process of multinationalization was not essentially a capital movement. It was, as the French put it, an implantation—the reaching out to one more location by an existing business network. Along the spokes and ribs of the network moved not only goods and money, but also—much more importantly—access to information, access to credit, the use of trade names and patents, and the application of organizational systems. To a considerable degree, too, such networks could substitute one type of asset for another. If money could not be sent, then credit guarantees could. If goods could not be sent, then blueprints or experts could take their place. With international transportation and communication so greatly improved, the network was flexible in what it moved across international boundaries. For the United States or any other country to control the spread of such enterprises, its measures would have to be draconian.

The spread of United States enterprises abroad during the 1950s turned the passive tolerance of many American businessmen for open international boundaries into active support. Expansive slogans such as "The world is our oyster" were voiced here and there in the United States business world. For international operations, parochial company names were often replaced by more universal designations: Minnesota Mining and Manufacturing by 3M; Food Machinery and Chemicals Corp. by FMC; and so on.

Meanwhile, however, the coalition that had supported an internationalist mood in the United States was beginning to lose one of its key elements, the leaders of labor. As labor leaders pursued their international interests during the decade of the 1950s, they found themselves exposed to increased sniping from their own rank and file. International trade was increasing and the American economy was confronting greater imports of steel, shoes, textiles, automobiles, and other products. To deal with the adjustment problems that these imports were generating, labor leaders began to pin their defenses on the concept of government-supported trade adjustment programs. The hope was that federal funds would assist ailing enterprises and workers pressed by competition from abroad to make the transition to other lines of work. But that proposal, first launched by the head of the United Steel Workers in 1954, drew practically no support from businessmen or academics.[16] It was not until the Trade Expansion Act was passed in 1962 that the concept was embodied in law. It was not until 1969 that the idea found tangible expression in any benefits to workers. And even then, the benefits took an especially sterile form, namely, a limited prolongation of unemployment compensation to the affected workers.

For the rank and file of labor, programs such as these were much too little and far too late. As they saw it, the psychic uncertainties and the pains of adjustment that went with open borders were being borne essentially by them. Of course, valid arguments could be made to the contrary: closed borders would reduce everybody's living standard including that of labor and would reduce the employment opportunities of their children. But these abstractions were not strong enough in the 1960s to stand up against the immediate fears that were generated by increased imports in some of the slow-growing industries. The leaders of labor had little choice: either they had to rejoin the troops or give up their claim to leadership. By the middle 1960s, most labor leaders had chosen to rejoin the troops; and having done so, most leaders infused their new position with a spirit of commitment that rivaled their earlier opposite views.

The change in their commitment, however, did little to change the fundamental facts. In practice, large American enterprises could still scan Western Europe and other areas for business opportunities. They could still exploit some of those opportunities by creating or expanding productive facilities in Europe. If capital was blocked, other means could be found to finance expansion abroad. Labor's negative policies for security and growth, as most labor leaders were privately aware, were unlikely to help labor in the end.

The inference I am inclined to draw from the American labor movement's present structure and behavior is that its role in future international relations is not irrevocably fixed—that, despite its current tone of belligerency and dogmatism, it still is capable of a wide range of choice. Its exposure to foreign competition is not nearly so great as that of labor in other countries. Moreover the effects of that exposure are both diverse and ambiguous: while the traditional sectors are pinched back, the dynamic ones seem to profit. If my reasoning is correct, the attitude of labor need not be thought of as cast in concrete.

Nor should it be assumed that labor's reactions can be projected as some simple function of the level of national economic activity. In the past, to be sure, depressions have heightened the fear of foreign imports; but they have also sharpened the countervailing fear of being shut out of foreign markets. It is no accident, for instance, that the first Trade Agreements Act was enacted in the economic trough of 1934, and the Trade Expansion Act in the shallower dip of 1962.

My disposition to think of labor's position as both diverse and fluid is strengthened by two factors. One is the strong tendency of multinational enterprises in the United States to increase the number and scope of their product lines, so that the typical large firm is engaged in a much wider range of product markets than has ever been the case before.[17] The other is the strong tendency for labor unions themselves to recruit their membership across product lines.[18] The consequences of these changes are too complex for easy generalization. But they offer new prospects for flexibility and change. If, for example, the political process in the United States promised much more generous and more imaginative support to labor in handling the problems of adjustment and change, I think a considerable section of the national labor leadership would turn away from its present dead-end policies with a sigh of obvious relief.

Today's situation, moreover, is being shaped by one more factor, of fundamental importance. The process of international implantation by national industries is no longer a one-way flow. Since the latter half of the 1960s, a considerable number of European firms have established themselves in the United States. In fact, by 1974, Europeans had acquired a stake of about $14 billion in their United States subsidiaries, a figure not wholly incommensurate with American firms' reported $45 billion commitment in Europe.[19] Major European firms, such as BASF, Hoechst, Imperial Chemical Industries, British Petroleum, Péchiney-Ugine-Kuhlmann, and Volvo, now have a long-run commitment to the United States economy. And American workers numbering in the several hundred thousands now have a stake in ensuring that the subsidiaries of foreign firms remain and grow.

The growth of foreign-owned enterprises in the United States does not mean that tensions will necessarily decline between the factors that are locked on national soil and those that can move across international boundaries. As recent statements of the head of the United Automobile Workers indicate, the reaction of labor leaders to the growth of foreign-owned subsidiaries in the United States is hardly more friendly than such leaders' reaction to the growth of U.S.-owned subsidiaries abroad.[20] These leaders feel a special sense of weakness whenever they negotiate their multinational enterprises, and that sense exists whether those enterprises are headquartered in the United States or headquartered abroad. The rank and file, though, may have different reactions; for them the foreign enterprises are possible employers as well as potential adversaries. So the possibility of moving labor from its neoprotectionist position seems real.

Interdependence in Future Relations

Revelations come in waves. In the years immediately after World War II, the revelations of the future international order came from a dazzling array of inspired men, including Marshall, Monnet, and Adenauer. In the years since the late 1960s, the durability of the nation state has been reasserted with varying degrees of eloquence by de Gaulle, Nixon, Wilson, and Schmidt. The time may now be ripe for still a third wave of revelation. The problem is to fashion a set of institutions that respond to two disturbing yet compelling facts: the costs of reducing the degree of interdependence between the United States and Western Europe are high; yet the interdependence inhibits governments in their efforts to respond to the tasks laid on them by their national political processes.

There is nothing new in the formulation of this dilemma. Much the same point was persuasively formulated in 1968 by one of the contributors to the present volume.[21] It was assumed at the time—rightly, no doubt—that nations were not yet prepared effectively to coordinate their national economic objectives and economic policies. A variety of cooperative approaches were suggested as second-best solutions, including variable exchange rates, wider currency bands, larger lines of short-term credit among central banks, and more intensive consultations among nations over their national restrictions. In the past few years, some of these measures have in fact been put in place; and already it is becoming clear that these measures by themselves will not dispose of the dilemma. There are various reasons why this is so. Not the least of these is the changing structure of industry.

It was once hoped that more flexible exchange rates might reduce the sensitivity of nations to the openness of their national boundaries. The reasoning was straightforward: flexible rates were seen as a way of allowing a country to pursue an independent national monetary policy while yet maintaining open boundaries. If a nation wished to increase national demand by running the printing press, the commitment to a fixed exchange rate would not stand in the way.

Today, the hope that flexible rates will reduce the problems of interdependence is a little less vigorous, weakened by a number of different concerns. With large quantities of short-term funds slopping about in international money markets, there is the fear that speculative capital movements may unsettle exchange rates and produce tremors inside some national economics. Moreover, frequent movements in exchange rates, whatever their cause, imply frequent shifts in the internal mix of industries; and since such shifts entail economic and social costs, continuous adjustments of that nature are not altogether welcome. Finally, the fear has developed that changes in exchange rates, which might have been expected a priori to reduce international prices as often as they increase such prices, in fact operate as one-way impulses, serving mainly to increase such prices; so flexible rates become a factor that feeds inflation.

The fear that exchange rates may prove too flexible is matched by the fear that they may not prove flexible enough. In this case, the changing structure of world industry has generated the concern. Transactions between the affiliates of multinational enterprises have come to represent perhaps one quarter or one third of the international trade in manufactured goods and industrial raw materials. There is reason for assuming that these interaffiliate transactions are relatively insensitive to changes in exchange rates. As long as international transactions are conducted at arm's length, importers presumably feel free to shift their sources of supply in accordance with changes in price. When affiliates trade with each other across an international border, however, they are probably much less prone to shift sources in response to relative price changes, especially if the shift entails the abandonment of an existing plant or the construction of a new one. The reason for this assumption has to do with the structure of costs as perceived by any multiplant system.

From the viewpoint of such a system, any plant that is in actual operation already has sunk a considerable part of the full cost of production. Buildings and machinery are in place. Local staff has been recruited and trained. Headquarters staff has been restructured to monitor and control the new entity. Governmental arrangements have been negotiated and are in operation. The running-in costs and learning costs have already been absorbed. So the cost of continuing to operate the plant is relatively low. When a multinational enterprise contemplates abandoning an old location for a new one in response to a change in exchange rates, it is obliged to compare the full cost of operating in the new location with the marginal cost of continuing in the old. There may be similar choices at times for an enterprise that is buying at arm's length from an independent supplier; in an effort to hold an important customer, such a supplier might offer to sell at long-term marginal cost. But it would be surprising if cases of this sort were very common.

The implications of these relationships are profound. They suggest a reduction in the efficacy of exchange rates in bringing about a change in patterns of international trade. And they suggest also that in industries made up of multinational enterprises the influence of tariffs, subsidies, and other policy instruments in stimulating locational shifts may be reduced.

There is also a possibility that the growth of multinational enterprises has tended to reduce the role of interest rate diffentials in determining international money movements. Multinational enterprises have two reasons for moving money from one currency area to another. One is to profit from interest rate differentials; the other is to avoid the adverse effects of a change in currency values. When the second motivation dominates, it leads to a speeding up or slowing down of payments that would eventually take place in any case, and thereby it places added pressure on a currency that is under stress.

This problem is, of course, a variant of the familiar problem of leads and lags in international payments. Difficulties of that sort would exist even if multinational enterprises did not. But it can be assumed that multinational enterprises by and large have a greater propensity to respond to the threat of currency instability than national enterprises. One reason is that changes in exchange rates have more immediate repercussions on multinational enterprises. As a result, multinational enterprises are more likely to gear up their organizations to respond to the risk. Moreover, when multinational enterprises respond through accelerated or delayed payments among affiliates, they do so without having to involve an outside party. They can move faster; hence are quicker to move.[22]

The role of multinational enterprises in monetary crises has been a matter of considerable public concern. To this, managers have replied with a simple, though self-serving, contention: that any time an enterprise takes some defensive action in a currency, the currency is already out of equilibrium and in need of adjustment. In that case, the precautionary measures of the enterprise serve the socially useful purpose of pushing the currencies in the "right" direction. That generalization, however, is no more plausible a priori than the rival view, namely, that the uncertainties which exist in the minds of the multinational managers can start up or amplify currency movements that are costly to the economic system; and further, that such costly movements are greater than those which would occur if multinational enterprises did not exist. This is a possibility that policymakers are obliged to confront.

If the power of exchange-rate policy and interest-rate policy as instruments of national policy is being reduced by the growth of multinational enterprises, as I think is the case, the implications of that tendency for relations between the United States and Western Europe are fairly critical. It suggests that as American enterprises spread further into Western Europe and as the enterprises of European nations establish themselves in other European states and in the United States, the efficacy of these tools of national policy will continue to decline; or, alternatively, that the spread of multinational enterprises across the Atlantic will be checked.

The probability that the spread will be checked does not seem very high. In times past, European nations that have threatened to impose restrictions on multinationals have tended to act very cautiously; even the well-advertised hostility of de Gaulle failed to generate much action. The reasons are always the same: the costs of restriction appear to outweigh the benefits. Moreover, with European enterprises rapidly implanting themselves in the United States, the seeming costs may well grow in European eyes. Finally, even if governments could bring themselves substantially to curb the establishment of foreign subsidiaries, it seems probable that the curbs would only change the form of the multinationalizing process, not its substance. In the modern world, the substitutability between information, money, and goods is high, and any effective regulations would have to cover not only the offending flow, but also its substitutes.

Nations are likely to be pushed, therefore, to other responses. One possibility, difficult as it may seem at the present moment, is the more effective coordination of relevant national policies. If flexible exchange rates prove as inadequate as fixed rates have already proven, the coordination of national policies is the only serious line of approach left to reduce the diversity of economic trends among countries. One must be realistic, however, about the degree of coordination that can be contemplated. To a man, the Europeans engaged in the preparation of this volume seem to feel that individual European states will resist any substantial new commitments on vital national economic policies, whether confined to Europe or broader in reach. *A fortiori*, this also must be assumed for the United States and Japan. That assumption limits what can be done; but it does not altogether eliminate the possibility of constructive action.

Areas for Policy Coordination

The implications of this formulation go well beyond policies relating to industry's structure. They bear on monetary and fiscal policy, medium-term growth policy, and many other issues. Sticking to my last, however, I intend to explore the possible lines of policy that relate to the issue of industrial structure.

The Functional Approach

The development of an agenda for action in this field is, in fact, already well under way. Half a dozen international agencies—UNCTAD, the OAS, the ILO, and the OECD—are bristling with programs of study and action. In the United States-European context, the OECD program has the greatest relevance. That group is in process of studying the following subjects: improving exchanges of information among governments on the subject of multinational enterprises; evaluating the role of such enterprises in contributing to short-term capital movements; analyzing the interaffiliate transactions of the enterprises; and analyzing their practices as they bear on taxation, industrial relations, and technological transfers. At the same time specific action is being pushed on three fronts: on the development of a code of conduct for multinational enterprises; on the development of rules regarding the national treatment of foreign-owned affiliates; and on the application of incentives or disincentives to foreign investors. This, therefore, is where one begins.

It would not be helpful or practical to comment on any of these issues in great detail; they are too complex, and the tactical twists of negotiation too unpredictable to render such a treatment very useful. But some of the issues illuminate certain larger choices.

The case of taxation is illustrative. Intrinsically, the problem itself is not of earthshaking importance. But it is one in which the individual states concerned seem likely to operate independently and aggressively during the next decade. If they do, it may be one of the early cases in which the multinational enterprises themselves will wish for a more effective means of coordinating national action than is presently available.

At the root of the problem is the unavoidable element of arbitrariness in deciding how much of the aggregate profit of a multinational enterprise has been generated by each affiliate unit—how much by the British unit, how much by the French, how much by the American. In some cases, the goods that are transferred between affiliates have a market price that can be objectively determined; but just as often, they do not. At least as important is the fact that the things of value which are transferred among the units of a multinational enterprise or are shared by them are commonly intangibles: access to a common body of knowledge, a common trade name, a common pool of patents, a joint credit rating, and a functioning organization. When assets of this sort are used by any unit of the organization, what is the appropriate charge for tax purposes?

A clash among the industrialized countries over this subject has been long a-building. National tax authorities, single-mindedly devoted to the collection of revenue in accordance with their national statutes, have neither the viewpoint nor the discretion for contemplating the problem in its international dimensions. Accordingly, the United States Internal Revenue Service has already promulgated regulations that unilaterally define the American share in certain kinds of interaffiliate transactions. And this is only a beginning; in the pipeline are much more comprehensive interpretations of United States tax law that will have a major impact on the way in which the American affiliate's profit is defined in this unavoidably difficult area.[23]

So far, the frictions that might otherwise arise among the industrialized countries in allocating taxable profits among the affiliates of multinational enterprises have been held in bounds by two factors. One factor has been the passivity of most European governments in tackling some of these thorny questions. The second is the network of bilateral international tax agreements; these agreements, many of them based on an OECD model, provide an instrument for reducing conflict.

But the outlook for the rest of the 1970s is one of greatly heightened interest of governments in the tax payments of multinational enterprises. The rise of a populist mood in the United States and Europe, as well as the increasing sophistication and concern for the tax authorities of Europe, would be reason enough. But the initiatives of the United States tax authorities almost guarantee the result.

The OECD initiative, therefore, is timely. There is a chance, however, that it may also prove too conservative. The need to find workable rules to allocate profits is complemented by the need to fashion an institution that can make the rules work. It would be surprising if the present network of bilateral agreements proved sufficient to handle the traffic that will likely be generated in this field in the years just ahead, including conflicts in interpretation, inadequacies in coverage, unavailability of remedies, and similar problems. In that case, it may be necessary to replace or supplement the network of bilateral agreements with a more effective and more flexible structure for intergovernmental coordination. Such a structure would probably need to be multilateral in character, with a capacity for developing information, settling disputes, and formulating new principles.

More important and more complex is the broad field of the regulation of market behavior. It does not much matter whether a country is bent on restraining its large national enterprises in order to promote competition, as the United States is inclined to do, or whether a country wants to merge its national enterprises for greater efficiency, as the Europeans often prefer to do. In either case, the determination of the relevant facts and the application of the appropriate action are rendered much more difficult by the multinational structure of industry.

The problems in the field of competition and monopoly are of several kinds. One is ignorance on the part of national authorities. The problem is not limited to assessing the operations of foreign-owned subsidiaries in a nation's jurisdiction; it also applies to understanding the implications of the overseas operations of national companies. Indeed, even when the national companies are government-owned, as in the case of British Petroleum or Renault, it is difficult for governments to grasp the full meaning of their multinational operations.

These difficulties take various forms. There are the conceptual difficulties of interpreting a complex global pattern of behavior, as well as the jurisdictional limitations upon the right to command information. For multinational enterprises, whatever their nationality or ownership, tend to shape their strategies on a global basis. These strategies entail many different forms of interaction with competitors. They include cooperative behavior, in the form of partnerships or other forms of conscious cooperation; but also independent behavior, in the form of follow-the-leader imitation or countervailing thrusts. The measures and countermeasures in these cooperative or conflicting relations among multinational enterprises take place all over the globe. Accordingly, authorities have more than the usual difficulties in determining what is going on.

Another kind of problem has to do with the fashioning of remedies. As with information gathering, the problem is partly jurisdictional: if national authorities were to direct the local subsidiaries of two different multinational enterprises to merge, for instance, they would not ordinarily obtain a very relevant response. But even when the companies involved in a government-sponsored merger are nationally owned, the fact that each is part of an international network tends to place limits on the power of local authorities. That is amply illustrated by the French government's frustrations in trying to encourage a merger between its Compagnie Générale d'Electricité and Thomson-Houston.[24] The two enterprises were each linked to a different technological and competitive network in international markets; each had its own allies, linked by licenses and shared interests; each soon found itself in adversary relationships with the other. The ministries of the French government were not strong enough to hold the two companies to a clearly coordinated French strategy.

The problems of harmonizing the national responses of different countries in this critical field are quite formidable. One type of problem rests on cultural and philosophical differences: the reactions of different nations to monopolies and to agreements in restraint of trade are fairly diverse. France has often promoted monopolies on the assumption that a strong tutelary ministry can guarantee that the monopoly's potential efficiencies will be realized and its potential abuses avoided.[25] The United Kingdom has typically picked and chosen among restrictive private arrangements, favoring them in some cases and striking them down in others.[26] The United States alone has defined some types of restrictive agreements as illegal per se.[27] Some reconciliation of these different approaches will be needed, and it will not be easy.

Moreover, there are ideological differences among countries regarding the distinction between public enterprises and private enterprises. In some countries of Western Europe, there is a presumption that publicly-owned enterprises are more solicitous of the public interest than private, and that in any event the remedies against predatory actions applicable to public enterprises ought to be different from the remedies applicable to private enterprises. This has proved a stumbling block in international discussions over restrictive business practices, as some nations have insisted on exempting publicly-owned enterprises from international agreement.

Indeed, the only issue that national authorities have effectively addressed so far with respect to international restrictive business practices is that of the overlap of national jurisdictions. On this point, however, effectiveness has been measured by success in avoiding political disputes, not by the ability to deal with a restrictive international practice. Nations intending to institute a procedure that might directly affect another have given notice and engaged in consultation. The virtual disappearance of international cases from the United States docket suggests that the consultative procedures have restrained nations from pursuing problems with international ramifications. Conflict has been reduced, but mainly at the price of leaving the problems themselves to fester. That approach is unlikely to suffice much longer.

With the oil crisis so fresh in mind, it is almost gratuitous to point out another implication of the multinationalization of large enterprises. When international markets break down, individual importing nations rarely are in a position to do much in the short run to deal with the situation. A governmental decision to go it alone is ordinarily a commitment to be ineffectual; the apparatus for international distribution lies largely beyond any single government's reach. Though the generalization applies with less force to large nations than to small, even the United States is not immune. With a third or so of its industrial output in the hands of businesss entities that have significant overseas interests, the United States has to think of itself as an open economy. The moral scarcely needs to be drawn. If nations wish to affect the behavior of international markets, they have to be able to influence the multinational enterprises. That possibility is more likely to be realized if the principal industrial nations are coordinating their efforts than if each attempts to go it alone. In this case, of course, the prototypical response is already in place, namely, the International Energy Agency. Its seminal provisions for "cooperation" among the member countries and with the international oil industry have yet to be tested. Inaction in this field could easily develop. If it does, the next emergency may well generate an uncoordinated scramble among frantic nations or a slipping back into informal rationing by the international companies. Neither of these outcomes would be palatable, either to the governments or to the companies.

Finally, in the context of the conflict-of-jurisdiction issue, there are the somewhat shopworn disputes over controlling trading with the "enemy." Shopworn though the issue may be, its capacity for doing mischief in relations between the United States and Europe is very high, since it stands for a class of issues that provoke special national sensitivities. The history of the trading-with-the-enemy issue is well chronicled.[28] In brief, the U.S. government during much of the 1950s and 1960s sought to impose some fairly severe restrictions on exports from NATO countries and Japan of goods that might contribute to the war-making power of the USSR. Part of the effort took place through an international organization designed for the purpose, the so-called Coordinating Committee, COCOM. In that committee, the United States sought to persuade Western European countries and Japan to impose restrictions that were as tight as the American restrictions; and characteristically, the United States was obliged to accept a lesser level of commitment on the part of the countries of Western Europe. Nonetheless, the United States persevered. Though it could not easily reach the European-owned firms located in Europe, it sought to impose its restrictive export standards on the U.S.-owned subsidiaries located in Western Europe, simply by leaning on their parents in the United States. These efforts led to explosive incidents from time to time, as United States authorities tried to limit the Soviet-bound exports of the French or British or German subsidiaries of United States firms. In the end, the political costliness of the policy became too painfully evident. Besides, the policy itself grew anachronistic with the coming of détente.

There is an excellent case to be made for the view that the American policy of security export controls was ill-conceived and ill-executed, and that it was more hurtful than helpful to United States security. Still, an underlying lesson remains. If and when such controls are regarded by any country as necessary for its security, the existence of multinational enterprises is likely to reduce the efficacy of any national policy. The need for coordination in this kind of field, therefore, is as great as it has ever been.

Sorting Out Jurisdictions

In this emphasis on the functional approach, a basic factor contributing to the underlying tension remains neglected. Many Europeans see U.S.-based enterprises as the extended arm of United States policy, supportive of and supported by the United States government. The occasional links between the CIA and U.S. firms in foreign countries have reinforced the conviction. The French, British, German, and Italian styles of association between ministries and enterprises may be even more intimate and reciprocally supportive at times. But Europeans do not see their own styles and practices as being so much a threat to international harmony.

The issue reflects a fundamental point, touched on again and again in this brief essay. Incompatibilities exist between the concept of the multinational enterprise and the concept of an international system composed of nation states. Nations are concerned about their ability to command the loyalty of foreign-owned subsidiaries in their jurisdiction and concerned about their ability to retain the loyalty of their own parent business entities. Meanwhile, the multinational enterprises themselves operate on a global level, dealing with these real or latent conflicts as best they can.

There is no sweeping way to eliminate the incompatibility; but there are ways of making it more manageable. One way is to support a treaty embodying the basic principle that governments would not seek to influence the behavior of business subsidiaries located in other jurisdictions. The principle would be applied only to certain specified fields, namely, those in which the signatory governments had put in place an effective multilateral machinery for the joint handling of issues. If the functional approach described earlier should generate results, machinery of this sort could be envisaged, to begin with, in the fields of taxation, competition and monopoly, trading with the enemy, and the disclosure requirements for corporations.

An obvious corollary of that proposition would be that no government would support the claims or complaints of one of its enterprises with respect to the treatment of a subsidiary located in another jurisdiction. Such an agreement would, however, require the adoption—or the readoption—of a companion principle, namely, that in the treatment of enterprises in their jurisdiction, distinctions based on the nationality of the owners would be rigorously and explicitly limited. Of course, the principle exists already in agreements between the United States and Western Europe, solemnized in numerous bilateral treaties of friendship, commerce, and navigation. But despite widespread violation in one degree or another, no government has felt free to press its treaty rights. This is a common affliction of bilateral treaties. To redress the situation and to revitalize the principle, it may prove necessary to create a multilateral apparatus. The Convention on the Settlement of Investment Disputes, which operates under the wing of the World Bank, moves in that direction. But its membership, its procedures, and its general outlook are all somewhat at variance with the proposals suggested here. More to the point would be an organization whose membership and sense of cohesion allowed its member countries to withdraw their protective national mantle from the overseas subsidiaries of their enterprises and to consider jointly with other countries what the basis of the operation of multinational enterprises should be.

The Technology Gap

None of these measures is likely to affect very much the tensions that are associated with the continued technological imbalance between the United States and Europe. Fundamentally, the American priority in industrial innovation that provoked the debate of the latter 1960s has hardly changed at all. To be sure, European industry has managed largely to obliterate, even to reverse, some of the large technological leads that U.S.-based enterprises managed to pile up during the war years and the decade immediately following. In automobiles, plastics, consumer electronics, consumer durables, and many other lines, no technological gap exists any longer. But that shift in the technological balance was to be anticipated, following a pattern that has been observed repeatedly over a century of industrial competition.

In individual product lines, a technological gap rarely persists for long periods. Where a technological gap appears to persist, it is because of the leading nation's ability to generate a succession of innovations that continually renew the lead. That capacity of the United States economy has not greatly changed, at least by comparison with Europe. The size of the United States market in general and of governmental needs in particular, as well as the open-ended nature of the high-technology industries in the United States, creates unique advantages in the race to develop costly new products at the outer perimeters of those industries. A unitary Europe with a genuinely integrated market could come close to duplicating such conditions; but the individual nations in a loosely structured Europe, which my European colleagues regard as more realistic, would have much greater difficulty.

The pervasive existence of multinational enterprises in these industries brings added dimensions to an already difficult problem. All nations try to hold inside their own territory any plants that produce advanced products with military applications, especially products whose development has been supported in one way or another by the government. Sometimes, though not often, governments succeed in their quarantine efforts. The singular indisposition of the aircraft industry to multinationalize, as nearly as an outsider can judge, represents a rare triumph of home governmental pressures over business predilections.

When such enterprises have managed to break out of their home territory and to spread into other countries, the nature of the tension has usually changed. A hauling and pulling has developed among potential host countries over whether and where such enterprises should establish some coveted production facility. But the countries that win in the hauling and pulling still do not remain content for very long. Though host countries prefer local production to imports, they prefer even more that nationally-owned firms should do the producing rather than foreigners. So the issue shifts; the question is how to ease the foreign-owned firm out of a position of control over its advanced technology.

The issue is too complex to invite any simple response. One can envisage a series of marginal changes in patent law, in government procurement policy, and in the allocation of research subsidies, all worked out by international agreement, which would blunt the sharp corners of the problem and maintain a tolerable *modus vivendi*. Some initiatives already have been taken in this direction, such as NASA's arrangements with a European consortium for the construction of a space shuttle, and the plans for a U.S.-related center for nuclear fusion research in Euratom. The risk is that projects of this sort may not move rapidly enough to offset the sense of tension in Europe arising out of a continued technological gap. On the other hand, the necessary conditions for any substantial alleviation of the problem probably lie mainly in European hands—in their capacity for merging certain critical areas of government procurement such as military hardware, for abandoning the principle of *le juste retour*, and for accepting a genuine commingling of national identities and institutions. In that case, the first critical choices lie with Europe, rather than with the United States.

If the European states fail to take the necessary integrative steps, as my European colleagues think likely, then the problem for the United States will be to manage its technological lead in ways that are not egregiously offensive to the Europeans. That will represent a tough challenge for the United States, a challenge that it may well handle badly.

The Problem of Labor

One key factor that may determine national reactions to the changing industrial structure of the West is the position of national labor movements. As was pointed out earlier, labor leaders believe that the managers they confront have greater flexibility and choice than they do; and that conviction applies both to the parent enterprise in the home country and to the foreign-owned subsidiary abroad. The labor leaders feel that they dare not be too successful in their negotiations or too stubborn in their demands, lest they lose the jobs created by multinational firms to other locations.[29]

For a time, it was thought that labor leaders might be able to develop some countervailing power against the managers of multinational enterprises by creating international movements that would represent the collective inerests of the national labor groups. Indeed, the International Chemical Workers Union, the International Metal Workers Union, and a number of other coalitions of national labor groups seemed for a while to be succeeding in just such a strategy.[30] But the potential of that kind of countervailing force was always limited. National labor movements confronting a common employer do not always see themselves as having common interests. In some cases, of course, the common interest is clear: few unions, for instance, would be inclined to encourage increases in local production that would undermine a labor unit which was on strike against the same firm in another country. On the other hand, each national movement is usually aware that its wages and benefits cannot be expected to deviate much from the norms of the national labor market in which it operates; accordingly, its community of interest with the labor unions of other countries is limited. Besides, no national movement can be oblivious of the fact that in the longer run it is in competition with other locations in which the multinational enterprise is implanted, and even with potential locations in which the multinational enterprise has not yet established itself.

In addition, the national labor movements in the different countries of the West—despite the seeming similarity in their interests—in fact have widely different objectives. In many countries of Europe, labor organizations are concerned not only with extracting greater rewards for labor, but also with achieving larger political objectives. The political diversity of European labor movements is illustrated, for instance, by the TUC's tie to the Labour party in Great Britain, by the Communist labor movements of France and Italy, by German labor's special concentration on the *Mitbestimmungsrecht* (right to participate in management), and so on. In any particular case, then, in order to bring about some coordination across borders, it may be necessary to a leader who sees his strength in national politics, another whose interests are confined to a given industry, a third who identifies with a single craft, and a fourth who identifies only with a single employer. Diverse labor movements of this sort may conceivably act together at times in order to countervail against the multinational enterprise; but the possibilities do seem rather limited.

By one means or another, the United States and Europe may be obliged to deal with labor's sense of uncertainty and relative impotence in the face of a multinationalizing world. Increasing labor's bargaining strength would not be very easy to do. But one step that would be responsive to labor's sense of relative weakness would be a program to limit governmental competition aimed at attracting foreign investors, particularly when that competition takes the form of subsidies to capital. The OECD initiative to study incentives and disincentives applicable to foreign investors therefore takes on a special importance.

Incentive programs affecting foreign investors are found in numerous variants: in subsidized credit for industrial structures, in tax forgiveness formulas based on invested capital, in abnormal depreciation allowances, and so on. Such programs have a double impact on labor: they draw facilities away from their established locations, and they encourage producers at times to favor capital-intensive methods of manufacture. Guidelines already exist within the European Community for limiting the use of devices of this sort on the part of member states. The problems of extending the approach to cover the United States are not inconsiderable, since many of the aids in the United States stem from state and local authorities. But the problems can probably be overcome.

Part of the response to labor's uncertainties may also have to come from national programs unrelated to any international agreement. Labor's problems of adjustment to the shifts of the multinational enterprise are analogous in many respects to those raised by the growth of international trade. One responsive line would be for the United States to extend the adjustment assistance provisions that already apply to dislocations associated with international trade. So far, to be sure, the United States government has conducted its trade adjustment programs rather badly: hedged in by domestic ideological disagreements, the government has framed such programs on a niggardly basis and in an unimaginative form. What is more, such programs have been confined to situations involving foreign imports and have not covered the case of labor adjustment associated with the creation of overseas investment. Programs of this sort must be drastically widened in coverage and substantially improved in efficiency. Otherwise, the inequality with which multinationalization distributes its benefits and its risks between labor and management could in the end prevent the process from realizing its full creative potential.

Reprise

The international environment in which the United States will be reconsidering its economic policies in the next decade or so will be shaped by many factors that are largely beyond American control. One of these is the continuing change in the technology of transportation and communication, which promises to reduce even further the insulation that space once provided between nation-states. Though this is a force that affects United States relations with all nations, its effect on relations with Europe is especially strong. A second factor largely beyond our control is Europe's choice between a tight coalition of European nations or a looser grouping.

Whatever Europe chooses, the interpenetration of the economies will still leave the United States a continental economic power, looking principally to its internal economic resources as the basis for its economic policies. The interaction of the economies and the multinationalization of industry will be significant factors in shaping United States perspectives and policies, but they will fall short of being vital elements in our environment. Moreover, the impact of the multinationalizing trend will fall unevenly on different elements in the United States. Some elements of labor will see themselves advantaged, some disadvantaged, by the trend. United States economic policy therefore will not be wholly predetermined by economic constraints or by economic promise; choices will be possible, keeping in mind the political and security consequences of different courses.

Europe is quite another story. Europe's ability to exercise freedom of choice on a level comparable to that of the United States turns on its ability to develop a substantially more integrated political structure. That goal requires among other things a much tighter economic alliance.

As long as Europe remains a system of nation-states joined principally by a customs union, the sense of vulnerability of each of those states will be very high. Each will react uneasily from time to time, not only to the presence of U.S.-owned enterprises in key positions, but also to the presence of subsidiaries owned by the enterprises of other European states. (According to the evidence so far, the presence of subsidiaries owned by other Europeans may be as disconcerting as the presence of the subsidiaries of U.S.-based enterprises.) If European interests became psychically adjusted to their European identity, however, this would no longer be the case. Presumably the problem of foreign ownership would then be one mainly associated with the role of U.S.-based—and to a much lesser extent, Japan-based—enterprises. In that event, the problem would be one of modest proportions, involving perhaps 10 or 15 per cent of Europe's industrial sector.

There is a larger point that lies behind these observations. In a genuinely unified Europe, the external sector would be relatively small, much smaller than the relative position it now occupies from the viewpoint of Europe's individual nation-states. The shift in perspective would place Europe in a position more nearly approximating that of the United States. The implications of such a shift in perspective could be quite profound. In economic terms, a country with a comparatively small external sector is relatively invulnerable to foreign influence; it can neither gain very much nor lose very much, relatively speaking, by changes in its economic policies toward other countries. One corollary is that other considerations—political, military, or social—will play a larger role in determining economic policy.

These statements are neutral as to the direction of the outcome. Nations freed from economic constraints may be more solicitous of global economic welfare or less so; all one can say with assurance is that in these circumstances neither the hope of short-run economic gain nor the fear of short-run economic loss is quite so important in national decisions. At the same time, a relatively invulnerable Europe will be in an improved position to cooperate with the United States on the issues that concern them both, provided initiatives are forthcoming. A key question for the United States is whether it will be capable of working with an independent Europe that equals it in size and flexibility.

If Europe remains a loose coalition of states, as seems more likely, the choice for the United States may prove even more difficult. Whereas a strong, unified Europe may be able to command United States attention on questions of mutual interest, individual European states joined only in a loose coalition may tend to generate reactions of indifference or of petulance. The risk of such a reaction is all the greater because a loose European coalition would find it hard to propose its own initiatives for cooperation with the United States; yet any proposal from the American side would run the risk of generating a veto from one or more European states. In these circumstances, the United States might be tempted to return to a self-righteous, withdrawn position, reasonably secure in the expectation that some sort of dilute economic hegemony would probably continue. The critical choice for the United States would be to resist that temptation and to continue its efforts at cooperative solutions in spite of all.

Notes

1. "Multinational Enterprises," a special issue of *Business History Review*, Autumn 1974.

2. Raymond Vernon, *Sovereignty at Bay* (New York: Basic Books, 1971), p. 62.

3. *Journal of International Law and Economics* 8, 1 (June 1973); Mira Wilkins, *The Maturing of Multinational Enterprise* (Cambridge: Harvard University Press, 1974); Heinrich Kronstein, *The Law of International Cartels* (Ithaca: Cornell University' Press, 1973).

4. See for instance R.N. Cooper, *The Economics of Interdependence: Economic Policy in the Atlantic Community* (New York: McGraw-Hill, 1968); also E.L. Morse, "Transnational Economic Processes," *International Organization* 3, 3 (Summer 1971):373-397; and Assar Lindbeck, 'The Changing Role of the National State," *Kyklos* 28 (1975):28-46.

5. Raymond Vernon (ed.), *Big Business and the State: Changing Relations in Western Europe* (Cambridge: Harvard University Press, 1974).

6. R. Rowthorn and S. Hymer, *International Big Business 1957-1967: A Study of Comparative Growth* (London: Cambridge University Press, 1971), pp. 75-80.

7. OECD, *Conditions for Success in Technological Innovation* (Paris: 1971), pp. 14-16, 113-118.

8. F.T. Knickerbocker, *Oligopolistic Reaction and Multinational Enterprise* (Boston: Division of Research, Graduate School of Business Administration, Harvard University, 1973). Also Raymond Vernon, "The Location of Economic Activity," in J.H. Dunning (ed.), *Economic Activity and Multinational Enterprise* (London: Allen & Unwin, 1974).

9. R.B. Stobaugh, "The Oil Companies in the Crisis," *Daedalus*, September 1975.

10. For instance, Harry Magdoff, *The Age of Imperialism: The Economics of U.S. Foreign Policy* (New York: Monthly Review, Inc., 1966), pp. 40-50.

11. For instance, Committee for Economic Development, *International Trade, Foreign Investment and Domestic Employment, including Bretton Woods Proposals: A Statement on National Policy by the Research Committee of the Committee for Economic Development* (New York, 1945).

12. For the viewpoints of the various groups, see the following hearings of U.S. Congress, House Committee on Ways and Means: *Tariffs and Foreign Trade, Testimony before a Subcommittee of the House Committee on Ways and Means on the Operation of the Trade Agreements Program*, 80th Congress, 2nd Session, 1948; *Trade Agreements Extension*, Parts I and II on H.R. 1, 84th Congress, 1st Session, 1955; *Renewal of Trade Agreements Act*, H.R. 6902, H.R. 1259, H.R. 8111, S1879, S2240, S3363, 85th Congress, 2nd Session, 1958. See also the following hearings of the Senate Committee on Finance: *Extending Authority to Negotiate Trade Agreements, Hearings before the Senate Committee on Finance* on H.R. 6566, 80th Congress, 2nd Session, 1948; *Trade Agreements Extension Act of 1951* on H.R. 1612, 81st Congress, 1st Session, 1951; *Trade Agreements Extension Act of 1953* on H.R. 5495, 82nd Congress, 2nd Session; *Trade Agreements Extension Act of 1955*, Parts 1, 2, 3, 4 on H.R. 1, 84th Congress, 1st Session, 1955. For a scholarly analysis of political factors at work in the period, see R.A. Bauer, I. de S. Pool, and L.A. Dexter, *American Business and Public Policy: The Politics of Foreign Trade* (New York: Atherton Press, 1963).

13. F.H. Preeg, *Traders and Diplomats, An Analysis of the Kennedy Round of Negotiations under the General Agreements on Tariffs and Trade* (Washington, D.C.: The Brookings Institution, 1970), pp. 208-211; P.B. Kenen, "United States Commercial Policy in a Program for the 1960's," in Bela Balassa (ed.), *Changing Patterns in Foreign Trade and Payments: An Introduction to a Current Issue of Public Policy* (New York: Norton and Company, Inc., 1964), pp. 65-69; J.W. Evans, *The Kennedy Round in American Trade Policy: The Twilight of G.A.T.T.* (Cambridge: Harvard University Press, 1971).

14. See Raymond Vernon, *Sovereignty at Bay*, p. 62.

15. Thomas Horst, "The Industrial Composition of U.S. Exports and Subsidiary Sales to the Canadian Market," *American Economic Review* 62, 1 (March 1972):37-45.

16. Commission on Foreign Policy, *Report to the President and the Congress* (Washington, D.C.: G.P.O., January 1954), pp. 54-61.

17. R.P. Rumelt, *Strategy, Structure and Economic Performance* (Boston: Division of Research, Graduate School of Business Administration, Harvard University, 1974), pp. 50-55.

18. D.C. Bok and J.T. Dunlop, *Labor and the American Community* (New York: Simon and Schuster, 1970), pp. 140-160.

19. *Survey of Current Business*, October 1975, pt. II, pp. 37, 46.

20. "U.A.W. President Cautions V.W.," *N.Y. Times*, July 13, 1974, p. 30.

21. R.N. Cooper, *The Economics of Interdependence: Economic Policy in the Atlantic Community* (New York: McGraw-Hill Book Co., 1968), pp. 148-177.

22. S.M. Robbins and R.B. Stobaugh, *Money in the Multinational Enterprise: A Study of Financial Policy* (New York: Basic Books, 1973), pp. 119-142.

23. "Administrative Survey," in *Law and Policy in International Business* 8, 2 (Spring 1975): 532-549.

24. "Commutation: l'offensive de la C.G.E." *Enterprise*, March 1974, pp. 19-20, 53.

25. V.G. Venturini, *Monopolies and Restrictive Trade Practices in France* (Leyden: A.W. Sijthoff, 1971), pp. 308-311.

26. Dennis Swann, *Competition in British Industry: Restrictive Practices Legislation in Theory and Practice* (London: Allen & Unwin, 1974).

27. M.A. Duggan, *Antitrust and the U.S. Supreme Court, 1829-1967* (New York: Federal Legal Publications, 1968).

28. J.N. Behrman, *National Interests and the Multinational Enterprise: Tensions Among the North Atlantic Countries* (Englewood Cliffs, New Jersey: Prentice-Hall, 1970), pp. 100-113.

29. The classic example cited is Henry Ford II's alleged threat to his British workers in 1971, after a series of strikes, to withdraw all his plants from Great Britain. See Everett M. Kassalow, "The International Metalworkers Federation and the Multinational Automobile Companies: A Study in Transnational Unionism" (mimeo), March 1974.

30. Duane Kujawa, *International Labor Relations Management in the Automobile Industry* (New York: Praeger Publishers, 1971), pp. 207-212; also H.R. Northrup and R.L. Rowan, "Multinational Collective Bargaining Activity: The Factual Record in Chemicals, Glass, and Rubber Tires, Parts I & II," *Columbia Journal of World Business*, Spring 1974, pp. 112-124, and Summer 1974, pp. 49-63.

XII Epilogue

David S. Landes

As the preceding articles make clear, the Western alliance is in midpassage, as are intra-European relations. In the crucial economic sphere, the Atlantic partnership of unequals has turned into a sometimes cacophonous concert of competitors; while the European community of war victims has turned into a partnership of unequals. In the political domain, a number of our allies are in the throes of interregnum or on the threshold (brink) of significant changes in government. We ourselves are in a convalescent state, trying to recover that sense of confidence and purpose that is prerequisite to an effective role abroad. Only in military matters have our relations with Europe changed relatively little: we continue to be the protector of last resort.

Europe as a unit has lost much of its momentum. The oil crisis of 1973 was a moment of truth, and Europe failed the test: it was almost, but not quite, every country for itself, and the devil take the Dutch.[a] Since then the faithful servants of the Commission have redoubled their efforts to get the common cause back on the track, and most diplomats are behaving as though they had learned a lesson about the dangers of selfishness and virtues of cooperation. The constitutional processes of building a united Europe—the preparation for direct elections, for example—pursues its bureaucratic course. Every once in a while a small agreement, such as the recent one on introduction of a standard passport, is saluted as a giant step forward; but then people realize that a standard passport is not a common passport and that each nation will continue to issue its own papers and police its own frontiers, and there is inevitably some disappoint-

---

[a]It was not only that certain European countries were falling over themselves to be accommodating to the Arabs. They also saw this as an opportunity to hurt Rotterdam's preeminence as an oil entrepot and build up their own ports and refineries.

ment. Similarly the Common Market continues to bind the member economies together in interdependence; but when home interests cannot take the competition, the market dissolves and the French embargo, then levy an import duty on, Italian wines. They are not supposed to do that, but they do; and unless one is prepared to see the whole Market go down the drain with the wine, a way will have to be found to tax all the members and subsidize French viticulture.

Today it is French wine; tomorrow, British cheese; the next day, the Italian lira. It is not easy to unify unequal economies unless the strong members are prepared to raise up the weak and each country is ready to sacrifice its own interest to the common good. But those are difficult conditions. They obtain best when the component members of a commercial union are bound by more than material purpose—as in the American Confederation that became the United States or the Zollverein that became Germany. (The assumption of many Europeanists was that a European Common Market would necessarily follow a similar course. The analogy is obviously far from complete.) They are not easy to achieve in a coalition of consciously separate states, especially when the loyalties of the populations remain overwhelmingly national, if not regional.

This, as we know, was precisely de Gaulle's point: that there was no hope of building a Europe unless it were an *Europe des patries*—a Europe resting on those units which alone command the energies, passions, and loyalties of their inhabitants. The trouble is that an *Europe des patries* may well prove in the long run a contradiction in terms, and that only the development of new loyalties will make it possible. This is why Europeanists set such store by the prospect of a popularly-elected European parliament in 1978.

In the meantime, the Gaullists have not disarmed. In a recent interview, Michel Jobert expressed his continued opposition to anything that might conduce to a unified, supranational Europe.[1] A parliament might be acceptable, but only if it were balanced by a second chamber representing the states. Direct elections sound good, but what are they supposed to achieve anyway? Majority voting in the ministerial Council might produce decisions, but one country, "perhaps Britain," would refuse to go along, and the agreement would then quickly collapse. As for trying to build on Common Market strength, giving the Commission political power "is a mistake."

You must understand that I am passionately in favour of Europe. But I want the reality, not just the appearance. I want a confederation [N.B.: not a federation] representing the will of the people of Europe, but as expressed through their governments. Attempts to make Europe progress by wishful thinking like direct elections could well kill the real Europe.

In short, Jobert gives us one more chorus of the hardheaded old refrain. Clearly it wants more than constitutional arrangements and periodic meetings to produce a united Europe, which will come about only when the member states are willing or compelled to subordinate what are perceived as national interests to what is voted as the common interest. The Americans found this difficult enough and fought a Civil War to clinch the point. The German states gave way to the superior might of Prussia. What is strong eough to make the *Europe des patries* take this path?

Meanwhile American-European relations have improved somewhat since the low point of 1973. It is not only that there has been some turnover in personnel; or that there has been a conscious effort on both sides to moderate the language and temper the recriminations. For a while, Henry Kissinger was so vexed by European fecklessness and refusal to cooperate with American policy that he could not refrain from barbed reflections—among other things, on the "legitimacy" of European governments. Some of the Europeans repaid him in kind, with personal comments thrown in. Watergate provided further ammunition, first for wonderment at American naïveté—how could we make such a fuss about the normal processes of government?—and then for animadversions on our morality. It is a wonder that the Alliance survived that unhappy time and a testimony to its fundamental importance and resilience.

Paradoxically, one of the factors that has most contributed to a friendlier climate is the growing European awareness of American weakness. It was one thing to condemn Vietnam, or even to gloat over "the decline of the United States" on the occasion of our precipitate withdrawal from the battle. A little reflection gave better counsel, and some of those who rejoiced at our discomfiture now began to worry about our health. Watergate produced a similar reconsideration. This has been particularly true of French attitudes, in the best Gaullist tradition: when the United States is down, it is time to help it up. Besides, Europe has had its own moments of anxiety, particularly in late 1974 and early 1975, when Portugal threatened to go Communist and the whole "southern tier" gave signs of following. We need each other.

The fact that we need each other is no guarantee of success in our relations. In 1965 Henry Kissinger published a book with a title not dissimilar to ours: *The Troubled Partnership.* It is a wise book and still of considerable use in understanding the American-European relationship. In his Introduction he offered a summary of the issues dividing us:

In recent years this promise [of a partnership between a united Europe and the United States] has been flawed by increasingly sharp disputes among the Allies. The absence of agreement on major policies is striking. On the Continent, the fear of a bilateral United States-Soviet arrangement is pervasive. The United States-British view with respect to disarmament is rejected by France and greeted with distrust and fear by the Federal Republic. The United States finds little support in Europe for its Asian or Latin American policies. The attempt to establish a common trade policy with the Communist world has been generally ineffective. For over a decade the Western Allies have been unable to agree on a common attitude toward the former colonial areas. Progress toward European political unity has been slowed. Britain has been excluded from the Common Market. Basic issues of strategic doctrine have gone unresolved. The issue of nuclear control threatens to divide the Alliance.[2]

Except for the reference to Britain's exclusion from the Common Market, nothing in that paragraph would not be more or less appropriate today. That it remains timely after more than ten years is testimony to Henry Kissinger's perspicacity: it is not easy to write anything in current politics that is not out of date or out of true by the time it appears in print. But even more, it points to the obstinacy of these issues, their resistance to manipulation, however statesmanlike. Kissinger's book is full of suggestions for American policy, most of which he has been unable to act on since entering government. (Indeed it has become something of a game in academe to cite the Professor's pronouncements and contrast them with the Secretary's behavior.) Does this mean that he was wrong originally and knows better now? In part, perhaps. Or that he has been led astray by power? Maybe somewhat. But surely it also means that it is one thing to know what to do and another to be able to do it. Washington has been witness again and again to men who came on a crusade and stayed to practice the art of the possible.

With these qualifications in mind, what suggestions can we offer about critical choices for the United States in Western Europe? The reader of the foregoing essays will have quickly understood that there is no single, coherent message. Raymond Aron thinks that we will have more of the same, on the principle that it is always easier to stay on course than to explore new paths. This is what Stanley Hoffmann said back in 1973, when he offered a considerably less ambitious program than he does in this volume: "And yet, so much initiative, foresight and drive would be required in so many places that it is far easier to predict that in the coming years the story will not be a sudden or even gradual mutation—but more of the same."[3]

Yet time does not stand still. There will be changes to cope with, and America will have to make choices. Let me take some of these *seriatim.*

1. There is a good possibility in the next few years that one or more of our European allies will admit Communists to government. The Portuguese are already in this situation. Can we live with this? All our contributors who deal with the subject argue that we can (thus Suzanne Berger on Italy and Juan Linz on Spain and Portugal); indeed, that we have no choice. Any attempt on our part to interfere in the domestic politics of European nations, they say, can only be self-defeating. (The clear assumption is that we are not the Soviet Union, and our European allies are not satellites—a distinction in alliances and hegemonies that some of America's critics are not prepared to make.)

Can NATO live with partially Communist allies? That is not the same thing as the inverse question—can "popular front" governments live with NATO?—which the Italian Communists at least answer in the affirmative. But it is a qualified affirmative, a concession to the inopportunity of withdrawal rather than a commitment to participation. However sincere the Italian and French Communists may be in their widely announced conversion to democracy—in politics, as in love, the road to hell is paved with good intentions[4]—they have made no comparable turnabout in matters of foreign policy.[5] There is every reason to fear that a left-wing, partially Communist government would be less sympathetic to the Atlantic alliance and to the United States and would tilt in the long run against NATO. At best it would be hostilely neutral. Thus Yugoslavia's much-vaunted independence of the Soviet Union, though contingent in the last analysis on NATO support, has not made it a friend or ally of the United States or the Western world. On the contrary: its credibility as a free Socialist entity seems to require it to play the game of nonalignment—a plague on both your houses.

In sum, my sense is that even if the Alliance wanted to live with partially Communist members, the nature of the tie would change. In particular, it would be increasingly difficult to share top-secret technology under conditions of questionable security. The character and substance of the integrated command would have to be altered, and the Alliance might well move in the direction of a non-Communist core or *ad hoc* multilateral cooperation of a more conventional type.[b] In the long run, such a change would probably hasten American withdrawal from Europe, and that in turn might produce a drastic change in Communist objectives, West as well as East.

How should American diplomacy respond to this prospect (threat) of Communist participation in Western governments? Some of our contributors feel that we should bow to inevitability and make the best of the new situation. It will be easier, they argue, to deal with these popular front governments later on if we are supple and forthcoming today. Maybe so; though one could as well argue that these same governments will respect power more than sweetness. If they are realists today, will they be less so tomorrow? They will not love us the more for our acquiescence; let them at least respect us for our principles or cater to our interest. Even more important, let those among their people who oppose Communism and stand for political freedom know that we have not abandoned the good cause. Is it reasonable to suppose that the Communist parties of Italy or Spain will not exploit cooperation or endorsement or appeasement by the United States to undermine the confidence and commitment of their opponents at home? Why should we cooperate in this new version of "the wave of the future?"

2. What should be the American attitude toward a united Europe? Should we work, as we once did, toward its accomplishment? Should we guide the process, with a view to ensuring our participation in European deliberations and decisions? Or should we let Europe take such shape as the Europeans want to give it, even though this may mean accepting it as an equal, unitary partner that makes up its mind without us? Again, the consensus of those who deal with this aspect is that we let the Europeans move to whatever unity they can achieve, even at the price of dissent from American policy.

---

[b]Compare the two-tier proposal of Leo Tindemans for the Common Market: that further integration take place among the stronger core countries of the EEC (Germany, Benelux, and probably France) while an outer ring of weak partners gather the strength to join.

Yet that is the kind of well-intentioned principle that is easier to pronounce than put into practice. Does it mean that we should eschew bilateral relations and avoid trying to influence members of the European Community before they have a chance to thrash things out among themselves? This has been the French position, and Stanley Hoffmann would agree with it. The French argument is that the United States is so much stronger than any West European nation that prior pressure from our side must needs distort any subsequent European deliberation. The point is well taken, and it is reinforced by the uncommon sensitivity of Europeans these days to anything smacking of American "intervention." This hypersensitivity has become so much of a political "given," I am told, that Machiavellian European statesmen have on occasion invited us to "send a letter" or take a position, the better to smite us with righteous indignation. If true, we should probably be less obliging in such matters. The contrast with the attitude toward European intervention is striking. "Olof Palme [then Swedish prime minister] could come to Germany and campaign for Willy Brandt at the last election, and nobody thought twice about it."[6] Imagine if Gerald Ford tried to barnstorm for Margaret Thatcher or Helmut Kohl.

Clearly a European sense of identity, of in-group vs. out-group, is emerging, and at least in matters not related to security, we are now seen as outsiders. This process of extrusion manifests itself most obviously in certain new forms of international intra-European collaboration. In particular the growing consultation and concentration among like political parties across frontiers necessarily leaves us out in the cold. When European Socialists get together to plan for the directly elected European parliament or to adopt a position on the Portuguese revolution, they constitute an organism that the United States cannot easily interact or deal with. We have no political parties that correspond to the European alignments. As a result, we usually have to act through government representatives, which gives our intervention a necessarily official character.

These new forms of nongovernmental collaboration hint at a revolution in international relations: the Marxist internationals generalized to the whole range of political parties. It may well be the means some day of by-passing the kind of tenacious nationalism represented by Jobert. It may even be a way to penetrate the Iron Curtain, for if Socialists can talk and work with Communists in the West, they may be able to do so in the East as well. To be sure, there is no way to predict the outcome of such a connection. We in the West are accustomed to believe that truth and virtue must triumph in the open market; but that is pure faith; there is nothing in historical experience that would justify such confidence.

In the meantime, the exclusion of the United States from some of these new forms of interaction makes the old channels that much more precious. For all the disadvantages, it would be undesirable for us to eschew bilateral contacts with individual European nations. The French themselves, who are, as we have seen, energetic logrollers in advance of European meetings, would not accept such a constraint. To say this, however, is not to argue for some kind of preferential axis between the United States and, say, Germany. This, as our contributors point out, would have negative consequences for European cooperation and unity.

3. As noted by a number of contributors, economic issues now hold the center of the stage. Ever since the suspension of convertibility in 1971 and the imposition of a temporary 10 per cent import surcharge, the United States and Europe have been bargaining at arm's length. Should we revert to a more self-sacrificing policy? Should we make allowance for our considerable economic weight and avoid throwing it around against weaker partners? Specifically, Stanley Hoffmann deplores our "hard sell" in the recent fighter battle—the "deal of the century." Should we subsidize a European armaments industry by refraining from competition in some areas and reserving it a substantial share of NATO contracts? What about monetary policy? Should we try to support the dollar and move to fixed parities more favorable to European exporters? What about American multinationals? Alfred Grosser feels that we should be less supportive of our companies abroad, lest we incur the hostility of important European interests (labor, for example) that are determined to bring these homeless enterprises under home control.

In general, our two economist contributors, Cooper and Vernon, are inclined to leave these things to the market. Floating exchange rates, notes Cooper, have a number of disadvantages, among others, a higher degree of uncertainty, which business abhors but must learn to live with.[c] On the other hand, they have important virtues; in particular, by adjusting to the balance of commodity flows in international trade, they in effect regulate them, thereby making the more abrupt and divisive device of tariff controls unnecessary. As a result, those commercial issues that were becoming serious sources of dissension between the United States and its allies have lost much of their passion and urgency. As for multinationals, Vernon points out that they are long since an international phenomenon: the Europeans have almost as much stake in their prosperity as we do. Insofar as they need closer watching and tighter regulation, only a truly international effort will work; as the French have learned, no one country can fight them unless it is prepared to see valuable investments go to competitors. Here, then, is a phenomenon that all the advanced industrial countries want to share in, yet want to control. On both counts it could be a stimulus to collaboration.

---

[c]I am not persuaded that the uncertainty is in fact greater with floating rates than in a system of fixed parities among trading partners with different monetary policies and rates of inflation. This is the system that prevailed until 1971, and it was characterized, especially toward the end, by tidal movements of speculative flights out of one currency into another and by surprise defensive changes in parity. It got to the point where nothing was more alarming than official assurances by some treasury official that country X had no intention of devaluing, especially when offered on the Friday before a long weekend. Floating rates do entail some uncertainty, but there is an active market in money futures for those who want to insure themselves against adverse fluctuations.

On armaments manufacture, Alastair Buchan agrees with Hoffmann that Europe should be encouraged and aided to play a bigger role. For Buchan the primary consideration is the contribution such sharing and collaboration could make to tightening the Alliance; for Hoffmann, it would be a means—one of several—of encouraging the military cooperation of France with its EEC partners and ultimately the creation of a truly autonomous European defense system. My own sense is that the United States should lean more to the former, that is, procurement sharing to reinforce and rationalize the Alliance. The French appeals to higher European loyalties in their campaign to secure the big fighter contract rang hollow, coming as they did from the odd-man-out of Western security arrangements. As Hoffmann points out, Giscard's "Europeanism" is confined for now to securing for France a share of European weapons procurement.[7] (Hence the sudden willingness to participate in Eurogroup meetings on arms coordination.) Success in this area will not increase French incentives to share in the common defense; quite the contrary.

4. It is generally agreed that the Atlantic alliance cannot be expected to apply outside its geographical domain and that the nations of Western Europe will more and more play a different role or favor other policies than the United States in the rest of the world (Buchan, Grosser, Hoffmann). This divergence is the result partly of competitive economic interests, partly of differences in philosophy and views. Cooper and Hoffmann both note that the European countries, for example, tend to be more forthcoming toward the nations of the Third World; and several contributors (Aron, Buchan, Cooper, Grosser, Hoffmann) lay particular stress on the divergence of American and European policies in the Middle East. What are the implications for American-European collaboration?

One experience will serve as illustration. The Yom Kippur War raised the fundamental problem of optimum deployment and control over one's armed forces. The refusal in that crisis by European nations to allow us to move men and equipment from or through NATO bases constituted a grievous constraint that we may not be able to live with in other circumstances. In effect, the Europeans were saying that even though the Alliance holds only for the North Atlantic region, the American forces in Europe must be reserved to Europe. But if that is so, how many men can we afford to keep there, especially when one takes into account the greater likelihood of trouble elsewhere? Compare the French decision in 1960 to pull its Mediterranean fleet units out of the NATO command, the better to use them in North Africa as required.

In general the United States has been inclined to resent European intervention unless supportive and, beginning with the Vietnam War, has sought to exclude Europe from negotiations and settlements in other parts of the world. Buchan and Hoffmann both feel that this has been a mistake, not only because the United States is not always right and can use some advice and assistance from its partners, but also because these, by virtue of historical connections or chosen vocation, sometimes have more leverage in these situations. Buchan feels we might have done better in Cyprus with outside help. Hoffmann argues that the Europeans might be better able than we to prod the Arabs toward moderation; and he has argued in another context that France especially, with its new *mondialiste* stance, might be uniquely equipped to mediate between the United States and the Third World.

Here again it may be easier to give the recipe than to use it. Buchan recognizes, for example, that the United States has interests in the Middle East that may not admit of the kind of solution envisaged by some of the European nations, which have their own interests to protect. (To which I would add that it is hard to see why the pro-Arab European position would conduce to Arab moderation.) There *is* such a thing as conflicts of interest, and in such situations it is hard to imagine why any nation should or would voluntarily reinforce the adverse camp. Similarly it would be ill-advised for the United States to allow other parties regularly to act on its behalf in dealings with the Third World; it would be too easy for the intermediary to play the generous, easy-going "good guy" while putting us in the role of the big, bad capitalist wolf—an image that already attaches to us and hurts us.

On the other hand, there have been and will be specific situations in which we would do well either to work with one or more of our European partners or to leave them a free hand. Juan Linz points out that Spain and Portugal might be able to do many things in Latin America better than we. And both France and Britain have valuable connections in ex-colonial Africa, and even in the West Indies. The appropriate tactics would be a function of the situation, and each situation should be judged in and of itself. In general, the United States would profit from the devolution of responsibilities. The consensus is that we have long tried to do too much.

The one area where, it seems to me, we would gain most by devolution is Europe itself. Portugal is a good case in point. Any interference by the United States in the evolution of the crisis would no doubt have produced a serious backlash in the aftermath of destabilization in Chile (Raymond Aron) and sundry other revelations about the CIA. By contrast, the support given by European Socialist parties to Soares has been viewed as a legitimate act of fraternal responsibility. What is more, it is good for Europe to take on such responsibilities. Portugal may be only the first of a number of countries on the brink of victimization by a tyranny of either Left or Right. If Europe is to become a significant factor in world politics, it had better learn to take care of its own house.

5. That raises the question of inequalities within the European Community. Shonfield and Berger stress the serious weaknesses of Great Britain and Italy respectively, and Shonfield cogently argues that if Britain is to "make it" as a part of the Community, it is going to need the forbearance and help of its fellows. And it was not so long ago that Italy needed a substantial loan from

Germany in order to stay afloat in the oil crisis. What should be the role of the United States in solving these difficulties?

There was a time when America could meet all these emergencies: all it had to do was lend dollars. Today, if Italy needed ten billions and we agreed to provide them, the dollar would sink 10 per cent on the exchanges. (It is common to speak of the monetary and financial discipline imposed by the gold standard. But floating rates impose their own discipline.) We can still help, along the lines suggested by Shonfield, by allowing these convalescents the kind of exemptions from rules of the game that were almost normal during the years of reconstruction. Yet with the best of will, our role in that regard cannot be so important as that of the stronger members of the Common Market. If they do not want to go along, all our concessions will avail little. Our greatest contribution, then, would seem to lie in using our good offices to encourage the stronger European nations to help the weaker. We are not, after all, without influence and incentives, military as well as economic.

When all is said and done, the choices presented to us are few, and none is really critical. And that in itself says something about the character of the Western alliance. We are in effect wedded to each other for better or worse, and for the moment, there does not seem to be an alternative. This is not to say that the bond will last forever, but then forever is a long time.

In the meantime, what can we do to improve the working of the Alliance, diminish friction, restore the sentimental ties of yesteryear? If I had to pinpoint any area to make an effort, I would single out the improvement of image and interpersonal relations. This may seem to some like trying to cure a disease by treating the symptoms—a typical American recourse to public relations and Madison Avenue. But that is the last thing in my mind. I am thinking of restoring a sense of community and affection that once existed and was based on the realities of what we are and what we have done, on both sides of the Atlantic: of getting behind the unhappy and inaccurate stereotypes to what I am convinced are the positive values we hold in common, to the realities that can bring us together. If I did not think there was this basis for friendship in shared values and common sympathies, I would give up hope for the Alliance as we know it.

How do we go about this task? As in so many other things, it is easier to prescribe here than to carry out. The emphasis would have to be on youth, for what we are talking about takes time, and it is the younger generation that needs consciousness-raising in these matters. We need, between the United States and Europe, the kind of exchanges that have become a feature of our relations with the Third World. Like the Church in regard to traditionally Catholic areas, we have allowed detachment to go on too long. Now we have to face facts and declare the home territory an area for missionary effort.

We also have to clean up our own house. Nothing will do more to improve our reputation in the world at large and enhance the esteem and affection of our friends than the restoration of our own forces, the healing of our divisions, the curing of our corruptions. At the moment we present an unhappy picture of a nation determined to hurt itself in front of the entire world. There is something depressing, even frightening, about the succession of disasters and disappointments that have afflicted us; but there is something sick about our need to feed on these revelations. In this sense the Republic, on its two hundredth anniversary, is at a nadir of self-respect and self-esteem; and our relations with the rest of the world cannot but be affected by this. Here, then, lies our most critical task at the start of our third century: to take ourselves in hand. This is not a critical choice. We have no choice in the matter.

Notes

1. Michel Jobert, in *The Economist*, January 24, 1976, p. 60.

2. Henry A. Kissinger, *The Troubled Partnership: A Re-appraisal of the Atlantic Alliance* (New York: McGraw-Hill, 1965), p. 4.

3. "Toward a Common European Foreign Policy?" in Wolfram Hanrieder (ed.), *The United States and Western Europe*, p. 105.

4. In regard to domestic matters: it is not unreasonable to expect that Communist participation in government in Italy, for example, would promote the disintegration of the Christian Democratic party, at least initially. This in turn might well encourage the Communists to reevaluate their own possibilities and objectives—the appetite grows with the eating. Or the hand of the Communists may be forced by less disciplined leftist *groupuscules*, as Allende's was in Chile. The fact that the Communist leadership wants to avoid a Chilean scenario is no assurance that the free Left will be equally prudent. The world has had reassurances about "agrarian reformers" and other allegedly democratic avatars of communism before. Cf. "Italy's Communists," *The Economist*, Feb. 28, 1976, pp. 53-60.

5. See Michael Ledeen and Claire Sterling, "Italy's Russian Sugar Daddies," *The New Republic*, April 3, 1976, pp. 16-21, on direct and indirect Soviet financial subsidies to the Italian Communist Party. The authors suggest that these monies may well be a leash; and I would add, a leash all the more effective when put on a party devoted to good housekeeping.

6. Klaus Ruprecht, a West German political analyst, as reported by Flora Lewis, *New York Times*, February 9, 1976, p. 18.

7. On May 22, 1975, the *New York Times* reported (p. 14) that Giscard d'Estaing felt there would be no point in discussing an independent and unified European defense system now, in part because of the "understandable Soviet fears of European military pressure," in part because France's European allies would want "an integrated defense with the United States," which France was

not ready to accept. Interestingly enough, at the same time as he recognized the Soviet Union's "understandable fears" of Western Europe, he asserted that the Soviet leaders "have no aggressive intentions against Europe. . . . My conversations with Leonid Brezhnev have convinced me of this." He conceded, however, that "the level of arms does mean that a danger continues for the future."

Index

Agricoles Familiales (MODEF), 155
Movimento Democratico Português-Comis-
são Democratica Eleitoral (MDP-CED),
251
Movimento das Forcas Armadas (MFA),
238, 247, 251, 254, 257
Moynihan, Pat, 2
Multilateral Nuclear Force (MLF), 58, 304
Multinational corporations, 37, 69, 248,
364, 368, 369; American, 391; and FRG,
182; and high-technology industries, 376;
profits of, 371; regulations of, 372. *See
also* Industry
Mutual and Balanced Force Reductions
(MBFR), 67, 99
Mutual Force Reductions (MFR), Vienna
negotiations on, 103, 300, 305-306, 309

NASA, 377
National Farmers' Association (Fédération
Nationale des Syndicats d'Exploitants
Agricoles) French, 155
Nationalism, 16; economic, 69; ethnic, 154;
European, 320; French military, 80; in
Germany, 194. *See also* Interdependence
Navigation, treaties of, 375
Nazism, 3
Neo-isolationism, 82
Netherlands, energy policy of, 345
Neues Deutschland, 195
Neutralism, 92; of EEC, 86
Neves, Jaime, 255
New Economic Policy, 20, 332
New York Times, 39
Nicoud, Gérard, 155
Nixon, Richard M., 22, 25, 38, 367; diplo-
macy of, 55; new economic policy of, 20,
332
Nixon Round, of trade negotiations, 36, 48
Nonproliferation doctrine, 33
North Atlantic Treaty Organization
(NATO), 3-4, 108, 301; conventional
forces of, 101; erosion of, 314; Eurogroup
within, 59; European allies in, 310-311;
European bases of, 317; and Communism,
388; France and, 16, 62, 165; and global
situation, 319; and Middle East, 305; mili-
tary command structure of, 310; and PCI,
230; U.S. in, 303
Northern Ireland, 134, 136, 320
North Sea, 346; British oil production in,
127
Norway, 346; energy policy of, 345
Nuclear energy, export quarrels over, 35
Nuclear industry, 35
"Nuclear parity," 65
Nuclear proliferation, 72

Nuclear Proliferation Treaty (NPT), 99
Nuclear strategies, nonproliferation doctrine, 33
Nuclear weapons, and U.S. foreign policy,
99; in Western Europe, 61. *See also* Weapon systems

Occitans, 154
Oil cake, 340
Oil crisis, 70, 307; and France, 148; and
Europe, 385, 394; and globalization, 361
Oil embargo, Arab, 23, 344
Oil-exporting countries, 42; and EEC, 105;
monetary policy of, 49-50, 338; reserves
of, 70; trade surpluses of, 337
Oil industry, 360
Oil prices, 339, 347
Organization for Economic Cooperation and
Development (OECD), 84, 108; fund,
336; international tax agreements of, 371
Organization for European Economic Co-
operation (OEEC), 5
Organization of Petroleum Exporting Coun-
tries (OPEC), 69, 346; American invest-
ment of, 71; and developing countries,
350; and EEC, 75, 76, 96; and European
security, 301; and Kissinger diplomacy, 71
Osgood, Robert, 57
Ostpolitik, 31, 63, 280, 297
Overvaluation, of dollar, 39. *See also* De-
valuations

Palme, Olof, 390
Partido Communista Portugues (PCP), 255,
256
Partido Democrata Cristão (PDC), Portu-
guese, 254
Partido Nacionalista Vasco (PNV), 278
Partido Popular Democratico (PPD), Portu-
guese, 252
Partido Socialista Obrero Español (PSOE),
251
Partito Socialista Italiano di Unità Proletaria
(PSIUP), 223
Passport, standard, 385
PCE, 265-266, 275
PCI. *See* Communism, Italian
Peaceful coexistence, 32. *See also* Détente
Pearson, Lester, 304
Peasants, French, 154, 155; Portuguese, 241
Péchiney-Ugine-Kuhlmann, 361, 366
Pensioners, European, 325
Petrodollars, 312. *See also* Monetary system
Petroleum, price of, 40, 41, 44, 329. *See
also* Oil-exporting countries
Pisani laws, French, 155
Pluralism, 96; of authoritarian regimes, 243;
in Italy, 227

About the Authors

DAVID S. LANDES is Robert Walton Goelet Professor of French History in Harvard University. He is a specialist in the economic and social history of modern Europe, with a side interest in the Middle East. His published works include: *Bankers and Pashas* (1958), *The Unbound Prometheus* (1968), and *History as Social Science* (with Charles Tilly; 1971). He has been a Junior Fellow of the Society of Fellows at Harvard (1950-1953); a Fellow of the Center for Advanced Study in the Behavioral Sciences at Stanford (1957-1958); Ellen MacArthur Lecturer in Cambridge University (1964); Overseas Fellow of Churchill College, Cambridge (1968-1969); and Professeur Associé of the Université de Paris IV (Sorbonne) in 1972-1973. He is Docteur *honoris causa* of the Université de Lille and President-Elect of the Economic History Association. His latest publication: "Palestine Before the Zionists," *Commentary*, February 1976.

RAYMOND ARON, Professor of Sociology at the Collège de France since 1970, has been Professor of Sociology at the Sorbonne, editor of *La France Libre* in London during the war, and columnist for *Le Figaro*. He is the author of numerous works, many of which have been translated into English and include *Introduction to the Philosophy of History, The Opium of the Intellectuals, War and Peace Among Nations, Main Currents in Sociological Thought,* and *The Imperial Republic.* Among his honorary degrees are those from Harvard, Columbia and Oxford universities. He is a member of the Académie des Sciences Morales et Politiques, the American Academy of Arts and Sciences and the British Academy.

STANLEY HOFFMANN is Professor of Government and Chairman of the Center for European Studies at Harvard University, where he has been teaching political science since 1955. Professor Hoffmann was born in Vienna and educated in France, where he resided for a quarter of a century. He is a student of France political and intellectual history and of international relations. He is the author of *Gulliver's Troubles* (1968), *Decline or Renewal: France since the 1930s* (1974) and *Social Science Policy in France* (OECD, 1975) and at present is working on a book on United States foreign policy while on leave teaching political science (1975-76) in Paris.

ANDREW SHONFIELD is Director of the Royal Institute of International Affairs (Chatham House) and a distinguished British economist. He has served as foreign editor of the *Financial Times*, economic editor of *The Observer*, and Director of the Social Science Research Council. He has been a member of the Royal Commission on Trade Unions and Employment Associations, the Duncan Committee on British Overseas Representation, the Vedel Committee on EEC Institutes, and the European Commission. He is the author of *British Economic Policy since the War* (1958), *The Attack on World Poverty* (1960), *A Man Beside Himself* (1964), *Modern Capitalism: The Changing Balance of Public and Private Power* (1965) and *Europe: Journey to an Unknown Destination* (1973).

SUZANNE BERGER is Professor of Political Science at the Massachusetts Institute of Technology and Research Fellow at the Center for European Studies at Harvard University. She is also Chairman of the Social Science Research Council's Joint Committee on Western Europe. She has published articles and books on France and Italy including *Peasants Against Politics* and *The French Political System*.

ALFRED GROSSER is Director of the Graduate Program and Professor at the Fondation Nationale des Sciences Politiques in Paris. Born in Frankfurt, Professor Grosser has served as a political columnist for *Le Monde*. He was Assistant Director of UNESCO in Germany in 1950-51; permanent Visiting Professor at the Bologna Center of the Johns Hopkins University, 1955-68; Kratter Professor of Modern European History at Stanford University in 1964-65; and Vice President of the International Political Science Association in 1970-73. Professor Grosser, who has published numerous books in both France and Germany, many of which have been translated into English, was awarded the German Peace Prize in 1975.

JUAN J. LINZ, Professor of Sociology and Political Science at Yale University, is a Spanish citizen and has published in English and Spanish on politics, social structure and modern history of Spain. Among his main research interests are nondemocratic politics, the breakdown of democracies, and the comparative study of fascism. He received a doctorate *honoris causa* from the University of Grenada, is chairman of the Committee on Political Sociology of the International Sociological Association and the International Political Science Association, and is president of DATA, a private survey research organization in Spain.

ALASTAIR FRANCIS BUCHAN was Montague Burton Professor of International Relations at Oxford from 1972 until his death in February of 1976. Son of John Buchan, novelist, he was on the staff of *The Economist* and *The Observer* for seven years, for which he served as Washington correspondent and then diplomatic and defense correspondent. He has served as Director of the Institute for Strategic Studies, Commandant of the Royal College of Defense Studies, Chairman of the British International Studies Association. His publications include *Europe's Future, Europe's Choices* (ed.), and *Power and Equilibrium in the 1970's.*

RICHARD N. COOPER is Frank Altschul Professor of International Economics at Yale University. He has served as Senior staff economist for President Kennedy's Council of Economic Advisors (1961-1963), as Deputy Asst. Secretary of State for International Monetary Affairs (1965-1966), as Economic Consultant to the National Security Council (1969-70), and as Provost of Yale University (1972-1974). He is author of *The Economics of Interdependence* (1968), *Economic Mobility and National Economic Policy* (1974), and many other works. He has been a Marshall scholar, a Ford Foundation Faculty Fellow, a Fellow of the Center for Advanced Study in Behavioral Sciences and is an elected Fellow of the American Academy of Arts and Sciences.

RAYMOND VERNON is the Director of Harvard University's Center for International Affairs and Professor of International Business Management at the Harvard Business School. He has published numerous articles and several books on the subject of international economic relations including *Sovereignty at Bay: The Multinational Spread of U.S. Enterprises* and *Big Business and the State: Changing Relations in Western Europe.*